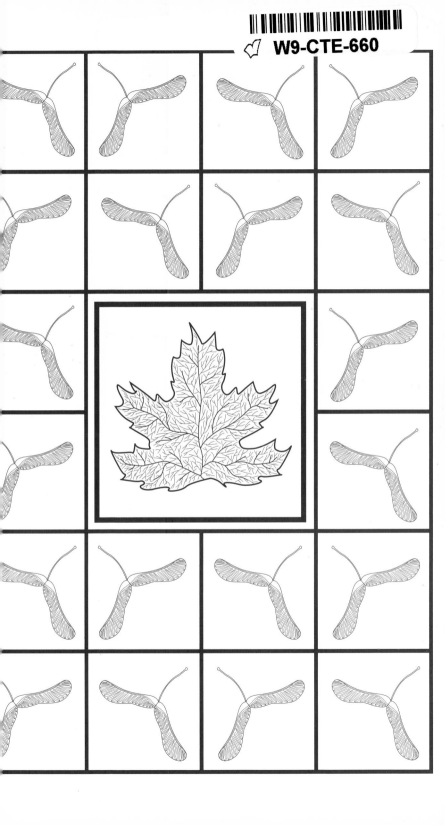

THE OLD SCHOOLHOUSE

ROUGHING IT IN THE BUSH

Or, FOREST LIFE IN CANADA

BY SUSANNA MOODIE

"THE poor exiles of wealthy and over-populous nations
have generally been the first founders of mighty empires.
Necessity and industry producing greater results
than rank and affluence, in the civilization
of barbarous countries."

ILLUSTRATIONS
BY R. A. STEWART

Unabridged

PROSPERO

CANADIAN COLLECTION

TORONTO
2000

Roughing It in the Bush
or
Forest Life in Canada

This edition first published by
Prospero Books in 2000
from the 1913 Bell & Cockburn edition

Prospero Canadian Collection edition © Prospero Books, 2000

Canadian Cataloguing in Publication Data

Moodie, Susanna, 1803-1885
Roughing it in the bush, or, Forest life in Canada

(Prospero Canadian Collection)
Facsim. reprint.
Originally published: Toronto: Bell & Cockburn, 1913.
ISBN 1-55267-140-2

1. Frontier and pioneer life - Ontario.
2. Ontario - Description and travel.
I. Title. II. Title: Forest life in Canada. III. Series.
FC3067.2.M67 2000   971.3'02   C00-931936-0
F1057.M82 2000

Prospero Books
90 Ronson Drive, Toronto, Ontario, Canada
M9W 1C1

Printed on acid free paper
Printed and bound in Canada

CONTENTS

CONTENTS

ILLUSTRATIONS

FOREWORD

IN presenting this edition of Mrs. Moodie's excellent book to the public, it still further emphasizes the contrast between life in Canada in 1830 and 1913. When first published in London it had especial value to the intending emigrant, because it told fearlessly of the hardships to be overcome in an unbroken country, but, always with an optimism that was an inducement to undertake the voyage. To the reader of the present day it has the additional charm of literary excellence, and as such should have a permanent place in Canadian literature. Editions have already been published in London and Toronto, but are now out of print, and, owing to the steadily increasing demand for Canadiana, are becoming scarce. I am indebted to Dr. George H. Locke, of the Toronto Public Library for the fine portrait of Mrs. Moodie, and to Mr. M. J. Cockburn for the portrait, and Book Plate of J. W. Dunbar Moodie.

W. C. BELL

TORONTO, *August* 1, 1913

ADVERTISEMENT TO THIRD EDITION

PUBLISHED BY RICHARD BENTLEY, IN 1854

IN JUSTICE TO MRS. MOODIE, IT IS RIGHT to state that being still resident in the far-west of Canada, she has not been able to superintend this work whilst passing through the press. From this circumstance some verbal mistakes and oversights may have occurred, but the greatest care has been taken to avoid them.

Although well known as an authoress in Canada, and a member of a family which has enriched English literature with works of very high popularity, Mrs. Moodie is chiefly remembered in this country by a volume of Poems published in 1831, under her maiden name of Susanna Strickland. During the rebellion in Canada, her loyal lyrics, prompted by strong affection for her native country, were circulated and sung throughout the colony, and produced a great effect in rousing an enthusiastic feeling in favour of law and order. Another of her lyrical compositions, the charming Sleigh Song, printed in the present work, p. 175, has been extremely popular in Canada. The warmth of feeling which beams through every line, and the touching truthfulness of its details, won for it a reception there as universal as it was favourable.

The glowing narrative of personal incident and suffering which she gives in the present work, will no doubt attract general attention. It would be difficult to point out delineations of fortitude under privation, more interesting or more pathetic than those contained in her second volume.

LONDON, *January* 22, 1852

INTRODUCTION TO THIRD EDITION

PUBLISHED BY RICHARD BENTLEY, IN 1854

IN MOST INSTANCES, EMIGRATION IS A
matter of necessity, not of choice; and this is more
especially true of the emigration of persons of respectable connections, or of any station or position
in the world. Few educated persons, accustomed to
the refinements and luxuries of European society,
ever willingly relinquish those advantages, and place
themselves beyond the protective influence of the
wise and revered institutions of their native land,
without the pressure of some urgent cause. Emigration may, indeed, generally be regarded as an act
of severe duty, performed at the expense of personal
enjoyment, and accompanied by the sacrifice of those
local attachments which stamp the scenes amid which
our childhood grew, in imperishable characters upon
the heart. Nor is it until adversity has pressed sorely upon the proud and wounded spirit of the well-educated sons and daughters of old but impoverished
families, that they gird up the loins of the mind, and
arm themselves with fortitude to meet and dare the
heart-breaking conflict.

The ordinary motives for the emigration of such
persons may be summed up in a few brief words;—
the emigrant's hope of bettering his condition, and of
escaping from the vulgar sarcasms too often hurled at
the less wealthy by the purse-proud, commonplace
people of the world. But there is a higher motive
still, which has its origin in that love of independence
which springs up spontaneously in the breasts of the
high-souled children of a glorious land. They cannot labour in a menial capacity in the country where

xv

they were born and educated to command. They can trace no difference between themselves and the more fortunate individuals of a race whose blood warms their veins, and whose name they bear. The want of wealth alone places an impassable barrier between them and the more favoured offspring of the same parent stock; and they go forth to make for themselves a new name and to find another country, to forget the past and to live in the future, to exult in the prospect of their children being free and the land of their adoption great.

The choice of the country to which they devote their talents and energies depends less upon their pecuniary means than upon the fancy of the emigrant or the popularity of a name. From the year 1826 to 1829, Australia and the Swan River were all the rage. No other portions of the habitable globe were deemed worthy of notice. These were the *El Dorados* and lands of Goshen to which all respectable emigrants eagerly flocked. Disappointment, as a matter of course, followed their high-raised expectations. Many of the most sanguine of these adventurers returned to their native shores in a worse condition than when they left them. In 1830, the great tide of emigration flowed westward. Canada became the great landmark for the rich in hope and poor in purse. Public newspapers and private letters teemed with the unheard-of advantages to be derived from a settlement in this highly-favoured region.

Its salubrious climate, its fertile soil, commercial advantages, great water privileges, its proximity to the mother country, and last, not least, its almost total

INTRODUCTION TO THIRD EDITION

exemption from taxation—that bugbear which keeps honest John Bull in a state of constant ferment—were the theme of every tongue, and lauded beyond all praise. The general interest, once excited, was industriously kept alive by pamphlets, published by interested parties, which prominently set forth all the *good* to be derived from a settlement in the Backwoods of Canada; while they carefully concealed the toil and hardship to be endured in order to secure these advantages. They told of lands yielding forty bushels to the acre, but they said nothing of the years when these lands, with the most careful cultivation, would barely return fifteen; when rust and smut, engendered by the vicinity of damp overhanging woods, would blast the fruits of the poor emigrant's labour, and almost deprive him of bread. They talked of log houses to be raised in a single day, by the generous exertions of friends and neighbours, but they never ventured upon a picture of the disgusting scenes of riot and low debauchery exhibited during the raising, or upon a description of the dwellings when raised—dens of dirt and misery, which would, in many instances, be shamed by an English pig-sty. The necessaries of life were described as inestimably cheap; but they forgot to add that in remote bush settlements, often twenty miles from a market town, and some of them even that distance from the nearest dwelling, the necessaries of life which would be deemed indispensable to the European, could not be procured at all, or, if obtained, could only be so by sending a man and team through a blazed forest road,—a process far too expensive for frequent repetition.

INTRODUCTION TO THIRD EDITION

Oh, ye dealers in wild lands—ye speculators in the folly and credulity of your fellow-men—what a mass of misery, and of misrepresentation productive of that misery, have ye not to answer for ! You had your acres to sell, and what to you were the worn-down frames and broken hearts of the infatuated purchasers? The public believed the plausible statements you made with such earnestness, and men of all grades rushed to hear your hired orators declaim upon the blessings to be obtained by the clearers of the wilderness.

Men who had been hopeless of supporting their families in comfort and independence at home, thought that they had only to come out to Canada to make their fortunes; almost even to realize the story told in the nursery, of the sheep and oxen that ran about the streets, ready roasted, and with knives and forks upon their backs. They were made to believe that if it did not actually rain gold, that precious metal could be obtained, as is now stated of California and Australia, by stooping to pick it up.

The infection became general. A Canada mania pervaded the middle ranks of British society; thousands and tens of thousands, for the space of three or four years, landed upon these shores. A large majority of the higher class were officers of the army and navy, with their families—a class perfectly unfitted by their previous habits and education for contending with the stern realities of emigrant life. The hand that has long held the sword, and been accustomed to receive implicit obedience from those under its control, is seldom adapted to wield the spade and guide the plough, or try its strength against the stubborn trees of the forest. Nor will such persons submit cheerfully to the saucy familiarity of servants, who, republicans in spirit, think themselves as good as their employers. Too many of these brave and honourable men were easy dupes to the designing land-speculators. Not having counted the cost, but only looked upon the bright side of the picture held up to their admiring gaze, they fell easily into the snares of their artful seducers.

To prove their zeal as colonists, they were induced to purchase large tracts of wild land in remote and unfavourable situations. This, while it impoverished and often proved the ruin of the unfortunate immigrant, possessed a double advantage to the seller. He obtained an exorbitant price for the land which he actually sold, while the residence of a respectable settler upon the spot greatly enhanced the value and price of all other lands in the neighbourhood.

It is not by such instruments as those I have just mentioned, that Providence works when it would reclaim the waste places of the earth, and make them subservient to the wants and happiness of its creatures. The Great Father of the souls and bodies of men knows the arm which wholesome labour from infancy has made strong, the nerves which have become iron by patient endurance, by exposure to weather, coarse fare, and rude shelter; and He chooses such, to send forth into the forest to hew out the rough paths for the advance of civilization. These men become wealthy and prosperous, and form the bones and sinews of a great and rising country. Their labour is wealth, not exhaustion; it produces independence and content, not home-sickness and despair. What the

INTRODUCTION TO THIRD EDITION

Backwoods of Canada are to the industrious and ever-to-be-honoured sons of honest poverty, and what they are to the refined and accomplished gentleman, these simple sketches will endeavour to portray. They are drawn principally from my own experience, during a sojourn of nineteen years in the colony.

In order to diversify my subject, and make it as amusing as possible, I have between the sketches introduced a few small poems, all written during my residence in Canada, and descriptive of the country.

In this pleasing task I have been assisted by my husband, J. W. Dunbar Moodie, author of "Ten Years in South Africa."

BELLEVILLE, UPPER CANADA

CANADA : A CONTRAST

A

IN THE YEAR 1832 I LANDED WITH my husband, J. W. Dunbar Moodie, in Canada. Mr. Moodie was the youngest son of Major Moodie, of Mellsetter, in the Orkney Islands; he was a lieutenant in the 21st Regiment of Fusileers, and had been severely wounded in the night-attack upon Bergen-op-Zoom, in Holland.

Not being overgifted with the good things of this world—the younger sons of old British families seldom are—he had, after mature deliberation, determined to try his fortunes in Canada, and settle upon the grant of 400 acres of land ceded by the Government to officers upon half-pay.

Emigration, in most cases—and ours was no exception to the general rule—is a matter of necessity, not of choice. It may, indeed, generally be regarded as an act of duty performed at the expense of personal enjoyment, and at the sacrifice of all those local attachments which stamp the scenes in which our childhood grew in imperishable characters upon the heart.

Nor is it, until adversity has pressed hard upon the wounded spirit of the sons and daughters of old, but impoverished, families, that they can subdue their proud and rebellious feelings, and submit to make the trial.

This was our case, and our motive for emigrating to one of the British colonies can be summed up in a few words.

The emigrant's hope of bettering his condition, and securing a sufficient competence to support his family, to free himself from the slighting remarks too often hurled at the poor gentleman by the practical people of the world, which is always galling to a proud man, but doubly so when he knows that the want of wealth constitutes the sole difference between him and the more favoured offspring of the same parent stock.

In 1830 the tide of emigration flowed westward, and Canada became the great landmark for the rich in hope and poor in purse. Public newspapers and private letters teemed with the almost fabulous advantages to be derived from a settlement in this highly favoured region. Men, who had been doubtful of supporting their families in comfort at home, thought that they had only to land in Canada to realize a fortune. The infection became general. Thousands and tens of thousands from the middle ranks of British society, for the space of three or four years, landed upon these shores. A large majority of these emigrants were officers of the army and navy, with their families: a class perfectly unfitted, by their previous habits and standing in society, for contending with the stern realities of emigrant life in the backwoods. A class formed mainly from the younger scions of great families, naturally proud, and not only accustomed to command, but to receive implicit obedience from the people under them, are not men adapted to the hard toil of the woodman's life. Nor will such persons submit cheerfully to the saucy familiarity of servants, who, republicans at heart, think themselves quite as good as their employers.

Too many of these brave and honest men took up their grants of wild land in remote and unfavourable localities, far from churches, schools, and markets, and

4

fell an easy prey to the land speculators that swarmed in every rising village on the borders of civilization.

It was to warn such settlers as these last mentioned, not to take up grants and pitch their tents in the wilderness, and by so doing reduce themselves and their families to hopeless poverty, that my work *Roughing it in the Bush* was written.

I gave the experience of the first seven years we passed in the woods, attempting to clear a bush farm, as a warning to others, and the number of persons who have since told me, that my book "told the history" of their own life in the woods, ought to be the best proof to every candid mind that I spoke the truth. It is not by such feeble instruments as the above that Providence works when it seeks to reclaim the waste places of the earth, and make them subservient to the wants and happiness of its creatures. The great Father of the souls and bodies of men knows the arm which wholesome labour from infancy has made strong, the nerves that have become iron by patient endurance, and He chooses such to send forth into the forest to hew out the rough paths for the advance of civilization.

These men become wealthy and prosperous, and are the bones and sinews of a great and rising country. Their labour is wealth, not exhaustion; it produces content, not home-sickness and despair.

What the backwoods of Canada are to the industrious and ever-to-be-honoured sons of honest poverty, and what they are to the refined and polished gentleman, these sketches have endeavoured to show.

5

ROUGHING IT IN THE BUSH

The poor man is in his native element; the poor gentleman totally unfitted, by his previous habits and education, to be a hewer of the forest and a tiller of the soil. What money he brought out with him is lavishly expended during the first two years in paying for labour to clear and fence lands which, from his ignorance of agricultural pursuits, will never make him the least profitable return and barely find coarse food for his family. Of clothing we say nothing. Bare feet and rags are too common in the bush.

Now, had the same means and the same labour been employed in the cultivation of a leased farm, or one purchased for a few hundred dollars, near a village, how different would have been the results, not only to the settler, but it would have added greatly to the wealth and social improvement of the country.

I am well aware that a great and, I must think, a most unjust prejudice has been felt against my book in Canada because I dared to give my opinion freely on a subject which had engrossed a great deal of my attention; nor do I believe that the account of our failure in the bush ever deterred a single emigrant from coming to the country, as the only circulation it ever had in the colony was chiefly through the volumes that often formed a portion of their baggage. The many who have condemned the work without reading it will be surprised to find that not one word has been said to prejudice intending emigrants from making Canada their home. Unless, indeed, they ascribe the regret expressed at having to leave my native land, so natural in the painful home-sickness which, for several months, preys upon the health and

6

spirits of the dejected exile, to a deep-rooted dislike to the country.

So far from this being the case, my love for the country has steadily increased from year to year, and my attachment to Canada is now so strong that I cannot imagine any inducement, short of absolute necessity, which could induce me to leave the colony where, as a wife and mother, some of the happiest years of my life have been spent.

Contrasting the first years of my life in the bush with Canada as she now is, my mind is filled with wonder and gratitude at the rapid strides she has made towards the fulfilment of a great and glorious destiny.

What important events have been brought to pass within the narrow circle of less than forty years! What a difference since *now* and *then*. The country is the same only in name. Its aspect is wholly changed. The rough has become smooth, the crooked has been made straight, the forests have been converted into fruitful fields, the rude log cabin of the woodsman has been replaced by the handsome, well-appointed homestead, and large populous cities have pushed the small clap-boarded village into the shade.

The solitary stroke of the axe that once broke the uniform silence of the vast woods is only heard in remote districts, and is superseded by the thundering tread of the iron horse and the ceaseless panting of the steam-engine in our sawmills and factories.

Canada is no longer a child, sleeping in the arms of nature, dependent for her very existence on the fostering care of her illustrious mother. She has outstepped infancy, and is in the full enjoyment of a strong and vigorous youth. What may not we hope for her maturity ere another forty summers have glided down the stream of time! Already she holds in her hand the crown of one of the mightiest empires that the world has seen, or is yet to see.

Look at her vast resources—her fine healthy climate—her fruitful soil—the inexhaustible wealth of her pine forests—the untold treasures hidden in her unexplored mines. What other country possesses such an internal navigation for transporting its products from distant Manitoba to the sea, and from thence to every port in the world!

If an excellent Government, defended by wise laws, a loyal people, and a free Church, can make people happy and proud of their country, surely we have every reason to rejoice in our new Dominion.

When we first came to the country it was a mere struggle for bread to the many, while all the offices of emolument and power were held by a favoured few. The country was rent to pieces by political factions, and a fierce hostility existed between the native born Canadians—the first pioneers of the forest—and the British emigrants, who looked upon each other as mutual enemies who were seeking to appropriate the larger share of the new country.

Those who had settled down in the woods were happily unconscious that these quarrels threatened to destroy the peace of the colony.

The insurrection of 1837 came upon them like a thunder clap; they could hardly believe such an incredible tale. Intensely loyal, the emigrant officers

J. W. DUNBAR MOODIE

rose to a man to defend the British flag and chastise the rebels and their rash leader.

In their zeal to uphold British authority, they made no excuse for the wrongs that the dominant party had heaped upon a clever and high-spirited man. *To them he was a traitor*, and, as such, a public enemy. Yet the blow struck by that injured man, weak as it was, without money, arms, or the necessary munitions of war, and defeated and broken in its first effort, gave freedom to Canada, and laid the foundation of the excellent constitution that we now enjoy. It drew the attention of the Home Government to the many abuses then practised in the colony, and made them aware of its vast importance in a political point of view, and ultimately led to all our great national improvements.

The settlement of the long-vexed clergy reserves question, and the establishment of common schools was a great boon to the colony. The opening up of new townships, the making of roads, the establishment of municipal councils in all the old districts, leaving to the citizens the free choice of their own members in the council for the management of their affairs, followed in rapid succession.

These changes of course took some years to accomplish, and led to others equally important. The Provincial Exhibitions have done much to improve the agricultural interests, and have led to better and more productive methods of cultivation than were formerly practised in the Province. The farmer gradually became a wealthy and intelligent landowner, proud of his improved flocks and herds, of his fine horses

9

and handsome homestead. He was able to send his sons to college and his daughters to boarding school, and not uncommonly became an honourable member of the Legislative Council.

While the sons of poor gentlemen have generally lost caste and sunk into useless sots, the children of these honest tillers of the soil have steadily risen to the highest class, and have given to Canada some of her best and wisest legislators.

Men who rest satisfied with the mere accident of birth for their claims to distinction, without energy and industry to maintain their position in society, are sadly at discount in a country which amply rewards the worker, but leaves the indolent loafer to die in indigence and obscurity.

Honest poverty is encouraged, not despised, in Canada. Few of her prosperous men have risen from obscurity to affluence without going through the mill, and therefore have a fellow-feeling for those who are struggling to gain the first rung on the ladder.

Men are allowed in this country a freedom enjoyed by few of the more polished countries in Europe— freedom in religion, politics, and speech; freedom to select their own friends and to visit with whom they please without consulting the Mrs. Grundys of society—and they can lead a more independent social life than in the mother country, because less restricted by the conventional prejudices that govern older communities.

Few people who have lived many years in Canada, and return to England to spend the remainder of their days, accomplish the fact. They almost invariably come back, and why? They feel more independent and happier here; they have no idea what a blessed country it is to live in until they go back and realize the want of social freedom. I have heard this from so many educated people, persons of taste and refinement, that I cannot doubt the truth of their statements.

Forty years has accomplished as great a change in the habits and tastes of the Canadian people as it has in the architecture of their fine cities and the appearance of the country. A young Canadian gentleman is as well educated as any of his compeers across the big water, and contrasts very favourably with them. Social and unaffected, he puts on no airs of offensive superiority, but meets a stranger with the courtesy and frankness best calculated to shorten the distance between them and to make his guest feel perfectly at home.

Few countries possess a more beautiful female population. The women are elegant in their tastes, graceful in their manners, and naturally kind and affectionate in their dispositions. Good housekeepers, sociable neighbours, and lively and active in speech and movement, they are capital companions and make excellent wives and mothers. Of course there must be exceptions to every rule; but cases of divorce, or desertion of their homes, are so rare an occurrence that it speaks volumes for their domestic worth. Numbers of British officers have chosen their wives in Canada, and I never heard that they had cause to repent of their choice.

In common with our American neighbours, we find that the worst members of our community are not Canadian born, but importations from other countries.

ROUGHING IT IN THE BUSH

The Dominion and Local Governments are now doing much to open up the resources of Canada by the Intercolonial and projected Pacific Railways and other Public Works, which, in time, will make a vast tract of land available for cultivation, and furnish homes for multitudes of the starving populations of Europe.

And again, the Government of the flourishing Province of Ontario—of which the Hon. J. Sandfield Macdonald is premier—has done wonders during the last four years by means of its Immigration policy, which has been most successfully carried out by the Hon. John Carling, the Commissioner, and greatly tended to the development of the country. By this policy liberal provision is made for free grants of land to actual settlers, for general education, and for the encouragement of the industrial Arts and Agriculture; by the construction of public roads and the improvement of the internal navigable waters of the Province; and by the assistance now given to an economical system of railways connecting these interior waters with the leading railroads and ports on the frontier; and not only are free grants of land given in the districts extending from the eastern to the western extremity of the Province, but one of the best of the new townships has been selected in which the Government is now making roads, and upon each lot is clearing five acres and erecting thereon a small house, which will be granted to heads of families, who, by six annual instalments, will be required to pay back to the Government the cost of these improvements—not exceeding $200, or £40 sterling—when a free patent (or deed) of the land will be given, without any charge whatever, under a protective Homestead Act. This wise and liberal policy would have astonished the Colonial Legislature of 1832, but will, no doubt, speedily give to the Province a noble and progressive back country, and add much to its strength and prosperity.

Our busy factories and foundries—our copper, silver, and plumbago mines—our salt and petroleum—the increasing exports of native produce—speak volumes for the prosperity of the Dominion and for the government of those who are at the head of affairs. It only requires the loyal co-operation of an intelligent and enlightened people to render this beautiful and free country the greatest and the happiest upon the face of the earth.

When we contrast forest life in Canada forty years ago with the present state of the country, my book will not be without interest and significance. We may truly say, old things have passed away, all things have become new.

What an advance in the arts and sciences and in the literature of the country has been made during the last few years. Canada can boast of many good and even distinguished authors, and the love of books and booklore is daily increasing.

Institutes and literary associations for the encouragement of learning are now to be found in all the cities and large towns in the Dominion. We are no longer dependent upon the States for the reproduction of the works of celebrated authors; our own publishers, both in Toronto and Montreal, are furnishing

13

our handsome book stores with volumes that rival, in cheapness and typographical excellence, the best issues from the large printing establishments in America. We have no lack of native talent or books, or of intelligent readers to appreciate them.

Our print shops are full of the well-educated designs of native artists. And the grand scenery of our lakes and forests, transferred to canvas, adorns the homes of our wealthy citizens.

We must not omit in this slight sketch to refer to the number of fine public buildings which meet us at every turn, most of which have been designed and executed by native architects. Montreal can point to her Victoria Bridge, and challenge the world to produce its equal. This prodigy of mechanical skill should be a sufficient inducement to strangers from other lands to visit our shores, and though designed by the son of the immortal George Stephenson, it was Canadian hands that helped him to execute his great project—to raise that glorious monument to his fame, which, we hope, will outlast a thousand years.

Our new Houses of Parliament, our churches, banks, public halls, asylums for the insane, the blind, and the deaf and dumb are buildings which must attract the attention of every intelligent traveller; and when we consider the few brief years that have elapsed since the Upper Province was reclaimed from the wilderness, our progress in mechanical arts, and all the comforts which pertain to modern civilization, is unprecedented in the history of older nations.

If the Canadian people will honestly unite in carrying out measures proposed by the Government for

CANADA : A CONTRAST

the good of the country, irrespective of self-interest
and party prejudices, they must, before the close of
the present century, become a great and prosperous
people, bearing their own flag and enjoying their own
nationality. May the blessing of God rest upon Canada and the Canadian people!

SUSANNA MOODIE

BELLEVILLE, 1871

ROUGHING IT IN THE BUSH

CANADA, THE BLEST—THE FREE!
With prophetic glance, I see
Visions of thy future glory,
Giving to the world's great story
A page, with mighty meaning fraught,
That asks a wider range of thought.
Borne onward on the wings of Time,
I trace thy future course sublime;
And feel my anxious lot grow bright,
While musing on the glorious sight;—
Yea, my heart leaps up with glee
To hail thy noble destiny!

Even now thy sons inherit
All thy British mother's spirit.
Ah ! no child of bondage thou;
With her blessing on thy brow,
And her deathless, old renown
Circling thee with freedom's crown,
And her love within thy heart,
Well may'st thou perform thy part,
And to coming years proclaim
Thou art worthy of her name.
Home of the homeless!—friend to all
Who suffer on this earthly ball!
On thy bosom sickly care
Quite forgets her squalid lair;
Gaunt famine, ghastly poverty
Before thy gracious aspect fly,
And hopes long crush'd, grow bright again,
And, smiling, point to hill and plain.
By thy winter's stainless snow,
Starry heavens of purer glow,
Glorious summers, fervid, bright,
Basking in one blaze of light;
By thy fair, salubrious clime;
By thy scenery sublime;
By thy mountains, streams, and woods;

CANADA : A CONTRAST

By thy everlasting floods;
If greatness dwells beneath the skies,
Thou to greatness shalt arise!

Nations old, and empires vast,
From the earth had darkly pass'd
Ere rose the fair auspicious morn
When thou, the last, not least, wast born.
Through the desert solitude
Of trackless waters, forests rude,
Thy guardian angel sent a cry
All jubilant of victory!
"Joy," she cried, "to th' untill'd earth,
Let her joy in a mighty nation's birth,—
Night from the land has pass'd away,
The desert basks in noon of day.
Joy, to the sullen wilderness,
I come, her gloomy shades to bless,
To bid the bear and wild-cat yield
Their savage haunts to town and field.
Joy, to stout hearts and willing hands,
That win a right to these broad lands,
And reap the fruit of honest toil,
Lords of the rich, abundant soil.

"Joy, to the sons of want, who groan
In lands that cannot feed their own;
And seek, in stern, determined mood,
Homes in the land of lake and wood,
And leave their heart's young hopes behind,
Friends in this distant world to find;
Led by that God, who from His throne
Regards the poor man's stifled moan.
Like one awaken'd from the dead,
The peasant lifts his drooping head,
Nerves his strong heart and sunburnt hand,
To win a portion of the land,
That glooms before him far and wide

ROUGHING IT IN THE BUSH

In frowning woods and surging tide
No more oppress'd, no more a slave,
Here freedom dwells beyond the wave.

" Joy, to those hardy sires who bore
The day's first heat—their toils are o'er;
Rude fathers of this rising land,
Theirs was a mission truly grand.
Brave peasants whom the Father, God,
Sent to reclaim the stubborn sod;
Well they perform'd their task, and won
Altar and hearth for the woodman's son.
Joy, to Canada's unborn heirs,
A deathless heritage is theirs;
For, sway'd by wise and holy laws,
Its voice shall aid the world's great cause,
Shall plead the rights of man, and claim
For humble worth an honest name;
Shall show the peasant-born can be,
When call'd to action, great and free.
Like fire, within the flint conceal'd,
By stern necessity reveal'd,
Kindles to life the stupid sod,
Image of perfect man and God.

" Joy, to thy unborn sons, for they
Shall hail a brighter, purer day;
When peace and Christian brotherhood
Shall form a stronger tie than blood—
And commerce, freed from tax and chain,
Shall build a bridge o'er earth and main
And man shall prize the wealth of mind,
The greatest blessing to mankind;
True Christians, both in word and deed,
Ready in virtue's cause to bleed,
Against a world combined to stand,
And guard the honour of the land.
Joy, to the earth, when this shall be,
Time verges on eternity."

CHAPTER ONE
A VISIT TO GROSSE ISLE

Alas! that man's stern spirit e'er should mar
A scene so pure—so exquisite as this.

ROUGHING IT IN THE BUSH, OR FOREST LIFE IN CANADA   CHAPTER ONE   A VISIT TO GROSSE ISLE

THE DREADFUL CHOLERA WAS DEPOPulating Quebec and Montreal when our ship cast anchor off Grosse Isle, on the 30th of August 1832, and we were boarded a few minutes after by the health-officers.

One of these gentlemen—a little, shrivelled-up Frenchman—from his solemn aspect and attenuated figure, would have made no bad representative of him who sat upon the pale horse. He was the only grave Frenchman I had ever seen, and I naturally enough regarded him as a phenomenon. His companion — a fine-looking, fair-haired Scotchman — though a little consequential in his manners, looked like one who in his own person could combat and vanquish all the evils which flesh is heir to. Such was the contrast between these doctors that they would have formed very good emblems, one, of vigorous health, the other, of hopeless decay.

Our captain, a rude, blunt north-country sailor, possessing certainly not more politeness than might be expected in a bear, received his sprucely dressed visitors on the deck, and, with very little courtesy, abruptly bade them follow him down to the cabin.

The officials were no sooner seated than, glancing hastily round the place, they commenced the following dialogue:—

"From what port, captain?"

Now, the captain had a peculiar language of his own, from which he commonly expunged all the connecting links. Small words, such as "and" and "the," he contrived to dispense with altogether.

"Scotland—sailed from port o' Leith, bound for Quebec, Montreal—general cargo—seventy-two steerage, four cabin passengers—brig *Anne*, one hundred and ninety-two tons burden, crew eight hands."

Here he produced his credentials, and handed them to the strangers. The Scotchman just glanced over the documents, and laid them on the table.

"Had you a good passage out?"

"Tedious, baffling winds, heavy fogs, detained three weeks on Banks—foul weather making Gulf—short of water, people out of provisions, steerage passengers starving."

"Any case of sickness or death on board?"

"All sound as crickets."

"Any births?" lisped the little Frenchman.

The captain screwed up his mouth, and after a moment's reflection he replied, "Births? Why, yes; now I think on't, gentlemen, we had one female on board, who produced three at a birth."

"That's uncommon," said the Scotch doctor, with an air of lively curiosity. "Are the children alive and well? I should like much to see them." He started up and knocked his head —for he was very tall— against the ceiling. "Confound your low cribs! I have nearly dashed out my brains."

"A hard task that," looked the captain to me. He did not speak, but I knew by his sarcastic grin what was uppermost in his thoughts. "The young ones all males—fine thriving fellows. Step upon deck. Sam

A VISIT TO GROSSE ISLE

Frazer," turning to his steward, "bring them down for doctors to see." Sam vanished, with a knowing wink to his superior, and quickly returned, bearing in his arms three fat, chuckle-headed bull terriers, the sagacious mother following close at his heels, and looking ready to give and take offence on the slighest provocation.

"Here, gentlemen, are the babies," said Frazer, depositing his burden on the floor. "They do credit to the nursing of the brindled slut."

The old tar laughed, chuckled, and rubbed his hands in ecstasy of delight at the indignation and disappointment visible in the countenance of the Scotch Esculapius, who, angry as he was, wisely held his tongue. Not so the Frenchman; his rage scarcely knew bounds —he danced in a state of most ludicrous excitement, he shook his fist at our rough captain, and screamed at the top of his voice—

"Sacré, you bête! You tink us dog, when you try to pass your puppies on us for babies?"

"Hout, man, don't be angry," said the Scotchman, stifling a laugh; "you see 'tis only a joke!"

"Joke! me no understand such joke. Bête!" returned the angry Frenchman, bestowing a savage kick on one of the unoffending pups which was frisking about his feet. The pup yelped; the slut barked and leaped furiously at the offender, and was only kept from biting him by Sam, who could scarcely hold her back for laughing; the captain was uproarious; the offended Frenchman alone maintained a severe and dignified aspect. The dogs were at length dismissed, and peace restored.

23

After some further questioning from the officials, a Bible was required for the captain to take an oath. Mine was mislaid, and there was none at hand.

"Confound it!" muttered the old sailor, tossing over the papers in his desk; "that scoundrel, Sam, always stows my traps out of the way." Then taking up from the table a book which I had been reading, which happened to be Voltaire's *History of Charles XII.*, he presented it, with as grave an air as he could assume, to the Frenchman. Taking for granted that it was the volume required, the little doctor was too polite to open the book, the captain was duly sworn, and the party returned to the deck.

Here a new difficulty occurred, which nearly ended in a serious quarrel. The gentlemen requested the old sailor to give them a few feet of old planking to repair some damage which their boat had sustained the day before. This the captain could not do. They seemed to think his refusal intentional, and took it as a personal affront. In no very gentle tones they ordered him instantly to prepare his boats, and put his passengers on shore.

"Stiff breeze—short sea," returned the bluff old seaman; "great risk in making land—boats heavily laden with women and children will be swamped. Not a soul goes on shore this night."

"If you refuse to comply with our orders, we will report you to the authorities."

"I know my duty—you stick to yours. When the wind falls off I'll see to it. Not a life shall be risked to please you or your authorities."

He turned upon his heel, and the medical men left

Susanna Moodie

the vessel in great disdain. We had every reason to be thankful for the firmness displayed by our rough commander. That same evening we saw eleven persons drowned, from another vessel close beside us, while attempting to make the shore.

By daybreak all was hurry and confusion on board the *Anne*. I watched boat after boat depart for the island, full of people and goods, and envied them the glorious privilege of once more standing firmly on the earth after two long months of rocking and rolling at sea. How ardently we anticipate pleasure, which often ends in positive pain! Such was my case when at last indulged in the gratification so eagerly desired. As cabin passengers we were not included in the general order of purification, but were only obliged to send our servant, with the clothes and bedding we had used during the voyage, on shore, to be washed.

The ship was soon emptied of all her live cargo. My husband went off with the boats, to reconnoitre the island, and I was left alone with my baby in the otherwise empty vessel. Even Oscar, the captain's Scotch terrier, who had formed a devoted attachment to me during the voyage, forgot his allegiance, became possessed of the land mania, and was away with the rest. With the most intense desire to go on shore, I was doomed to look and long and envy every boatful of emigrants that glided past. Nor was this all; the ship was out of provisions, and I was condemned to undergo a rigid fast until the return of the boat, when the captain had promised a supply of fresh butter and bread. The vessel had been nine weeks at sea; the poor steerage passengers for the two last weeks had

25

been out of food, and the captain had been obliged to feed them from the ship's stores. The promised bread was to be obtained from a small steam-boat which plied daily between Quebec and the island, transporting convalescent emigrants and their goods in her upward trip and provisions for the sick on her return.

How I reckoned on once more tasting bread and butter! The very thought of the treat in store served to sharpen my appetite and render the long fast more irksome. I could now fully realize all Mrs. Bowdich's longings for English bread and butter, after her three years' travel through the burning African deserts with her talented husband.

"When we arrived at the hotel at Plymouth," said she, "and were asked what refreshment we chose— 'Tea, and home-made bread and butter,' was my instant reply. 'Brown bread, if you please, and plenty of it.' I never enjoyed any luxury like it. I was positively ashamed of asking the waiter to refill the plate. After the execrable messes, and the hard ship-biscuit, imagine the luxury of a good slice of English bread and butter!"

At home, I laughed heartily at the lively energy with which that charming woman of genius related this little incident in her eventual history—but off Grosse Isle I realized it all.

As the sun rose above the horizon, all these matter-of-fact circumstances were gradually forgotten and merged in the surpassing grandeur of the scene that rose majestically before me. The previous day had been dark and stormy, and a heavy fog had concealed the mountain chain, which forms the stupendous background to this sublime view, entirely from our sight. As the clouds rolled away from their grey, bald brows, and cast into denser shadow the vast forest belt that girdled them round, they loomed out like mighty giants—Titans of the earth, in all their rugged and awful beauty—a thrill of wonder and delight pervaded my mind. The spectacle floated dimly on my sight—my eyes were blinded with tears—blinded by the excess of beauty. I turned to the right and to the left, I looked up and down the glorious river; never had I beheld so many striking objects blended into one mighty whole! Nature had lavished all her noblest features in producing that enchanting scene.

The rocky isle in front, with its neat farmhouses at the eastern point, and its high bluff at the western extremity, crowned with the telegraph—the middle space occupied by tents and sheds for the cholera patients, and its wooded shores dotted over with motley groups—added greatly to the picturesque effect of the land scene. Then the broad glittering river, covered with boats darting to and fro, conveying passengers from twenty-five vessels, of various size and tonnage, which rode at anchor, with their flags flying from the masthead, gave an air of life and interest to the whole. Turning to the south side of the St. Lawrence, I was not less struck with its low fertile shores, white houses, and neat churches, whose slender spires and bright tin roofs shone like silver as they caught the first rays of the sun. As far as the eye could reach, a line of white buildings extended along the bank, their background formed by the purple hue of the

ROUGHING IT IN THE BUSH

dense, interminable forest. It was a scene unlike any I had ever beheld, and to which Britain contains no parallel. Mackenzie, an old Scotch dragoon, who was one of our passengers, when he rose in the morning and saw the parish of St. Thomas for the first time, exclaimed: "Weel, it beats a'! Can thae white clouts be a' houses? They look like claes hung out to drie!" There was some truth in this odd comparison, and for some minutes I could scarcely convince myself that the white patches scattered so thickly over the opposite shore could be the dwellings of a busy, lively population.

"What sublime views of the north side of the river those *habitans* of St. Thomas must enjoy," thought I. Perhaps familiarity with the scene has rendered them indifferent to its astonishing beauty.

Eastward, the view down the St. Lawrence towards the Gulf is the finest of all, scarcely surpassed by anything in the world. Your eye follows the long range of lofty mountains until their blue summits are blended and lost in the blue of the sky. Some of these, partially cleared round the base, are sprinkled over with neat cottages, and the green slopes that spread around them are covered with flocks and herds. The surface of the splendid river is diversified with islands of every size and shape, some in wood, others partially cleared, and adorned with orchards and white farmhouses. As the early sun streamed upon the most prominent of these, leaving the others in deep shade, the effect was strangely novel and imposing. In more remote regions, where the forest has never yet echoed to the woodman's axe, or received the impress of civilization, the first approach to the shore inspires a melancholy awe which becomes painful in its intensity.

> And silence—awful silence broods
> Profoundly o'er these solitudes;
> Not but the lapsing of the floods
> Breaks the deep stillness of the woods;
> A sense of desolation reigns
> O'er these unpeopled forest plains
> Where sounds of life ne'er wake a tone
> Of cheerful praise round Nature's throne,
> Man finds himself with God—alone.

My daydreams were dispelled by the return of the boat, which brought my husband and the captain from the island.

"No bread," said the latter, shaking his head; "you must be content to starve a little longer. Provision-ship not in till four o'clock." My husband smiled at the look of blank disappointment with which I received these unwelcome tidings. "Never mind, I have news which will comfort you. The officer who commands the station sent a note to me by an orderly, inviting us to spend the afternoon with him. He promises to show us everything worthy of notice on the island. Captain —— claims acquaintance with me; but I have not the least recollection of him. Would you like to go?"

"Oh, by all means. I long to see the lovely island. It looks a perfect paradise at this distance."

The rough sailor-captain screwed his mouth on one side, and gave me one of his comical looks; but he said nothing until he assisted in placing me and the baby in the boat.

"Don't be too sanguine, Mrs. Moodie; many things

look well at a distance which are bad enough when near."

I scarcely regarded the old sailor's warning. So eager was I to go on shore—to put my foot upon the soil of the new world for the first time—I was in no humour to listen to any depreciation of what seemed so beautiful.

It was four o'clock when we landed on the rocks, which the rays of an intensely scorching sun had rendered so hot that I could scarcely place my foot upon them. How the people without shoes bore it I cannot imagine. Never shall I forget the extraordinary spectacle that met our sight the moment we passed the low range of bushes which formed a screen in front of the river. A crowd of many hundred Irish emigrants had been landed during the present and former day and all this motley crew—men, women, and children, who were not confined by sickness to the sheds (which greatly resembled cattle-pens)—were employed in washing clothes or spreading them out on the rocks and bushes to dry.

The men and boys were *in* the water, while the women, with their scanty garments tucked above their knees, were tramping their bedding in tubs or in holes in the rocks, which the retiring tide had left half full of water. Those who did not possess washing tubs, pails, or iron pots, or could not obtain access to a hole in the rocks, were running to and fro, screaming and scolding in no measured terms. The confusion of Babel was among them. All talkers and no hearers—each shouting and yelling in his or her uncouth dialect, and all accompanying their vociferations with violent and

A VISIT TO GROSS ISLE

extraordinary gestures, quite incomprehensible to the uninitiated. We were literally stunned by the strife of tongues. I shrank, with feelings almost akin to fear, from the hard-featured, sunburnt women as they elbowed rudely past me.

I had heard and read much of savages, and have since seen, during my long residence in the bush, somewhat of uncivilized life, but the Indian is one of Nature's gentlemen—he never says or does a rude or vulgar thing. The vicious, uneducated barbarians, who form the surplus of overpopulous European countries, are far behind the wild man in delicacy of feeling or natural courtesy. The people who covered the island appeared perfectly destitute of shame, or even a sense of common decency. Many were almost naked, still more but partially clothed. We turned in disgust from the revolting scene, but were unable to leave the spot until the captain had satisfied a noisy group of his own people, who were demanding a supply of stores.

And here I must observe that our passengers, who were chiefly honest Scotch labourers and mechanics from the vicinity of Edinburgh, and who while on board ship had conducted themselves with the greatest propriety, and appeared the most quiet, orderly set of people in the world, no sooner set foot upon the island than they became infected by the same spirit of insubordination and misrule, and were just as insolent and noisy as the rest.

While our captain was vainly endeavouring to satisfy the unreasonable demands of his rebellious people, Moodie had discovered a woodland path that led to the back of the island. Sheltered by some hazel-bushes from the intense heat of the sun, we sat down by the cool, gushing river, out of sight, but, alas! not out of hearing of the noisy, riotous crowd. Could we have shut out the profane sounds which came to us on every breeze, how deeply should we have enjoyed an hour amid the tranquil beauties of that retired and lovely spot!

The rocky banks of the island were adorned with beautiful evergreens, which sprang up spontaneously in every nook and crevice. I remarked many of our favourite garden shrubs among these wildings of nature: the fillagree, with its narrow, dark glossy-green leaves; the privet, with its modest white blossoms and purple berries; the lignum-vitæ, with its strong resinous odour; the burnet-rose; and a great variety of elegant unknowns.

Here, the shores of the island and mainland, receding from each other, formed a small cove, overhung with lofty trees, clothed from the base to the summit with wild vines, that hung in graceful festoons from the topmost branches to the water's edge. The dark shadows of the mountains, thrown upon the water, as they towered to the height of some thousand feet above us, gave to the surface of the river an ebon hue. The sunbeams, dancing through the thick, quivering foliage, fell in stars of gold, or long lines of dazzling brightness, upon the deep black waters, producing the most novel and beautiful effects. It was a scene over which the spirit of peace might brood in silent adoration; but how spoiled by the discordant yells of the filthy beings who were sullying the purity of the air and water with contaminating sights and sounds!

We were now joined by the sergeant, who very kindly brought us his capful of ripe plums and hazel-nuts, the growth of the island: a joyful present, but marred by a note from Captain ——, who had found that he had been mistaken in his supposed knowledge of us, and politely apologized for not being allowed by the health-officers to receive any emigrant beyond the bounds appointed for the performance of quarantine.

I was deeply disappointed, but my husband laughingly told me that I had seen enough of the island, and, turning to the good-natured soldier, remarked that "it could be no easy task to keep such wild savages in order."

"You may well say that, sir—but our night scenes far exceed those of the day. You would think they were incarnate devils, singing, drinking, dancing, shouting, and cutting antics that would surprise the leader of a circus. They have no shame—are under no restraint—nobody knows them here, and they think they can speak and act as they please; and they are such thieves that they rob one another of the little they possess. The healthy actually run the risk of taking the cholera by robbing the sick. If you have not hired one or two stout, honest fellows from among your fellow-passengers to guard your clothes while they are drying, you will never see half of them again. They are a sad set, sir, a sad set. We could, perhaps, manage the men; but the women, sir!—the women! Oh, sir!"

Anxious as we were to return to the ship, we were obliged to remain until sundown in our retired nook. We were hungry, tired, and out of spirits; the mosquitoes swarmed in myriads around us, tormenting the poor baby, who, not at all pleased with her visit to the new world, filled the air with cries, when the captain came to tell us that the boat was ready. It was a welcome sound. Forcing our way once more through the still squabbling crowd, we gained the landing place. Here we encountered a boat, just landing a fresh cargo of emigrants from the Emerald Isle. One fellow, of gigantic proportions, whose long, tattered great-coat just reached below the middle of his bare red legs and, like charity, hid the defects of his other garments, or perhaps concealed his want of them, leaped upon the rocks, and flourishing aloft his shilelagh, bounded and capered like a wild goat from his native mountains. "Whurrah! my boys!" he cried. "Shure we'll all be jintlemen!"

"Pull away, my lads!" said the captain. Then turning to me, "Well, Mrs. Moodie, I hope that you have had enough of Grosse Isle. But could you have witnessed the scenes that I did this morning——"

Here he was interrupted by the wife of the old Scotch dragoon, Mackenzie, running down to the boat and laying her hand familiarly upon his shoulder, "Captain, dinna forget."

"Forget what?"

She whispered something confidentially in his ear.

"Oh, ho! the brandy!" he responded aloud. "I should have thought, Mrs. Mackenzie, that you had had enough of *that same* on yon island?"

"Aye, sic a place for *decent* folk," returned the drunken body, shaking her head. "One needs a drap o' comfort, captain, to keep up one's heart avá."

The captain set up one of his boisterous laughs as he pushed the boat from the shore. "Hollo! Sam Frazer! steer in, we have forgotten the stores."

"I hope not, captain," said I; "I have been starving since daybreak."

"The bread, the butter, the beef, the onions, and potatoes are here, sir," said honest Sam, particularizing each article.

"All right; pull for the ship. Mrs. Moodie, we will have a glorious supper, and mind you don't dream of Grosse Isle."

In a few minutes we were again on board. Thus ended my first day's experience of the land of all our hopes.

CHAPTER TWO
QUEBEC

Queen of the West!—upon thy rocky throne,
   In solitary grandeur sternly placed;
In awful Majesty thou sitt'st alone,
   By Nature's master-hand supremely graced.
The world has not thy counterpart—thy dower,
Eternal beauty, strength, and matchless power.

The clouds enfold thee in their misty vest,
   The lightning glances harmless round thy brow;
The loud-voiced thunder cannot shake thy nest,
   Or warring waves that idly chafe below;
The storm above—the waters at thy feet—
May rage and foam, they but secure thy seat.

The mighty river, as it onward rushes
   To pour its floods in ocean's dread abyss,
Checks at thy feet its fierce impetuous gushes,
   And gently fawns thy rocky base to kiss.
Stern eagle of the crag! thy hold should be
The mountain home of heaven-born liberty!

True to themselves, thy children may defy
   The power and malice of a world combined;
While Britain's flag, beneath thy deep blue sky,
   Spreads its rich folds and wantons in the wind;
The offsprings of her glorious race of old
May rest securely in their mountain hold.

ON THE FIFTH OF SEPTEMBER THE AN-
chor was weighed, and we bade a long farewell to
Grosse Isle. As our vessel struck into mid-channel, I
cast a last lingering look at the beautiful shores we
were leaving. Cradled in the arms of the St. Lawrence,
and basking in the bright rays of the morning sun, the
island and its sister group looked like a second Eden
just emerged from the waters of chàos. With what
joy could I have spent the rest of the fall in exploring
the romantic features of that enchanting scene! But

39

ROUGHING IT IN THE BUSH

our bark spread her white wings to the favouring breeze, and the fairy vision gradually receded from my sight, to remain for ever on the tablets of memory.

The day was warm, and the cloudless heavens of that peculiar azure tint which gives to the Canadian skies and waters a brilliancy unknown in more favoured latitudes. The air was pure and elastic, the sun shone out in uncommon splendour, lighting up the changing woods with a rich mellow colouring, composed of a thousand brilliant and vivid dyes. The mighty river rolled flashing and sparkling onward, impelled by a strong breeze, that tipped its short rolling surges with a crest of snowy foam.

Had there been no other object of interest in the landscape than this majestic river, its vast magnitude, and the depth and clearness of its waters, and its great importance to the colony would have been sufficient to have riveted the attention and claimed the admiration of every thinking mind.

Never shall I forget that short voyage from Grosse Isle to Quebec. I love to recall, after the lapse of so many years, every object that awoke in my breast emotions of astonishment and delight. What wonderful combinations of beauty, and grandeur, and power, at every winding of that noble river! How the mind expands with the sublimity of the spectacle, and soars upward in gratitude and adoration to the Author of all being, to thank Him for having made this lower world so wondrously fair—a living temple, heaven-arched, and capable of receiving the homage of all worshippers.

Every perception of my mind became absorbed in-

QUEBEC FROM THE WALLS, 1830

to the one sense of seeing, when, upon rounding Point
Levi, we cast anchor before Quebec. What a scene!
—Can the world produce such another? Edinburgh
had been the *beau idéal* to me of all that was beautiful in Nature—a vision of the northern Highlands
had haunted my dreams across the Atlantic; but all
these past recollections faded before the *present* of
Quebec.

Nature has lavished all her grandest elements to
form this astonishing panorama. There frowns the
cloud-capped mountain, and below, the cataract foams
and thunders; wood, and rock, and river combined to
lend their aid in making the picture perfect and worthy of its Divine Originator.

The precipitous bank upon which the city lies piled,
reflected in the still deep waters at its base, greatly
enhances the romantic beauty of the situation. The
mellow and serene glow of the autumnal day harm-
onized so perfectly with the solemn grandeur of the
scene around me, and sank so silently and deeply into my soul, that my spirit fell prostrate before it, and
I melted involuntarily into tears. Yes, regardless of
the eager crowds around me, I leant upon the side of
the vessel and cried like a child—not tears of sorrow,
but a gush from the heart of pure and unalloyed delight. I heard not the many voices murmuring in my
ears—I saw not the anxious beings that thronged our
narrow deck—my soul at that moment was alone with
God. The shadow of His glory rested visibly on the
stupendous objects that composed that magnificent
scene; words are perfectly inadequate to describe the
impression it made upon my mind—the emotions it

41

produced. The only homage I was capable of offering at such a shrine was tears—tears the most heartfelt and sincere that ever flowed from human eyes. I never before felt so overpowering my own insignificance, and the boundless might and majesty of the Eternal.

Canadians, rejoice in your beautiful city! Rejoice and be worthy of her—for few, very few, of the sons of men can point to such a spot as Quebec—and exclaim, "She is ours!—God gave her to us in her beauty and strength!—We will live for her glory—we will die to defend her liberty and rights—to raise her majestic brow high above the nations!"

Look at the situation of Quebec!—the city founded on the rock that proudly holds the height of the hill. The queen sitting enthroned above the waters, that curb their swiftness and their strength to kiss her lovely feet.

Canadians!—as long as you remain true to yourselves and her, what foreign invader could ever dare to plant a hostile flag upon that rock-defended height, or set his foot upon a fortress rendered impregnable by the hand of Nature? United in friendship, loyalty, and love, what wonders may you not achieve? to what an enormous altitude of wealth and importance may you not arrive? Look at the St. Lawrence, that king of streams, that great artery flowing from the heart of the world, through the length and breadth of the land, carrying wealth and fertility in its course, and transporting from town to town along its beautiful shores the riches and produce of a thousand distant climes. What elements of future greatness and prosperity encircle you on every side! Never yield up these solid advantages to become an humble dependant on the great republic—wait patiently, loyally, lovingly upon the illustrious parent from whom you sprang, and by whom you have been fostered into life and political importance; in the fulness of time she will proclaim your childhood past, and bid you stand up in your own strength, a free Canadian people!

British mothers of Canadian sons!—learn to feel for their country the same enthusiasm which fills your hearts when thinking of the glory of your own. Teach them to love Canada—to look upon her as the first, the happiest, the most independent country in the world! Exhort them to be worthy of her—to have faith in her present prosperity, in her future greatness, and to devote all their talents, when they themselves are men, to accomplish this noble object. Make your children proud of the land of their birth, the land which has given them bread—the land in which you have found an altar and a home; do this, and you will soon cease to lament your separation from the mother country, and the loss of those luxuries which you could not, in honour to yourself, enjoy; you will soon learn to love Canada as I now love it, who once viewed it with hatred so intense that I longed to die, that death might effectually separate us for ever.

But, oh! beware of drawing disparaging contrasts between the colony and its illustrious parent. All such comparisons are cruel and unjust;—you cannot exalt the one at the expense of the other without committing an act of treason against both.

But I have wandered away from my subject into

the regions of thought, and must again descend to common workaday realities.

The pleasure we experienced upon our first glance at Quebec was greatly damped by the sad conviction that the cholera-plague raged within her walls, while the almost ceaseless tolling of bells proclaimed a mournful tale of woe and death. Scarcely a person visited the vessel who was not in black, or who spoke not in tones of subdued grief. They advised us not to go on shore if we valued our lives, as strangers most commonly fell the first victims to this fatal malady. This was to me a severe disappointment, who felt an intense desire to climb to the crown of the rock, and survey the noble landscape at my feet. I yielded at last to the wishes of my husband, who did not himself resist the temptation in his own person, and en‐ deavoured to content myself with the means of enjoyment placed within my reach. My eyes were never tired of wandering over the scene before me.

It is curious to observe how differently the objects which call forth intense admiration in some minds will affect others. The Scotch dragoon, Mackenzie, see‐ ing me look long and intently at the distant Falls of Montmorency, dryly observed—

" It may be a' vera fine ; but it looks na' better to my thinken than hanks o' white woo' hung out o'er the bushes."

" Weel," cried another, " thae fa's are just bonnie; 'tis a braw land, nae doubt; but no' just so braw as auld Scotland."

" Hout, man! hauld your clavers, we shall a' be lairds here," said a third; "and ye maun wait a muckle time before they wad think aucht of you at hame."

I was not a little amused at the extravagant expectations entertained by some of our steerage passengers. The sight of the Canadian shores had changed them into persons of great consequence. The poorest and the worst-dressed, the least-deserving and the most repulsive in mind and morals exhibited most disgusting traits of self-importance. Vanity and presumption seemed to possess them altogether. They talked loudly of the rank and wealth of their connexions at home, and lamented the great sacrifices they had made in order to join brothers and cousins who had foolishly settled in this beggarly wooden country.

Girls, who were scarcely able to wash a floor decently, talked of service with contempt, unless tempted to change their resolution by the offer of twelve dollars a month. To endeavour to undeceive them was a useless and ungracious task. After having tried it with several without success, I left it to time and bitter experience to restore them to their sober senses. In spite of the remonstrances of the captain and the dread of the cholera, they all rushed on shore to inspect the land of Goshen, and to endeavour to realize their absurd anticipations.

We were favoured, a few minutes after our arrival, with another visit from the health-officers; but in this instance both the gentlemen were Canadians. Grave, melancholy-looking men, who talked much and ominously of the prevailing disorder, and the impossibility of strangers escaping from its fearful ravages. This was not very consoling, and served to depress

45

the cheerful tone of mind which, after all, is one of the best antidotes against this awful scourge. The cabin seemed to lighten, and the air to circulate more freely, after the departure of these professional ravens. The captain, as if by instinct, took an additional glass of grog, to shake off the sepulchral gloom their presence had inspired.

The visit of the doctors was followed by that of two of the officials of the Customs—vulgar, illiterate men, who, seating themselves at the cabin table, with a familiar nod to the captain and a blank stare at us, commenced the following dialogue :—

Custom-house officer (*after making inquiries as to the general cargo of the vessel*): " Any good brandy on board, captain? "

Captain (*gruffly*): "Yes."

Officer: "Best remedy for the cholera known. The only one the doctors can depend upon."

Captain (*taking the hint*): "Gentlemen, I'll send you up a dozen bottles this afternoon."

Officer: "Oh, thank you. We are sure to get it *genuine* from you. Any Edinburgh ale in your freight? "

Captain (*with a slight shrug*): "A few hundreds in cases. I'll send you a dozen with the brandy."

Both: "Capital!"

First officer: "Any short, large-bowled, Scotch pipes, with metallic lids? "

Captain (*quite impatiently*): "Yes, yes; I'll send you some to smoke, with the brandy.—What else? "

Officer: "We will now proceed to business."

My readers would have laughed, as I did, could they have seen how doggedly the old man shook his fist after these worthies as they left the vessel. "Scoundrels!" he muttered to himself; and then turning to me, "They rob us in this barefaced manner, and we dare not resist or complain, for fear of the trouble they can put us to. If I had those villains at sea, I'd give them a taste of brandy and ale that they would not relish."

The day wore away, and the lengthened shadows of the mountains fell upon the waters, when the *Horsley Hill*, a large three-masted vessel from Waterford, that we had left at the quarantine station, cast anchor a little above us. She was quickly boarded by the health-officers, and ordered round to take up her station below the castle. To accomplish this object she had to heave her anchor; when lo! a great pine-tree, which had been sunk in the river, became entangled in the chains. Uproarious was the mirth to which the incident gave rise among the crowds that thronged the decks of the many vessels then at anchor in the river. Speaking trumpets resounded on every side; and my readers may be assured that the sea-serpent was not forgotten in the multitude of jokes which followed.

Laughter resounded on all sides; and in the midst of the noise and confusion, the captain of the *Horsley Hill* hoisted his colours downwards, as if making signals of distress, a mistake which provoked renewed and long-continued mirth.

I laughed until my sides ached, little thinking how the *Horsley Hill* would pay us off for our mistimed hilarity.

Towards night, most of the steerage passengers returned, greatly dissatisfied with their first visit to the city, which they declared to be a filthy hole, that looked a great deal better from the ship's side than it did on shore. This, I have often been told, is literally the case. Here, as elsewhere, man has marred the magnificent creation of his Maker.

A dark and starless night closed in, accompanied by cold winds and drizzling rain. We seemed to have made a sudden leap from the torrid to the frigid zone. Two hours before, my light summer clothing was almost insupportable, and now a heavy and well-lined plaid formed but an inefficient screen from the inclemency of the weather. After watching for some time the singular effect produced by the lights in the town reflected in the water, and weary with a long day of anticipation and excitement, I made up my mind to leave the deck and retire to rest. I had just settled down my baby in her berth, when the vessel struck, with a sudden crash that sent a shiver through her whole frame. Alarmed, but not aware of the real danger that hung over us, I groped my way to the cabin, and thence ascended to the deck.

Here a scene of confusion prevailed that baffles description. By some strange fatality, the *Horsley Hill* had changed her position, and run foul of us in the dark. The *Anne* was a small brig, and her unlucky neighbour a heavy three-masted vessel, with three hundred Irish emigrants on board; and as her bowsprit was directly across the bows of the *Anne*, and she anchored and unable to free herself from the deadly embrace, there was no small danger of the poor brig going down in the unequal struggle.

48

QUEBEC

Unable to comprehend what was going on, I raised my head above the companion ladder, just at the critical moment when the vessels were grappled together. The shrieks of the women, the shouts and oaths of the men, and the barking of the dogs in either ship aided the dense darkness of the night in producing a most awful and stunning effect.

"What is the matter?" I gasped out. "What is the reason of this dreadful confusion?"

The captain was raging like a chafed bull, in the grasp of several frantic women, who were clinging, shrieking, to his knees.

With great difficulty I persuaded the women to accompany me below. The mate hurried off with the cabin light upon the deck, and we were left in total darkness to await the result.

A deep, strange silence fell upon my heart. It was not exactly fear, but a sort of nerving of my spirit to meet the worst. The cowardly behaviour of my companions inspired me with courage. I was ashamed of their pusillanimity and want of faith in the Divine Providence. I sat down, and calmly begged them to follow my example.

An old woman, called Williamson, a sad reprobate, in attempting to do so set her foot within the fender, which the captain had converted into a repository for empty glass bottles; the smash that ensued was echoed by a shriek from the whole party.

"God guide us," cried the ancient dame; "but we are going into eternity. I shall be lost; my sins are more in number than the hairs of my head." This

49   D

confession was followed by oaths and imprecations too blasphemous to repeat.

Shocked and disgusted at her profanity, I bade her pray, and not waste the few moments that might be hers in using oaths and bad language.

"Did you not hear the crash?" said she.

"I did; it was of your own making. Sit down and be quiet."

Here followed another shock, that made the vessel heave and tremble; and the dragging of the anchor increased the uneasy motion which began to fill the boldest of us with alarm.

"Mrs. Moodie, we are lost," said Margaret Williamson, the youngest granddaughter of the old woman, a pretty girl, who had been the belle of the ship, flinging herself on her knees before me, and grasping both my hands in hers. "Oh, pray for me! pray for me! I cannot, I dare not pray for myself; I was never taught a prayer." Her voice was choked with convulsive sobs, and scalding tears fell in torrents from her eyes over my hands. I never witnessed such an agony of despair. Before I could say one word to comfort her, another shock seemed to lift the vessel upwards. I felt my own blood run cold, expecting instantly to go down; and thoughts of death, and the unknown eternity at our feet, flitted vaguely through my mind.

"If we stay here, we shall perish," cried the girl, springing to her feet. "Let us go on deck, mother, and take our chance with the rest."

"Stay," said I; "you are safer here. British sailors never leave women to perish. You have fathers, husbands, brothers on board, who will not forget you. I beseech you to remain patiently here until the danger is past." I might as well have preached to the winds. The headstrong creatures would no longer be controlled. They rushed simultaneously upon deck, just as the *Horsley Hill* swung off, carrying with her part of the outer frame of our deck and the larger portion of our stern. When tranquillity was restored, fatigued both in mind and body, I sunk into a profound sleep, and did not wake until the sun had risen high above the wave-encircled fortress of Quebec.

The stormy clouds had all dispersed during the night; the air was clear and balmy; the giant hills were robed in a blue, soft mist, which rolled around them in fleecy volumes. As the beams of the sun penetrated their shadowy folds, they gradually drew up like a curtain, and dissolved like wreaths of smoke into the clear air.

The moment I came on deck, my old friend Oscar greeted me with his usual joyous bark, and, with the sagacity peculiar to his species, proceeded to show me all the damage done to the vessel during the night. It was laughable to watch the motions of the poor brute as he ran from place to place, stopping before, or jumping upon, every fractured portion of the deck, and barking out his indignation at the ruinous condition in which he found his marine home. Oscar had made eleven voyages in the *Anne*, and had twice saved the life of the captain. He was an ugly specimen of the Scotch terrier, and greatly resembled a bundle of old rope-yarn; but a more faithful or attached creature I never saw. The captain was not a little jealous of Oscar's friendship for me. I was the only person the dog had ever deigned to notice, and his master regarded it as an act of treason on the part of his four-footed favourite. When my arms were tired with nursing, I had only to lay my baby on my cloak on deck and tell Oscar to watch her, and the good dog would lie down by her, and suffer her to tangle his long curls in her little hands, and pull his tail and ears in the most approved baby fashion, without offering the least opposition; but if any one dared to approach his charge, he was alive on the instant, placing his paws over the child and growling furiously. He would have been a bold man who had approached the child to do her an injury. Oscar was the best plaything and as sure a protector as Katie had.

During the day, many of our passengers took their departure; tired of the close confinement of the ship and the long voyage, they were too impatient to remain on board until we reached Montreal. The mechanics obtained instant employment, and the girls, who were old enough to work, procured situations as servants in the city. Before night, our numbers were greatly reduced. The old dragoon and his family, two Scotch fiddlers of the name of Duncan, a Highlander called Tam Grant, and his wife and little son, and our own party were all that remained of the seventy-two passengers that left the port of Leith in the brig *Anne*.

In spite of the earnest entreaties of his young wife, the said Tam Grant, who was the most mercurial fellow in the world, would insist upon going on shore to see all the lions of the place. " Ah, Tam! Tam! ye will die o' the cholera," cried the weeping Maggie. " My

QUEBEC

heart will brak if ye dinna bide wi' me an' the bairnie."
Tam was deaf as Ailsa Craig. Regardless of tears and
entreaties, he jumped into the boat, like a wilful man
as he was, and my husband went with him. Fortunately for me, the latter returned safe to the vessel, in
time to proceed with her to Montreal, in tow of the
noble steamer, *British America*; but Tam, the volatile Tam was missing. During the reign of the cholera,
what at another time would have appeared but a trifling incident was now invested with doubt and terror.
The distress of the poor wife knew no bounds. I think
I see her now, as I saw her then, sitting upon the floor
of the deck, her head buried between her knees, rocking herself to and fro, and weeping in the utter abandonment of her grief. "He is dead! he is dead! My
dear, dear Tam! The pestilence has seized upon him;
and I and the puir bairn are left alone in the strange
land." All attempts at consolation were useless; she
obstinately refused to listen to probabilities, or to be
comforted. All through the night I heard her deep
and bitter sobs and the oft-repeated name of him that
she had lost.

The sun was sinking over the plague-stricken city,
gilding the changing woods and mountain peaks with
ruddy light; the river mirrored back the gorgeous
sky, and moved in billows of liquid gold; the very air
seemed lighted up with heavenly fires, and sparkled
with myriads of luminous particles, as I gazed my
last upon that beautiful scene.

The tow-line was now attached from our ship to
the *British America,* and in company with two other
vessels, we followed fast in her foaming wake. Day

lingered on the horizon just long enough to enable me to examine, with deep interest, the rocky heights of Abraham, the scene of our immortal Wolfe's victory and death; and when the twilight faded into night, the moon arose in solemn beauty, and cast mysterious gleams upon the strange stern landscape. The wide river, flowing rapidly between its rugged banks, rolled in inky blackness beneath the overshadowing crags; while the waves in mid-channel flashed along in dazzling light, rendered more intense by the surrounding darkness. In this luminous track the huge steamer glided majestically forward, flinging showers of red earth-stars from the funnel into the clear air, and looking like some fiery demon of the night enveloped in smoke and flame.

The lofty groves of pine frowned down in hearse-like gloom upon the mighty river, and the deep stillness of the night, broken alone by its hoarse wailings, filled my mind with sad forebodings—alas! too prophetic of the future. Keenly, for the first time, I felt that I was a stranger in a strange land; my heart yearned intensely for my absent home. Home! the word had ceased to belong to my *present*—it was doomed to live for ever in the *past*; for what emigrant ever regarded the country of his exile as his *home*? To the land he has left that name belongs for ever, and in no instance does he bestow it upon another. "I have got a letter from home!" "I have seen a friend from home!" "I dreamt last night that I was at home!" are expressions of everyday occurrence, to prove that the heart acknowledges no other home than the land of its birth.

QUEBEC

From these sad reveries I was roused by the hoarse notes of the bagpipe. That well-known sound brought every Scotchman upon deck, and set every limb in motion on the decks of the other vessels. Determined not to be outdone, our fiddlers took up the strain, and a lively contest ensued between the rival musicians, which continued during the greater part of the night. The shouts of noisy revelry were in no way congenial to my feelings. Nothing tends so much to increase our melancholy as merry music when the heart is sad; and I left the scene with eyes brimful of tears, and my mind painfully agitated by sorrowful recollections and vain regrets.

CHAPTER THREE
OUR JOURNEY UP THE COUNTRY

CHAPTER   THREE

OUR JOURNEY UP THE COUNTRY

Fly this plague-stricken spot! The hot, foul air
Is rank with pestilence—the crowded marts
And public ways, once populous with life,
Are still and noisome as a churchyard vault;
Aghast and shuddering, Nature holds her breath
In abject fear, and feels at her strong heart
The deadly pangs of death.

OF MONTREAL I CAN SAY BUT LITTLE. The cholera was at its height, and the fear of infection, which increased the nearer we approached its shores, cast a gloom over the scene, and prevented us from exploring its infected streets. That the feelings of all on board very nearly resembled our own might be read in the anxious faces of both passengers and crew. Our captain, who had never before hinted that he entertained any apprehensions on the subject, now confided to us his conviction that he should never quit the city alive: "This cursed cholera! Left it in Russia—found it on my return to Leith—meets me again in Canada. No escape the third time." If the captain's prediction proved true in his case, it was not so in ours. We left the cholera in England, we met it again in Scotland, and, under the providence of God, we escaped its fatal visitation in Canada.

Yet the fear and the dread of it on that first day caused me to throw many an anxious glance on my husband and my child. I had been very ill during the three weeks that our vessel was becalmed upon the Banks of Newfoundland, and to this circumstance I attribute my deliverance from the pestilence. I was weak and nervous when the vessel arrived at Quebec, but the voyage up the St. Lawrence, the fresh air and beautiful scenery were rapidly restoring me to health.

Montreal from the river wears a pleasing aspect, but it lacks the grandeur, the stern sublimity of Quebec. The fine mountain that forms the background to the city, the Island of St. Helens in front, and the junction of the St. Lawrence and the Ottawa—which run side by side, their respective boundaries only marked by a long ripple of white foam, and the darker blue tint of the former river—constitute the most remarkable features in the landscape.

The town itself was, at that period, dirty and ill-paved; and the opening of all the sewers, in order to purify the place and stop the ravages of the pestilence, rendered the public thoroughfares almost impassable and loaded the air with intolerable effluvia, more likely to produce than stay the course of the plague, the violence of which had, in all probability, been increased by these long-neglected receptacles of uncleanliness.

The dismal stories told us by the excise-officer who came to inspect the unloading of the vessel, of the frightful ravages of the cholera, by no means increased our desire to go on shore.

" It will be a miracle if you escape," he said. " Hundreds of emigrants die daily; and if Stephen Ayres had not providentially come among us, not a soul would have been alive at this moment in Montreal."

" And who is Stephen Ayres? " said I.

"God only knows," was the grave reply. " There was a man sent from heaven, and his name was John."

" But I thought this man was called Stephen? "

" Ay, so he calls himself; but 'tis certain that he is not of the earth. Flesh and blood could never do what he has done—the hand of God is in it. Besides, no one knows who he is, or whence he comes. When the cholera was at the worst, and the hearts of all men stood still with fear, and our doctors could do nothing to stop its progress, this man, or angel, or saint suddenly made his appearance in our streets. He came in great humility, seated in an ox-cart, and drawn by two lean oxen and a rope harness. Only think of that! Such a man in an *old ox-cart*, drawn by *rope harness*! The thing itself was a miracle. He made no parade about what he could do, but only fixed up a plain pasteboard notice, informing the public that he possessed an infallible remedy for the cholera, and would engage to cure all who sent for him."

" And was he successful? "

" Successful! It beats all belief; and his remedy so simple! For some days we all took him for a quack, and would have no faith in him at all, although he performed some wonderful cures upon poor folks, who could not afford to send for the doctor. The Indian village was attacked by the disease, and he went out to them, and restored upwards of a hundred of the Indians to perfect health. They took the old lean oxen out of the cart, and drew him back to Montreal in triumph. This 'stablished him at once, and in a few days' time he made a fortune. The very doctors sent for him to cure them; and it is to be hoped that, in a few days, he will banish the cholera from the city."

" Do you know his famous remedy? "

" Do I not?—Did he not cure me when I was at

the last gasp? Why, he makes no secret of it. It is all drawn from the maple-tree. First he rubs the patient all over with an ointment, made of hog's lard and maple-sugar and ashes from the maple-tree; and he gives him a hot draught of maple-sugar and ley, which throws him into a violent perspiration. In about an hour the cramps subside; he falls into a quiet sleep, and when he awakes he is perfectly restored to health." Such were our first tidings of Stephen Ayres, the cholera doctor, who is universally believed to have effected some wonderful cures. He obtained a wide celebrity throughout the colony.*

The day of our arrival in the port of Montreal was spent in packing and preparing for our long journey up the country. At sunset I went upon deck to enjoy the refreshing breeze that swept from the river. The evening was delightful; the white tents of the soldiers on the Island of St. Helens glittered in the beams of the sun, and the bugle-call, wafted over the waters, sounded so cheery and inspiring that it banished all fears of the cholera, and the heavy gloom that had clouded my mind since we left Quebec. I could once more hold sweet converse with nature, and enjoy the soft loveliness of the rich and harmonious scene.

A loud cry from one of the crew startled me; I turned to the river, and beheld a man struggling in the water a short distance from our vessel. He was a young sailor, who had fallen from the bowsprit of a ship near us.

* A friend of mine, in this town, has an original portrait of this notable empiric—this man sent from heaven. The face is rather handsome, but has a keen, designing expression, and is evidently that of an American from its complexion and features.

OUR JOURNEY UP THE COUNTRY

There is something terribly exciting in beholding a fellow-creature in imminent peril, without having the power to help him. To witness his death-struggles —to feel in your own person all the dreadful alternations of hope and fear—and, finally, to see him die, with scarcely an effort made for his preservation. This was our case.

At the moment he fell into the water, a boat with three men was within a few yards of the spot, and actually sailed over the spot where he sank. Cries of "Shame!" from the crowd collected upon the bank of the river had no effect in rousing these people to attempt the rescue of a perishing fellow-creature. The boat passed on. The drowning man again rose to the surface, the convulsive motion of his hands and feet visible above the water, but it was evident that the struggle would be his last.

"Is it possible that they will let a human being perish, and so near the shore, when an oar held out would save his life?" was the agonizing question at my heart, as I gazed, half-maddened by excitement, on the fearful spectacle. The eyes of a multitude were fixed upon the same object—but not a hand stirred. Every one seemed to expect from his fellow an effort which he was incapable of attempting himself.

At this moment—splash! a sailor plunged into the water from the deck of a neighbouring vessel, and dived after the drowning man. A deep "Thank God!" burst from my heart. I drew a freer breath as the brave fellow's head appeared above the water. He called to the men in the boat to throw him an oar, or the drowning man would be the death of them both. Slowly they put back the boat—the oar was handed; but it came too late! The sailor, whose name was Cook, had been obliged to shake off the hold of the dying man to save his own life. He dived again to the bottom, and succeeded in bringing to shore the body of the unfortunate being he had vainly endeavoured to succour. Shortly after, he came on board our vessel, foaming with passion at the barbarous indifference manifested by the men in the boat.

"Had they given me the oar in time, I could have saved him. I knew him well—he was an excellent fellow, and a good seaman. He has left a wife and three children in Liverpool. Poor Jane!—how can I tell her that I could not save her husband?"

He wept bitterly, and it was impossible for any of us to witness his emotion without joining in his grief.

From the mate I learned that this same young man had saved the lives of three women and a child when the boat was swamped at Grosse Isle, in attempting to land the passengers from the *Horsley Hill*.

Such acts of heroism are common in the lower walks of life. Thus, the purest gems are often encased in the rudest crust, and the finest feelings of the human heart are fostered in the chilling atmosphere of poverty.

While this sad event occupied all our thoughts, and gave rise to many painful reflections, an exclamation of unqualified delight at once changed the current of our thoughts, and filled us with surprise and pleasure. Maggie Grant had fainted in the arms of her husband.

Yes, there was Tam—her dear, reckless Tam, after all her tears and lamentations, pressing his young wife to his heart, and calling her by a thousand endearing pet names.

He had met with some countrymen at Quebec, had taken too much whiskey on the joyful occasion, and lost his passage in the *Anne*, but had followed a few hours later in another steam-boat; and he assured the now happy Maggie, as he kissed the infant Tam, whom she held up to his admiring gaze, that he never would be guilty of the like again. Perhaps he kept his word; but I much fear that the first temptation would make the lively laddie forget his promise.

Our luggage having been removed to the Customhouse, including our bedding, the captain collected all the ship's flags for our accommodation, of which we formed a tolerably comfortable bed; and if our dreams were of England, could it be otherwise, with her glorious flag wrapped around us, and our heads resting upon the Union Jack?

In the morning we were obliged to visit the city to make the necessary arrangements for our upward journey.

The day was intensely hot. A bank of thunderclouds lowered heavily above the mountain, and the close, dusty streets were silent, and nearly deserted. Here and there might be seen a group of anxious-looking, care-worn, sickly emigrants, seated against a wall among their packages, and sadly ruminating upon their future prospects.

The sullen toll of the death-bell, the exposure of ready-made coffins in the undertakers' windows, and the oft-recurring notice placarded on the walls, of fun-

E

erals furnished at such and such a place, at cheapest rate and shortest notice, painfully reminded us, at every turning of the street, that death was everywhere —perhaps lurking in our very path; we felt no desire to examine the beauties of the place. With this ominous feeling pervading our minds, public buildings possessed few attractions, and we determined to make our stay as short as possible.

Compared with the infected city, our ship appeared an ark of safety, and we returned to it with joy and confidence, too soon to be destroyed. We had scarcely re-entered our cabin, when tidings were brought to us that the cholera had made its appearance: a brother of the captain had been attacked.

It was advisable that we should leave the vessel immediately, before the intelligence could reach the health-officers. A few minutes sufficed to make the necessary preparations; and in less than half an hour we found ourselves occupying comfortable apartments in Goodenough's hotel, and our passage taken in the stage for the following morning.

The transition was like a dream. The change from the close, rank ship to large, airy, well-furnished rooms and clean attendants, was a luxury we should have enjoyed had not the dread of the cholera involved all things around us in gloom and apprehension. No one spoke upon the subject; and yet it was evident that it was uppermost in the thoughts of all. Several emigrants had died of the terrible disorder during the week, beneath the very roof that sheltered us, and its ravages, we were told, had extended up the country as far as Kingston; so that it was still to be the phantom of our coming journey, if we were fortunate enough to escape from its headquarters.

At six o'clock the following morning, we took our places in the coach for Lachine, and our fears of the plague greatly diminished as we left the spires of Montreal in the distance. The journey from Montreal westward has been so well described by many gifted pens that I shall say little about it. The banks of the St. Lawrence are picturesque and beautiful, particularly in those spots where there is a good view of the American side. The neat farmhouses looked to me, whose eyes had been so long accustomed to the watery waste, homes of beauty and happiness; and the splendid orchards, the trees at that season of the year being loaded with ripening fruit of all hues, were refreshing and delicious.

My partiality for the apples was regarded by a fellow-traveller with a species of horror. "Touch them not, if you value your life." Every draught of fresh air and water inspired me with renewed health and spirits, and I disregarded the well-meant advice: the gentleman who gave it had just recovered from the terrible disease. He was a middle-aged man, a farmer from the Upper Province, Canadian born. He had visited Montreal on business for the first time. "Well, sir," he said, in answer to some questions put to him by my husband respecting the disease, "I can tell you what it is: a man smitten with the cholera stares death right in the face; and the torment he is suffering is so great that he would gladly die to get rid of it."

"You were fortunate, C——, to escape," said a backwoods settler, who occupied the opposite seat; "many a younger man has died of it."

"Ay; but I believe I never should have taken it had it not been for some things they gave me for supper at the hotel; oysters they called them, oysters: they were alive! I was persuaded by a friend to eat them, and I liked them well enough at the time. But I declare to you that I felt them crawling over one another in my stomach all night. The next morning I was seized with cholera."

"Did you swallow them whole, C——?" said the former spokesman, who seemed highly tickled by the evil doings of the oysters.

"To be sure. I tell you, the creatures are alive. You put them on your tongue, and I'll be bound you'll be glad to let them slip down as fast as you can."

"No wonder you had the cholera," said the backwoodsman; "you deserved it for your barbarity. If I had a good plate of oysters here, I'd teach you the way to eat them."

Our journey during the first day was performed partly by coach, partly by steam. It was nine o'clock in the evening when we landed at Cornwall, and took coach for Prescott. The country through which we passed appeared beautiful in the clear light of the moon; but the air was cold, and slightly sharpened by frost. This seemed strange to me in the early part of September, but it is very common in Canada. Nine passengers were closely packed into our narrow vehicle, but the sides being of canvas, and the open space allowed for windows unglazed, I shivered with cold, which amounted to a state of suffering, when the day broke, and we approached the little village of Matilda. It was unanimously voted by all hands that we should stop and breakfast at a small inn by the roadside, and warm ourselves before proceeding to Prescott.

The people in the tavern were not stirring, and it was some time before an old white-headed man unclosed the door, and showed us into a room, redolent with fumes of tobacco, and darkened by paper blinds. I asked him if he would allow me to take my infant into a room with a fire.

"I guess it was a pretty considerable cold night for the like of her," said he. "Come, I'll show you to the kitchen; there's always a fire there." I cheerfully followed, accompanied by our servant.

Our entrance was unexpected, and by no means agreeable to the persons we found there. A half-clothed, red-haired Irish servant was upon her knees, kindling up the fire; and a long thin woman, with a sharp face, and an eye like a black snake, was just emerging from a bed in the corner. We soon discovered this apparition to be the mistress of the house.

"The people can't come in here!" she screamed in a shrill voice, darting daggers at the poor old man.

"Sure there's a baby, and the two women critters are perished with cold," pleaded the good old man.

"What's that to me? They have no business in my kitchen."

"Now, Almira, do hold on. It's the coach has stopped to breakfast with us; and you know we don't often get the chance."

All this time the fair Almira was dressing as fast as

she could, and eyeing her unwelcome female guests as we stood shivering over the fire.

"Breakfast!" she muttered, "what can we give them to eat? They pass our door a thousand times without any one alighting; and now, when we are out of everything, they must stop and order breakfast at such an unreasonable hour. How many are there of you?" turning fiercely to me.

"Nine," I answered laconically, continuing to chafe the cold hands and feet of the child.

"Nine! That bit of beef will be nothing, cut into steaks for nine. What's to be done, Joe?" (to the old man).

"Eggs and ham, summat of that dried venison, and pumpkin pie," responded the *aide-de-camp* thoughtfully. "I don't know of any other fixings."

"Bestir yourself, then, and lay out the table, for the coach can't stay long," cried the virago, seizing a frying-pan from the wall, and preparing it for the reception of the eggs and ham. "I must have the fire to myself. People can't come crowding here, when I have to fix breakfast for nine; particularly when there is a good room elsewhere provided for their accommodation." I took the hint, and retreated to the parlour, where I found the rest of the passengers walking to and fro, and impatiently awaiting the advent of the breakfast.

To do Almira justice, she prepared from her scanty materials a very substantial breakfast in an incredibly short time, for which she charged us a quarter of a dollar per head.

At Prescott we embarked on board a fine new steam-boat, *William IV.*, crowded with Irish emigrants, proceeding to Cobourg and Toronto.

While pacing the deck, my husband was greatly struck by the appearance of a middle-aged man and his wife, who sat apart from the rest, and seemed struggling with intense grief, which, in spite of all their efforts at concealment, was strongly impressed upon their features. Some time after, I fell into conversation with the woman, from whom I learned their little history. The husband was factor to a Scotch gentleman of large landed property, who had employed him to visit Canada, and report the capabilities of the country, prior to his investing a large sum of money in wild lands. The expenses of their voyage had been paid, and everything up to that morning had prospered with them. They had been blessed with a speedy passage, and were greatly pleased with the country and the people; but of what avail was all this? Their only son, a fine lad of fourteen, had died that day of the cholera, and all their hopes for the future were buried in his grave. For his sake they had sought a home in this far land; and here, at the very onset of their new career, the fell disease had taken him from them for ever —here, where, in such a crowd, the poor heart-broken mother could not even indulge her natural grief!

"Ah for a place where I might greet!" she said; "it would relieve the burning weight at my heart. But with sae many strange eyes glowering upon me, I tak' shame to mysel' to greet."

"Ah, Jeannie, my puir woman," said the husband, grasping her hand, "ye maun bear up; 'tis God's will; and sinfu' creatures like us mauna repine. But oh, madam," turning to me, "we have sair hearts the day!"

Poor bereaved creatures, how deeply I commiserated their grief—how I respected the poor father, in the stern efforts he made to conceal from indifferent spectators the anguish that weighed upon his mind! Tears are the best balm that can be applied to the anguish of the heart. Religion teaches man to bear his sorrows with becoming fortitude, but tears contribute largely both to soften and to heal the wounds from whence they flow.

At Brockville we took in a party of ladies, which somewhat relieved the monotony of the cabin, and I was amused by listening to their lively prattle, and the little gossip with which they strove to wile away the tedium of the voyage. The day was too stormy to go upon deck—thunder and lightning, accompanied with torrents of rain. Amid the confusion of the elements, I tried to get a peep at the Lake of the Thousand Isles; but the driving storm blended all objects into one, and I returned wet and disappointed to my berth. We passed Kingston at midnight, and lost all our lady passengers but two. The gale continued until daybreak, and noise and confusion prevailed all night, which was greatly increased by the uproarious conduct of a wild Irish emigrant, who thought fit to make his bed upon the mat before the cabin door. He sang, he shouted, he harangued his countrymen on the political state of the Emerald Isle, in a style which was loud if not eloquent. Sleep was impossible whilst his stentorian lungs continued to pour forth torrents of unmeaning sound.

THE FARM OF 1871

OUR JOURNEY UP THE COUNTRY

Our Dutch stewardess was highly enraged. His conduct, she said, "was perfectly ondacent." She opened the door, and, bestowing upon him several kicks, bade him get away "out of that," or she would complain to the captain.

In answer to this remonstrance, he caught her by the foot, and pulled her down. Then, waving the tattered remains of his straw hat in the air, he shouted with an air of triumph, "Git out wid you, you ould witch! Shure the ladies, the purty darlints, never sent you wid that ugly message to Pat, who loves them so intirely that he means to kape watch over them through the blessed night." Then, making us a ludicrous bow, he continued, "Ladies, I'm at yer sarvice; I only wish I could get a dispensation from the Pope, and I'd marry yeas all." The stewardess bolted the door, and the mad fellow kept up such a racket that we all wished him at the bottom of the Ontario.

The following day was wet and gloomy. The storm had protracted the length of our voyage for several hours, and it was midnight when we landed at Cobourg.

CHAPTER FOUR
TOM WILSON'S EMIGRATION

IV.   TOM WILSON'S EMIGRATION

"Of all odd fellows, this fellow was the oddest. I have seen many strange fish in my days, but I never met with his equal."

ABOUT A MONTH PREVIOUS TO OUR emigration to Canada, my husband said to me, "You need not expect me home to dinner to-day; I am going with my friend Wilson to Y——, to hear Mr. C—— lecture upon emigration to Canada. He has just returned from the North American provinces, and his lectures are attended by vast numbers of persons who are anxious to obtain information on the subject. I got a note from your friend B—— this morning, begging me to come over and listen to his palaver; and as Wilson thinks of emigrating in the spring, he will be my walking companion."

"Tom Wilson going to Canada!" said I, as the door closed on my better-half. "What a backwoodsman he will make! What a loss to the single ladies of S——! What will they do without him at their balls and picnics?"

One of my sisters, who was writing at a table near me, was highly amused at this unexpected announcement. She fell back in her chair and indulged in a long and hearty laugh. I am certain that most of my readers would have joined in her laugh had they known the object which provoked her mirth. "Poor Tom is such a dreamer," said my sister, "it would be an act of charity in Moodie to persuade him from undertaking such a wild-goose chase; only that I fancy my good brother is possessed with the same mania."

"Nay, God forbid!" said I. "I hope this Mr. ——, with the unpronounceable name, will disgust them with his eloquence; for B—— writes me word, in his

77

droll way, that he is a coarse, vulgar fellow, and lacks the dignity of a bear. Oh! I am certain they will return quite sickened with the Canadian project." Thus I laid the flattering unction to my soul, little dreaming that I and mine should share in the strange adventures of this oddest of all odd creatures.

It might be made a subject of curious inquiry, to those who delight in human absurdities, if ever there were a character drawn in works of fiction so extravagantly ridiculous as some which daily experience presents to our view. We have encountered people in the broad thoroughfares of life more eccentric than ever we read of in books; people who, if all their foolish sayings and doings were duly recorded, would vie with the drollest creations of Hood or George Colman, and put to shame the flights of Baron Munchausen. Not that Tom Wilson was a romancer; oh no! He was the very prose of prose, a man in a mist, who seemed afraid of moving about for fear of knocking his head against a tree, and finding a halter suspended to its branches—a man as helpless and as indolent as a baby.

Mr. Thomas, or Tom Wilson, as he was familiarly called by all his friends and acquaintances, was the son of a gentleman who once possessed a large landed property in the neighbourhood; but an extravagant and profligate expenditure of the income which he derived from a fine estate which had descended from father to son through many generations had greatly reduced the circumstances of the elder Wilson. Still, his family held a certain rank and standing in their native county, of which his evil courses, bad as they were, could not wholly deprive them. The young people—and a very large family they made of sons and daughters, twelve in number—were objects of interest and commiseration to all who knew them, while the worthless father was justly held in contempt. Our hero was the youngest of the six sons; and from his childhood he was famous for his nothing-to-doishness. He was too indolent to engage heart and soul in the manly sports of his comrades; and he never thought it necessary to commence learning his lessons until the school had been in an hour. As he grew up to man's estate, he might be seen dawdling about in a black frock-coat, jean trousers, and white kid gloves, making lazy bows to the pretty girls of his acquaintance; or dressed in a green shooting-jacket, with a gun across his shoulder, sauntering down the wooded lanes, with a brown spaniel dodging at his heels, and looking as sleepy and indolent as his master.

The slowness of all Tom's movements was strangely contrasted with his slight, elegant, and symmetrical figure; that looked as if it only awaited the will of the owner to be the most active piece of human machinery that ever responded to the impulses of youth and health. But then, his face! What pencil could faithfully delineate features at once so comical and lugubrious—features that one moment expressed the most solemn seriousness, and the next the most grotesque and absurd abandonment to mirth? In him, all extremes appeared to meet; the man was a contradiction to himself. Tom was a person of few words, and so intensely lazy that it required a strong effort of will to enable him to answer the questions of inquiring friends; and when at length aroused to exercise his colloquial powers, he performed the task in so original a manner that it never failed to upset the gravity of the interrogator. When he raised his large, prominent, leaden-coloured eyes from the ground, and looked the inquirer steadily in the face, the effect was irresistible; the laugh would come—do your best to resist it.

Poor Tom took this mistimed merriment in very good part, generally answering with a ghastly contortion which he meant for a smile, or, if he did trouble himself to find words, with, "Well, that's funny! What makes you laugh? At me, I suppose? I don't wonder at it; I often laugh at myself."

Tom would have been a treasure to an undertaker. He would have been celebrated as a mute; he looked as if he had been born in a shroud, and rocked in a coffin. The gravity with which he could answer a ridiculous or impertinent question completely disarmed and turned the shafts of malice back upon his opponent. If Tom was himself an object of ridicule to many, he had a way of quietly ridiculing others that bade defiance to all competition. He could quiz with a smile, and put down insolence with an incredulous stare. A grave wink from those dreamy eyes would destroy the veracity of a travelled dandy for ever.

Tom was not without use in his day and generation; queer and awkward as he was, he was the soul of truth and honour. You might suspect his sanity—a matter always doubtful—but his honesty of heart and purpose, never.

TOM WILSON'S EMIGRATION

When you met Tom in the streets, he was dressed with such neatness and care (to be sure it took him half the day to make his toilet), that it led many persons to imagine that this very ugly young man considered himself an Adonis; and I must confess that I rather inclined to this opinion. He always paced the public streets with a slow, deliberate tread, and with his eyes fixed intently on the ground—like a man who had lost his ideas, and was diligently employed in searching for them. I chanced to meet him one day in this dreamy mood.

"How do you do, Mr. Wilson?" He stared at me for several minutes, as if doubtful of my presence or identity.

"What was that you said?"

I repeated the question; and he answered, with one of his incredulous smiles—

"Was it to me you spoke? Oh, I am quite well, or I should not be walking here. By the way, did you see my dog?"

"How should I know your dog?"

"They say he resembles me. He's a queer dog, too; but I never could find out the likeness. Good night!"

This was at noonday; but Tom had a habit of taking light for darkness, and darkness for light, in all he did or said. He must have had different eyes and ears, and a different way of seeing, hearing, and comprehending, than is possessed by the generality of his species; and to such a length did he carry this abstraction of soul and sense that he would often leave you abruptly in the middle of a sentence; and if you chanced to meet him some weeks after, he would resume the conversation with the very word at which he had cut short the thread of your discourse.

A lady once told him in jest that her youngest brother, a lad of twelve years old, had called his donkey Braham, in honour of the great singer of that name. Tom made no answer, but started abruptly away. Three months after, she happened to encounter him on the same spot, when he accosted her, without any previous salutation—

"You were telling me about a donkey, Miss ——, a donkey of your brother's—Braham, I think you called him—yes, Braham; a strange name for an ass! I wonder what the great Mr. Braham would say to that. Ha, ha, ha!"

"Your memory must be excellent, Mr. Wilson, to enable you to remember such a trifling circumstance all this time."

"Trifling, do you call it? Why, I have thought of nothing else ever since."

From traits such as these my readers will be tempted to imagine him brother to the animal who had dwelt so long in his thoughts; but there were times when he surmounted this strange absence of mind, and could talk and act as sensibly as other folks.

On the death of his father, he emigrated to New South Wales, where he contrived to doze away seven years of his valueless existence, suffering his convict servants to rob him of everything, and finally to burn his dwelling. He returned to his native village, dressed as an Italian mendicant, with a monkey perched upon his shoulder, and playing airs of his own composition upon a hurdy-gurdy. In this disguise he sought the dwelling of an old bachelor uncle, and solicited his charity. But who that had once seen our friend Tom could ever forget him? Nature had no counterpart of one who in mind and form was alike original. The good-natured old soldier, at a glance, discovered his hopeful nephew, received him into his house with kindness, and had afforded him an asylum ever since.

One little anecdote of him at this period will illustrate the quiet love of mischief with which he was imbued. Travelling from W —— to London in the stagecoach (railways were not invented in those days), he entered into conversation with an intelligent farmer who sat next him; New South Wales, and his residence in that colony, forming the leading topic. A Dissenting minister who happened to be his *vis-à-vis*, and who had annoyed him by making several impertinent remarks, suddenly asked him, with a sneer, how many years he had been there.

"Seven," returned Tom, in a solemn tone, without deigning a glance at his companion.

"I thought so," responded the other, thrusting his hands into his breeches pockets. "And pray, sir, what were you sent there for?"

"Stealing pigs," returned the incorrigible Tom, with the gravity of a judge. The words were scarcely pronounced when the questioner called the coachman to stop, preferring a ride outside in the rain to a seat within with a thief. Tom greatly enjoyed the hoax, which he used to tell with the merriest of all grave faces.

Besides being a devoted admirer of the fair sex, and always imagining himself in love with some unattainable beauty, he had a passionate craze for music, and

83

played upon the violin and flute with considerable taste and execution. The sound of a favourite melody operated upon the breathing automaton like magic, his frozen faculties experienced a sudden thaw, and the stream of life leaped and gambolled for a while with uncontrollable vivacity. He laughed, danced, sang, and made love in a breath, committing a thousand mad vagaries to make you acquainted with his existence.

My husband had a remarkably sweet-toned flute, and this flute Tom regarded with a species of idolatry.

"I break the Tenth Commandment, Moodie, whenever I hear you play upon that flute. Take care of your black wife" (a name he had bestowed upon the coveted treasure), "or I shall certainly run off with her."

"I am half afraid of you, Tom. I am sure if I were to die, and leave you my black wife as a legacy, you would be too much overjoyed to lament my death."

Such was the strange, helpless, whimsical being who contemplated an emigration to Canada. How he succeeded in the speculation the sequel will show.

It was late in the evening before my husband and his friend Tom Wilson returned from Y——. I had provided a hot supper and a cup of coffee after their long walk, and they did ample justice to my care.

Tom was in unusually high spirits, and appeared wholly bent upon his Canadian expedition.

"Mr. C—— must have been very eloquent, Mr. Wilson," said I, "to engage your attention for so many hours."

"Perhaps he was," returned Tom, after a pause of

some minutes, during which he seemed to be grop-
ing for words in the salt-cellar, having deliberately
turned out its contents upon the table-cloth. "We
were hungry after our long walk, and he gave us an
excellent dinner."

"But that had nothing to do with the substance of
his lecture."

"It was the substance, after all," said Moodie, laughing; "and his audience seemed to think so, by the attention they paid to it during the discussion. But
come, Wilson, give my wife some account of the intellectual part of the entertainment."

"What! I—I—I—I give an account of the lecture? Why, my dear fellow, I never listened to one
word of it!"

"I thought you went to Y—— on purpose to obtain information on the subject of emigration to
Canada?"

"Well, and so I did; but when the fellow pulled out
his pamphlet, and said that it contained the substance
of his lecture, and would only cost a shilling, I thought
that it was better to secure the substance than endeavour to catch the shadow—so I bought the book, and
spared myself the pain of listening to the oratory of
the writer. Mrs. Moodie! he had a shocking delivery;
a drawling, vulgar voice; and he spoke with such a
nasal twang that I could not bear to look at him or
listen to him. He made such grammatical blunders
that my sides ached with laughing at him. Oh, I wish
you could have seen the wretch! But here is the document, written in the same style in which it was spoken.
Read it; you have a rich treat in store."

85

I took the pamphlet, not a little amused at his description of Mr. C——, for whom I felt an uncharitable dislike.

"And how did you contrive to entertain yourself, Mr. Wilson, during his long address?"

"By thinking how many fools were collected together, to listen to one greater than the rest. By the way, Moodie, did you notice Parmer Flitch?"

"No; where did he sit?"

"At the foot of the table. You must have seen him; he was too big to be overlooked. What a delightful squint he had! What a ridiculous likeness there was between him and the roast pig he was carving! I was wondering all dinner-time how that man contrived to cut up that pig; for one eye was fixed upon the ceiling, and the other leering very affectionately at me. It was very droll, was it not?"

"And what do you intend doing with yourself when you arrive in Canada?" said I.

"Find out some large hollow tree, and live like Bruin in the winter by sucking my paws. In the summer there will be plenty of mast and acorns to satisfy the wants of an abstemious fellow."

"But, joking apart, my dear fellow," said my husband, anxious to induce him to abandon a scheme so hopeless, "do you think that you are at all qualified for a life of toil and hardship?"

"*Are you?*" returned Tom, raising his large, bushy, black eyebrows to the top of his forehead, and fixing his leaden eyes steadfastly upon his interrogator, with an air of such absurd gravity that we burst into a hearty laugh.

TOM WILSON'S EMIGRATION

"Now what do you laugh for? I am sure I asked you a very serious question."

"But your method of putting it is so unusual that you must excuse us for laughing."

"I don't want you to weep," said Tom; "but as to our qualifications, Moodie, I think them pretty equal. I know you think otherwise, but I will explain. Let me see; what was I going to say?—ah, I have it! You go with the intention of clearing land, and working for yourself, and doing a great deal. I have tried that before in New South Wales, and I know that it won't answer. Gentlemen can't work like labourers, and if they could they won't—it is not in them, and that you will find out. You expect, by going to Canada, to make your fortune, or at least secure a comfortable independence. I anticipate no such results; yet I mean to go, partly out of a whim, partly to satisfy my curiosity whether it is a better country than New South Wales; and lastly, in the hope of bettering my condition in a small way, which at present is so bad that it can scarcely be worse. I mean to purchase a farm with the three hundred pounds I received last week from the sale of my father's property; and if the Canadian soil yields only half what Mr. C—— says it does, I need not starve. But the refined habits in which you have been brought up, and your unfortunate literary propensities—(I say unfortunate, because you will seldom meet people in a colony who can or will sympathize with you in these pursuits)—they will make you an object of mistrust and envy to those who cannot appreciate them, and will be a source of constant mortification and disappointment to yourself. Thank God! I have no literary propensities; but, in spite of the latter advantage, in all probability I shall make no exertion at all; so that your energy, damped by disgust and disappointment, and my laziness will end in the same thing, and we shall both return like bad pennies to our native shores. But, as I have neither wife nor child to involve in my failure, I think, without much self-flattery, that my prospects are better than yours."

This was the longest speech I ever heard Tom utter; and, evidently astonished at himself, he sprang up abruptly from the table, overset a cup of coffee into my lap, and, wishing us *good day* (it was eleven o'clock at night), he ran out of the house.

There was more truth in poor Tom's words than at that moment we were willing to allow; for youth and hope were on our side in those days, and we were most ready to believe the suggestions of the latter.

My husband finally determined to emigrate to Canada, and in the hurry and bustle of a sudden preparation to depart, Tom and his affairs for a while were forgotten.

How dark and heavily did that frightful anticipation weigh upon my heart! As the time for our departure drew near, the thought of leaving my friends and native land became so intensely painful that it haunted me even in sleep. I seldom awoke without finding my pillow wet with tears. The glory of May was upon the earth—of an English May. The woods were bursting into leaf, the meadows and hedgerows were flushed with flowers, and every grove and copsewood echoed to the warblings of birds and the hum-

ming of bees. To leave England at all was dreadful
—to leave her at such a season was doubly so. I went
to take a last look at the old Hall, the beloved home
of my childhood and youth; to wander once more beneath the shades of its venerable oaks—to rest once
more upon the velvet sward that carpeted their roots.
It was while reposing beneath those noble trees that
I had first indulged in those delicious dreams which
are a foretaste of the enjoyments of the spirit-land.
In them the soul breathes forth its aspirations in a
language unknown to common minds; and that language is *Poetry*. Here annually, from year to year, I
had renewed my friendship with the first primroses
and violets, and listened with the untiring ear of love
to the spring roundelay of the blackbird, whistled
from among his bower of May blossoms. Here I had
discoursed sweet words to the tinkling brook, and
learned from the melody of waters the music of natural sounds. In these beloved solitudes all the holy
emotions which stir the human heart in its depths had
been freely poured forth, and found a response in the
harmonious voice of Nature, bearing aloft the choral
song of earth to the throne of the Creator.

How hard it was to tear myself from scenes endeared to me by the most beautiful and sorrowful recollections, let those who have loved and suffered as
I did say. However the world has frowned upon me,
Nature, arrayed in her green loveliness, had ever smiled upon me like an indulgent mother, holding out her
loving arms to enfold to her bosom her erring but devoted child.

Dear, dear England! why was I forced by a stern

necessity to leave you? What heinous crime had I committed that I, who adored you, should be torn from your sacred bosom, to pine out my joyless existence in a foreign clime? Oh that I might be permitted to return and die upon your wave-encircled shores, and rest my weary head and heart beneath your daisy-covered sod at last! Ah, these are vain outbursts of feeling—melancholy relapses of the spring home-sickness! Canada! thou art a noble, free, and rising country—the great fostering mother of the orphans of civilization. The offspring of Britain, thou must be great, and I will and do love thee, land of my adoption, and of my children's birth; and oh—dearer still to a mother's heart—land of their graves!

*   *   *   *   *   *

Whilst talking over our coming separation with my sister C——, we observed Tom Wilson walking slowly up the path that led to the house. He was dressed in a new shooting-jacket, with his gun lying carelessly across his shoulder, and an ugly pointer dog following at a little distance.

"Well, Mrs. Moodie, I am off," said Tom, shaking hands with my sister instead of me. "I suppose I shall see Moodie in London. What do you think of my dog?" patting him affectionately.

"I think him an ugly beast," said C——. "Do you mean to take him with you?"

"An ugly beast!—Duchess a beast? Why, she is a perfect beauty!—Beauty and the beast! Ha, ha, ha! I gave two guineas for her last night." (I thought of the old adage.) "Mrs. Moodie, your sister is no judge of a dog."

"Very likely," returned C——, laughing. "And you go to town to-night, Mr. Wilson? I thought as you came up to the house that you were equipped for shooting."

"To be sure; there is capital shooting in Canada."

"So I have heard—plenty of bears and wolves. I suppose you take out your dog and gun in anticipation?"

"True," said Tom.

"But you surely are not going to take that dog with you?"

"Indeed I am. She is a most valuable brute. The very best venture I could take. My brother Charles has engaged our passage in the same vessel."

"It would be a pity to part you," said I. "May you prove as lucky a pair as Whittington and his cat."

"Whittington! Whittington!" said Tom, staring at my sister, and beginning to dream, which he invariably did in the company of women. "Who was the gentleman?"

"A very old friend of mine, one whom I have known since I was a very little girl," said my sister; "but I have not time to tell you more about him now. If you go to St. Paul's Churchyard, and inquire for Sir Richard Whittington and his cat, you will get his history for a mere trifle."

"Do not mind her, Mr. Wilson; she is quizzing you," quoth I. "I wish you a safe voyage across the Atlantic; I wish I could add a happy meeting with your friends. But where shall we find friends in a strange land?"

"All in good time," said Tom. "I hope to have the

pleasure of meeting you in the backwoods of Canada before three months are over. What adventures we shall have to tell one another! It will be capital. Good-bye."

* * * * * *

"Tom has sailed," said Captain Charles Wilson, stepping into my little parlour a few days after his eccentric brother's last visit. "I saw him and Duchess safe on board. Odd as he is, I parted with him with a full heart; I felt as if we never should meet again. Poor Tom! he is the only brother left me now that I can love. Robert and I never agreed very well, and there is little chance of our meeting in this world. He is married, and settled down for life in New South Wales; and the rest—John, Richard, George—are all gone—all!"

"Was Tom in good spirits when you parted?"

"Yes. He is a perfect contradiction. He always laughs and cries in the wrong place. 'Charles,' he said, with a loud laugh, 'tell the girls to get some new music against I return: and, hark ye! if I never come back, I leave them my Kangaroo Waltz as a legacy.'"

"What a strange creature!"

"Strange, indeed; you don't know half his oddities. He has very little money to take out with him, but he actually paid for two berths in the ship, that he might not chance to have a person who snored sleep near him. Thirty pounds thrown away upon the mere chance of a snoring companion! 'Besides, Charles,' quoth he, 'I cannot endure to share my little cabin with others; they will use my towels, and combs, and brushes, like that confounded rascal who slept in the same berth with me coming from New South Wales, who had the impudence to clean his teeth with my tooth-brush. Here I shall be all alone, happy and comfortable as a prince, and Duchess shall sleep in the after-berth, and be my queen.' And so we parted," continued Captain Charles. "May God take care of him, for he never could take care of himself."

"That puts me in mind of the reason he gave for not going with us. He was afraid that my baby would keep him awake of a night. He hates children, and says that he never will marry on that account."

* * * * * *

We left the British shores on the 1st of July, and cast anchor, as I have already shown, under the Castle of St. Louis, at Quebec, on the 2nd of September 1832. Tom Wilson sailed the 1st of May, and had a speedy passage, and was, as we heard from his friends, comfortably settled in the bush, had bought a farm, and meant to commence operations in the fall. All this was good news, and as he was settled near my brother's location, we congratulated ourselves that our eccentric friend had found a home in the wilderness at last, and that we should soon see him again.

On the 9th of September, the steam-boat *William IV.* landed us at the then small but rising town of ——, on Lake Ontario. The night was dark and rainy; the boat was crowded with emigrants; and when we arrived at the inn, we learnt that there was no room for us—not a bed to be had; nor was it likely, owing to the number of strangers that had arrived for several weeks, that we could obtain one by searching farther. Moodie requested the use of a sofa for me during

93

ROUGHING IT IN THE BUSH

the night; but even that produced a demur from the landlord. Whilst I awaited the result in a passage crowded with strange faces, a pair of eyes glanced upon me through the throng. Was it possible?—could it be Tom Wilson? Did any other human being possess such eyes, or use them in such an eccentric manner? In another second he had pushed his way to my side, whispering in my ear, "We met, 'twas in a crowd."

"Tom Wilson, is that you?"

"Do you doubt it? I flatter myself that there is no likeness of such a handsome fellow to be found in the world. It is I, I swear!—although very little of me is left to swear by. The best part of me I have left to fatten the mosquitoes and black flies in that infernal bush. But where is Moodie?"

"There he is—trying to induce Mr. S——, for love or money, to let me have a bed for the night."

"You shall have mine," said Tom. "I can sleep upon the floor of the parlour in a blanket, Indian fashion. It's a bargain—I'll go and settle it with the Yankee directly; he's the best fellow in the world! In the meanwhile here is a little parlour, which is a joint-stock affair between some of us young hopefuls for the time being. Step in here, and I will go for Moodie. I long to tell him what I think of this confounded country. But you will find it out all in good time;" and, rubbing his hands together with a most lively and mischievous expression, he shouldered his way through trunks, and boxes, and anxious faces, to communicate to my husband the arrangement he had so kindly made for us.

"Accept this gentleman's offer, sir, till to-morrow,"

said Mr. S——; "I can then make more comfortable arrangements for your family. But we are crowded—crowded to excess. My wife and daughters are obliged to sleep in a little chamber over the stable, to give our guests more room. Hard that, I guess, for decent people to locate over the horses."

These matters settled, Moodie returned with Tom Wilson to the little parlour, in which I had already made myself at home.

"Well, now, is it not funny that I should be the first to welcome you to Canada?" said Tom.

"But what are you doing here, my dear fellow?"

"Shaking every day with the ague. But I could laugh in spite of my teeth to hear them make such a confounded rattling; you would think they were all quarrelling which should first get out of my mouth. This shaking mania forms one of the chief attractions of this new country."

"I fear," said I, remarking how thin and pale he had become, "that this climate cannot agree with you."

"Nor I with the climate. Well, we shall soon be quits, for, to let you into a secret, I am now on my way to England."

"Impossible!"

"It is true."

"And the farm—what have you done with it?"

"Sold it."

"And your outfit?"

"Sold that too."

"To whom?"

"To one who will take better care of both than I did. Ah! such a country!—such people!—such rogues!

ROUGHING IT IN THE BUSH

It beats Australia hollow: you know your customers there—but here you have to find them out. Such a take-in!—God forgive them! I never could take care of money; and, one way or other, they have cheated me out of all mine. I have scarcely enough left to pay my passage home. But, to provide against the worst, I have bought a young bear, a splendid fellow, to make my peace with my uncle. You must see him; he is close by in the stable."

"To-morrow we will pay a visit to Bruin; but to-night do tell us something about yourself, and your residence in the Bush."

"You will know enough about the Bush by-and-by. I am a bad historian," he continued, stretching out his legs, and yawning horribly, "a worse biographer. I never can find words to relate facts. But I will try what I can do. Mind, don't laugh at my blunders."

We promised to be serious—no easy matter while looking at and listening to Tom Wilson; and he gave us, at detached intervals, the following account of himself:—

"My troubles began at sea. We had a fair voyage, and all that; but my poor dog, my beautiful Duchess! —that beauty in the beast—died. I wanted to read the funeral service over her, but the captain interfered —the brute!—and threatened to throw me into the sea along with the dead bitch, as the unmannerly ruffian persisted in calling my canine friend. I never spoke to him again during the rest of the voyage. Nothing happened worth relating until I got to this place, where I chanced to meet a friend who knew your brother, and I went up with him to the woods.

TOM WILSON'S EMIGRATION

Most of the wise men of Gotham we met on the road
were bound to the woods; so I felt happy that I was,
at least, in the fashion. Mr. —— was very kind, and
spoke in raptures of the woods, which formed the
theme of conversation during our journey—their
beauty, their vastness, the comfort and independence
enjoyed by those who had settled in them; and he so
inspired me with the subject that I did nothing all
day but sing as we rode along—

'A life in the woods for me;'

until we came to the woods, and then I soon learned
to sing that same, as the Irishman says, on the other
side of my mouth."

Here succeeded a long pause, during which friend
Tom seemed mightily tickled with his reminiscences,
for he leaned back in his chair, and, from time to time,
gave way to loud, hollow bursts of laughter.

"Tom, Tom! are you going mad?" said my husband, shaking him.

"I never was sane, that I know of," returned he.
"You know that it runs in the family. But do let me
have my laugh out. The woods! Ha! ha! When I
used to be roaming through those woods, shooting,—
though not a thing could I ever find to shoot, for birds
and beasts are not such fools as our English emigrants
—and I chanced to think of you coming to spend the
rest of your lives in the woods—I used to stop, and
hold my sides, and laugh until the woods rang again
It was the only consolation I had."

"Good heavens!" said I, "let us never go to the
woods."

"You will repent if you do," continued Tom. "But

G

let me proceed on my journey. My bones were well-nigh dislocated before we got to D——. The roads for the last twelve miles were nothing but a succession of mud-holes, covered with the most ingenious invention ever thought of for racking the limbs, called corduroy bridges; not breeches, mind you,—for I thought, whilst jolting up and down over them, that I should arrive at my destination minus that indispensable covering. It was night when we got to Mr. ——'s place. I was tired and hungry, my face disfigured and blistered by the unremitting attentions of the black flies that rose in swarms from the river. I thought to get a private room to wash and dress in, but there is no such thing as privacy in this country. In the bush, all things are in common; you cannot even get a bed without having to share it with a companion. A bed on the floor in a public sleeping-room! Think of that; a public sleeping-room!—men, women, and children, only divided by a paltry curtain. Oh, ye gods! think of the snoring, squalling, grumbling, puffing; think of the kicking, elbowing, and crowding; the suffocating heat, the mosquitoes, with their infernal buzzing—and you will form some idea of the misery I endured the first night of my arrival in the bush.

"But these are not half the evils with which you have to contend. You are pestered with nocturnal visitants far more disagreeable than even the mosquitoes, and must put up with annoyances more disgusting than the crowded close room. And then, to appease the cravings of hunger, fat pork is served to you three times a day. No wonder that the Jews eschewed the vile animal; they were people of taste. Pork, morning, noon, and night, swimming in its own grease! The bishop who complained of partridges every day should have been condemned to three months' feeding upon pork in the bush; and he would have become an anchorite, to escape the horrid sight of swine's flesh for ever spread before him. No wonder I am thin; I have been starved—starved upon pritters and pork, and that disgusting specimen of unleavened bread, yclept cakes in the pan.

"I had such a horror of the pork diet, that whenever I saw the dinner in progress I fled to the canoe, in the hope of drowning upon the waters all reminiscences of the hateful banquet; but even here the very fowls of the air and the reptiles of the deep lifted up their voices, and shouted, 'Pork, pork, pork!'"

M—— remonstrated with his friend for deserting the country for such minor evils as these, which, after all, he said, could easily be borne.

"Easily borne!" exclaimed the indignant Wilson. "Go and try them; and then tell me that. I did try to bear them with a good grace, but it would not do. I offended everybody with my grumbling. I was constantly reminded by the ladies of the house that gentlemen should not come to this country without they were able to put up with a *little* inconvenience; that I should make as good a settler as a butterfly in a beehive; that it was impossible to be nice about food and *dress* in the *bush*; that people must learn to eat what they could get, and be content to be shabby and dirty, like their neighbours in the *bush*,—until that horrid word *bush* became synonymous with all that was hateful and revolting in my mind.

99

" It was impossible to keep anything to myself. The children pulled my books to pieces to look at the pictures; and an impudent, bare-legged Irish servant girl took my towels to wipe the dishes with, and my clothes-brush to black the shoes—an operation which she performed with a mixture of soot and grease. I thought I should be better off in a place of my own, so I bought a wild farm that was recommended to me, and paid for it double what it was worth. When I came to examine my estate, I found there was no house upon it, and I should have to wait until the fall to get one put up, and a few acres cleared for cultivation. I was glad to return to my old quarters.

" Finding nothing to shoot in the woods, I determined to amuse myself with fishing; but Mr. —— could not always lend his canoe, and there was no other to be had. To pass away the time, I set about making one. I bought an axe, and went to the forest to select a tree. About a mile from the lake, I found the largest pine I ever saw. I did not much like to try my maiden hand upon it, for it was the first and the last tree I ever cut down. But to it I went; and I blessed God that it reached the ground without killing me in its way thither. When I was about it, I thought I might as well make the canoe big enough; but the bulk of the tree deceived me in the length of my vessel, and I forgot to measure the one that belonged to Mr.——. It took me six weeks hollowing it out, and when it was finished, it was as long as a sloop-of-war, and too unwieldy for all the oxen in the township to draw it to the water. After all my labour, my combats with those wood-demons the black-flies, sand-flies, and mosquitoes, my boat remains a useless monument of my industry. And worse than this, the fatigue I had endured, while working at it late and early, brought on the ague; which so disgusted me with the country that I sold my farm and all my traps for an old song; purchased Bruin to bear me company on my voyage home; and the moment I am able to get rid of this tormenting fever, I am off."

Argument and remonstrance were alike in vain, he could not be dissuaded from his purpose. Tom was as obstinate as his bear.

The next morning he conducted us to the stable to see Bruin. The young denizen of the forest was tied to the manger, quietly masticating a cob of Indian corn, which he held in his paw, and looked half human as he sat upon his haunches, regarding us with a solemn, melancholy air. There was an extraordinary likeness, quite ludicrous, between Tom and the bear. We said nothing, but exchanged glances. Tom read our thoughts.

"Yes," said he, "there is a strong resemblance; I saw it when I bought him. Perhaps we are brothers;" and taking in his hand the chain that held the bear, he bestowed upon him sundry fraternal caresses, which the ungrateful Bruin returned with low and savage growls.

"He can't flatter. He's all truth and sincerity. A child of nature, and worthy to be my friend; the only Canadian I ever mean to acknowledge as such."

About an hour after this, poor Tom was shaking with ague, which in a few days reduced him so low that I began to think he never would see his native

shores again. He bore the affliction very philosophically, and all his well days he spent with us.

One day my husband was absent, having accompanied Mr. S—— to inspect a farm, which he afterwards purchased, and I had to get through the long
day in the best manner I could. The local papers were
soon exhausted. At that period, they possessed little
or no interest for me. I was astonished and disgusted
at the abusive manner in which they were written, the
freedom of the press being enjoyed to an extent in
this province unknown in more civilized communities.

Men, in Canada, may call one another rogues and
miscreants, in the most approved Billingsgate, through the medium of the newspapers, which are a sort
of safety-valve to let off all the bad feelings and malignant passions floating through the country, without
any dread of the horsewhip. Hence it is the common-
est thing in the world to hear one editor abusing, like
a pickpocket, an opposition brother; calling him a
*reptile—a crawling thing—a calumniator—a hired
vendor of lies; and his paper a smut-machine—a vile
engine of corruption, as base* and *degraded* as the *pro-
prietor*, &c. Of this description was the paper I now
held in my hand, which had the impudence to style itself the *Reformer*—not of morals or manners, certainly, if one might judge by the vulgar abuse that defiled
every page of the precious document. I soon flung it
from me, thinking it worthy of the fate of many a
better production in the olden times, that of being
burned by the common hangman; but, happily, the
office of hangman has become obsolete in Canada, and

the editors of these refined journals may go on abusing their betters with impunity.

Books I had none, and I wished that Tom would make his appearance, and amuse me with his oddities; but he had suffered so much from the ague the day before that when he did enter the room to lead me to dinner, he looked like a walking corpse—the dead among the living! so dark, so livid, so melancholy, it was really painful to look upon him.

"I hope the ladies who frequent the ordinary won't fall in love with me," said he, grinning at himself in the miserable looking-glass that formed the case of the Yankee clock, and was ostentatiously displayed on a side table; "I look quite killing to-day. What a comfort it is, Mrs. M——, to be above all rivalry."

In the middle of dinner, the company was disturbed by the entrance of a person who had the appearance of a gentleman, but who was evidently much flustered with drinking. He thrust his chair in between two gentlemen who sat near the head of the table, and in a loud voice demanded fish.

"Fish, sir?" said the obsequious waiter, a great favourite with all persons who frequented the hotel; "there is no fish, sir. There was a fine salmon, sir, had you come sooner; but 'tis all eaten, sir."

"Then fetch me something, smart!"

"I'll see what I can do, sir," said the obliging Tim, hurrying out.

Tom Wilson was at the head of the table, carving a roast pig, and was in the act of helping a lady, when the rude fellow thrust his fork into the pig, calling out as he did so—

"Hold, sir! give me some of that pig! You have eaten among you all the fish, and now you are going to appropriate the best parts of the pig."

Tom raised his eyebrows, and stared at the stranger in his peculiar manner, then very coolly placed the whole of the pig on his plate. "I have heard," he said, "of dog eating dog, but I never before saw pig eating pig."

"Sir! do you mean to insult me?" cried the stranger, his face crimsoning with anger.

"Only to tell you, sir, that you are no gentleman. Here, Tim," turning to the waiter, "go to the stable and bring in my bear; we will place him at the table to teach this man how to behave himself in the presence of ladies."

A general uproar ensued; the women left the table, while the entrance of the bear threw the gentlemen present into convulsions of laughter. It was too much for the human biped; he was forced to leave the room, and succumb to the bear.

My husband concluded his purchase of the farm, and invited Wilson to go with us into the country and try if change of air would be beneficial to him; for in his then weak state it was impossible for him to return to England. His funds were getting very low, and Tom thankfully accepted the offer. Leaving Bruin in the charge of Tim (who delighted in the oddities of the strange English gentleman), Tom made one of our party to ——.

CHAPTER FIVE

OUR FIRST SETTLEMENT, AND THE BORROWING SYSTEM

CHAPTER V.　　OUR FIRST SETTLE-MENT, & THE BORROWING SYSTEM

To lend, or not to lend—is that the question?

"THOSE WHO GO A-BORROWING, GO A-sorrowing," saith the old adage; and a wiser saw never came out of the mouth of experience. I have tested the truth of this proverb since my settlement in Canada, many, many times, to my cost; and what emigrant has not? So averse have I ever been to this practice, that I would at all times rather quietly submit to a temporary inconvenience than obtain anything I wanted in this manner. I verily believe that a demon of mischief presides over borrowed goods, and takes a wicked pleasure in playing off a thousand malicious pranks upon you the moment he enters your dwelling. Plates and dishes, that had been the pride and ornament of their own cupboard for years, no sooner enter upon foreign service than they are broken; wine-glasses and tumblers, that have been handled by a hundred careless wenches in safety, scarcely pass into the hands of your servants when they are sure to tumble upon the floor, and the accident turns out a compound fracture. If you borrow a garment of any kind, be sure that you will tear it; a watch, that you will break it; a jewel, that you will lose it; a book, that it will be stolen from you. There is no end to the trouble and vexation arising out of this evil habit. If you borrow a horse, and he has the reputation of being the best-behaved animal in the district, you no sooner become responsible for his conduct than he loses his character. The moment that you attempt to drive him, he shows that he has a will of his own, by taking the reins into his own management, and running away in a contrary direction to the road that you wished him to travel. He never gives over his eccentric capers until he has broken his own knees, and the borrowed carriage and harness. So anxious are you about his safety, that you have not a moment to bestow upon your own. And why?—the beast is borrowed, and you are expected to return him in as good condition as he came to you.

But of all evils, to borrow money is perhaps the worst. If of a friend, he ceases to be one the moment you feel that you are bound to him by the heavy clog of obligation. If of a usurer, the interest, in this country, soon doubles the original sum, and you owe an increasing debt, which in time swallows up all you possess.

When we first came to the colony, nothing surprised me more than the extent to which this pernicious custom was carried, both by the native Canadians, the European settlers, and the lower order of Americans. Many of the latter had spied out the goodness of the land, and *borrowed* various portions of it, without so much as asking leave of the absentee owners. Unfortunately, our new home was surrounded by these odious squatters, whom we found as ignorant as savages, without their courtesy and kindness.

The place we first occupied was purchased of Mr. B——, a merchant, who took it in payment of sundry large debts which the owner, a New England loyalist, had been unable to settle. Old Joe R——, the present occupant, had promised to quit it with his family, at the commencement of sleighing; and as the bargain was concluded in the month of September, and we were anxious to plough for fall wheat, it was necessary to be upon the spot. No house was to be found in the immediate neighbourhood, save a small dilapidated log tenement, on an adjoining farm (which was scarcely reclaimed from the bush) that had been some months without an owner. The merchant assured us that this could be made very comfortable until such time as it suited R—— to remove, and the owner was willing to let us have it for the moderate sum of four dollars a month.

Trusting to Mr. B——'s word, and being strangers in the land, we never took the precaution to examine this delightful summer residence before entering upon it, but thought ourselves very fortunate in obtaining a temporary home so near our own property, the distance not exceeding half a mile. The agreement was drawn up, and we were told that we could take possession whenever it suited us.

The few weeks that I had sojourned in the country had by no means prepossessed me in its favour. The home-sickness was sore upon me, and all my solitary hours were spent in tears. My whole soul yielded itself up to a strong and overpowering grief. One simple word dwelt for ever in my heart, and swelled it to bursting—"Home!" I repeated it waking a thousand times a day, and my last prayer before I sank to sleep was still "Home! Oh, that I could return, if only to die at home!" And nightly I did return; my feet again trod the daisied meadows of England; the song of her birds was in my ears; I wept with delight to find myself once more wandering beneath the fragrant shade of her green hedge-rows; and I awoke to weep in earnest when I found it but a dream. But this is all digression, and has nothing to do with our unseen dwelling. The reader must bear with me in my fits of melancholy, and take me as I am.

It was the 22nd September that we left the Steamboat Hotel, to take possession of our new abode. During the three weeks we had sojourned at ——, I had not seen a drop of rain, and I began to think that the fine weather would last for ever; but this eventful day arose in clouds. Moodie had hired a covered carriage to convey the baby, the servant-maid, and myself to the farm, as our driver prognosticated a wet day; while he followed with Tom Wilson and the teams that conveyed our luggage.

The scenery through which we were passing was so new to me, so unlike anything that I had ever beheld before, that, in spite of its monotonous character, it won me from my melancholy, and I began to look about me with considerable interest. Not so my English servant, who declared that the woods were frightful to look upon; that it was a country only fit for wild beasts; that she hated it with all her heart and soul, and would go back as soon as she was able.

About a mile from the place of our destination the rain began to fall in torrents, and the air, which had been balmy as a spring morning, turned as chilly as that of a November day. Hannah shivered; the baby cried, and I drew my summer shawl as closely round as possible, to protect her from the sudden change in our hitherto delightful temperature. Just then, the carriage turned into a narrow, steep path, overhung with lofty woods, and, after labouring up it with considerable difficulty, and at the risk of breaking our necks, it brought us at length to a rocky upland clearing, partially covered with a second growth of timber, and surrounded on all sides by the dark forest.

"I guess," quoth our Yankee driver, "that at the bottom of this 'ere swell you'll find yourself *to hum*;" and plunging into a short path cut through the wood, he pointed to a miserable hut, at the bottom of a steep descent, and cracking his whip, exclaimed, " 'Tis a smart location that. I wish you Britishers may enjoy it."

I gazed upon the place in perfect dismay, for I had never seen such a shed called a house before. "You must be mistaken; that is not a house, but a cattle-shed, or pig-sty."

The man turned his knowing, keen eye upon me, and smiled, half-humorously, half-maliciously, as he said—

"You were raised in the old country, I guess; you have much to learn, and more, perhaps, than you'll like to know, before the winter is over."

I was perfectly bewildered—I could only stare at the place, with my eyes swimming in tears; but, as the horses plunged down into the broken hollow, my attention was drawn from my new residence to the perils which endangered life and limb at every step. The driver, however, was well used to such roads, and, steering as dexterously between the black stumps, at length drove up, not to the door, for there was none to the house, but to the open space from which that absent, but very necessary, appendage had been removed. Three young steers and two heifers, which the driver proceeded to drive out, were quietly reposing upon the floor. A few strokes of his whip, and a loud burst of gratuitous curses, soon effected an ejectment; and I dismounted, and took possession of this untenable tenement. Moodie was not yet in sight with the teams. I begged the man to stay until he arrived, as I felt terrified at being left alone in this wild, strange-looking place. He laughed, as well he might, at our fears, and said he had a long way to go, and must be off; then, cracking his whip, and nodding to the girl, who was crying aloud, he went his way, and Hannah and myself were left standing in the middle of the dirty floor.

The prospect was indeed dreary. Without, pouring rain; within, a fireless hearth; a room with but one window, and that containing only one whole pane of glass; not an article of furniture to be seen, save an old painted pine-wood cradle, which had been left there by some freak of fortune. This, turned upon its side, served us for a seat, and there we impatiently awaited the arrival of Moodie, Wilson, and a man whom the former had hired that morning to assist on the farm. Where they were all to be stowed might have puzzled a more sagacious brain than mine. It is true there was a loft, but I could see no way of reaching it, for ladder there was none, so we amused ourselves, while waiting for the coming of our party, by abusing the place, the country, and our own dear selves for our folly in coming to it.

Now, when not only reconciled to Canada, but loving it, and feeling a deep interest in its present welfare, and the fair prospect of its future greatness, I often look back and laugh at the feelings with which I then regarded this noble country.

OUR FIRST SETTLEMENT

When things come to the worst, they generally mend. The males of our party no sooner arrived than they set about making things more comfortable. James, our servant, pulled up some of the decayed stumps, with which the small clearing that surrounded the shanty was thickly covered, and made a fire, and Hannah roused herself from the stupor of despair, seized the corn-broom from the top of the loaded waggon, and began to sweep the house, raising such an intolerable cloud of dust that I was glad to throw my cloak over my head, and run out of doors, to avoid suffocation. Then commenced the awful bustle of unloading the two heavily loaded waggons. The small space within the house was soon entirely blocked up with several trunks and packages of all descriptions. There was scarcely room to move, without stumbling over some article of household stuff.

The rain poured in at the open door, beat in at the shattered window, and dropped upon our heads from the holes in the roof. The wind blew keenly through a thousand apertures in the log walls; and nothing could exceed the uncomfortableness of our situation. For a long time the box which contained a hammer and nails was not to be found. At length Hannah discovered it, tied up with some bedding which she was opening out in order to dry. I fortunately spied the door lying among some old boards at the back of the house, and Moodie immediately commenced fitting it to its place. This, once accomplished, was a great addition to our comfort. We then nailed a piece of white cloth entirely over the broken window, which, without diminishing the light, kept out the rain.

H

James constructed a ladder out of the old bits of boards, and Tom Wilson assisted him in stowing the luggage away in the loft.

But what has this picture of misery and discomfort to do with borrowing? Patience, my dear, good friends; I will tell you all about it by-and-by.

While we were all busily employed—even the poor baby, who was lying upon a pillow in the old cradle, trying the strength of her lungs, and not a little irritated that no one was at leisure to regard her laudable endeavours to make herself heard—the door was suddenly pushed open, and the apparition of a woman squeezed itself into the crowded room. I left off arranging the furniture of a bed, that had been just put up in a corner, to meet my unexpected, and at that moment, not very welcome guest. Her whole appearance was so extraordinary that I felt quite at a loss how to address her.

Imagine a girl of seventeen or eighteen years of age, with sharp, knowing-looking features, a forward, impudent carriage, and a pert, flippant voice, standing upon one of the trunks, and surveying all our proceedings in the most impertinent manner. The creature was dressed in a ragged, dirty purple stuff gown, cut very low in the neck, with an old red cotton handkerchief tied over her head; her uncombed, tangled locks falling over her thin, inquisitive face, in a state of perfect nature. Her legs and feet were bare, and, in her coarse, dirty red hands, she swung to and fro an empty glass decanter.

"What can she want?" I asked myself. "What a strange creature!"

OUR FIRST SETTLEMENT

And there she stood, staring at me in the most un-ceremonious manner, her keen black eyes glancing obliquely to every corner of the room, which she examined with critical exactness.

Before I could speak to her, she commenced the conversation by drawling through her nose—

"Well, I guess you are fixing here."

I thought she had come to offer her services; and I told her that I did not want a girl, for I had brought one out with me.

"How!" responded the creature, "I hope you don't take me for a help. I'd have you to know that I'm as good a lady as yourself. No; I just stepped over to see what was going on. I see'd the teams pass our'n about noon, and I says to father, 'Them strangers are cum; I'll go and look arter them.' 'Yes,' says he, 'do—and take the decanter along. May be they'll want one to put their whiskey in.' 'I'm goin' to,' says I; so I cum across with it, an' here it is. But, mind —don't break it—'tis the only one we have to hum; and father says 'tis so mean to drink out of green glass."

My surprise increased every minute. It seemed such an act of disinterested generosity thus to anticipate wants we had never thought of. I was regularly taken in.

"My good girl," I began, "this is really very kind— but——"

"Now, don't go to call me 'gal'—and pass off your English airs on us. We are *genuine* Yankees, and think ourselves as good—yes, a great deal better than you. I am a young lady."

"Indeed!" said I, striving to repress my astonishment. "I am a stranger in the country, and my acquaintance with Canadian ladies and gentlemen is very small. I did not mean to offend you by using the term girl; I was going to assure you that we had no need of the decanter. We have bottles of our own—and we don't drink whiskey."

"How! Not drink whiskey? Why, you don't say! How ignorant you must be! May be they have no whiskey in the old country?"

"Yes, we have; but it is not like the Canadian whiskey. But, pray take the decanter home again—I am afraid that it will get broken in this confusion."

"No, no; father told me to leave it—and there it is;" and she planted it resolutely down on the trunk. "You will find a use for it till you have unpacked your own."

Seeing that she was determined to leave the bottle, I said no more about it, but asked her to tell me where the well was to be found.

"The well!" she repeated after me, with a sneer. "Who thinks of digging wells where they can get plenty of water from the creek? There is a fine water privilege not a stone's-throw from the door," and, jumping off the box, she disappeared as abruptly as she had entered. We all looked at each other; Tom Wilson was highly amused, and laughed until he held his sides.

"What tempted her to bring this empty bottle here?" said Moodie. "It is all an excuse; the visit, Tom, was meant for you."

"You'll know more about it in a few days," said

James, looking up from his work. "That bottle is not brought here for nought."

I could not unravel the mystery, and thought no more about it, until it was again brought to my recollection by the damsel herself.

Our united efforts had effected complete transformation in our uncouth dwelling. Sleeping-berths had been partitioned off for the men; shelves had been put up for the accommodation of books and crockery, a carpet covered the floor, and the chairs and tables we had brought from —— gave an air of comfort to the place, which, on the first view of it, I deemed impossible. My husband, Mr. Wilson, and James, had walked over to inspect the farm, and I was sitting at the table at work, the baby creeping upon the floor, and Hannah preparing dinner. The sun shone warm and bright, and the open door admitted a current of fresh air, which tempered the heat of the fire.

"Well, I guess you look smart," said the Yankee damsel, presenting herself once more before me. "You old country folks are so stiff, you must have everything nice or you fret. But, then, you can easily do it; you have *stacks* of money; and you can fix everything right off with money."

"Pray take a seat," and I offered her a chair, "and be kind enough to tell me your name. I suppose you must live in the neighbourhood, although I cannot perceive any dwelling near us."

"My name! So you want to know my name. I arn't ashamed of my own; 'tis Emily S——. I am eldest daughter to the *gentleman* who owns this house."

"What must the father be," thought I, "if he resembles the young *lady*, his daughter?"

Imagine a young lady, dressed in ragged petticoats, through whose yawning rents peered forth, from time to time, her bare red knees, with uncombed elf-locks, and a face and hands that looked as if they had been unwashed for a month—who did not know A from B, and despised those who did. While these reflections, combined with a thousand ludicrous images, were flitting through my mind, my strange visitor suddenly exclaimed—

"Have you done with that 'ere decanter I brought across yesterday?"

"Oh yes! I have no occasion for it." I rose, took it from the shelf, and placed it in her hand.

"I guess you won't return it empty; that would be mean, father says. He wants it filled with whiskey."

The mystery was solved, the riddle made clear. I could contain my gravity no longer, but burst into a hearty fit of laughter, in which I was joined by Hannah. Our young lady was mortally offended; she tossed the decanter from hand to hand, and glared at us with her tiger-like eyes.

"You think yourselves smart! Why do you laugh in that way?"

"Excuse me—but you have such an odd way of borrowing that I cannot help it. This bottle, it seems, was brought over for your own convenience, not for mine. I am sorry to disappoint you, but I have no whiskey."

"I guess spirits will do as well; I know there is some in that keg, for I smells it."

"It contains rum for the workmen."

"Better still. I calculate when you've been here a few months, you'll be too knowing to give rum to your helps. But old country folks are all fools, and that's the reason they get so easily sucked in, and be so soon wound-up. Cum, fill the bottle, and don't be stingy. In this country we all live by borrowing. If you want anything, why, just send and borrow from us."

Thinking that this might be the custom of the country, I hastened to fill the decanter, hoping that I might get a little new milk for the poor weanling child in return; but when I asked my liberal visitor if she kept cows, and would lend me a little new milk for the baby, she burst out into high disdain. "Milk! Lend milk? I guess milk in the fall is worth a York shilling a quart. I cannot sell you a drop under."

This was a wicked piece of extortion, as the same article in the towns, where, of course, it was in greater request, only brought three-pence the quart.

"If you'll pay me for it, I'll bring you some to-morrow. But mind—cash down."

"And when do you mean to return the rum," I said, with some asperity.

"When father goes to the creek." This was the name given by my neighbours to the village of P——, distant about four miles.

Day after day I was tormented by this importunate creature; she borrowed of me tea, sugar, candles, starch, blueing, irons, pots, bowls—in short, every article in common domestic use—while it was with the utmost difficulty we could get them returned. Articles of food, such as tea and sugar, or of convenience, like candles, starch, and soap, she never dreamed of being required at her hands. This method of living upon their neighbours is a most convenient one to unprincipled people, as it does not involve the penalty of stealing; and they can keep the goods without the unpleasant necessity of returning them, or feeling the moral obligation of being grateful for their use. Living eight miles from ——, I found these constant encroachments a heavy burden on our poor purse; and being ignorant of the country, and residing in such a lonely, out-of-the-way place, surrounded by these savages, I was really afraid of denying their requests.

The very day our new plough came home, the father of this bright damsel, who went by the familiar and unenviable title of *Old Satan*, came over to borrow it (though we afterwards found out that he had a good one of his own). The land had never been broken up, and was full of rocks and stumps, and he was anxious to save his own from injury; the consequence was that the borrowed implement came home unfit for use, just at the very time that we wanted to plough for fall wheat. The same happened to a spade and trowel, bought in order to plaster the house. Satan asked the loan of them for *one* hour for the same purpose, and we never saw them again.

The daughter came one morning, as usual, on one of these swindling expeditions, and demanded of me the loan of some *fine slack*. Not knowing what she meant by *fine slack*, and weary of her importunities, I said I had none. She went away in a rage. Shortly after she came again for some pepper. I was at work, and my work-box was open upon the table, well stored with threads and spools of all descriptions.

OUR FIRST SETTLEMENT

Miss Satan cast her hawk's eye into it, and burst out in her usual rude manner—

"I guess you told me a tarnation big lie the other day."

Unaccustomed to such language, I rose from my seat, and pointing to the door, told her to walk out, as I did not choose to be insulted in my own house.

"Your house! I'm sure it's father's," returned the incorrigible wretch. "You told me that you had no *fine slack*, and you have *stacks* of it."

"What is fine slack?" said I, very pettishly.

"The stuff that's wound upon these 'ere pieces of wood," pouncing as she spoke upon one of my most serviceable spools.

"I cannot give you that; I want that myself."

"I didn't ask you to give it. I only wants to borrow it till father goes to the creek."

"I wish he would make haste, then, as I want a number of things which you have borrowed of me, and which I cannot longer do without."

She gave me a knowing look, and carried off my spool in triumph.

I happened to mention the manner in which I was constantly annoyed by these people, to a worthy English farmer who resided near us; and he fell a-laughing, and told me that I did not know the Canadian Yankees as well as he did, or I should not be troubled with them long.

"The best way," says he, "to get rid of them, is to ask them sharply what they want; and if they give you no satisfactory answer, order them to leave the house; but I believe I can put you in a better way still.

Buy some small article of them, and pay them a trifle over the price, and tell them to bring the change. I will lay my life upon it that it will be long before they trouble you again."

I was impatient to test the efficacy of his scheme. That very afternoon Miss Satan brought me a plate of butter for sale. The price was three and ninepence; twice the sum, by the by, that it was worth.

"I have no change," giving her a dollar; "but you can bring it me to-morrow."

Oh, blessed experiment! for the value of one quarter dollar I got rid of this dishonest girl for ever; rather than pay me, she never entered the house again.

About a month after this, I was busy making an apple-pie in the kithen. A cadaverous-looking woman, very long-faced and witch-like, popped her ill-looking visage into the door, and drawled through her nose—

"Do you want to buy a *rooster*?"

Now, the sucking-pigs with which we had been re-galed every day for three weeks at the tavern, were called roasters; and not understanding the familiar phrases of the country, I thought she had a sucking-pig to sell.

"Is it a good one?"

"I guess 'tis."

"What do you ask for it?"

"Two Yorkers."

"That is very cheap, if it is any weight. I don't like them under ten or twelve pounds."

"Ten or twelve pounds! Why, woman, what do you mean? Would you expect a rooster to be bigger nor a turkey?"

OUR FIRST SETTLEMENT

We stared at each other. There was evidently some misconception on my part.

"Bring the roaster up; and if I like it, I will buy it, though I must confess that I am not very fond of roast pig."

"Do you call this a pig?" said my she-merchant, drawing a fine game-cock from under her cloak.

I laughed heartily at my mistake, as I paid her down the money for the bonny bird. This little matter settled, I thought she would take her departure; but that rooster proved the dearest fowl to me that ever was bought.

"Do you keep backy and snuff here?" says she, sidling close up to me.

"We make no use of those articles."

"How! Not use backy and snuff? That's oncommon."

She paused, then added in a mysterious, confidential tone—

"I want to ask you how your tea-caddy stands?"

"It stands in the cupboard," said I, wondering what all this might mean.

"I know that; but have you any tea to spare?"

I now began to suspect what sort of a customer the stranger was.

"Oh, you want to borrow some? I have none to spare."

"You don't say so. Well, now, that's stingy. I never asked anything of you before. I am poor, and you are rich; besides, I'm troubled so with the headache, and nothing does me any good but a cup of strong tea."

"The money I have just given you will buy a quarter of a pound of the best."

"I guess that isn't mine. The fowl belonged to my neighbour. She's sick; and I promised to sell it for her to buy some physic. Money!" she added, in a coaxing tone, "Where should I get money? Lord bless you! people in this country have no money; and those who come out with piles of it, soon lose it. But Emily S—— told me that you are tarnation rich, and draw your money from the old country. So I guess you can well afford to lend a neighbour a spoonful of tea."

"Neighbour! Where do you live, and what is your name?"

"My name is Betty Fye—old Betty Fye; I live in the log shanty over the creek, at the back of your'n. The farm belongs to my eldest son. I'm a widow with twelve sons; and 'tis —— hard to scratch along."

"Do you swear?"

"Swear! What harm? It eases one's mind when one's vexed. Everybody swears in this country. My boys all swear like Sam Hill; and I used to swear mighty big oaths till about a month ago, when the Methody parson told me that if I did not leave it off I should go to a tarnation bad place; so I dropped some of the worst of them."

"You would do wisely to drop the rest; women never swear in my country."

"Well, you don't say! I always heer'd they were very ignorant. Will you lend me the tea?"

The woman was such an original that I gave her

what she wanted. As she was going off, she took up one of the apples I was peeling.

"I guess you have a fine orchard?"

"They say the best in the district."

"We have no orchard to hum, and I guess you'll want *sarce*."

"Sarce! What is sarce?"

"Not know what sarce is? You are clever! Sarce is apples cut up and dried, to make into pies in the winter. Now do you comprehend?"

I nodded.

"Well, I was going to say that I have no apples, and that you have a tarnation big few of them; and if you'll give me twenty bushels of your best apples, and find me with half a pound of coarse thread to string them upon, I will make you a barrel of sarce on shares—that is, give you one, and keep one for myself."

I had plenty of apples, and I gladly accepted her offer, and Mrs. Betty Fye departed, elated with the success of her expedition.

I found to my cost, that, once admitted into the house, there was no keeping her away. She borrowed everything she could think of, without once dreaming of restitution. I tried all ways of affronting her, but without success. Winter came, and she was still at her old pranks. Whenever I saw her coming down the lane, I used involuntarily to exclaim, "Betty Fye! Betty Fye! Fye upon Betty Fye! The Lord deliver me from Betty Fye!" The last time I was honoured with a visit from this worthy, she meant to favour me with a very large order upon my goods and chattels.

"Well, Mrs. Fye, what do you want *to-day*?"

125

" So many things that I scarce know where to begin. Ah, what a thing 'tis to be poor! First, I want you to lend me ten pounds of flour to make some Johnnie cakes."

" I thought they were made of Indian meal?"

"Yes, yes, when you've got the meal? I'm out of it, and this is a new fixing of my own invention. Lend me the flour, woman, and I'll bring you one of the cakes to taste."

This was said very coaxingly.

"Oh, pray don't trouble yourself. What next?" I was anxious to see how far her impudence would go, and determined to affront her if possible.

"I want you to lend me a gown, and a pair of stockings. I have to go to Oswego to see my husband's sister, and I'd like to look decent."

"Mrs. Fye, I never lend my clothes to any one. If I lent them to you, I should never wear them again."

" So much the better for me " (with a knowing grin). " I guess if you won't lend me the gown, you will let me have some black slack to quilt a stuff petticoat, a quarter of a pound of tea and some sugar; and I will bring them back as soon as I can."

" I wonder when that will be. You owe me so many things that it will cost you more than you imagine to repay me."

"Sure you're not going to mention what's past; I can't owe you much. But I will let you off the tea and the sugar, if you will lend me a five-dollar bill." This was too much for my patience longer to endure, and I answered sharply—

"Mrs. Fye, it surprises me that such proud people

MONTREAL FROM THE ST LAWRENCE

as you Americans should condescend to the meanness
of borrowing from those whom you affect to despise.
Besides, as you never repay us for what you pretend
to borrow, I look upon it as a system of robbery. If
strangers unfortunately settle among you, their good-
nature is taxed to supply your domestic wants, at a
ruinous expense, besides the mortification of finding
that they have been deceived and tricked out of their
property. If you would come honestly to me and say,
'I want these things, I am too poor to buy them myself, and would be obliged to you to give them to me,'
I should then acknowledge you as a common beggar,
and treat you accordingly; give or not give, as it suited
my convenience. But in the way in which you obtain
these articles from me you are spared even a debt of
gratitude; for you well know that the many things
which you have borrowed from me will be a debt owing to the Day of Judgment."

"S'pose they are," quoth Betty, not in the least a-
bashed at my lecture on honesty, "you know what
the Scripture saith, 'It is more blessed to give than
to receive.'"

"Ay, there is an answer to that in the same book
which doubtless you may have heard," said I, disgusted with her hypocrisy, "'The wicked borroweth, and
payeth not again.'"

Never shall I forget the furious passion into which
this too apt quotation threw my unprincipled ap-
plicant. She lifted up her voice and cursed me, using
some of the big oaths temporarily discarded for *conscience*' sake. And so she left me, and I never looked
upon her face again.

ROUGHING IT IN THE BUSH

When I removed to our own house, the history of which, and its former owner, I will give by-and-by, we had a bony, red-headed, ruffianly American squatter, who had "left his country for his country's good," for an opposite neighbour. I had scarcely time to put my house in order before his family commenced borrowing or stealing from me. It is even worse than stealing, the things procured from you being obtained on false pretences—adding lying to theft. Not having either an oven or a cooking-stove, which at that period were not so cheap or so common as they are now, I had provided myself with a large bake-kettle as a substitute. In this kettle we always cooked hot cakes for breakfast, preferring that to the trouble of thawing the frozen bread. This man's wife was in the habit of sending over for my kettle whenever she wanted to bake, which, as she had a large family, happened nearly every day, and I found her importunity a great nuisance.

I told the impudent lad so, who was generally sent for it; and asked him what they did to bake their bread before I came.

"I guess we had to eat cakes in the pan; but now we can borrow this kettle of your'n, mother can fix bread."

I told him that he could have the kettle this time; but I must decline letting his mother have it in future, for I wanted it for the same purpose.

The next day passed over. The night was intensely cold, and I did not rise so early as usual in the morning. My servant was away at a quilting bee, and we were still in bed, when I heard the latch of the kitchen-door lifted up, and a step crossed the floor. I jumped out of bed, and began to dress as fast as I could, when Philander called out in his well-known nasal twang—

"Missus! I'm come for the kettle."

I (*through the partition*): "You can't have it this morning. We cannot get our breakfast without it."

Philander: "Nor more can the old woman to hum," and, snatching up the kettle, which had been left to warm on the hearth, he rushed out of the house, singing, at the top of his voice—

"Hurrah for the Yankee Boys!"

When James came home for his breakfast, I sent him across to demand the kettle, and the dame very coolly told him that when she had done with it I *might* have it, but she defied him to take it out of her house with her bread in it.

One word more about this lad, Philander, before we part with him. Without the least intimation that his company would be agreeable, or even tolerated, he favoured us with it at all hours of the day, opening the door and walking in and out whenever he felt inclined. I had given him many broad hints that his presence was not required, but he paid not the slightest attention to what I said. One morning he marched in with his hat on, and threw himself down in the rocking-chair, just as I was going to dress my baby.

"Philander, I want to attend to the child; I cannot do it with you here. Will you oblige me by going into the kitchen?"

No answer. He seldom spoke during these visits,

but wandered about the room, turning over our books and papers, looking at and handling everything. Nay, I have even known him to take a lid off from the pot on the fire to examine its contents.

I repeated my request.

Philander: "Well, I guess I shan't hurt the young 'un. You can dress her."

I: "But not with you here."

Philander: "Why not? *We* never do anything that we are ashamed of."

I: "So it seems. But I want to sweep the room—you had better get out of the dust."

I took the broom from the corner, and began to sweep; still my visitor did not stir. The dust rose in clouds; he rubbed his eyes, and moved a little nearer to the door. Another sweep, and, to escape its inflictions, he mounted the threshold. I had him now at a fair advantage, and fairly swept him out, and shut the door in his face.

Philander (*looking through the window*): "Well, I guess you did me then; but 'tis deuced hard to outwit a Yankee."

When a sufficient time had elapsed for the drying of my twenty bushels of apples, I sent a Cornish lad, in our employ, to Betty Fye's, to inquire if they were ready, and when I should send the cart for them.

Dan returned with a yellow, smoke-dried string of pieces dangling from his arm. Thinking that these were a specimen of the whole, I inquired when we were to send the barrel for the rest.

"Lord, ma'am, this is all there be."

"Impossible! All out of twenty bushels of apples?"

"Yes," said the boy, with a grin. "The old witch told me that this was all that was left of your share; that when they were fixed enough she put them under her bed for safety, and the mice and the children had eaten them all up but this string."

This ended my dealings with Betty Fye.

I had another incorrigible borrower in the person of old Betty B——. This Betty was unlike the rest of my Yankee borrowers; she was handsome in her person, and remarkably civil, and she asked for the loan of everything in such a frank, pleasant manner, that for some time I hardly knew how to refuse her. After I had been a loser to a considerable extent, and declined lending her any more, she refrained from coming to the house herself, but sent in her name the most beautiful boy in the world: a perfect cherub, with regular features, blue, smiling eyes, rosy cheeks, and lovely curling auburn hair, who said, in the softest tones imaginable, that mammy had sent him, with her *compliments*, to the English lady to ask the loan of a little sugar or tea. I could easily have refused the mother, but I could not find it in my heart to say nay to her sweet boy.

There was something original about Betty B——, and I must give a slight sketch of her.

She lived in a lone shanty in the woods, which had been erected by lumberers some years before, and which was destitute of a single acre of clearing; yet Betty had plenty of potatoes without the trouble of planting, or the expense of buying; she never kept a cow, yet she sold butter and milk; but she had a fashion, and it proved a convenient one to her, of making pets of the cattle of her neighbours. If our cows strayed from their pastures, they were always found near Betty's shanty, for she regularly supplied them with salt, which formed a sort of bond of union between them; and, in return for these little attentions, they suffered themselves to be milked before they returned to their respective owners. Her mode of obtaining eggs and fowls was on the same economical plan, and we all looked upon Betty as a sort of freebooter, living upon the property of others. She had had three husbands, and he with whom she now lived was not her husband, although the father of the splendid child whose beauty so won upon my woman's heart. Her first husband was still living (a thing by no means uncommon among persons of her class in Canada), and though they had quarrelled and parted years ago, he occasionally visited his wife to see her eldest daughter, Betty the younger, who was his child. She was now a fine girl of sixteen, as beautiful as her little brother. Betty's second husband had been killed in one of our fields, by a tree falling upon him while ploughing under it. He was buried upon the spot, part of the blackened stump forming his monument. In truth, Betty's character was none of the best, and many of the respectable farmers' wives regarded her with a jealous eye.

"I am so jealous of that nasty Betty B——," said the wife of an Irish captain in the army, and our near neighbour, to me, one day as we were sitting at work together. She was a West Indian, and a negro by the mother's side, but an uncommonly fine-looking mulatto, very passionate, and very watchful over the conduct of her husband.

OUR FIRST SETTLEMENT

"Are you not afraid of letting Captain Moodie go near her shanty?"

"No, indeed; and if I were so foolish as to be jealous, it would not be of old Betty, but of the beautiful young Betty, her daughter." Perhaps this was rather mischievous on my part, for the poor dark lady went off in a frantic fit of jealousy, but this time it was not of old Betty.

Another American squatter was always sending over to borrow a small-tooth comb, which she called a *vermin destroyer*; and once the same person asked the loan of a towel, as a friend had come from the States to visit her, and the only one she had had been made into a best "pinny" for the child; she likewise begged a sight in the looking-glass, as she wanted to try on a new cap to see if it were fixed to her mind. This woman must have been a mirror of neatness when compared with her dirty neighbours.

One night I was roused up from my bed for the loan of a pair of "steelyards." For what purpose, think you, gentle reader? To weigh a new-born infant. The process was performed by tying the poor squalling thing up in a small shawl, and suspending it to one of the hooks. The child was a fine boy, and weighed ten pounds, greatly to the delight of the Yankee father.

One of the drollest instances of borrowing I have ever heard of was told me by a friend. A maid-servant asked her mistress to go out on a particular afternoon, as she was going to have a party of her friends, and wanted the loan of the drawing-room.

It would be endless to enumerate our losses in this way; but, fortunately for us, the arrival of an English family in our immediate vicinity drew off the attention of our neighbours in that direction, and left us time to recover a little from their persecutions.

This system of borrowing is not wholly confined to the poor and ignorant; it pervades every class of society. If a party is given in any of the small villages, a boy is sent round from house to house to collect all the plates and dishes, knives and forks, teaspoons and candlesticks, that are presentable, for the use of the company.

After removing to the bush, many misfortunes befell us, which deprived us of our income, and reduced us to great poverty. In fact we were strangers, and the knowing ones took us in; and for many years we struggled with hardships which would have broken stouter hearts than ours, had not our trust been placed in the Almighty, who among all our troubles never wholly deserted us.

While my husband was absent on the frontier during the rebellion, my youngest boy fell very sick, and required my utmost care both by night and day. To attend to him properly, a candle burning during the night was necessary. The last candle was burnt out; I had no money to buy another, and no fat from which I could make one. I hated borrowing, but, for the dear child's sake I overcame my scruples, and succeeded in procuring a candle from a good neighbour, but with strict injunctions (for it was *her last*) that I must return it if I did not require it during the night.

I went home quite grateful with my prize. It was a clear moonlight night—the dear boy was better, so I told old Jenny, my Irish servant, to go to bed, as I would lie down in my clothes by the child, and if he were worse I would get up and light the candle. It happened that a pane of glass was broken out of the window-frame, and I had supplied its place by fitting in a shingle; my friend Emilia S——had a large Tom-cat, who, when his mistress was absent, often paid me a predatory or borrowing visit; and Tom had a practice of pushing in this wooden pane in order to pursue his lawless depredations. I had forgotten all this, and never dreaming that Tom would appropriate such light food, I left the candle lying in the middle of the table, just under the window.

Between sleeping and waking, I heard the pane gently pushed in. The thought instantly struck me that it was Tom, and that, for lack of something better, he might steal my precious candle.

I sprang up from the bed, just in time to see him dart through the broken window, dragging the long white candle after him. I flew to the door, and pursued him *half* over the field, but all to no purpose. I can see him now, as I saw him then, scampering away for dear life, with his prize trailing behind him, gleaming like a silver tail in the bright light of the moon.

Ah! never did I feel more acutely the truth of the proverb, "Those that go a-borrowing go a-sorrowing," than I did that night. My poor boy awoke ill and feverish, and I had no light to assist him, or even to look into his sweet face, to see how far I dared hope that the light of day would find him better.

CHAPTER SIX
OLD SATAN AND TOM WILSON'S NOSE

CHAPTER   SIX

OLD SATAN AND TOM WILSON'S NOSE

> A nose, kind sir! Sure mother Nature,
> With all her freaks, ne'er formed this feature.
> If such were mine, I'd try and trade it,
> And swear the gods had never made it.

AFTER REDUCING THE LOG CABIN INTO some sort of order, we contrived, with the aid of a few boards, to make a bed-closet for poor Tom Wilson, who continued to shake every day with the pitiless ague. There was no way of admitting light and air into this domicile, which opened into the general a-partment, but through a square hole cut in one of the planks, just wide enough to admit a man's head through the aperture. Here we made Tom a comfortable bed on the floor, and did the best we could to nurse him through his sickness. His long thin face, emaciated with disease, and surrounded by huge black whiskers and a beard of a week's growth, looked perfectly unearthly. He had only to stare at the baby to frighten her almost out of her wits.

"How fond that young one is of me," he would say; "she cries for joy at the sight of me."

Among his curiosities, and he had many, he held in great esteem a huge nose, made hollow to fit his face, which his father, a being almost as eccentric as himself, had carved out of boxwood. When he slipped this nose over his own (which was no beautiful classical specimen of the nasal organ), it made a most perfect and hideous disguise. The mother who bore him never would have recognized her accomplished son.

Numberless were the tricks he played off with this nose. Once he walked through the streets of ——,
139

with this proboscis attached to his face. "What a nose! Look at the man with the nose!" cried all the boys in the street. A party of Irish emigrants passed at the moment. The men, with the courtesy natural to their nation, forbore to laugh in the gentleman's face; but after they had passed, Tom looked back, and saw them bent half double in convulsions of mirth. Tom made the party a low bow, gravely took off his nose, and put it in his pocket.

The day after this frolic he had a very severe fit of the ague, and looked so ill that I really entertained fears for his life. The hot fit had just left him, and he lay upon his bed bedewed with a cold perspiration, in a state of complete exhaustion.

"Poor Tom," said I, "he has passed a horrible day, but the worst is over, and I will make him a cup of coffee." While preparing it, Old Satan came in and began to talk to my husband. He happened to sit directly opposite the aperture which gave light and air to Tom's berth. This man was disgustingly ugly. He had lost one eye in a quarrel. It had been gouged out in a free fight, and the side of his face presented a succession of horrible scars inflicted by the teeth of his savage adversary. The nickname he had acquired through the country sufficiently testified to the respectability of his character, and dreadful tales were told of him in the neighbourhood, where he was alike feared and hated.

The rude fellow, with his accustomed insolence, began abusing the Old Country folks.

The English were great bullies, he said; they thought no one could fight but themselves; but the Yankees had whipped them, and would whip them again. He was not afear'd of them, he never was afear'd in his life.

Scarcely were the words out of his mouth, when a horrible apparition presented itself to his view. Slowly rising from his bed, and putting on the fictitious nose, while he drew his white night-cap over his ghastly and livid brow, Tom thrust his face through the aperture, and uttered a diabolical cry; then sank down upon his unseen couch as noiselessly as he had arisen. The cry was like nothing human, and it was echoed by an involuntary scream from the lips of our maid-servant and myself.

"Good God! what's that?" cried Satan, falling back in his chair, and pointing to the vacant aperture. "Did you hear it? did you see it? It beats the universe. I never saw a ghost or the devil before!"

Moodie, who had recognized the ghost, and greatly enjoyed the fun, pretended profound ignorance, and coolly insinuated that Old Satan had lost his senses. The man was bewildered; he stared at the vacant aperture, then at us in turn, as if he doubted the accuracy of his own vision. "'Tis tarnation odd," he said; "but the women heard it too."

"I heard a sound," I said, "a dreadful sound, but I saw no ghost."

"Sure an' 'twas himsel'," said my Lowland Scotch girl, who now perceived the joke; "he was a-seekin' to gie us puir bodies a wee fricht."

"How long have you been subject to these sort of fits?" said I. "You had better speak to the doctor about them. Such fancies, if they are not attended to, often end in madness."

141

"Mad!" (*very indignantly*), "I guess I'm not mad, but as wide awake as you are. Did I not see it with my own eyes? And then the noise —I could not make such a tarnation outcry to save my life. But be it man or devil, I don't care, I'm not afear'd," doubling his fist very undecidedly at the hole. Again the ghastly head was protruded—the dreadful eyes rolled wildly in their hollow sockets, and a yell more appalling than the former rang through the room. The man sprang from his chair, which he overturned in his fright, and stood for an instant with his one eyeball starting from his head, and glaring upon the spectre; his cheeks deadly pale; the cold perspiration streaming from his face; his lips dissevered, and his teeth chattering in his head.

"There—there—there. Look—look, it comes a-gain!—the devil!—the devil!"

Here Tom, who still kept his eyes fixed upon his victim, gave a knowing wink, and thrust his tongue out of his mouth.

"He is coming!—he is coming!" cried the affrighted wretch; and clearing the open doorway with one leap, he fled across the field at full speed. The stream intercepted his path—he passed it at a bound, plunged into the forest, and was out of sight.

"Ha, ha, ha!" chuckled poor Tom, sinking down exhausted on his bed. "Oh that I had strength to follow up my advantage, I would lead Old Satan such a chase that he should think his namesake was in truth behind him."

During the six weeks that we inhabited that wretched cabin, we never were troubled by Old Satan again.

142

OLD SATAN AND TOM WILSON'S NOSE

As Tom slowly recovered, and began to regain his appetite, his soul sickened over the salt beef and pork, which, owing to our distance from ——, formed our principal fare. He positively refused to touch the *sad* bread, as my Yankee neighbours very appropriately termed the unleavened cakes in the pan; and it was no easy matter to send a man on horseback eight miles to fetch a loaf of bread.

"Do, my dear Mrs. Moodie, like a good Christian as you are, give me a morsel of the baby's biscuit, and try and make us some decent bread. The stuff your servant gives us is uneatable," said Wilson to me, in most imploring accents.

"Most willingly. But I have no yeast; and I never baked in one of those strange kettles in my life."

"I'll go to old Joe's wife and borrow some," said he; "they are always borrowing of you." Away he went across the field, but soon returned. I looked into his jug—it was empty. "No luck," said he; "those stingy wretches had just baked a fine batch of bread, and they would neither lend nor sell a loaf; but they told me how to make their milk-emptyings."

"Well, discuss the same;" but I much doubted if he could remember the recipe.

"You are to take an old tin pan," said he, sitting down on the stool, and poking the fire with a stick.

"Must it be an old one?" said I, laughing.

"Of course; they said so."

"And what am I to put into it?"

"Patience; let me begin at the beginning. Some flour and some milk—but, by George! I've forgot all about it. I was wondering as I came across the field

143

ROUGHING IT IN THE BUSH

why they called the yeast *milk*-emptyings, and that put the way to make it quite out of my head. But never mind; it is only ten o'clock by my watch. I have nothing to do; I will go again."

He went. Would I had been there to hear the colloquy between him and Mrs. Joe; he described it something to this effect:—

Mrs. Joe: "Well, stranger, what do you want now?"

Tom: "I have forgotten the way you told me how to make the bread."

Mrs. Joe: "I never told you how to make bread. I guess you are a fool. People have to raise bread before they can bake it. Pray who sent you to make game of me? I guess somebody as wise as yourself."

Tom: "The lady at whose house I am staying."

Mrs. Joe: "*Lady!* I can tell you that we have no *ladies* here. So the woman who lives in the old log shanty in the hollow don't know how to make bread. A clever wife that! Are you her husband?" (*Tom shakes his head.*)—"Her brother?"—(*Another shake.*) —"Her son? Do you hear? or are you deaf?" (*going quite close up to him*).

Tom (*moving back*): "Mistress, I'm not deaf; and who or what I am is nothing to you. Will you oblige me by telling me how to make the *mill-emptyings?* and this time I'll put it down in my pocket-book."

Mrs. Joe (*with a strong sneer*): "*Mill-emptyings!* Milk, I told you. So you expect me to answer your questions, and give back nothing in return. Get you gone; I'll tell you no more about it."

Tom (*bowing very low*): "Thank you for your *civ-*

144

ility. Is the old woman who lives in the little shanty near the apple-trees more obliging?"

Mrs. Joe: "That's my husband's mother. You may try. I guess she'll give you an answer." (*Exit, slamming the door in his face.*)

"And what did you do then?" said I.

"Oh, went of course. The door was open, and I reconnoitred the premises before I ventured in. I liked the phiz of the old woman a deal better than that of her daughter-in-law, although it was cunning and inquisitive, and as sharp as a needle. She was busy shelling cobs of Indian corn into a barrel. I rapped at the door. She told me to come in, and in I stepped. She asked me if I wanted her. I told her my errand, at which she laughed heartily."

Old woman: "You are from the old country, I guess, or you would know how to make *milk*-emptyings. Now, I always prefer *bran-emptyings*. They make the best bread. The milk, I opine, gives it a sourish taste, and the bran is the least trouble."

Tom: "Then let us have the bran, by all means. How do you make it?"

Old woman: "I put a double handful of bran into a small pot, or kettle, but a jug will do, and a teaspoonful of salt; but mind you don't kill it with salt, for if you do, it won't rise. I then add as much warm water, at blood-heat, as will mix it into a stiff batter. I then put the jug into a pan of warm water, and set it on the hearth near the fire, and keep it at the same heat until it rises, which it generally will do, if you attend to it, in two or three hours' time. When the bran cracks at the top, and you see white bubbles rising through it,

145   K

you may strain it into your flour, and lay your bread. It makes good bread."

Tom: "My good woman, I am greatly obliged to you. We have no bran; can you give me a small quantity?"

Old woman: "I never give anything. You English-ers, who come out with stacks of money, can afford to buy."

Tom: "Sell me a small quantity."

Old woman: "I guess I will." (*Edging quite close, and fixing her sharp eyes on him.*) "You must be very rich to buy bran."

Tom (*quizzically*): "Oh, very rich."

Old woman: "How do you get your money?"

Tom (*sarcastically*): "I don't steal it."

Old woman: "Pr'aps not. I guess you'll soon let others do that for you, if you don't take care. Are the people you live with related to you?"

Tom (*hardly able to keep his gravity*): "On Eve's side. They are my friends."

Old woman (*in surprise*): "And do they keep you for nothing, or do you work for your meat?"

Tom (*impatiently*): "Is that bran ready?" (*The old woman goes to the binn, and measures out a quart of bran.*) "What am I to pay you?"

Old woman: "A York shilling."

Tom (*wishing to test her honesty*): "Is there any difference between a York shilling and a shilling of British currency?"

Old woman (*evasively*): "I guess not. Is there not a place in England called York?" (*Looking up, and leering knowingly in his face.*)

146

OLD SATAN AND TOM WILSON'S NOSE

Tom (*laughing*): "You are not going to come York over me in that way, or Yankee either. There is three-pence for your pound of bran; you are enormously paid."

Old woman (*calling after him*): "But the recipe; do you allow nothing for the recipe?"

Tom: "It is included in the price of the bran."

"And so," said he, "I came away laughing, rejoicing in my sleeve that I had disappointed the avaricious old cheat."

The next thing to be done was to set the bran rising. By the help of Tom's recipe, it was duly mixed in the coffee-pot, and placed within a tin pan, full of hot water, by the side of the fire. I have often heard it said that a watched pot never boils; and there certainly was no lack of watchers in this case. Tom sat for hours regarding it with his large heavy eyes, the maid inspected it from time to time, and scarce ten minutes were suffered to elapse without my testing the heat of the water, and the state of the emptyings; but the day slipped slowly away, and night drew on, and yet the watched pot gave no signs of vitality. Tom sighed deeply when we sat down to tea with the old fare.

"Never mind," said he, "we shall get some good bread in the morning; it must get up by that time. I will wait till then. I could almost starve before I could touch these leaden cakes."

The tea-things were removed. Tom took up his flute, and commenced a series of the wildest voluntary airs that ever were breathed forth by human lungs. Mad jigs, to which the gravest of mankind might have

ROUGHING IT IN THE BUSH

cut eccentric capers. We were all convulsed with laughter. In the midst of one of these droll movements, Tom suddenly hopped like a kangaroo (which feat he performed by raising himself upon tip-toes, then flinging himself forward with a stooping jerk), towards the hearth, and squinting down into the coffee-pot in the most quizzical manner, exclaimed, "Miserable chaff! If that does not make you rise nothing will."

I left the bran all night by the fire. Early in the morning I had the satisfaction of finding that it had risen high above the rim of the pot, and was surrounded by a fine crown of bubbles.

"Better late than never," thought I, as I emptied the emptyings into my flour. "Tom is not up yet. I will make him so happy with a loaf of new bread, nice home-baked bread, for his breakfast."

It was my first Canadian loaf. I felt quite proud of it, as I placed it in the odd machine in which it was to be baked. I did not understand the method of baking in these ovens; or that my bread should have remained in the kettle for half an hour until it had risen the second time, before I applied the fire to it, in order that the bread should be light. It not only required experience to know when it was in a fit state for baking, but the oven should have been brought to a proper temperature to receive the bread. Ignorant of all this, I put my unrisen loaf into a cold kettle, and heaped a large quantity of hot ashes above and below it. The first intimation I had of the result of my experiment was the disagreeable odour of burning bread filling the house.

OLD SATAN AND TOM WILSON'S NOSE

"What is this horrid smell?" cried Tom, issuing from his domicile in his shirt sleeves. "Do open the door, Bell (*to the maid*); I feel quite sick."

"It is the bread," said I, taking off the lid of the oven with the tongs. "Dear me, it is all burnt!"

"And smells as sour as vinegar," says he. "The black bread of Sparta!"

Alas! for my maiden loaf! With a rueful face I placed it on the breakfast-table. "I hoped to have given you a treat, but I fear you will find it worse than the cakes in the pan."

"You may be sure of that," said Tom, as he stuck his knife into the loaf, and drew it forth covered with raw dough. "Oh, Mrs. Moodie, I hope you make better books than bread."

We were all sadly disappointed. The others submitted to my failure good-naturedly, and made it the subject of many droll, but not unkindly, witticisms. For myself, I could have borne the severest infliction from the pen of the most formidable critic with more fortitude than I bore the cutting up of my first loaf of bread.

After breakfast, Moodie and Wilson rode into the town, and when they returned at night, brought several long letters for me. Ah! those first kind letters from home! Never shall I forget the rapture with which I grasped them—the eager, trembling haste with which I tore them open, while the blinding tears which filled my eyes hindered me for some minutes from reading a word which they contained. Sixteen years have slowly passed away—it appears half a century—but never, never can home letters give me the intense joy those letters did. After seven years' exile, the hope of return grows feeble, the means are still less in our power, and our friends give up all hope of our return; their letters grow fewer and colder, their expressions of attachment are less vivid; the heart has formed new ties, and the poor emigrant is nearly forgotten. Double those years, and it is as if the grave had closed over you, and the hearts that once knew and loved you know you no more.

Tom, too, had a large packet of letters, which he read with great glee. After re-perusing them, he declared his intention of setting off on his return home the next day. We tried to persuade him to stay until the following spring, and make a fair trial of the country. Arguments were thrown away upon him; the next morning our eccentric friend was ready to start.

"Good-bye!" quoth he, shaking me by the hand as if he meant to sever it from the wrist. "When next we meet it will be in New South Wales, and I hope by that time you will know how to make better bread."

And thus ended Tom Wilson's emigration to Canada. He brought out three hundred pounds, British currency; he remained in the country just four months, and returned to England with barely enough to pay his passage home.

CHAPTER SEVEN
UNCLE JOE AND HIS FAMILY

VII.   UNCLE JOE AND HIS FAMILY

Ay, your rogue is a laughing rogue, and not a whit the less
dangerous for the smile on his lip, which comes not from an
honest heart, which reflects the light of the soul through the
eye. All is hollow and dark within; and the contortion of the
lip, like the phosphoric glow upon decayed timber, only serves
to point out the rottenness within.

UNCLE JOE! I SEE HIM NOW BEFORE ME,
with his jolly red face, twinkling black eyes, and rubi-
cund nose. No thin, weasel-faced Yankee was he, looking as if he had lived upon 'cute ideas and speculations all his life; yet Yankee he was by birth, ay, and
in mind, too; for a more knowing fellow at a bargain
never crossed the lakes to abuse British institutions
and locate himself comfortably among the despised
Britishers. But, then, he had such a good-natured,
fat face, such a mischievous, mirth-loving smile, and
such a merry, roguish expression in those small, jet-
black, glittering eyes, that you suffered yourself to be
taken in by him, without offering the least resistance
to his impositions.

Uncle Joe's father had been a New England loyalist, and his doubtful attachment to the British Government had been repaid by a grant of land in the township of H——. He was the first settler in that township, and chose his location in a remote spot, for the
sake of a beautiful natural spring, which bubbled up
in a small stone basin in the green bank at the back
of the house.

"Father might have had the pick of the township,"
quoth Uncle Joe; "but the old coon preferred that sup
of good water to the site of a town. Well, I guess it's
seldom I trouble the spring; and whenever I step that
way to water the horses, I think what a tarnation fool

153

the old one was, to throw away such a chance of making his fortune for such cold lap."

"Your father was a temperance man?"

"Temperance!—He had been fond enough of the whiskey bottle in his day. He drank up a good farm in the United States, and then he thought he could not do better than turn loyal, and get one here for nothing. He did not care a cent, not he, for the King of England. He thought himself as good, anyhow. But he found that he would have to work hard here to scratch along, and he was mightily plagued with the rheumatics, and some old woman told him that good spring water was the best cure for that; so he chose this poor, light, stony land on account of the spring, and took to hard work and drinking cold water in his old age."

"How did the change agree with him?"

"I guess better than could have been expected. He planted that fine orchard, and cleared his hundred acres, and we got along slick enough as long as the old fellow lived."

"And what happened after his death, that obliged you to part with your land?"

"Bad times—bad crops," said Uncle Joe, lifting his shoulders. "I had not my father's way of scraping money together. I made some deuced clever speculations, but they all failed. I married young, and got a large family; and the women critters ran up heavy bills at the stores, and the crops did not yield enough to pay them; and from bad we got to worse, and Mr. B—— put in an execution, and seized upon the whole concern. He sold it to your man for double what it

154

cost him; and you got all that my father toiled for during the last twenty years of his life for less than half the cash he laid out upon clearing it."

" And had the whiskey nothing to do with this change?" said I, looking him in the face suspiciously.

" Not a bit! When a man gets into difficulties, it is the only thing to keep him from sinking outright. When your husband has had as many troubles as I have had, he will know how to value the whiskey bottle."

This conversation was interrupted by a queer-looking urchin of five years old, dressed in a long-tailed coat and trousers, popping his black shock head in at the door, and calling out—

"Uncle Joe!—You're wanted to hum."

" Is that your nephew?"

" No! I guess 'tis my woman's eldest son," said Uncle Joe, rising, "but they call me Uncle Joe. 'Tis a spry chap that—as cunning as a fox. I tell you what it is—he will make a smart man. Go home, Ammon, and tell your ma that I am coming."

" I won't," said the boy; "you may go hum and tell her yourself. She has wanted wood cut this hour, and you'll catch it!"

Away ran the dutiful son, but not before he had applied his forefinger significantly to the side of his nose, and, with a knowing wink, pointed in the direction of home.

Uncle Joe obeyed the signal, drily remarking that he could not leave the barn door without the old hen clucking him back.

At this period we were still living in Old Satan's

log house, and anxiously looking out for the first snow to put us in possession of the good substantial log dwelling occupied by Uncle Joe and his family, which consisted of a brown brood of seven girls, and the highly-prized boy who rejoiced in the extraordinary name of Ammon.

Strange names are to be found in this free country. What think you, gentle reader, of *Solomon Sly*, *Reynard Fox*, *Hiram Dolittle*, and *Prudence Fidget*; all veritable names, and belonging to substantial yeomen?, After Ammon and Ichabod, I should not be at all surprised to meet with Judas Iscariot, Pilate, and Herod. And then the female appellations! But the subject is a delicate one, and I will forbear to touch upon it. I have enjoyed many a hearty laugh over the strange affectations which people designate here *very handsome names*. I prefer the old homely Jewish names, such as that which it pleased my godfather and godmothers to bestow upon me, to one of those high-sounding Christianities, the Minervas, Cinderellas, and Almerias of Canada. The love of singular names is here carried to a marvellous extent. It was only yesterday that, in passing through one busy village, I stopped in astonishment before a tombstone headed thus: "Sacred to the memory of *Silence* Sharman, the beloved wife of Asa Sharman." Was the woman deaf and dumb, or did her friends hope by bestowing upon her such an impossible name to still the voice of Nature, and check, by an admonitory appellative, the active spirit that lives in the tongue of woman? Truly, Asa Sharman, if thy wife was silent by name as well as by nature, thou wert a fortunate man!

UNCLE JOE AND HIS FAMILY

But to return to Uncle Joe. He made many fair promises of leaving the residence we had bought, the moment he had sold his crops and could remove his family. We could see no interest which could be served by his deceiving us, and therefore we believed him, striving to make ourselves as comfortable as we could in the meantime in our present wretched abode. But matters are never so bad but that they may be worse.

One day when we were at dinner, a waggon drove up to the door, and Mr.——— alighted, accompanied by a fine-looking, middle-aged man, who proved to be Captain S———, who had just arrived from Demerara with his wife and family. Mr. ———, who had purchased the farm of Old Satan, had brought Captain S——— over to inspect the land, as he wished to buy a farm and settle in that neighbourhood. With some difficulty I contrived to accommodate the visitors with seats, and provide them with a tolerable dinner. Fortunately, Moodie had brought in a brace of fine fat partridges that morning; these the servant transferred to a pot of boiling water, in which she immersed them for the space of a minute—a novel but very expeditious way of removing the feathers, which then come off at the least touch. In less than ten minutes they were stuffed, trussed, and in the bake-kettle; and before the gentleman returned from walking over the farm, the dinner was on the table.

To our utter consternation, Captain S——— agreed to purchase, and asked if we could give him possession in a week!

"Good heavens!" cried I, glancing reproachfully at

Mr.——, who was discussing his partridge with stoical indifference. "What will become of us? Where are we to go?"

"Oh, make yourself easy; I will force that old witch Joe's mother to clear out."

"But 'tis impossible to stow ourselves into that pig-sty."

"It will only be for a week or two, at farthest. This is October; Joe will be sure to be off by the first of sleighing."

"But if she refuses to give up the place?"

"Oh, leave her to me. I'll talk her over," said the knowing land speculator. "Let it come to the worst," he said, turning to my husband, "she will go out for the sake of a few dollars. By the bye, she refused to bar the dower when I bought the place; we must cajole her out of that. It is a fine afternoon; suppose we walk over the hill, and try our luck with the old nigger?"

I felt so anxious about the result of the negotiation, that, throwing my cloak over my shoulders, and tying on my bonnet without the assistance of a glass, I took my husband's arm, and we walked forth.

It was a bright, clear afternoon, the first week in October, and the fading woods, not yet denuded of their gorgeous foliage, glowed in a mellow, golden light. A soft, purple haze rested on the bold outline of the Haldimand hills, and in the rugged beauty of the wild landscape I soon forgot the purport of our visit to the old woman's log hut.

On reaching the ridge of the hill, the lovely valley in which our future home lay smiled peacefully upon us from amidst its fruitful orchards, still loaded with their rich, ripe fruit.

"What a pretty place it is!" thought I, for the first time feeling something like a local interest in the spot springing up in my heart. "How I wish those odious people would give us possession of the home which for some time has been our own!"

The log hut that we were approaching, and in which the old woman, R——, resided by herself—having quarrelled years ago with her son's wife—was of the smallest dimensions, only containing one room, which served the old dame for kitchen, and bedroom, and all. The open door and a few glazed panes supplied it with light and air, while a huge hearth, on which crackled two enormous logs—which are technically termed a front and a back stick—took up nearly half the domicile; and the old woman's bed, which was covered with an unexceptionably clean patched quilt, nearly the other half, leaving just room for a small home-made deal table, of the rudest workmanship, two basswood-bottomed chairs, stained red, one of which was a rocking-chair, appropriated solely to the old woman's use, and a spinning-wheel. Amidst this muddle of things—for, small as was the quantum of furniture, it was all crowded into such a tiny space that you had to squeeze your way through it in the best manner you could—we found the old woman, with a red cotton handkerchief tied over her grey locks, hood-fashion, shelling white bush-beans into a wooden bowl. Without rising from her seat, she pointed to the only remaining chair. "I guess, miss, you can sit there; and if the others can't stand, they can make a seat of my bed."

The gentlemen assured her that they were not tired, and could dispense with seats. Mr. —— then went up to the old woman, and proffering his hand, asked after her health in his blandest manner.

"I'm none the better for seeing you, or the like of you," was the ungracious reply. "You have cheated my poor boy out of his good farm; and I hope it may prove a bad bargain to you and yours."

"Mrs. R——," returned the land speculator, nothing ruffled by her unceremonious greeting, "I could not help your son giving way to drink, and getting into my debt. If people will be so imprudent, they cannot be so stupid as to imagine that others can suffer for their folly."

"*Suffer!*" repeated the old woman, flashing her small, keen black eyes upon him with a glance of withering scorn. "You suffer! I wonder what the widows and orphans you have cheated would say to that? My son was a poor, weak, silly fool to be sucked in by the like of you. For a debt of eight hundred dollars—the goods never cost you four hundred—you take from us our good farm; and these, I s'pose," pointing to my husband and me, "are the folk you sold it to. Pray, miss," turning quickly to me, "what might your man give for the place?"

"Three hundred pounds in cash."

"Poor sufferer!" again sneered the hag. "Four hundred dollars is a very *small* profit in as many weeks. Well, I guess, you beat the Yankees hollow. And pray, what brought you here to-day, scenting about you like a carrion-crow? We have no more land for you to seize from us."

UNCLE JOE AND HIS FAMILY

Moodie now stepped forward, and briefly explained our situation, offering the old woman anything in reason to give up the cottage and reside with her son until he removed from the premises; which, he added, must be in a very short time.

The old dame regarded him with a sarcastic smile. "I guess Joe will take his own time. The house is not built which is to receive him; and he is not the man to turn his back upon a warm hearth to camp in the wilderness. You were *green* when you bought a farm of that man, without getting along with it the right of possession."

"But, Mrs. R ——, your son promised to go out the first of sleighing."

"Wheugh!" said the old woman. "Would you have a man give away his hat and leave his own head bare? It's neither the first snow nor the last frost that will turn Joe out of his comfortable home. I tell you all that he will stay here, if it is only to plague you."

Threats and remonstrances were alike useless, the old woman remained inexorable; and we were just turning to leave the house, when the cunning old fox exclaimed, "And now, what will you give me to leave my place?"

"Twelve dollars, if you give us possession next Monday," said my husband.

"Twelve dollars! I guess you won't get me out for that."

"The rent would not be worth more than a dollar a month," said Mr. ——, pointing with his cane to the dilapidated walls. "Mr. Moodie has offered you a year's rent for the place."

"It may not be worth a cent," returned the woman, "for it will give everybody the rheumatism that stays a week in it—but it is worth that to me, and more nor double that just now to him. But I will not be hard with him," continued she, rocking herself to and fro. "Say twenty dollars, and I will turn out on Monday."

"I dare say you will," said Mr.——, "and who do you think would be fool enough to give you such an exorbitant sum for a ruined old shed like this?"

"Mind your own business, and make your own bargains," returned the old woman tartly. "The devil himself could not deal with you, for I guess he would have the worst of it. What do you say, sir?" and she fixed her keen eyes upon my husband as if she would read his thoughts. "Will you agree to my price?"

"It is a very high one, Mrs. R——; but as I cannot help myself, and you take advantage of that, I suppose I must give it."

"'Tis a bargain," cried the old crone, holding out her hard, bony hand. "Come, cash down!"

"Not until you give me possession on Monday next; or you might serve me as your son has done."

"Ha!" said the old woman, laughing and rubbing her hands together; "you begin to see daylight, do you? In a few months, with the help of him," pointing to Mr.——, "you will be able to go alone; but have a care of your teacher, for it's no good that you will learn from him. But will you *really* stand to your word, mister?" she added, in a coaxing tone, "if I go out on Monday?"

"To be sure I will; I never break my word."

"Well, I guess you are not so clever as our people,

for they only keep it as long as it suits them. You have an honest look; I will trust you; but I will not trust him," nodding to Mr.——, "he can buy and sell his word as fast as a horse can trot. So on Monday I will turn out my traps. I have lived here six-and-thirty years; 'tis a pretty place, and it vexes me to leave it," continued the poor creature, as a touch of natural feeling softened and agitated her world-burdened heart. "There is not an acre in cultivation but that I helped to clear it, nor a tree in yonder orchard but I held it while my poor man, who is dead and gone, planted it; and I have watched the trees bud from year to year, until their boughs overshadowed the hut, where all my children, but Joe, were born. Yes, I came here young, and in my prime; and must leave it in age and poverty. My children and husband are dead, and their bones rest beneath the turf in the burying-ground on the side of the hill. Of all that once gathered about my knees, Joe and his young ones alone remain. And it is hard, very hard, that I must leave their graves to be turned by the plough of a stranger."

I felt for the desolate old creature—the tears rushed to my eyes; but there was no moisture in hers. No rain from the heart could filter through that iron soil.

"Be assured, Mrs. R——," said Moodie, "that the dead will be held sacred; the place will never be disturbed by me."

"Perhaps not; but it is not long that you will remain here. I have seen a good deal in my time; but I never saw a gentleman from the old country make a good Canadian farmer. The work is rough and hard, and they get out of humour with it, and leave it to their

163

hired helps, and then all goes wrong. They are cheated on all sides, and in despair take to the whiskey bottle, and that fixes them. I tell you what it is, mister—I give you just three years to spend your money and ruin yourself; and then you will become a confirmed drunkard, like the rest."

The first part of her prophecy was only too true. Thank God! the last has never been fulfilled, and never can be.

Perceiving that the old woman was not a little elated with her bargain, Mr.——urged upon her the propriety of barring the dower. At first, she was outrageous, and very abusive, and rejected all his proposals with contempt; vowing that she would meet him in a certain place below, before she would sign away her right to the property.

"Listen to reason, Mrs. R——," said the land speculator. "If you will sign the papers before the proper authorities, the next time that your son drives you to C——, I will give you a silk gown."

"Pshaw! Buy a shroud for yourself; you will need it before I want a silk gown," was the ungracious reply.

"Consider, woman; a black silk of the best quality."

"To mourn in for my sins, or for the loss of the farm."

"Twelve yards," continued Mr.——, without noticing her rejoinder, "at a dollar a yard. Think what a nice church-going gown it will make."

"To the devil with you! I never go to church."

"I thought as much," said Mr.——, winking to us. "Well, my dear madam, what will satisfy you?"

"I'll do it for twenty dollars," returned the old woman, rocking herself to and fro in her chair; her eyes twinkling, and her hands moving convulsively, as if she already grasped the money so dear to her soul.

"Agreed," said the land speculator. "When will you be in town?"

"On Tuesday, if I be alive. But, remember, I'll not sign till I have my hand on the money."

"Never fear," said Mr.——, as we quitted the house; then, turning to me, he added, with a peculiar smile, "That's a devilish smart woman. She would have made a clever lawyer."

Monday came, and with it all the bustle of moving, and, as is generally the case on such occasions, it turned out a very wet day. I left Old Satan's hut without regret, glad, at any rate, to be in a place of my own, however humble. Our new habitation, though small, had a decided advantage over the one we were leaving. It stood on a gentle slope, and a narrow but lovely stream, full of speckled trout, ran murmuring under the little window; the house, also, was surrounded by fine fruit trees.

I know not how it was, but the sound of that tinkling brook, for ever rolling by, filled my heart with a strange melancholy, which for many nights deprived me of rest. I loved it, too. The voice of waters, in the stillness of night, always had an extraordinary effect upon my mind. Their ceaseless motion and perpetual sound convey to me the idea of life—eternal life; and looking upon them, glancing and flashing on, now in sunshine, now in shade, now hoarsely chiding with the opposing rock, now leaping triumphantly over it,—creates within me a feeling of mysterious awe of which I never could wholly divest myself.

165

A portion of my own spirit seemed to pass into that little stream. In its deep wailings and fretful sighs, I fancied myself lamenting for the land I had left for ever; and its restless and impetuous rushings against the stones which choked its passage, were mournful types of my own mental struggles against the strange destiny which hemmed me in. Through the day the stream moaned and travelled on,—but, engaged in my novel and distasteful occupations, I heard it not; but whenever my winged thoughts flew homeward, then the voice of the brook spoke deeply and sadly to my heart, and my tears flowed unchecked to its plaintive and harmonious music.

In a few hours I had my new abode more comfortably arranged than the old one, although its dimensions were much smaller. The location was beautiful, and I was greatly consoled by this circumstance. The aspect of Nature ever did, and I hope ever will, continue—

"To shoot marvellous strength into my heart."

As long as we remain true to the Divine Mother, so long will she remain faithful to her suffering children.

At that period my love for Canada was a feeling very nearly allied to that which the condemned criminal entertains for his cell—his only hope of escape being through the portals of the grave.

The fall rains had commenced. In a few days the cold wintry showers swept all the gorgeous crimson from the trees, and a bleak and desolate waste presented itself to the shuddering spectator. But, in spite of wind and rain, my little tenement was never free from the intrusion of Uncle Joe's wife and children. Their house stood about a stone's-throw from the hut we occupied, in the same meadow, and they seemed to look upon it still as their own, although we had literally paid for it twice over. Fine strapping girls they were, from five years old to fourteen, but rude and unnurtured as so many bears. They would come in without the least ceremony, and, young as they were, ask me a thousand impertinent questions; and when I civilly requested them to leave the room, they would range themselves upon the door-step, watching my motions, with their black eyes gleaming upon me through their tangled, uncombed locks. Their company was a great annoyance, for it obliged me to put a painful restraint upon the thoughtfulness in which it was so delightful to me to indulge. Their visits were not visits of love, but of mere idle curiosity, not unmingled with malicious pleasure at my awkward attempts at Canadian house-wiferies.

For a week I was alone, my good Scotch girl having left me to visit her father. Some small baby-articles were needed to be washed, and after making a great preparation, I determined to try my unskilled hand upon the operation. The fact is, I knew nothing about the task I had imposed upon myself, and in a few minutes rubbed the skin off my wrists without getting the clothes clean.

The door was open, as it generally was, even during the coldest winter days, in order to let in more light, and let out the smoke, which otherwise would have enveloped us like a cloud. I was so busy that I did not perceive that I was watched by the cold, heavy, dark eyes of Mrs. Joe, who, with a sneering laugh, exclaimed—

"Well! I am glad to see you brought to work at last. I hope you may have to work as hard as I have. I don't see, not I, why you, who are no better than me, should sit still all day, like a lady!"

"R——," said I, not a little annoyed at her presence, "what concern is it of yours whether I work or sit still? I never interfere with you. If you took it into your head to lie in bed all day, I should never trouble myself about it."

"Ah, I guess you don't look upon us as fellow-critters, you are so proud and grand. I s'pose you Britishers are not made of flesh and blood, like us. You don't choose to sit down at meat with your helps. Now, I calculate, we think them a great deal better nor you."

"Of course," said I, "they are more suited to you than we are; they are uneducated, and so are you. This is no fault in either; but it might teach you to pay a little more respect to those who are possessed of superior advantages. But, R——, my helps, as you call them, are civil and obliging, and never make unprovoked and malicious speeches. If they could so far forget themselves, I should order them to leave the house."

"Oh, I see what you are up to," replied the insolent dame; "you mean to say that if I were your help, you would turn me out of your house; but I'm a free-born American, and I won't go at your bidding. Don't think I come here out of regard to you. No, I hate you all; and I rejoice to see you at the wash-tub, and I wish

SCENE ON THE RIVER ST LAWRENCE NEAR MONTREAL

that you may be brought down upon your knees to scrub the floors."

This speech only caused a smile, and yet I felt hurt and astonished that a woman whom I had never done anything to offend should be so gratuitously spiteful.

In the evening she sent two of her brood over to borrow my "long iron," as she called an Italian iron. I was just getting my baby to sleep, sitting upon a low stool by the fire. I pointed to the iron upon the shelf, and told the girl to take it. She did so, but stood beside me, holding it carelessly in her hand, and staring at the baby, who had just sunk to sleep upon my lap.

The next moment the heavy iron fell from her relaxed grasp, giving me a severe blow upon my knee and foot; and glanced so near the child's head that it drew from me a cry of terror.

"I guess that was nigh braining the child," quoth Miss Amanda, with the greatest coolness, and without making the least apology. Master Ammon burst into a loud laugh. "If it had, Mandy, I guess we'd have cotched it." Provoked at their insolence, I told them to leave the house. The tears were in my eyes, for I felt certain that had they injured the child, it would not have caused them the least regret.

The next day, as we were standing at the door, my husband was greatly amused by seeing fat Uncle Joe chasing the rebellious Ammon over the meadow in front of the house. Joe was out of breath, panting and puffing like a steam-engine, and his face flushed to deep red with excitement and passion.

169

"You —— young scoundrel!" he cried, half choked with fury, "if I catch up to you, I'll take the skin off you!"

"You —— old scoundrel, you may have my skin if you can get at me," retorted the precocious child, as he jumped up upon the top of the high fence, and doubled his fist in a menacing manner at his father.

"That boy is growing too bad," said Uncle Joe, coming up to us out of breath, the perspiration streaming down his face. "It is time to break him in, or he'll get the master of us all."

"You should have begun that before," said Moodie. "He seems a hopeful pupil."

"Oh, as to that, a little swearing is manly," returned the father; "I swear myself, I know, and as the old cock crows, so crows the young one. It is not his swearing that I care a pin for, but he will not do a thing I tell him to."

"Swearing is a dreadful vice," said I, "and, wicked as it is in the mouth of a grown-up person, it is perfectly shocking in a child; it painfully tells he has been brought up without the fear of God."

"Pooh! pooh! that's all cant; there is no harm in a few oaths, and I cannot drive oxen and horses without swearing. I dare say that you can swear, too, when you are riled, but you are too cunning to let us hear you."

I could not help laughing outright at this supposition, but replied very quietly, "Those who practise such iniquities never take any pains to conceal them. The concealment would infer a feeling of shame; and when

UNCLE JOE AND HIS FAMILY

people are conscious of their guilt, they are in the road to improvement." The man walked whistling away, and the wicked child returned unpunished to his home.

The next minute the old woman came in. "I guess you can give me a piece of silk for a hood," said she, "the weather is growing considerable cold."

"Surely it cannot well be colder than it is at present," said I, giving her the rocking-chair by the fire.

"Wait a while; you know nothing of a Canadian winter. This is only November; after the Christmas thaw, you'll know something about cold. It is seven-and-thirty years ago since I and my man left the U-ni-ted States. It was called the year of the great winter. I tell you, woman, that the snow lay so deep on the earth, that it blocked up all the roads, and we could drive a sleigh whither we pleased, right over the snake fences. All the cleared land was one wide white level plain; it was a year of scarcity, and we were half starved; but the severe cold was far worse nor the want of provisions. A long and bitter journey we had of it; but I was young then, and pretty well used to trouble and fatigue; my man stuck to the British government. More fool he! I was an American born, and my heart was with the true cause. But his father was English, and, says he, 'I'll live and die under their flag.' So he dragged me from my comfortable fireside to seek a home in the far Canadian wilderness. Trouble! I guess you think you have your troubles; but what are they to mine?" She paused, took a pinch of snuff, offered me the box, sighed painfully, pushed the red handkerchief from her high, narrow, wrinkled

171

brow, and continued: "Joe was a baby then, and I had another helpless critter in my lap—an adopted child. My sister had died from it, and I was nursing it at the same breast with my boy. Well, we had to perform a journey of four hundred miles in an ox-cart, which carried, besides me and the children, all our household stuff. Our way lay chiefly through the forest, and we made but slow progress. Oh! what a bitter cold night it was when we reached the swampy woods where the city of Rochester now stands. The oxen were covered with icicles, and their breath sent up clouds of steam. 'Nathan,' says I to my man, 'you must stop and kindle a fire; I am dead with cold, and I fear the babes will be frozen.' We began looking about for a good spot to camp in, when I spied a light through the trees. It was a lone shanty, occupied by two French lumberers. The men were kind; they rubbed our frozen limbs with snow, and shared with us their supper and buffalo-skins. On that very spot where we camped that night, where we heard nothing but the wind soughing amongst the trees, and the rushing of the river, now stands the great city of Rochester. I went there two years ago, to the funeral of a brother. It seemed to me like a dream. Where we foddered our beasts by the shanty fire, now stands the largest hotel in the city; and my husband left this fine growing country to starve here."

I was so much interested in the old woman's narrative—for she was really possessed of no ordinary capacity, and, though rude and uneducated, might have been a very superior person under different circumstances—that I rummaged among my stores, and soon found a piece of black silk, which I gave her for the hood she required.

The old woman examined it carefully over, smiled to herself, but, like all her people, was too proud to return a word of thanks. One gift to the family always involved another.

"Have you any cotton-batting, or black sewing-silk, to give me, to quilt it with?"

"No."

"Humph!" returned the old dame, in a tone which seemed to contradict my assertion. She then settled herself in her chair, and, after shaking her foot a while, and fixing her piercing eyes upon me for some minutes, she commenced the following list of interrogatories:—

"Is your father alive?"

"No; he died many years ago, when I was a young girl."

"Is your mother alive?"

"Yes."

"What is her name?" I satisfied her on this point.

"Did she ever marry again?"

"She might have done so, but she loved her husband too well, and preferred living single."

"Humph! We have no such notions here. What was your father?"

"A gentleman, who lived upon his own estate."

"Did he die rich?"

"He lost the greater part of his property from being surety for another."

"That's a foolish business. My man burnt his fingers with that. And what brought you out to this poor country—you, who are no more fit for it than I am to be a fine lady?"

"The promise of a large grant of land, and the false statements we heard regarding it."

"Do you like the country?"

"No; and I fear I never shall."

"I thought not; for the drop is always on your cheek, the children tell me; and those young ones have keen eyes. Now, take my advice: return while your money lasts; the longer you remain in Canada the less you will like it, and when your money is all spent, you will be like a bird in a cage; you may beat your wings against the bars, but you can't get out." There was a long pause. I hoped that my guest had sufficiently gratified her curiosity, when she again commenced—

"How do you get your money? Do you draw it from the old country, or have you it with you in cash?"

Provoked by her pertinacity, and seeing no end to her cross-questioning, I replied very impatiently, "Mrs. R——, is it the custom in your country to catechize strangers whenever you meet with them?"

"What do you mean?" she said, colouring, I believe, for the first time in her life.

"I mean," quoth I, "an evil habit of asking impertinent questions."

The old woman got up, and left the house without speaking another word.

UNCLE JOE AND HIS FAMILY

THE SLEIGH-BELLS.*

'Tis merry to hear, at evening time,
By the blazing hearth the sleigh-bells' chime;
To know the bounding steeds bring near
The loved one to our bosoms dear.
Ah, lightly we spring the fire to raise,
Till the rafters glow with the ruddy blaze;
Those merry sleigh-bells, our hearts keep time
Responsive to their fairy chime.
Ding-dong, ding-dong, o'er vale and hill,
Their welcome notes are trembling still.

'Tis he, and blithely the gay bells sound,
As his sleigh glides over the frozen ground;
Hark! he has pass'd the dark pine wood,
He crosses now the ice-bound flood,
And hails the light at the open door
That tells his toilsome journey's o'er.
The merry sleigh-bells!   My fond heart swells
And throbs to hear the welcome bells;
Ding-dong, ding-dong, o'er ice and snow,
A voice of gladness, on they go.

Our hut is small, and rude our cheer,
But love has spread the banquet here;
And childhood springs to be caress'd
By our beloved and welcome guest.
With a smiling brow his tale he tells,
The urchins ring the merry sleigh-bells;
The merry sleigh-bells, with shout and song
They drag the noisy string along;
Ding-dong, ding-dong, the father's come,
The gay bells ring his welcome home.

* Many versions have been given of this song, and it has been set to music in the States. I here give the original copy, written whilst leaning on the open door of my shanty, and watching for the return of my husband.

175

ROUGHING IT IN THE BUSH

From the cedar swamp the gaunt wolves howl,
From the oak loud whoops the felon owl;
The snow-storm sweeps in thunder past,
The forest creaks beneath the blast;
No more I list, with boding fear,
The sleigh-bells' distant chime to hear.
The merry sleigh-bells with soothing power
Shed gladness on the evening hour.
Ding-dong, ding-dong, what rapture swells
The music of those joyous bells!

CHAPTER EIGHT
JOHN MONAGHAN

CHAPTER EIGHT   JOHN MONAGHAN

Dear mother Nature; on thy ample breast
Hast thou not room for thy neglected son?
A stern necessity has driven him forth
Alone and friendless. He has naught but thee,
And the strong hand and stronger heart thou gavest,
To win with patient toil his daily bread.

A FEW DAYS AFTER THE OLD WOMAN'S
visit to the cottage, our servant James absented himself for a week without asking leave, or giving any intimation of his intention. He had under his care a
fine pair of horses, a yoke of oxen, three cows, and a
numerous family of pigs, besides having to chop all
the firewood required for our use. His unexpected
departure caused no small trouble in the family; and
when the truant at last made his appearance, Moodie
discharged him altogether.

The winter had now fairly set in—the iron winter
of 1833. The snow was unusually deep, and it being
our first winter in Canada, and passed in such a miserable dwelling, we felt it very severely. In spite of all
my boasted fortitude—and I think my powers of endurance have been tried to the utmost since my sojourn in this country—the rigour of the climate subdued my proud, independent English spirit, and I actually shamed my womanhood, and cried with the
cold. Yes, I ought to blush at confessing such unpar-
donable weakness; but I was foolish and inexperi-
enced, and unaccustomed to the yoke.

My husband did not much relish performing the
menial duties of a servant in such weather, but he did
not complain, and in the meantime commenced an active inquiry for a man to supply the place of the one

we had lost; but at that season of the year no one was to be had.

It was a bitter, freezing night. A sharp wind howled without, and drove the fine snow through the chinks in the door, almost to the hearthstone, on which two immense blocks of maple shed forth a cheering glow, brightening the narrow window-panes, and making the blackened rafters ruddy with the heart-invigorating blaze.

The toils of the day were over, the supper things cleared away, and the door closed for the night. Moodie had taken up his flute, the sweet companion of happier days, at the earnest request of our home-sick Scotch servant-girl, to cheer her drooping spirits by playing some of the touching national airs of the glorious mountain land, the land of chivalry and song, the heroic North. Before retiring to rest, Bell, who had an exquisite ear for music, kept time with foot and hand, while large tears gathered in her soft blue eyes.

"Ay, 'tis bonnie thae songs; but they mak' me greet, an' my puir heart is sair, sair when I think on the bonnie braes and the days o' lang syne."

Poor Bell! Her heart was among the hills, and mine had wandered far, far away to the green groves and meadows of my own fair land. The music and our reveries were alike abruptly banished by a sharp blow upon the door. Bell rose and opened it, when a strange, wild-looking lad, barefooted, and with no other covering to his head than the thick, matted locks of raven blackness that hung like a cloud over his swarthy, sunburnt visage, burst into the room.

"Guidness defend us! Wha ha'e we here?" screamed Bell, retreating into a corner. "The puir callant's no cannie."

My husband turned hastily round to meet the intruder, and I raised the candle from the table the better to distinguish his face; while Bell, from her hiding-place, regarded him with unequivocal glances of fear and mistrust, waving her hands to me, and pointing significantly to the open door, as if silently beseeching me to tell her master to turn him out.

"Shut the door, man," said Moodie, whose long scrutiny of the strange being before us seemed, upon the whole, satisfactory; "we shall be frozen."

"Thin, faith, sir, that's what I am," said the lad, in a rich brogue, which told, without asking, the country to which he belonged. Then, stretching his bare hands to the fire, he continued, "By Jove, sir, I was never so near gone in my life!"

"Where do you come from, and what is your business here? You must be aware that this is a very late hour to take a house by storm in this way."

"Thrue for you, sir. But necessity knows no law; and the condition you see me in must plade for me. First, thin, sir, I come from the township of D——, and want a masther; and next to that, bedad! I want something to ate. As I'm alive, and 'tis a thousand pities that I'm alive at all at all, for shure God Almighty never made sich a misfortunate crather afore nor since —I have had nothing to put in my head since I ran away from my ould masther, Mr. F——, yesterday at noon. Money I have none, sir; the divil a cent. I have neither a shoe to my foot nor a hat to my head, and if you refuse to shelter me the night, I must be contint

181

to perish in the snow, for I have not a frind in the wide wurld."

The lad covered his face with his hands, and sobbed aloud.

"Bell," I whispered, "go to the cupboard and get the poor fellow something to eat. The boy is starving."

"Dinna heed him, mistress, dinna credit his lees. He is ane o' thae wicked Papists wha ha'e just stepped in to rob and kill us."

"Nonsense! Do as I bid you."

"I winna be fashed aboot him. An' if he bides here, I'll e'en flit by the first blink o' the morn."

"Isabel, for shame! Is this acting like a Christian, or doing as you would be done by?"

Bell was as obstinate as a rock, not only refusing to put down any food for the famished lad, but reiterating her threat of leaving the house if he were suffered to remain. My husband, no longer able to endure her selfish and absurd conduct, got angry in good earnest, and told her that she might please herself; that he did not mean to ask her leave as to whom he received into his house. I, for my part, had no idea that she would realize her threat. She was an excellent servant, clean, honest, and industrious, and loved the dear baby.

"You will think better of it in the morning," said I, as I rose and placed before the lad some cold beef and bread, and a bowl of milk, to which the runaway did ample justice.

"Why did you quit your master, my lad?" said Moodie.

"Because I could live wid him no longer. You see,

sir, I'm a poor foundling from the Belfast Asylum, shoved out, by the mother that bore me, upon the wide wurld, long before I knew that I was in it. As I was too young to spake for myself intirely, she put me into a basket, wid a label round my neck, to tell the folks that my name was John Monaghan. This was all I ever got from my parents; and who or what they were, I never knew, not I, for they never claimed me; bad cess to them! But I've no doubt it's a fine illigant gintleman he was, and herself a handsome rich young lady, who dared not own me for fear of affronting the rich jintry, her father and mother. Poor folk, sir, are never ashamed of their children; 'tis all the threasure they have, sir; but my parents were ashamed of me, and they thrust me out to the stranger and the hard bread of depindence." The poor lad sighed deeply, and I began to feel a growing interest in his sad history.

"Have you been in the country long?"

"Four years, madam. You know my masther, Mr. F——; he brought me out wid him as his apprentice, and during the voyage he trated me well. But the young men, his sons, are tyrants, and full of durty pride; and I could not agree wid them at all at all. Yesterday, I forgot to take the oxen out of the yoke, and Musther William tied me up to a stump, and bate me with the rawhide. Shure the marks are on myshowlthers yet. I left the oxen and the yoke, and turned my back upon them all, for the hot blood was bilin' widin me; and I felt that if I stayed it would be him that would get the worst of it. No one had ever cared for me since I was born, so I thought it was high time to take care of myself. I had heard your name, sir, and

I thought I would find you out; and if you want a lad, I will work for you for my kape, and a few dacent clothes."

A bargain was soon made. Moodie agreed to give Monaghan six dollars a month, which he thankfully accepted; and I told Bell to prepare his bed in a corner of the kitchen. But Mistress Bell thought fit to rebel. Having been guilty of one act of insubordination, she determined to be consistent, and throw off the yoke altogether. She declared that she would do no such thing; that her life and that all our lives were in danger; and that she would never stay another night under the same roof with that Papist vagabond.

"Papist!" cried the indignant lad, his dark eyes flashing fire, "I'm no Papist, but a Protestant like yourself; and I hope a deuced dale better Christian. You take me for a thief; yet shure a thief would have waited till you were all in bed and asleep, and not stepped in forenint you all in this fashion."

There was both truth and nature in the lad's argument; but Bell, like an obstinate woman as she was, chose to adhere to her own opinion. Nay, she even carried her absurd prejudices so far that she brought her mattress and laid it down on the floor in my room, for fear that the Irish vagabond should murder her during the night. By the break of day she was off; leaving me for the rest of the winter without a servant. Monaghan did all in his power to supply her place; he lighted the fires, swept the house, milked the cows, nursed the baby, and often cooked the dinner for me, and endeavoured by a thousand little attentions to show the gratitude he really felt for our kindness. To little Katie he attached himself in an extraordinary manner. All his spare time he spent in making little sleighs and toys for her, or in dragging her in the said sleighs up and down the steep hills in front of the house, wrapped up in a blanket. Of a night, he cooked her mess of bread and milk, as she sat by the fire, and his greatest delight was to feed her himself. After this operation was over, he would carry her round the floor on his back, and sing her songs in native Irish. Katie always greeted his return from the woods with a scream of joy, holding up her fair arms to clasp the neck of her dark favourite.

"Now the Lord love you for a darlint!" he would cry, as he caught her to his heart. "Shure you are the only one of the *crathers* he ever made who can love poor John Monaghan. Brothers and sisters I have none—I stand alone in the wurld, and your *bonny wee face* is the sweetest thing it contains for me. Och, jewil! I could lay down my life for you, and be proud to do that same."

Though careless and reckless about everything that concerned himself, John was honest and true. He loved us for the compassion we had shown him; and he would have resented any injury offered to our persons with his best blood.

But if we were pleased with our new servant, Uncle Joe and his family were not, and they commenced a series of petty persecutions that annoyed him greatly, and kindled into a flame all the fiery particles of his irritable nature.

Moodie had purchased several tons of hay of a neighbouring farmer, for the use of his cattle, and it had to be stowed into the same barn with some flax and straw that belonged to Uncle Joe. Going early one morning to fodder the cattle, John found Uncle Joe feeding his cows with his master's hay, and as it had diminished greatly in a very short time, he accused him in no measured terms of being the thief. The other very coolly replied that he had taken a little of the hay in order to repay himself for his flax, that Monaghan had stolen for the oxen. "Now by the powers!" quoth John, kindling into wrath, "that is adding a big lie to a dhirty petty larceny. I take your flax, you owld villain! Shure I know that flax is grown to make linen wid, not to feed oxen. God Almighty has given the crathers a good warm coat of their own; they neither require shifts nor shirts."

"I saw you take it, you ragged Irish vagabond, with my own eyes."

"Thin yer two eyes showed you a wicked illusion. You had betther shut up yer head, or I'll give you that for an eye-salve that shall make you see thrue for the time to come."

Relying upon his great size, and thinking that the slight stripling, who, by the bye, was all bones and sinews, was no match for him, Uncle Joe struck Monaghan over the head with the pitchfork. In a moment the active lad was upon him like a wild cat, and in spite of the difference of his age and weight, gave the big man such a thorough dressing that he was fain to roar aloud for mercy.

"Own that you are a thief and a liar, or I'll murther you!"

"I'll own to anything whilst your knee is pressing

me into a pancake. Come now—there's a good lad—let me get up." Monaghan felt irresolute, but after extorting from Uncle Joe a promise never to purloin any of the hay again, he let him rise.

"For shure," he said, "he began to turn so black in the face, I thought he'd burst intirely."

The fat man neither forgot nor forgave this injury; and though he dared not attack John personally, he set the children to insult and affront him upon all occasions. The boy was without socks, and I sent him to old Mrs. R——, to inquire of her what she would charge for knitting him two pairs of socks. The reply was a dollar. This was agreed to, and dear enough they were; but the weather was very cold, and the lad was barefooted, and there was no other alternative than either to accept her offer or for him to go without.

In a few days, Monaghan brought them home; but I found upon inspecting them that they were old socks new-footed. This was rather too glaring a cheat, and I sent the lad back with them, and told him to inform Mrs. R—— that as he had agreed to give the price for new socks, he expected them to be new altogether.

The avaricious old woman did not deny the fact; but she fell to cursing and swearing in an awful manner, and wished so much evil to the lad, that, with the superstitious fear so common to the natives of his country, he left her under the impression that she was gifted with the evil eye, and was an "owld witch." He never went out of the yard with the waggon and horses, but she rushed to the door and cursed him for a bare-heeled Irish blackguard, and wished that he might overturn the waggon, kill the horses, and break his own worthless neck.

"Ma'am," said John to me one day, after returning from C—— with the team, "it would be betther for me to lave the masther intirely; for shure if I do not, some mischief will befall me or the crathers. That wicked owld wretch! I cannot thole her curses. Shure it's in purgatory I am all the while."

"Nonsense, Monaghan! you are not a Catholic, and need not fear purgatory. The next time the old woman commences her reprobate conduct, tell her to hold her tongue, and mind her own business, for curses, like chickens, come home to roost."

The boy laughed heartily at the old Turkish proverb, but did not reckon much on its efficacy to still the clamorous tongue of the ill-natured old jade. The next day he had to pass her door with the horses. No sooner did she hear the sound of the wheels, than out she hobbled, and commenced her usual anathemas.

"Bad luck to yer croaking, yer ill-conditioned owld raven. It is not me you are desthroying shure, but yer own poor miserable sinful sowl. The owld one has the grip of ye already; for 'curses, like chickens, come home to roost'; so get in wid ye, and hatch them to yerself in the chimley corner. They'll all be roosting wid ye by and by; and a nice warm nest they'll make for you, considering the brave brood that belongs to you."

Whether the old woman was as superstitious as John, I know not; or whether she was impressed with the moral truth of the proverb—for, as I have before

JOHN MONAGHAN

stated, she was no fool—is difficult to tell; but she shrunk back into her den, and never attacked the lad again.

Poor John bore no malice in his heart, not he; for in spite of all the ill-natured things he had to endure from Uncle Joe and his family, he never attempted to return evil for evil. In proof of this, he was one day chopping firewood in the bush, at some distance from Joe, who was engaged in the same employment with another man. A tree in falling caught upon another, which, although a very large maple, was hollow, and very much decayed, and liable to be blown down by the least shock of the wind. The tree hung directly over the path that Uncle Joe was obliged to traverse daily with his team. He looked up and perceived, from the situation it occupied, that it was necessary for his own safety to cut it down; but he lacked courage to undertake so hazardous a job which might be attended, if the supporting tree gave way during the operation, with very serious consequences. In a careless tone he called to his companion to cut down the tree.

"Do it yourself, H——," said the axe man, with a grin. "My wife and children want their man as much as your Hannah wants you."

"I'll not put axe to it," quoth Joe. Then, making signs to his comrade to hold his tongue, he shouted to Monaghan, "Hollo, boy! you're wanted here to cut down this tree. Don't you see that your master's cattle might be killed if they should happen to pass under it, and it should fall upon them?"

"Thrue for you, Masther Joe; but your own cattle

would have the first chance. Why should I risk my life and limbs by cutting down the tree, when it was yerself that threw it so awkwardly over the other?"

"Oh, but you are a boy, and have no wife and children to depend upon you for bread," said Joe gravely. "We are both family men. Don't you see that 'tis your duty to cut down the tree?"

The lad swung the axe to and fro in his hand, eyeing Joe and the tree alternately; but the natural kindheartedness of the creature, and his reckless courage, overcame all idea of self-preservation, and raising aloft his slender but muscular arm, he cried out, "If it's a life that must be sacrificed, why not mine as well as another? Here goes! and the Lord have mercy on my sinful sowl!"

The tree fell, and, contrary to their expectations, without any injury to John. The knowing Yankee burst into a loud laugh. "Well, if you arn't a tarnation soft fool, I never saw one."

"What do you mane?" exclaimed John, his dark eyes flashing fire. "If 'tis to insult me for doing that which neither of you dared to do, you had better not thry that same. You have just seen the strength of my spirit. You had better not thry again the strength of my arm, or, may be, you and the tree would chance to share the same fate;" and, shouldering his axe, the boy strode down the hill, to get scolded by me for his foolhardiness.

The first week in March all the people were busy making maple sugar. "Did you ever taste any maple sugar, ma'am?" asked Monaghan, as he sat feeding Katie one evening by the fire.

JOHN MONAGHAN

"No, John."

"Well, then, you've a thrate to come; and it's my-self that will make Miss Katie, the darlint, an illigant lump of that same."

Early in the morning John was up, hard at work, making troughs for the sap. By noon he had complet-ed a dozen, which he showed me with great pride of heart. I felt a little curious about this far-famed maple sugar, and asked a thousand questions about the use to which the troughs were to be applied; how the trees were to be tapped, the sugar made, and if it were real-ly good when made?

To all my queries John responded, "Och! 'tis ill-igant. It bates all the sugar that ever was made in Jamaky. But you'll see before to-morrow night."

Moodie was away at P——, and the prospect of the maple sugar relieved the dulness occasioned by his absence. I reckoned on showing him a piece of sugar of our own making when he came home, and never dreamt of the possibility of disappointment.

John tapped his trees after the most approved fash-ion, and set his troughs to catch the sap; but Miss Amanda and Master Ammon upset them as fast as they filled, and spilt all the sap. With great difficulty Monaghan saved the contents of one large iron pot. This he brought in about nightfall, and made up a roaring fire in order to boil it down into sugar. Hour after hour passed away, and the sugar-maker looked as hot and black as the stoker in a steam-boat. Many times I peeped into the large pot, but the sap never seemed to diminish.

"This is a tedious piece of business," thought I, but

seeing the lad so anxious, I said nothing. About twelve o'clock he asked me very mysteriously for a piece of pork to hang over the sugar.

"Pork!" said I, looking into the pot, which was half full of a very black-looking liquid; "what do you want with pork?"

"Shure, an' 'tis to keep the sugar from burning."

"But, John, I see no sugar!"

"Och, but 'tis all sugar, only 'tis molasses jist now. See how it sticks to the ladle. Aha! but Miss Katie will have the fine lumps of sugar when she awakes in the morning."

I grew so tired and sleepy that I left John to finish his job, went to bed, and soon forgot all about the maple sugar. At breakfast I observed a small plate upon the table, placed in a very conspicuous manner on the tea-tray, the bottom covered with a hard, black substance, which very much resembled pitch. "What is that dirty-looking stuff, John?"

"Shure an' 'tis the maple sugar."

"Can people eat that?"

"By dad, an' they can; only thry it, ma'am."

"Why, 'tis so hard I cannot cut it."

With some difficulty, and not without cutting his finger, John broke a piece off, and stuffed it into the baby's mouth. The poor child made a horrible face, and rejected it as if it had been poison. For my own part, I never tasted anything more nauseous. It tasted like a compound of pork-grease and tobacco juice. "Well, Monaghan, if this be maple sugar, I never wish to taste any again."

"Och, bad luck to it!" said the lad, flinging it away,

plate and all. "It would have been first-rate but for the dhirty pot, and the blackguard cinders, and its burning to the bottom of the pot. That owld hag, Mrs. R——, betwitched it with her evil eye."

"She is not so clever as you think, John," said I, laughing. "You have forgotten how to make the sugar since you left D——; but let us forget the maple sugar, and think of something else. Had you not better get old Mrs. R—— to mend that jacket for you? it is too ragged."

"Ay, by dad! an' it's mysel' is the illigant tailor. Wasn't I brought up to the thrade in the Foundling Hospital?"

"And why did you quit it?"

"Because it's a low, mane thrade for a jintleman's son."

"But, John, who told you that you were a gentleman's son?"

"Och! but I'm shure of it, thin. All my propensities are gintale. I love horses, and dogs, and fine clothes, and money. Och! that I was but a jintleman! I'd show them what life is intirely, and I'd challenge Master William, and have my revenge out of him for the blows he gave me."

"You had better mend your trousers," said I, giving him a tailor's needle, a pair of scissors, and some strong thread.

"Shure, an' I'll do that same in a brace of shakes," and sitting down upon a rickety three-legged stool of his own manufacturing, he commenced his tailoring by tearing a piece of his trousers to patch the elbows of his jacket. And this trifling act, simple as it **may** appear, was a perfect type of the boy's general conduct, and marked his progress through life. The present for him was everything; he had no future. While he supplied stuff from the trousers to repair the fractures in the jacket, he never reflected that both would be required on the morrow. Poor John! in his brief and reckless career, how often have I recalled that foolish act of his. It now appears to me that his whole life was spent in tearing his trousers to repair his jacket.

In the evening John asked me for a piece of soap.

"What do you want with soap, John?"

"To wash my shirt, ma'am. Shure an' I am a baste to be seen, as black as the pots. Sorra a shirt have I but the one, an' it has stuck on my back so long that I can thole it no longer."

I looked at the wrists and collar of the condemned garment, which was all of it that John allowed to be visible. They were much in need of soap and water.

"Well, John, I will leave you the soap; but can you wash?"

"Och, shure, an' I can thry. If I soap it enough, and rub long enough, the shirt must come clane at last."

I thought the matter rather doubtful; but when I went to bed I left what he required, and soon saw through the chinks in the boards a roaring fire, and heard John whistling over the tub. He whistled and rubbed, and washed and scrubbed, but as there seemed no end to the job, and he was as long washing this one garment as Bell would have been performing the same operation on fifty, I laughed to myself, and thought of my own abortive attempts in that way, and went fast asleep. In the morning John came to his breakfast with his jacket buttoned up to his throat.

"Could you not dry your shirt by the fire, John? You will get cold wanting it."

"Aha, by dad! it's dhry enough now. The divil has made tinder of it long afore this."

"Why, what has happened to it? I heard you washing all night."

"Washing! Faith, an' I did scrub it till my hands were all ruined intirely, and thin I took the brush to it; but sorra a bit of the dhirt could I get out of it. The more I rubbed the blacker it got, until I had used up all the soap, and the perspiration was pouring off me like rain. 'You dhirty owld bit of a blackguard of a rag,' says I, in an exthremity of rage, 'you're not fit for the back of a dacent lad an' a jintleman. The divil may take ye to cover one of his imps;' an' wid that I sthirred up the fire, and sent it plump into the middle of the blaze."

"And what will you do for a shirt?"

"Faith, do as many a betther man has done afore me, go widout."

I looked up two old shirts of my husband's, which John received with an ecstasy of delight. He retired instantly to the stable, but soon returned, with as much of the linen breast of the garment displayed as his waistcoat would allow. No peacock was ever prouder of his tail than the wild Irish lad was of the old shirt.

John had been treated very much like a spoiled child, and, like most spoiled children, he was rather fond of having his own way. Moodie had set him to do something which was rather contrary to his own inclinations; he did not object to the task in words, for he was rarely saucy to his employers, but he left the following stave upon the table, written in pencil upon a scrap of paper torn from the back of an old letter:—

"A man alive, an ox may drive
　Unto a springing well;
To make him drink, as he may think,
　No man can him compel.
                    "JOHN MONAGHAN."

CHAPTER NINE

PHŒBE R——, AND OUR SECOND MOVING

CHAPTER NINE   PHŒBE R——, AND OUR SECOND MOVING

> She died in early womanhood,
> Sweet scion of a stem so rude;
> A child of Nature, free from art,
> With candid brow and open heart;
> The flowers she loved now gently wave
> Above her low and nameless grave.

IT WAS DURING THE MONTH OF MARCH that Uncle Joe's eldest daughter, Phœbe, a very handsome girl, and the best of the family, fell sick. I went over to see her. The poor girl was very depressed, and stood but a slight chance for her life, being under the medical treatment of three or four old women, who all recommended different treatment and administered different nostrums. Seeing that the poor girl was dangerously ill, I took her mother aside, and begged her to lose no time in procuring proper medical advice. Mrs. Joe listened to me very sullenly, and said there was no danger; that Phœbe had caught a violent cold by going hot from the wash-tub to fetch a pail of water from the spring; that the neighbours knew the nature of her complaint, and would soon cure her.

The invalid turned upon me her fine dark eyes, in which the light of fever painfully burned, and motioned me to come near her. I sat down by her, and took her burning hand in mine.

"I am dying, Mrs. Moodie, but they won't believe me. I wish you would talk to mother to send for the doctor."

"I will. Is there anything I can do for you?—anything I can make for you, that you would like to take?"

She shook her head. "I can't eat. But I want to

199

ask you one thing, which I wish very much to know." She grasped my hands tightly between her own. Her eyes looked darker, and her feverish cheek paled. "What becomes of people when they die?"

"My poor girl!" I exclaimed involuntarily; "can you be ignorant of a future state?"

"What is a future state?"

I endeavoured, as well as I was able, to explain to her the nature of the soul, its endless duration, and responsibility to God for the actions done in the flesh; its natural depravity and need of a Saviour; urging her, in the gentlest manner, to lose no time in obtain ing forgiveness of her sins, through the atoning blood of Christ.

The poor girl looked at me with surprise and horror. These things were all new to her. She sat like one in a dream; yet the truth seemed to flash upon her at once.

"How can I speak to God, who never knew Him? How can I ask Him to forgive me?"

"You must pray to Him?"

"Pray! I don't know how to pray. I never said a prayer in my life. Mother, can you teach me how to pray?"

"Nonsense!" said Mrs. Joe, hurrying forward "Why should you trouble yourself about *such things*? Mrs. Moodie, I desire you not to put such thoughts into my daughter's head. We don't want to know anything about Jesus Christ here."

"Oh, mother, don't speak so to the lady! Do, Mrs. Moodie, tell me more about God and my soul. I never knew until now that I had a soul."

COBURG

PHŒBE, AND OUR SECOND MOVING

Deeply compassionating the ignorance of the poor girl, in spite of the menaces of the heathen mother—for she was no better, but rather worse, seeing that the heathen worships in ignorance a false god, while this woman lived without acknowledging a God at all, and therefore considered herself free from all moral restraint—I bid Phœbe good-bye, and promised to bring my Bible and read to her the next day.

The gratitude manifested by this sick girl was such a contrast to the rudeness and brutality of the rest of the family, that I soon felt a powerful interest in her fate.

The mother did not actually forbid me the house, because she saw that my visits raised the drooping spirits of her child, whom she fiercely loved, and, to save her life, would cheerfully have sacrificed her own. But she never failed to make all the noise she could to disturb my reading and conversation with Phœbe. She could not be persuaded that her daughter was really in any danger until the doctor told her that her case was hopeless; then the grief of the mother burst forth, and she gave way to the most frantic and impious complainings.

The rigour of the winter began to abate. The beams of the sun during the day were warm and penetrating, and a soft wind blew from the south. I watched, from day to day, the snow disappearing from the earth, with indescribable pleasure, and at length it wholly vanished, not even a solitary patch lingered under the shade of the forest trees; but Uncle Joe gave no sign of removing his family.

"Does he mean to stay all the summer?" thought I,

"Perhaps he never intends going at all. I will ask him, the next time he comes to borrow whiskey."

In the afternoon he walked in to light his pipe, and, with some anxiety, I made the inquiry.

"Well, I guess we can't be moving afore the end of May. My missus expects to be confined the fore part of the month, and I shan't move till she be quite smart agin."

"You are not using us well, in keeping us out of the house so long."

"Oh, I don't care a curse about any of you. It is my house as long as I choose to remain in it, and you may put up with it the best way you can;" and, humming a Yankee tune, he departed.

I had borne patiently the odious, cribbed-up place during the winter, but now the hot weather was coming, it seemed almost insupportable, as we were obliged to have a fire in the close room, in order to cook our provisions. I consoled myself as well as I could by roaming about the fields and woods, and making acquaintance with every wild flower as it blossomed, and in writing long letters to home friends, in which I abused one of the finest countries in the world as the worst that God ever called out of chaos. I can recall to memory, at this moment, the few lines of a poem which commenced in this strain; nor am I sorry that the rest of it has passed into oblivion:—

Oh! land of waters, how my spirit tires
  In the dark prison of thy boundless woods;
No rural charm poetic thought inspires,
  No music murmurs in thy mighty floods;
Though vast the features that compose thy frame,
Turn where we will, the landscape's still the same.

PHŒBE, AND OUR SECOND MOVING

The swampy margin of thy inland seas,
   The eternal forest girdling either shore,
Its belt of dark pines sighing in the breeze,
   And rugged fields, with rude huts dotted o'er,
Show cultivation unimproved by art,
That sheds a barren chillness on the heart.

How many home-sick emigrants, during their first winter in Canada, will respond to this gloomy picture! Let them wait a few years; the sun of hope will arise and beautify the landscape, and they will proclaim the country one of the finest in the world.

The middle of May at length arrived, and, by the number of long, lean women, with handkerchiefs of all colours tied over their heads, who passed my door, and swarmed into Mrs. Joe's house, I rightly concluded that another young one had been added to the tribe; and, shortly after, Uncle Joe himself announced the important fact, by putting his jolly red face in at the door, and telling me that his missus had got a chopping boy; and he was right glad of it, for he was tired of so many gals, and that he should move in a fortnight, if his woman did kindly."

I had been so often disappointed that I paid very little heed to him, but this time he kept his word.

The *last* day of May they went, bag and baggage, the poor sick Phœbe, who still lingered on, and the new-born infant; and right joyfully I sent a Scotch girl (another Bell, whom I had hired in lieu of her I had lost), and Monaghan, to clean out the Augean stable. In a few minutes John returned, panting with indignation.

"The house," he said, "was more filthy than a pigsty." But that was not the worst of it; Uncle Joe, before he went, had undermined the brick chimney, and let all the water into the house. "Oh, but if he comes here agin," he continued, grinding his teeth and doubling his fist, "I'll thrash him for it. And thin, ma'am, he has girdled round all the best graft apple-trees, the murtherin' owld villain, as if it could spile his digestion our ating them."

"It would require a strong stomach to digest apple-trees, John; but never mind, it can't be helped, and we may be very thankful that these people are gone at last."

John and Bell scrubbed at the house all day, and in the evening they carried over the furniture, and I went to inspect our new dwelling.

It looked beautifully clean and neat. Bell had whitewashed all the black, smoky walls and boarded ceilings, and scrubbed the dirty window-frames, and polished the fly-spotted panes of glass, until they actually admitted a glimpse of the clear air and the blue sky. Snow-white fringed curtains, and a bed, with furniture to correspond, a carpeted floor, and a large pot of green boughs on the hearth-stone, gave an air of comfort and cleanliness to a room which, only a few hours before, had been a loathsome den of filth and impurity.

This change would have been very gratifying, had not a strong, disagreeable odour almost deprived me of my breath as I entered the room. It was unlike anything I had ever smelt before, and turned me so sick and faint that I had to cling to the door-post for support.

"Where does this dreadful smell come from?"

PHŒBE, AND OUR SECOND MOVING

"The guidness knows, ma'am; John and I have searched the house from the loft to the cellar, but we canna find out the cause of thae stink."

"It must be in the room, Bell; and it is impossible to remain here, or live in this house, until it is removed."

Glancing my eyes all round the place, I spied what seemed to me a little cupboard over the mantel-shelf, and I told John to see if I was right. The lad mounted upon a chair and pulled open a small door, but almost fell to the ground with the dreadful stench which seemed to rush from the closet.

"What is it, John?" I cried from the open door.

"A skunk, ma'am, a skunk! Shure, I thought the divil had scorched his tail, and left the grizzled hair behind him. What a strong perfume it has!" he continued, holding up the beautiful but odious little creature by the tail.

"By dad! I know all about it now. I saw Ned Layton, only two days ago, crossing the field with Uncle Joe, with his gun on his shoulder, and this wee bit baste in his hand. They were both laughing like sixty. 'Well, if this does not stink the Scotchman out of the house,' said Joe, 'I'll be contint to be tarred and feathered;' and thin they both laughed until they stopped to draw breath."

I could hardly help laughing myself; but I begged Monaghan to convey the horrid creature away, and putting some salt and sulphur into a tin plate, and setting fire to it, I placed it on the floor in the middle of the room, and closed all the doors for an hour, which greatly assisted in purifying the house from the skunkification. Bell then washed out the closet with strong

205

ley, and in a short time no vestige remained of the malicious trick that Uncle Joe had played off upon us.

The next day we took possession of our new mansion, and no one was better pleased with the change than little Katie. She was now fifteen months old, and could just begin to prattle, but she dared not venture to step alone, although she would stand by a chair all day, and even climb upon it. She crept from room to room, feeling and admiring everything, and talking to it in her baby language. So fond was the dear child of flowers, that her father used to hold her up to the apple-trees, then rich in their full spring beauty, that she might kiss the blossoms. She would pat them with her soft, white hands, murmuring like a bee in the branches. To keep her quiet whilst I was busy, I had only to give her a bunch of wild flowers. She would sit as still as a lamb, looking first at one and then at another, pressing them to her little breast in a sort of ecstasy, as if she comprehended the worth of this most beautiful of God's gifts to man.

She was a sweet, lovely flower herself, and her charming infant graces reconciled me, more than aught else, to a weary lot. Was she not purely British? Did not her soft blue eyes, and sunny curls, and bright rosy cheeks for ever remind me of her Saxon origin, and bring before me dear forms and faces I could never hope to behold again?

The first night we slept in the new house, a demon of unrest had taken possession of it in the shape of a countless swarm of mice. They scampered over our pillows, and jumped upon our faces, squeaking and cutting a thousand capers over the floor. I never could realize the true value of Whittington's invaluable cat until that night. At first we laughed until our sides ached, but in reality it was no laughing matter. Moodie remembered that we had left a mouse-trap in the old house; he went and brought it over, baited it, and set it on the table near the bed. During the night no less than fourteen of the provoki ngvermin were captured, and for several succeeding nights the trap did equal execution. How Uncle Joe's family could have allowed such a nuisance to exist, astonished me; to sleep with these creatures continually running over us was impossible; and they were not the only evils in the shape of vermin we had to contend with. The old logs which composed the walls of the house were full of bugs and large black ants; and the place, owing to the number of dogs that always had slept under the beds with the children, was infested with fleas. It required the utmost care to rid the place of these noisome and disgusting tenants.

Arriving in the country in the autumn, we had never experienced any inconvenience from the mosquitoes, but after the first moist, warm spring days, particularly after the showers, these tormenting insects annoyed us greatly. The farm lying in a valley cut up with little streams in every direction, made us more liable to their inflictions. The hands, arms, and face of the poor babe were covered every morning with red inflamed bumps, which often threw out blisters.

The banks of the little streams abounded with wild strawberries, which, although small, were of a delicious flavour. Thither Bell and I, and the baby, daily repaired to gather the bright red berries of Nature's own providing. Katie, young as she was, was very expert at helping herself, and we used to seat her in the middle of a fine bed, whilst we gathered farther on. Hearing her talking very lovingly to something in the grass, which she tried to clutch between her white hands, calling it "Pitty, pitty," I ran to the spot, and found that it was a large garter-snake that she was so affectionately courting to her embrace. Not then aware that this formidable-looking reptile was perfectly harmless, I snatched the child up in my arms and ran with her home, never stopping until I gained the house, and saw her safely seated in her cradle.

It had been a very late, cold spring, but the trees had fully expanded into leaf, and the forest world was glorious in its beauty. Every patch of cleared land presented a vivid green to the eye; the brook brawled in the gay sunshine, and the warm air was filled with soft murmurs. Gorgeous butterflies floated about like winged flowers, and feelings allied to poetry and gladness once more pervaded my heart. In the evenings we wandered through the woodland paths, beneath the glowing Canadian sunset, and gathered rare specimens of strange plants and flowers. Every object that met my eyes was new to me, and produced that peculiar excitement which has its origin in a thirst for knowledge and a love of variety.

We had commenced gardening, too, and my vegetables did great credit to my skill and care; and, when once the warm weather sets in, the rapid advance of vegetation in Canada is astonishing.

Not understanding much about farming, especially in a climate like Canada, Moodie was advised by a neighbouring settler to farm his farm upon shares. This advice seemed very reasonable; and had it been given disinterestedly, and had the persons recommended (a man and his wife) been worthy or honest people, we might have done very well. But the farmer had found out their encroaching ways, was anxious to get rid of them himself, and saw no better way of doing so than by palming them upon us.

From our engagement with these people commenced that long series of losses and troubles to which their conduct formed the prelude. They were to live in the little shanty that we had just left, and work the farm. Moodie was to find them the land, the use of his implements and cattle, and all the seed for the crops; and to share with them the returns. Besides this, they unfortunately were allowed to keep their own cows, pigs, and poultry. The produce of the orchard, with which they had nothing to do, was reserved for our own use.

For the first few weeks they were civil and obliging enough; and had the man been left to himself, I believe we should have done pretty well; but the wife was a coarse-minded, bold woman, who instigated him to every mischief. They took advantage of us in every way they could, and were constantly committing petty depredations.

From our own experience of this mode of farming, I would strenuously advise all new settlers never to embrace any such offer, without they are well acquainted with the parties, and can thoroughly rely upon their honesty; or else, like Mrs. O———, they may impudently tell you that they can cheat you as they

ROUGHING IT IN THE BUSH

please, and defy you to help yourself. All the money we expended upon the farm was entirely for these people's benefit, for by the joint contrivances very little of the crops fell to our share; and when any division was made, it was always when Moodie was absent from home and there was no person present to see fair play. They sold what apples and potatoes they pleased, and fed their hogs *ad libitum*. But even their roguery was more tolerable than the irksome restraint which their near vicinity, and constantly having to come into contact with them, imposed. We had no longer any privacy, our servants were cross-questioned, and our family affairs canvassed by these gossiping people, who spread about a thousand falsehoods regarding us. I was so much disgusted with this shareship, that I would gladly have given them all the proceeds of the farm to get rid of them, but the bargain was for twelve months, and, bad as it was, we could not break our engagement.

One little trick of this woman's will serve to illustrate her general conduct. A neighbouring farmer's wife had presented me with some very pretty hens, who followed to the call of old Betty Fye's handsome game-cock. I was always fond of fowls, and the innocent Katie delighted in her chicks, and would call them round her to the sill of the door to feed from her hand. Mrs. O—— had the same number as I had, and I often admired them when marshalled forth by her splendid black rooster. One morning I saw her eldest son chop off the head of the fine bird, and I asked his mother why she had allowed him to kill the beautiful creature. She laughed, and merely replied that she wanted it for the pot. The next day my sultan walked over to the widowed hens, and took all his seraglio with him. From that hour I never gathered a single egg; the hens deposited all their eggs in Mrs. O——'s hen-house. She used to boast of this as an excellent joke among her neighbours.

On the 9th of June, my dear little Agnes was born. A few days after this joyful event, I heard a great bustle in the room adjoining to mine, and old Dolly Rowe, my Cornish nurse, informed me that it was occasioned by the people who came to attend the funeral of Phœbe R——. She only survived the removal of the family a week; and at her own request had been brought all the way from the —— lake plains to be interred in the burying-ground on the hill which overlooked the stream.

As I lay upon my pillow I could distinctly see the spot, and mark the long funeral procession, as it wound along the banks of the brook. It was a solemn and imposing spectacle, that humble funeral. When the waggons reached the rude enclosure, the coffin was carefully lifted to the ground, the door in the lid opened, and old and young approached, one after another, to take a last look at the dead before consigning her to the oblivion of the grave.

Poor Phœbe! Gentle child of coarse, unfeeling parents, few shed more sincerely a tear for thy early fate than the stranger whom they hated and despised. Often have I stood beside that humble mound, when the song of the lark was above me, and the bee murmuring at my feet, and thought that it was well for thee that God opened the eyes of thy soul, and called

211

thee out of the darkness of ignorance and sin to glory in His marvellous light. Sixteen years have passed away since I heard anything of the family or what had become of them, when I was told by a neighbour of theirs, whom I accidentally met last winter, that the old woman, who now nearly numbers a hundred years, is still living, and inhabits a corner of her son's barn, as she still quarrels too much with his wife to reside with Joe; that the girls are all married and gone; and that Joe himself, although he does not know a letter, has commenced travelling preacher. After this, who can doubt the existence of miracles in the nineteenth century?

CHAPTER TEN
BRIAN, THE STILL-HUNTER

O'er memory's glass I see his shadow flit,
Though he was gathered to the silent dust
Long years ago. A strange and wayward man,
That shunn'd companionship, and lived apart;
The leafy covert of the dark brown woods,
The gleamy lakes, hid in their gloomy depths,
Whose still, deep waters never knew the stroke
Of cleaving oar, or echoed to the sound
Of social life, contained for him the sum
Of human happiness. With dog and gun
Day after day he track'd the nimble deer
Through all the tangled mazes of the forest.

IT WAS EARLY DAY. I WAS ALONE IN the old shanty, preparing breakfast, and now and then stirring the cradle with my foot, when a tall, thin, middle-aged man walked into the house, followed by two large, strong dogs.

Placing the rifle he had carried on his shoulder in a corner of the room, he advanced to the hearth, and, without speaking, or seemingly looking at me, lighted his pipe and commenced smoking. The dogs, after growling and snapping at the cat, who had not given the strangers a very courteous reception, sat down on the hearth-stone on either side of their taciturn master, eyeing him from time to time, as if long habit had made them understand all his motions. There was a great contrast between the dogs. The one was a brindled bull-dog of the largest size, a most formidable and powerful brute; the other a stag-hound, tawny, deep-chested, and strong-limbed. I regarded the man and his hairy companions with silent curiosity.

He was between forty and fifty years of age; his head, nearly bald, was studded at the sides with strong, coarse, black curling hair. His features were high, his complexion brightly dark, and his eyes, in size, shape, and colour, greatly resembling the eyes of a hawk. The face itself was sorrowful and taciturn; and his thin, compressed lips looked as if they were not much accustomed to smile, or often to unclose to hold social communion with any one. He stood at the side of the huge hearth, silently smoking, his eyes bent on the fire, and now and then he patted the heads of his dogs, reproving their exuberant expressions of attachment with—"Down, Music; down, Chance!"

"A cold, clear morning," said I, in order to attract his attention and draw him into conversation.

A nod, without raising his head, or withdrawing his eyes from the fire, was his only answer; and, turning from my unsociable guest, I took up the baby, who just then awoke, sat down on a low stool by the table, and began feeding her. During this operation, I once or twice caught the stranger's hawk-eye fixed upon me and the child, but word spoke he none; and presently, after whistling to his dogs, he resumed his gun, and strode out.

When Moodie and Monaghan came in to breakfast, I told them what a strange visitor I had had; and Moodie laughed at my vain attempt to induce him to talk.

"He is a strange being," I said; "I must find out who and what he is."

In the afternoon an old soldier, called Layton, who had served during the American war, and got a grant of land about a mile in the rear of our location, came in to trade for a cow. Now, this Layton was a perfect ruffian, a man whom no one liked, and whom all feared. He was a deep drinker, a great swearer, in short, a perfect reprobate, who never cultivated his land, but went jobbing about from farm to farm, trading horses and cattle, and cheating in a pettifogging way. Uncle Joe had employed him to sell Moodie a young heifer, and he had brought her over for him to look at. When he came in to be paid, I described the stranger of the morning; and as I knew that he was familiar with every one in the neighbourhood, I asked if he knew him.

"No one should know him better than myself," he said; "'tis old Brian B——, the still-hunter, and a near neighbour of your'n. A sour, morose, queer chap he is, and as mad as a March hare! He's from Lancashire, in England, and came to this country some twenty years ago, with his wife, who was a pretty young lass in those days, and slim enough then, though she's so awfully fleshy now. He had lots of money, too, and he bought four hundred acres of land, just at the corner of the concession line, where it meets the main road. And excellent land it is; and a better farmer, while he stuck to his business, never went into the bush, for it was all bush here then. He was a dashing, handsome fellow, too, and did not hoard the money either; he loved his pipe and his pot too well; and at last he left off farming, and gave himself to them altogether. Many a jolly booze he and I have had, I can tell you. Brian was an awful passionate man, and, when the liquor was in, and the wit was out, as savage and as quarrelsome as a bear. At such times there was no one but Ned Layton dared go near him. We once had a pitched battle, in which I was conqueror, and ever

arter he yielded a sort of sulky obedience to all I said
to him. Arter being on the spree for a week or two,
he would take fits of remorse, and return home to his
wife; would fall down at her knees, and ask her forgiveness, and cry like a child. At other times he would
hide himself up in the woods, and steal home at night,
and get what he wanted out of the pantry, without
speaking a word to any one. He went on with these
pranks for some years, till he took a fit of the blue
devils.

"'Come away, Ned, to the ———— lake, with me,'
said he; 'I am weary of my life, and I want a change.'

"'Shall we take the fishing-tackle?' says I. 'The
black bass are in prime season, and F—— will lend
us the old canoe. He's got some capital rum up from
Kingston. We'll fish all day, and have a spree at
night.'

"'It's not to fish I'm going,' says he.

"'To shoot, then? I've bought Rockwood's new
rifle.'

"'It's neither to fish nor to shoot, Ned; it's a new
game I'm going to try; so come along.'"

"Well, to the —— lake we went. The day was very
hot, and our path lay through the woods, and over
those scorching plains, for eight long miles. I thought
I should have dropped by the way; but during our
long walk my companion never opened his lips. He
strode on before me, at a half-run, never once turning
his head.

"'The man must be a devil!' says I, 'and accustomed to a warmer place, or he must feel this. Hollo,
Brian! Stop there! Do you mean to kill me?'

"'Take it easy,' says he; 'you'll see another day arter this—I've business on hand and cannot wait.'

"Well, on we went, at the same awful rate, and it was midday when we got to the little tavern on the lake shore, kept by one F——, who had a boat for the convenience of strangers who came to visit the place. Here we got our dinner, and a glass of rum to wash it down. But Brian was moody, and to all my jokes he only returned a sort of grunt; and while I was talking with F——, he steps out and a few minutes arter we saw him crossing the lake in the old canoe.

"'What's the matter with Brian?' says F——; 'all does not seem right with him, Ned. You had better take the boat and look arter him.'

"'Pooh!' says I; 'he's often so, and grows so glum nowadays that I will cut his acquaintance altogether if he does not improve.'

"'He drinks awful hard,' says F——; 'may be he's got a fit of the delirium-tremulous. There is no telling what he may be up to at this minute.'"

"My mind misgave me too, so I e'en takes the oars, and pushes out, right upon Brian's track; and by the Lord Harry! if I did not find him, upon my landing on the opposite shore, lying wallowing in his blood, with his throat cut. 'Is that you, Brian?' says I, giving him a kick with my foot, to see if he was alive or dead. 'What upon earth tempted you to play me and F—— such a dirty, mean trick, as to go and stick yourself like a pig, bringing such a discredit upon the house?—and you so far from home and those who should nurse you.'"

"I was so mad with him, that (saving your presence, ma'am) I swore awfully, and called him names that would be ondacent to repeat here; but he only answered with groans and a horrid gurgling in his throat. 'It's a choking you are,' said I; 'but you shan't have your own way and die so easily either, if I can punish you by keeping you alive.' So I just turned him upon his stomach, with his head down the steep bank; but he still kept choking and growing black in the face."

Layton then detailed some particulars of his surgical practice which it is not necessary to repeat. He continued—

"I bound up his throat with my handkerchief, and took him neck and heels, and threw him into the bottom of the boat. Presently he came to himself a little, and sat up in the boat; and—would you believe it?—made several attempts to throw himself into the water. 'This will not do,' says I; 'you've done mischief enough already by cutting your weasand! If you dare to try that again, I will kill you with the oar.' I held it up to threaten him; he was scared, and lay down as quiet as a lamb. I put my foot upon his breast. 'Lie still, now! or you'll catch it.' He looked piteously at me; he could not speak, but his eyes seemed to say, 'Have pity upon me, Ned; don't kill me.'

"Yes, ma'am, this man, who had just cut his throat, and twice arter that had tried to drown himself, was afraid that I should knock him on the head and kill him. Ha! ha! I never shall forget the work that F—— and I had with him arter I got him up to the house.

BRIAN, THE STILL-HUNTER

"The doctor came and sewed up his throat; and his wife—poor crittur!—came to nurse him. Bad as he was, she was mortal fond of him. He lay there, sick and unable to leave his bed, for three months, and did nothing but pray to God to forgive him, for he thought the devil would surely have him for cutting his own throat; and when he got about again, which is now twelve years ago, he left off drinking entirely, and wanders about the woods with his dogs, hunting. He seldom speaks to any one, and his wife's brother carries on the farm for the family. He is so shy of strangers that 'tis a wonder he came in here. The old wives are afraid of him; but you need not heed him —his troubles are to himself, he harms no one."

Layton departed, and left me brooding over the sad tale which he had told in such an absurd and jesting manner. It was evident from the account he had given of Brian's attempt at suicide, that the hapless hunter was not wholly answerable for his conduct— that he was a harmless maniac.

The next morning, at the very same hour, Brian again made his appearance; but instead of the rifle across his shoulder, a large stone jar occupied the place, suspended by a stout leather thong. Without saying a word, but with a truly benevolent smile that flitted slowly over his stern features, and lighted them up like a sunbeam breaking from beneath a stormy cloud, he advanced to the table, and unslinging the jar, set it down before me, and in a low and gruff, but by no means an unfriendly, voice, said, "Milk, for the child," and vanished.

"How good it was of him! How kind!" I exclaimed,

as I poured the precious gift of four quarts of pure new milk out into a deep pan. I had not asked him —had never said that the poor weanling wanted milk. It was the courtesy of a gentleman—of a man of benevolence and refinement.

For weeks did my strange, silent friend steal in, take up the empty jar, and supply its place with another replenished with milk. The baby knew his step, and would hold out her hands to him and cry, "Milk!" and Brian would stoop down and kiss her, and his two great dogs lick her face.

"Have you any children, Mr. B——?"

"Yes, five; but none like this."

"My little girl is greatly indebted to you for your kindness."

"She's welcome, or she would not get it. You are strangers; but I like you all. You look kind, and I would like to know more about you."

Moodie shook hands with the old hunter, and assured him that we should always be glad to see him. After this invitation, Brian became a frequent guest. He would sit and listen with delight to Moodie while he described to him elephant-hunting at the Cape, grasping his rifle in a determined manner, and whistling an encouraging air to his dogs. I asked him one evening what made him so fond of hunting.

"'Tis the excitement," he said; "it drowns thought, and I love to be alone. I am sorry for the creatures, too, for they are free and happy; yet I am led by an instinct I cannot restrain to kill them. Sometimes the sight of their dying agonies recalls painful feelings, and then I lay aside the gun, and do not hunt for days. But 'tis fine to be alone with God in the great woods—to watch the sunbeams stealing through the thick branches, the blue sky breaking in upon you in patches, and to know that all is bright and shiny above you, in spite of the gloom that surrounds you."

After a long pause, he continued, with much solemn feeling in his look and tone—

"I lived a life of folly for years, for I was respectably born and educated, and had seen something of the world, perhaps more than was good, before I left home for the woods; and from the teaching I had received from kind relatives and parents I should have known how to have conducted myself better. But, madam, if we associate long with the depraved and ignorant, we learn to become even worse than they. I felt deeply my degradation—felt that I had become the slave to low vice, and, in order to emancipate myself from the hateful tyranny of evil passions, I did a very rash and foolish thing. I need not mention the manner in which I transgressed God's holy laws; all the neighbours know it, and must have told you long ago. I could have borne reproof, but they turned my sorrow into indecent jests, and, unable to bear their coarse ridicule, I made companions of my dogs and gun, and went forth into the wilderness. Hunting became a habit. I could no longer live without it, and it supplies the stimulant which I lost when I renounced the cursed whiskey-bottle.

"I remember the first hunting excursion I took alone in the forest. How sad and gloomy I felt! I thought that there was no creature in the world so miserable as myself. I was tired and hungry, and I sat down upon a fallen tree to rest. All was still as death around me, and I was fast sinking to sleep, when my attention was aroused by a long, wild cry. My dog, for I had not Chance then, and he's no hunter, pricked up his ears, but instead of answering with a bark of defiance, he crouched down, trembling, at my feet. 'What does this mean?' I cried, and I cocked my rifle and sprang upon the log. The sound came nearer upon the wind. It was like the deep baying of a pack of hounds in full cry. Presently a noble deer rushed past me, and fast upon his trail—I see them now, like so many black devils—swept by a pack of ten or fifteen large, fierce wolves, with fiery eyes and bristling hair, and paws that seemed hardly to touch the ground in their eager haste. I thought not of danger, for, with their prey in view, I was safe; but I felt every nerve within me tremble for the fate of the poor deer. The wolves gained upon him at every bound. A close thicket intercepted his path, and, rendered desperate, he turned at bay. His nostrils were dilated, and his eyes seemed to send forth long streams of light. It was wonderful to witness the courage of the beast. How bravely he repelled the attacks of his deadly enemies, how gallantly he tossed them to the right and left, and spurned them from beneath his hoofs; yet all his struggles were useless, and he was quickly overcome and torn to pieces by his ravenous foes. At that moment he seemed more unfortunate even than myself, for I could not see in what manner he had deserved his fate. All his speed and energy, his courage and fortitude, had been exerted in vain. I had tried to destroy myself; but he, with every effort vigorously made for self-preservation, was doomed to meet the fate he dreaded! Is God just to his creatures?"

With this sentence on his lips, he started abruptly from his seat and left the house.

One day he found me painting some wild flowers, and was greatly interested in watching the progress I made in the group. Late in the afternoon of the following day he brought me a large bunch of splendid spring flowers.

"Draw these," said he; "I have been all the way to the —— lake plains to find them for you."

Little Katie, grasping them one by one, with infantile joy, kissed every lovely blossom.

"These are God's pictures," said the hunter, "and the child, who is all nature, understands them in a minute. Is it not strange that these beautiful things are hid away in the wilderness, where no eyes but the birds of the air, and the wild beasts of the wood, and the insects that live upon them, ever see them? Does God provide, for the pleasure of such creatures, these flowers? Is His benevolence gratified by the admiration of animals whom we have been taught to consider as having neither thought nor reflection? When I am alone in the forest, these thoughts puzzle me."

Knowing that to argue with Brian was only to call into action the slumbering fires of his fatal malady, I turned the conversation by asking him why he called his favourite dog Chance?

"I found him," he said, "forty miles back in the bush. He was a mere skeleton. At first I took him for a wolf, but the shape of his head undeceived me. I opened my wallet, and called him to me. He came slowly, stopping and wagging his tail at every step, and looking me wistfully in the face. I offered him a bit of dried venison, and he soon became friendly, and followed me home, and has never left me since. I called him Chance, after the manner I happened with him; and I would not part with him for twenty dollars."

Alas, for poor Chance! he had, unknown to his master, contracted a private liking for fresh mutton, and one night he killed no less than eight sheep that belonged to Mr. D——, on the front road; the culprit, who had been long suspected, was caught in the very act, and this *mischance* cost him his life. Brian was sad and gloomy for many weeks after his favourite's death.

"I would have restored the sheep fourfold," he said, "if he would but have spared the life of my dog."

My recollections of Brian seem more particularly to concentrate in the adventures of one night, when I happened to be left alone, for the first time since my arrival in Canada. I cannot now imagine how I could have been such a fool as to give way for four-and-twenty hours to such childish fears; but so it was, and I will not disguise my weakness from my indulgent reader.

Moodie had bought a very fine cow of a black man, named Mollineux, for which he was to give twenty-seven dollars. The man lived twelve miles back in the woods, and one fine frosty spring day—(don't smile at the term frosty, thus connected with the genial season of the year; the term is perfectly correct when applied to the Canadian spring, which, until the mid-

dle of May, is the most dismal season in the year)—
he and John Monaghan took a rope and the dog,
and sallied forth to fetch the cow home. Moodie said
that they should be back by six o'clock in the evening,
and charged me to have something cooked for supper
when they returned, as he doubted not their long walk
in the sharp air would give them a good appetite.
This was during the time that I was without a servant,
and living in old Mrs. ——'s shanty.

The day was so bright and clear, and Katie was so
full of frolic and play, rolling upon the floor, or tod-
dling from chair to chair, that the day passed on without my feeling remarkably lonely. At length the
evening drew nigh, and I began to expect my husband's return, and to think of the supper that I was to
prepare for his reception. The red heifer that we had
bought of Layton, came lowing to the door to be milked, but I did not know how to milk in those days, and,
besides this, I was terribly afraid of cattle. Yet, as I
knew that milk would be required for the tea, I ran
across the meadow to Mrs. Joe, and begged that one
of her girls would be so kind as to milk for me. My
request was greeted with a rude burst of laughter from
the whole set.

"If you can't milk," said Mrs. Joe, "it's high time
you should learn. My girls are above being helps."

"I would not ask you but as a great favour; I am
afraid of cows."

"*Afraid of cows!* Lord bless the woman! A farmer's
wife and afraid of cows!"

Here followed another laugh at my expense; and,
indignant at the refusal of my first and last request,

when they had all borrowed so much from me, I shut the inhospitable door, and returned home.

After many ineffectual attempts, I succeeded at last, and bore my half-pail of milk in triumph to the house. Yes! I felt prouder of that milk than many an author of the best thing he ever wrote, whether in verse or prose; and it was doubly sweet when I considered that I had procured it without being under any obligation to my ill-natured neighbours. I had learned a useful lesson of independence, to which in after years I had often again to refer. I fed little Katie and put her to bed, made the hot cakes for tea, boiled the potatoes, and laid the ham, cut in nice slices, in the pan, ready to cook the moment I saw the men enter the meadow, and arranged the little room with scrupulous care and neatness. A glorious fire was blazing on the hearth, and everything was ready for their supper, and I began to look out anxiously for their arrival.

The night had closed in cold and foggy, and I could no longer distinguish any object at more than a few yards from the door. Bringing in as much wood as I thought would last me for several hours, I closed the door; and for the first time in my life I found myself at night in a house entirely alone. Then I began to ask myself a thousand torturing questions as to the reason of their unusual absence. Had they lost their way in the woods? Could they have fallen in with wolves (one of my early bugbears)? Could any fatal accident have befallen them? I started up, opened the door, held my breath, and listened. The little brook lifted up its voice in loud, hoarse wailing, or mocked, in its babbling to the stones, the sound of human voices. As it became later, my fears increased in proportion. I grew too superstitious and nervous to keep the door open. I not only closed it, but dragged a heavy box in front, for bolt there was none. Several ill-looking men had, during the day, asked their way to Toronto. I felt alarmed lest such rude wayfarers should come to-night and demand a lodging, and find me alone and unprotected. Once I thought of running across to Mrs. Joe, and asking her to let one of the girls stay with me until Moodie returned; but the way in which I had been repulsed in the evening prevented me from making a second appeal to their charity.

Hour after hour wore away, and the crowing of the cocks proclaimed midnight, and yet they came not. I had burnt out all my wood, and I dared not open the door to fetch in more. The candle was expiring in the socket, and I had not courage to go up into the loft and procure another before it went finally out. Cold, heart-weary, and faint, I sat and cried. Every now and then the furious barking of the dogs at the neighbouring farms, and the loud cackling of the geese upon our own, made me hope that they were coming; and then I listened till the beating of my own heart excluded all other sounds. Oh, that unwearied brook! how it sobbed and moaned like a fretful child;—what unreal terrors and fanciful illusions my too active mind conjured up, whilst listening to its mysterious tones!

Just as the moon rose, the howling of a pack of wolves, from the great swamp in our rear, filled the whole air. Their yells were answered by the barking of all the dogs in the vicinity, and the geese, unwilling to be behind-hand in the general confusion, set up the most discordant screams. I had often heard, and even been amused, during the winter, particularly on thaw nights, with hearing the howls of these formidable wild beasts, but I had never before heard them alone, and when one dear to me was abroad amid their haunts. They were directly in the track that Moodie and Monaghan must have taken; and I now made no doubt that they had been attacked and killed on their return through the woods with the cow, and I wept and sobbed until the cold grey dawn peered in upon me through the small dim window. I have passed many a long cheerless night, when my dear husband was away from me during the rebellion, and I was left in my forest home with five little children, and only an old Irishwoman to draw and cut wood for my fire and attend to the wants of the family, but that was the saddest and longest night I ever remember.

Just as the day broke my friends the wolves set up a parting benediction, so loud and wild, and near to the house, that I was afraid lest they should break through the frail window, or come down the low, wide chimney, and rob me of my child. But their detestable howls died away in the distance, and the bright sun rose up and dispersed the wild horrors of the night, and I looked once more timidly around me. The sight of the table spread, and the uneaten supper, renewed my grief, for I could not divest myself of the idea that Moodie was dead. I opened the door, and stepped forth into the pure air of the early day. A solemn and beautiful repose still hung like a veil over the face of Nature. The mists of night still rested upon the majestic woods, and not a sound but the flowing of the waters went up in the vast stillness. The earth had not yet raised her matin hymn to the throne of the Creator. Sad at heart, and weary and worn in spirit, I went down to the spring and washed my face and head, and drank a deep draught of its icy waters. On returning to the house, I met, near the door, old Brian the hunter, with a large fox dangling across his shoulder, and the dogs following at his heels.

"Why! Mrs. Moodie, what is the matter? You are early abroad this morning, and look dreadful ill. Is anything wrong at home? Is the baby or your husband sick?"

"Oh!" I cried, bursting into tears, "I fear he is killed by the wolves."

The man stared at me, as if he doubted the evidence of his senses, and well he might; but this one idea had taken such strong possession of my mind that I could admit no other. I then told him, as well as I could find words, the cause of my alarm, to which he listened very kindly and patiently.

"Set your heart at rest; your husband is safe. It is a long journey on foot to Mollineux, to one unacquainted with a blazed path in a bush road. They have stayed all night at the black man's shanty, and you will see them back at noon."

I shook my head, and continued to weep.

"Well, now, in order to satisfy you, I will saddle my mare and ride over to the nigger's, and bring you word as fast as I can."

I thanked him sincerely for his kindness, and returned, in somewhat better spirits, to the house. At

231

ten o'clock my good messenger returned with the glad tidings that all was well.

The day before, when half the journey had been accomplished, John Monaghan let go the rope by which he led the cow, and she had broken away through the woods and returned to her old master; and when they again reached his place, night had set in, and they were obliged to wait until the return of day. Moodie laughed heartily at all my fears; but indeed I found them no joke.

Brian's eldest son, a lad of fourteen, was not exactly an idiot, but what, in the old country, is very expressively termed by the poor people a "natural." He could feed and assist himself, had been taught imperfectly to read and write, and could go to and from the town on errands, and carry a message from one farmhouse to another, but he was a strange, wayward creature, and evidently inherited, in no small degree, his father's malady.

During the summer months he lived entirely in the woods, near his father's dwelling, only returning to obtain food, which was generally left for him in an outhouse. In the winter, driven home by the severity of the weather, he would sit for days together moping in the chimney-corner, without taking the least notice of what was passing around him. Brian never mentioned this boy—who had a strong, active figure, a handsome, but very inexpressive, face—without a deep sigh; and I feel certain that half his own dejection was occasioned by the mental aberration of his child.

One day he sent the lad with a note to our house, to

know if Moodie would purchase the half of an ox that he was going to kill. There happened to stand in the corner of the room an open wood box, into which several bushels of fine apples had been thrown, and, while Moodie was writing an answer to the note, the eyes of the idiot were fastened as if by some magnetic influence, upon the apples. Knowing that Brian had a very fine orchard, I did not offer the boy any of the fruit. When the note was finished, I handed it to him. The lad grasped it mechanically, without removing his fixed gaze from the apples.

"Give that to your father, Tom."

The boy answered not—his ears, his eyes, his whole soul, were concentrated in the apples. Ten minutes elapsed, but he stood motionless, like a pointer at a dead set.

"My good boy, you can go."

He did not stir.

"Is there anything you want?"

"I want," said the lad, without moving his eyes from the objects of his intense desire, and speaking in a slow, pointed manner, which ought to have been heard to be fully appreciated, "I want ap-ples!"

"Oh, if that's all, take what you like."

The permission once obtained, the boy flung himself upon the box with the rapacity of a hawk upon its prey after being long poised in the air to fix its certain aim; thrusting his hands to the right and left, in order to secure the finest specimens of the devoted fruit, scarcely allowing himself time to breathe until he had filled his old straw hat and all his pockets with apples. To help laughing was impossible; while this new Tom

233

o'Bedlam darted from the house, and scampered across the field for dear life, as if afraid that we should pursue him to rob him of his prize.

It was during this winter that our friend Brian was left a fortune of three hundred pounds per annum; but it was necessary for him to return to his native country in order to take possession of the property. This he positively refused to do; and when we remonstrated with him on the apparent imbecility of this resolution, he declared that he would not risk his life, in crossing the Atlantic twice, for twenty times that sum. What strange inconsistency was this, in a being who had three times attempted to take away that which he dreaded so much to lose accidentally!

I was much amused with an account which he gave me, in his quaint way, of an excursion he went upon with a botanist, to collect specimens of the plants and flowers of Upper Canada.

"It was a fine spring day, some ten years ago, and I was yoking my oxen to drag in some oats I had just sown, when a little, fat, punchy man, with a broad, red, good-natured face, and carrying a small black leathern wallet across his shoulder, called to me over the fence, and asked me if my name was Brian B——? I said 'Yes; what of that?'

"'Only you are the man I want to see. They tell me that you are better acquainted with the woods than any person in these parts; and I will pay you anything in reason if you will be my guide for a few days.'

"'Where do you want to go?' said I.

"'Nowhere in particular,' says he. 'I want to go

here and there, in all directions, to collect plants and flowers.'

"That is still-hunting with a vengeance," thought I. 'To-day I must drag in my oats. If to-morrow will suit, we will be off.'

"'And your charge?' said he. 'I like to be certain of that.'

"'A dollar a day. My time and labour upon my farm, at this busy season, is worth more than that.'

"'True,' said he. 'Well, I'll give you what you ask. At what time will you be ready to start?'

"'By daybreak, if you wish it.'

"Away he went; and by daylight next morning he was at my door, mounted upon a stout French pony. 'What are you going to do with that beast?' said I. 'Horses are of no use on the road that you and I are to travel. You had better leave him in my stable.'

"'I want him to carry my traps,' said he; 'it may be some days that we shall be absent.'

"I assured him that he must be his own beast of burthen, and carry his axe, and blanket, and wallet of food upon his own back. The little body did not much relish this arrangement; but as there was no help for it, he very good-naturedly complied. Off we set, and soon climbed the steep ridge at the back of your farm, and got upon —— lake plains. The woods were flush with flowers, and the little man grew into such an ecstasy, that at every fresh specimen he uttered a yell of joy, cut a caper in the air, and flung himself down upon them, as if he was drunk with delight. 'Oh, what treasures! what treasures!' he cried. 'I shall make my fortune!'

ROUGHING IT IN THE BUSH

"It is seldom I laugh," quoth Brian, "but I could not help laughing at this odd little man; for it was not the beautiful blossoms, such as you delight to paint, that drew forth these exclamations, but the queer little plants which he had rummaged for at the roots of old trees, among the moss and long grass. He sat upon a decayed trunk, which lay in our path, I do believe for a long hour, making an oration over some greyish things, spotted with red, that grew upon it, which looked more like mould than plants, declaring himself repaid for all the trouble and expense he had been at, if it were only to obtain a sight of them. I gathered him a beautiful blossom of the lady's slipper, but he pushed it back when I presented it to him, saying, 'Yes, yes; 'tis very fine. I have seen that often before; but these lichens are splendid.'

"The man had so little taste that I thought him a fool, and so I left him to talk to his dear plants, while I shot partridges for our supper. We spent six days in the woods, and the little man filled his tin case with all sorts of rubbish, as if he wilfully shut his eyes to the beautiful flowers and chose only to admire ugly, insignificant plants that everybody else passes by without noticing, and which, often as I had been in the woods, I never had observed before. I never pursued a deer with such earnestness as he continued his hunt for what he called 'specimens.'

"When we came to the Cold Creek, which is pretty deep in places, he was in such a hurry to get at some plants that grew under the water, that in reaching after them he lost his balance, and fell head over heels into the stream. He got a thorough ducking, and was in a terrible fright; but he held on to the flowers, which had caused the trouble, and thanked his stars that he had saved them as well as his life. Well, he was an innocent man," continued Brian; "a very little made him happy, and at night he would sing and amuse himself like a child. He gave me ten dollars for my trouble, and I never saw him again; but I often think of him, when hunting in the woods that we wandered through together, and I pluck the wee plants that he used to admire, and wonder why he preferred them to the fine flowers."

When our resolution was formed to sell our farm, and take up our grant of land in the backwoods, no one was so earnest in trying to persuade us to give up this ruinous scheme as our friend Brian B——, who became quite eloquent in his description of the trials and sorrows that awaited us. During the last week of our stay in the township of H ——, he visited us every evening, and never bade us good-night without a tear moistening his cheek. We parted with the hunter as with an old friend; and we never met again. His fate was a sad one. After we left that part of the country, he fell into a moping melancholy, which ended in self-destruction. But a kinder or warmer-hearted man, while he enjoyed the light of reason, has seldom crossed our path.

CHAPTER ELEVEN
THE CHARIVARI

CHAPTER ELEVEN   THE CHARIVARI

Our fate is seal'd!   'Tis now in vain to sigh,
  For home, or friends, or country left behind.
Come, dry those tears, and lift the downcast eye
  To the high heaven of hope, and be resign'd;
Wisdom and time will justify the deed,
The eye will cease to weep, the heart to bleed.

Love's thrilling sympathies, affections pure,
  All that endear'd and hallow'd your lost home,
Shall on a broad foundation, firm and sure,
  Establish peace; the wilderness become
Dear as the distant land you fondly prize,
Or dearer visions that in memory rise.

THE MOAN OF THE WIND TELLS OF
the coming rain that it bears upon its wings; the deep
stillness of the woods, and the lengthened shadows
they cast upon the stream, silently but surely foreshow
the bursting of the thunder-cloud; and who that has
lived for any time upon the coast, can mistake the
language of the waves—that deep prophetic surging
that ushers in the terrible gale? So it is with the human
heart—it has its mysterious warnings, its fits of sunshine and shade, of storm and calm, now elevated
with anticipations of joy, now depressed by dark pre-
sentiments of ill.

All who have ever trodden this earth, possessed of
the powers of thought and reflection, of tracing effects
back to their causes, have listened to these voices of
the soul, and secretly acknowledged their power; but
few, very few, have had courage boldly to declare their
belief in them: the wisest and the best have given
credence to them, and the experience of every day
proves their truth; yea, the proverbs of past ages a-
bound with allusions to the same subject, and though

the worldly may sneer, and the good man reprobate the belief in a theory which he considers dangerous, yet the former, when he appears led by an irresistible impulse to enter into some fortunate, but until then unthought of, speculation; and the latter, when he devoutly exclaims that God has met him in prayer, unconsciously acknowledges the same spiritual a-gency. For my own part, I have no doubts upon the subject, and have found many times, and at different periods of my life, that the voice in the soul speaks truly; that if we gave stricter heed to its mysterious warnings, we should be saved much after-sorrow.

Well do I remember how sternly and solemnly this inward monitor warned me of approaching ill, the last night I spent at home; how it strove to draw me back as from a fearful abyss, beseeching me not to leave England and emigrate to Canada, and how glad-ly would I have obeyed the injunction had it still been in my power. I had bowed to a superior mandate, the command of duty; for my husband's sake, for the sake of the infant, whose little bosom heaved against my swelling heart, I had consented to bid adieu for ever to my native shores, and it seemed both useless and sinful to draw back.

Yet, by what stern necessity were we driven forth to seek a new home amid the western wilds? We were not compelled to emigrate. Bound to England by a thousand holy and endearing ties, surrounded by a circle of chosen friends, and happy in each other's love, we possessed all that the world can bestow of good— but *wealth*. The half-pay of a subaltern officer, man-aged with the most rigid economy, is too small to supply the wants of a family; and if of a good family, not enough to maintain his original standing in society. True, it may find his children bread, it may clothe them indifferently, but it leaves nothing for the indispensable requirements of education, or the painful contingencies of sickness and misfortune. In such a case, it is both wise and right to emigrate. Nature points it out as the only safe remedy for the evils arising out of an over-dense population, and her advice is always founded upon justice and truth.

Up to the period of which I now speak, we had not experienced much inconvenience from our very limited means. Our wants were few, and we enjoyed many of the comforts and even some of the luxuries of life; and all had gone on smoothly and lovingly with us until the birth of our first child. It was then that prudence whispered to the father, "You are happy and contented now, but this cannot always last; the birth of that child, whom you have hailed with as much rapture as though she were born to inherit a noble estate, is to you the beginning of care. Your family may increase, and your wants will increase in proportion; out of what fund can you satisfy their demands? Some provision must be made for the future, and made quickly, while youth and health enable you to combat successfully with the ills of life. When you married for inclination, you knew that emigration must be the result of such an act of imprudence in over-populated England. Up and be doing, while you still possess the means of transporting yourself to a land where the industrious can never lack bread, and where there is a chance that wealth and independence may reward virtuous toil."

Alas! that truth should ever whisper such unpleasant realities to the lover of ease—to the poet, the author, the musician, the man of books, of refined taste and gentlemanly habits. Yet he took the hint, and began to bestir himself with the spirit and energy so characteristic of the glorious North, from whence he sprung.

"The sacrifice," he said, "must be made, and the sooner the better. My dear wife, I feel confident that you will respond to the call of duty; and hand-in-hand and heart-in-heart we will go forth to meet difficulties, and, by the help of God, to subdue them."

Dear husband! I take shame to myself that my purpose was less firm, that my heart lingered so far behind yours in preparing for this great epoch in our lives; that, like Lot's wife, I still turned and looked back, and clung with all my strength to the land I was leaving. It was not the hardships of an emigrant's life I dreaded. I could bear mere physical privations philosophically enough; it was the loss of the society in which I had moved, the want of congenial minds, of persons engaged in congenial pursuits, that made me so reluctant to respond to my husband's call.

I was the youngest in a family remarkable for their literary attainments; and, while yet a child, I had seen riches melt away from our once prosperous home, as the Canadian snows dissolve before the first warm days of spring, leaving the verdureless earth naked and bare.

There was, however, a spirit in my family that rose

superior to the crushing influences of adversity. Poverty, which so often degrades the weak mind, became their best teacher, the stern but fruitful parent of high resolve and ennobling thought. The very misfortunes that overwhelmed, became the source from whence they derived both energy and strength, as the inundation of some mighty river fertilizes the shores over which it spreads ruin and desolation. Without losing aught of their former position in society, they dared to be poor; to place mind above matter, and make the talents with which the great Father had liberally endowed them, work out their appointed end. The world sneered, and summer friends forsook them; they turned their backs upon the world, and upon the ephemeral tribes that live but in its smiles.

From out the solitude in which they dwelt, their names went forth through the crowded cities of that cold, sneering world, and were mentioned with respect by the wise and good; and what they lost in wealth, they more than regained in well-earned reputation.

Brought up in this school of self-denial, it would have been strange indeed if all its wise and holy precepts had brought forth no corresponding fruit. I endeavoured to reconcile myself to the change that awaited me, to accommodate my mind and pursuits to the new position in which I found myself placed.

Many a hard battle had we to fight with old prejudices, and many proud swellings of the heart to subdue, before we could feel the least interest in the land of our adoption, or look upon it as our home.

All was new, strange, and distasteful to us; we

shrank from the rude, coarse familiarity of the uneducated people among whom we were thrown; and they in return viewed us as innovators, who wished to curtail their independence by expecting from them the kindly civilities and gentle courtesies of a more refined community. They considered us proud and shy, when we were only anxious not to give offence. The semi-barbarous Yankee squatters, who had "left their country for their country's good," and by whom we were surrounded in our first settlement, detested us, and with them we could have no feeling in common. We could neither lie nor cheat in our dealings with them; and they despised us for our ignorance in trading and our want of smartness.

The utter want of that common courtesy with which a well-brought-up European addresses the poorest of his brethren, is severely felt at first by settlers in Canada. At the period of which I am now speaking, the titles of "sir," or " madam," were very rarely applied by inferiors. They entered your house without knocking; and while boasting of their freedom, violated one of its dearest laws, which considers even the cottage of the poorest labourer his castle, and his privacy sacred.

"Is your man to hum?"—"Is the woman within?" were the general inquiries made to me by such guests, while my bare-legged, ragged Irish servants were always spoken to as "sir" and "*mem*," as if to make the distinction more pointed.

Why they treated our claims to their respect with marked insult and rudeness, I never could satisfactorily determine, in any way that could reflect honour

THE CHARIVARI

on the species, or even plead an excuse for its brutality, until I found that this insolence was more generally practised by the low, uneducated emigrants from Britain, who better understood your claims to their civility, than by the natives themselves. Then I discovered the secret.

The unnatural restraint which society imposes upon these people at home forces them to treat their more fortunate brethren with a servile deference which is repugnant to their feelings, and is thrust upon them by the dependent circumstances in which they are placed. This homage to rank and education is not sincere. Hatred and envy lie rankling at their heart, although hidden by outward obsequiousness. Necessity compels their obedience; they fawn, and cringe, and flatter the wealth on which they depend for bread. But let them once emigrate, the clog which fettered them is suddenly removed; they are free; and the dearest privilege of this freedom is to wreak upon their superiors the long-locked-up hatred of their hearts. They think they can debase you to their level by disallowing all your claims to distinction; while they hope to exalt themselves and their fellows into ladies and gentlemen by sinking you back to the only title you received from Nature—plain "man" and "woman." Oh, how much more honourable than their vulgar pretensions!

I never knew the real dignity of these simple epithets until they were insultingly thrust upon us by the working-classes of Canada.

But from this folly the native-born Canadian is exempt; it is only practised by the low-born Yankee, or

247

the Yankeefied British peasantry and mechanics. It originates in the enormous reaction springing out of a sudden emancipation from a state of utter dependence into one of unrestrained liberty. As such, I not only excuse, but forgive it, for the principle is founded in nature; and, however disgusting and distasteful to those accustomed to different treatment from their inferiors, it is better than a hollow profession of duty and attachment urged upon us by a false and unnatural position. Still, it is very irksome until you think more deeply upon it; and then it serves to amuse rather than to irritate.

And here I would observe, before quitting this subject, that of all follies, that of taking out servants from the old country is one of the greatest, and is sure to end in the loss of the money expended in their passage, and to become the cause of deep disappointment and mortification to yourself.

They no sooner set foot upon the Canadian shores than they become possessed with this ultra-republican spirit. All respect for their employers, all subordination is at an end; the very air of Canada severs the tie of mutual obligation which bound you together. They fancy themselves not only equal to you in rank, but that ignorance and vulgarity give them superior claims to notice. They demand the highest wages, and grumble at doing half the work, in return, which they cheerfully performed at home. They demand to eat at your table, and to sit in your company, and if you refuse to listen to their dishonest and extravagant claims, they tell you that "they are free; that no contract signed in the old country is binding

KINGSTON (LAKE ONTARIO)

in 'Meriky'; that you may look out for another person to fill their place as soon as you like; and that you may get the money expended in their passage and outfit in the best manner you can."

I was unfortunately persuaded to take out a woman with me as a nurse for my child during the voyage, as I was in very poor health; and her conduct, and the trouble and expense she occasioned, were a perfect illustration of what I have described.

When we consider the different position in which servants are placed in the old and new world, this conduct, ungrateful as it then appeared to me, ought not to create the least surprise. In Britain, for instance, they are too often dependent upon the caprice of their employers for bread. Their wages are low; their moral condition still lower. They are brought up in the most servile fear of the higher classes, and they feel most keenly their hopeless degradation, for no effort on their part can better their position. They know that if once they get a bad character they must starve or steal; and to this conviction we are indebted for a great deal of their seeming fidelity and long and laborious service in our families, which we owe less to any moral perception on their part of the superior kindness or excellence of their employers, than to the mere feeling of assurance, that as long as they do their work well, and are cheerful and obedient, they will be punctually paid their wages, and well housed and fed.

Happy is it for them and their masters when even this selfish bond of union exists between them!

But in Canada the state of things in this respect

is wholly reversed. The serving class, comparatively speaking, is small, and admits of little competition. Servants that understand the work of the country are not easily procured, and such always can command the highest wages. The possession of a good servant is such an addition to comfort, that they are persons of no small consequence, for the dread of starving no longer frightens them into servile obedience. They can live without you, and they well know that you cannot do without them. If you attempt to practise upon them that common vice of English mistresses, to scold them for any slight omission or offence, you rouse into active operation all their new-found spirit of freedom and opposition. They turn upon you with a torrent of abuse; they demand their wages, and declare their intention of quitting you instantly. The more inconvenient the time for you, the more bitter become their insulting remarks. They tell you, with a high hand, that "they are as good as you; that they can get twenty better places by the morrow, and that they don't care a snap for your anger." And away they bounce, leaving you to finish a large wash, or a heavy job of ironing, in the best way you can.

When we look upon such conduct as the reaction arising out of their former state, we cannot so much blame them, and are obliged to own that it is the natural result of a sudden emancipation from former restraint. With all their insolent airs of independence, I must confess that I prefer the Canadian to the European servant. If they turn out good and faithful, it springs more from real respect and affection, and you possess in your domestic a valuable assistant and friend; but this will never be the case with a servant brought out with you from the old country, for the reasons before assigned. The happy independence enjoyed in this highly-favoured land is nowhere better illustrated than in the fact that no domestic can be treated with cruelty or insolence by an unbenevolent or arrogant master.

Forty years has made as great a difference in the state of society in Canada as it has in its commercial and political importance. When we came to the Canadas, society was composed of elements which did not always amalgamate in the best possible manner.

The Canadian women, while they retain the bloom and freshness of youth, are exceedingly pretty; but these charms soon fade, owing, perhaps, to the fierce extremes of their climate, or the withering effect of the dry metallic air of stoves, and their going too early into company and being exposed, while yet children, to the noxious influence of late hours, and the sudden change from heated rooms to the cold, biting, bitter winter blast.

Though small in stature, they are generally well and symmetrically formed, and possess a graceful easy carriage. The early age at which they marry and are introduced into society, takes from them all awkwardness and restraint.

They have excellent practical abilities, which, with a little mental culture, would render them intellectual and charming companions. At present, too many of these truly lovely girls remind one of choice flowers half-buried in weeds.

Music and dancing are their chief accomplishments.

Though possessing an excellent general taste for music, it is seldom in their power to bestow upon its study the time which is required to make a really good musician. They are admirable proficients in the other art, which they acquire readily, with the least instruction, often without any instruction at all, beyond that which is given almost intuitively by a good ear for time, and a quick perception of the harmony of motion.

The waltz is their favourite dance, in which old and young join with the greatest avidity; it is not unusual to see parents and their grown-up children dancing in the same set in a public ballroom.

On entering one of the public ballrooms, a stranger would be delighted with such a display of pretty faces and neat figures. I have hardly ever seen a really plain Canadian girl in her teens; and a downright ugly one is almost unknown.

The high cheek-bones, wide mouth, and turned-up nose of the Saxon race, so common among the lower classes in Britain, are here succeeded in the next generation, by the small oval face, straight nose, and beautifully-cut mouth of the American; while the glowing tint of the Albion rose pales before the withering influence of late hours and stove-heat.

They are naturally a fine people, and possess capabilities and talents, which, when improved by cultivation, will render them second to no people in the world; and that period is not far distant.

To the benevolent philanthropist, whose heart has bled over the misery and pauperism of the lower classes in Great Britain, the almost entire absence of mendicity from Canada would be highly gratifying. Canada has few, if any, native beggars; her objects of charity are generally imported from the mother country, and these are never suffered to want food or clothing. The Canadians are a truly charitable people; no person in distress is driven with harsh and cruel language from their doors; they not only generously relieve the wants of suffering strangers cast upon their bounty, but they nurse them in sickness, and use every means in their power to procure them employment. The number of orphan children yearly adopted by wealthy Canadians, and treated in every respect as their own, is almost incredible.

It is a glorious country for the labouring classes, for while blessed with health, they are always certain of employment, and certain also to derive from it ample means of support for their families. An industrious, hard-working man in a few years is able to purchase from his savings a homestead of his own; and in process of time becomes one of the most important and prosperous class of settlers in Canada, her free and independent yeomen, who form the bones and sinews of this rising country, and from among whom she already begins to draw her senators, while their educated sons become the aristocrats of the rising generation.

It has often been remarked to me by people long resident in the colony, that those who come to the country destitute of means, but able and willing to work, invariably improve their condition and become independent; while the gentleman who brings out with him a small capital is too often tricked and cheated out of his property, and drawn into rash and dangerous speculations which terminate in his ruin. His children, neglected and uneducated, but brought up with ideas far beyond their means, and suffered to waste their time in idleness, seldom take to work, and not unfrequently sink down to the lowest class.

It was towards the close of the summer of 1833, which had been unusually cold and wet for Canada, while Moodie was absent at D———, inspecting a portion of his government grant of land, that I was startled one night, just before retiring to rest, by the sudden firing of guns in our near vicinity, accompanied by shouts and yells, the braying of horns, the beating of drums, and the barking of all the dogs in the neighbourhood. I never heard a more stunning uproar of discordant and hideous sounds.

What could it all mean? The maid-servant, as much alarmed as myself, opened the door and listened.

"The goodness defend us!" she exclaimed, quickly closing it, and drawing a bolt seldom used. "We shall be murdered. The Yankees must have taken Canada, and are marching hither."

"Nonsense! that cannot be. Besides, they would never leave the main road to attack a poor place like this. Yet the noise is very near. Hark! they are firing again. Bring me the hammer and some nails, and let us secure the windows."

The next moment I laughed at my folly in attempting to secure a log hut, when the application of a match to its rotten walls would consume it in a few minutes. Still, as the noise increased, I was really frightened. My servant, who was Irish (for my Scotch girl, Bell, had taken to herself a husband, and I had been obliged to hire another in her place, who had been only a few days in the country), began to cry and wring her hands, and lament her hard fate in coming to Canada.

Just at this critical moment, when we were both self-convicted of an arrant cowardice, which would have shamed a Canadian girl of six years old, Mrs. O—— tapped at the door, and although generally a most unwelcome visitor, from her gossiping, mischievous propensities, I gladly let her in.

"Do tell me," I cried, "the meaning of this strange uproar?"

"Oh, 'tis nothing," she replied, laughing. "You and Mary look as white as a sheet; but you need not be alarmed. A set of wild fellows have met to charivari Old Satan, who has married his fourth wife to-night, a young girl of sixteen. I should not wonder if some mischief happens among them, for they are a bad set, made up of all the idle loafers about Port H—— and C——."

"What is a charivari?" said I. "Do, pray, enlighten me."

"Have you been nine months in Canada, and ask that question? Why, I thought you knew everything! Well, I will tell you what it is. The charivari is a custom that the Canadians got from the French, in the Lower Province, and a queer custom it is. When an old man marries a young wife, or an old woman a young husband, or two old people, who ought to be thinking of their graves, enter for the second or third time into the holy estate of wedlock, as the priest calls it, all the idle young fellows in the neighbourhood meet together to charivari them. For this purpose they disguise themselves, blackening their faces, putting their clothes on hind part before, and wearing horrible masks, with grotesque caps on their heads, adorned with cocks' feathers and bells. They then form in a regular body, and proceed to the bridegroom's house, to the sound of tin kettles, horns, and drums, cracked fiddles, and all the discordant instruments they can collect together. Thus equipped, they surround the house where the wedding is held, just at the hour when the happy couple are supposed to be about to retire to rest—beating upon the door with clubs and staves, and demanding of the bridegroom admittance to drink the bride's health, or in lieu thereof to receive a certain sum of money to treat the band at the nearest tavern.

"If the bridegroom refuses to appear and grant their request, they commence the horrible din you heard, firing guns charged with peas against the doors and windows, rattling old pots and kettles, and abusing him for his stinginess in no measured terms. Sometimes they break open the doors, and seize upon the bridegroom; and he may esteem himself a very fortunate man, under such circumstances, if he escapes being ridden upon a rail, tarred and feathered, and otherwise maltreated. I have known many fatal accidents arise out of an imprudent refusal to satisfy the demands of the assailants. People have even lost their lives in the fray; and I think the Government should interfere, and put down these riotous meetings. Surely it is very hard that an old man cannot marry a young gal, if she is willing to take him, without asking the leave of such a rabble as that. What right have they to interfere with his private affairs?"

"What, indeed?" said I, feeling a truly British indignation at such a lawless infringement upon the natural rights of man.

"I remember," continued Mrs. O——, who had got fairly started upon a favourite subject, "a scene of this kind, that was acted two years ago, at——, when old Mr. P—— took his third wife. He was a very rich store-keeper, and had made during the war a great deal of money. He felt lonely in his old age, and married a young, handsome widow, to enliven his house. The lads in the village were determined to make him pay for his frolic. This got wind, and Mr. P—— was advised to spend the honeymoon in Toronto; but he only laughed, and said that 'he was not going to be frightened from his comfortable home by the threats of a few wild boys.' In the morning, he was married at the church, and spent the day at home, where he entertained a large party of his own and the bride's friends. During the evening all the idle chaps in the town collected round the house, headed by a mad young bookseller, who had offered himself for their captain, and, in the usual forms, demanded a sight of the bride, and liquor to drink her health. They were very good-naturedly received by Mr. P——, who sent a friend down to them to bid them welcome, and to inquire on what terms they would consent to let him off, and disperse.

"The captain of the band demanded sixty dollars, as he, Mr. P——, could well afford to pay it.

"'That's too much, my fine fellows!' cried Mr. P——

from the open window. 'Say twenty-five, and I will send you down a cheque upon the Bank of Montreal for the money.'

"'Thirty! thirty! thirty! old boy!' roared a hundred voices. 'Your wife's worth that. Down with the cash, and we will give you three cheers, and three times three for the bride, and leave you to sleep in peace. If you hang back, we will raise such a 'larum about your ears that you shan't know that your wife's your own for a month to come!'

"'I'll give you twenty-five,' remonstrated the bridegroom, not the least alarmed at their threats, and laughing all the time in his sleeve.

"'Thirty; not one copper less!' Here they gave him such a salute of diabolical sounds that he ran from the window with his hands to his ears, and his friend came down to the verandah, and gave them the sum they required. They did not expect that the old man would have been so liberal, and they gave him the 'Hip, hip, hip, hurrah!' in fine style, and marched off to finish the night and spend the money at the tavern."

"And do people allow themselves to be bullied out of their property by such ruffians?"

"Ah, my dear! 'tis the custom of the country, and 'tis not so easy to put it down. But I can tell you that a charivari is not always a joke.

"There was another affair that happened just before you came to the place, that occasioned no small talk in the neighbourhood; and well it might, for it was a most disgraceful piece of business, and attended with very serious consequences. Some of the charivari party had to fly, or they might have ended their days in the penitentiary.

"There was a runaway nigger from the States came to the village, and set up a barber's poll, and settled among us. I am no friend to the blacks; but really Tom Smith was such a quiet, good-natured fellow, and so civil and obliging, that he soon got a good business. He was clever, too, and cleaned old clothes until they looked almost as good as new. Well, after a time he persuaded a white girl to marry him. She was not a bad-looking Irishwoman, and I can't think what bewitched the creature to take him.

"Her marriage with the black man created a great sensation in the town. All the young fellows were indignant at his presumption and her folly, and they determined to give them the charivari in fine style, and punish them both for the insult they had put upon the place.

"Some of the young gentlemen in the town joined in the frolic. They went so far as to enter the house, drag the poor nigger from his bed, and in spite of his shrieks for mercy, they hurried him out into the cold air—for it was winter—and almost naked as he was, rode him upon a rail, and so ill-treated him that he died under their hands.

"They left the body, when they found what had happened, and fled. The ringleaders escaped across the lake to the other side; and those who remained could not be sufficiently identified to bring them to trial. The affair was hushed up; but it gave great uneasiness to several respectable families whose sons were in the scrape."

"But scenes like these must be of rare occurrence?"

"They are more common than you imagine. A man was killed up at W—— the other day, and two others dangerously wounded, at a charivari. The bridegroom was a man in middle life, a desperately resolute and passionate man, and he swore that if such riff-raff dared to interfere with him, he would shoot at them with as little compunction as he would at so many crows. His threats only increased the mischievous determination of the mob to torment him; and when he refused to admit their deputation, or even to give them a portion of the wedding cheer, they determined to frighten him into compliance by firing several guns, loaded with peas, at his door. Their salute was returned, from the chamber window, by the discharge of a double-barrelled gun, loaded with buckshot. The crowd gave back with a tremendous yell. Their leader was shot through the heart, and two of the foremost in the scuffle dangerously wounded. They vowed they would set fire to the house, but the bridegroom boldly stepped to the window, and told them to try it, and before they could light a torch he would fire among them again, as his gun was reloaded, and he would discharge it at them as long as one of them dared to remain on his premises.

"They cleared off; but though Mr. A—— was not punished for the *accident*, as it was called, he became a marked man, and lately left the colony to settle in the United States.

"Why, Mrs. Moodie, you look quite serious. I can,

however, tell you a less dismal tale. A charivari would seldom be attended with bad consequences if people would take it as a joke, and join in the spree."

"A very dignified proceeding, for a bride and bridegroom to make themselves the laughing-stock of such people!"

"Oh, but custom reconciles us to everything; and 'tis better to give up a little of our pride than endanger the lives of our fellow-creatures. I have been told a story of a lady in the Lower Province, who took for her second husband a young fellow, who, as far as his age was concerned, might have been her son. The mob surrounded her house at night, carrying her effigy in an open coffin, supported by six young lads, with white favours in their hats; and they buried the poor bride, amid shouts of laughter, and the usual accompaniments, just opposite her drawing-room windows. The widow was highly amused by the whole of their proceedings, but she wisely let them have their own way. She lived in a strong stone house, and she barred the doors, and closed the iron shutters, and set them at defiance.

"'As long as she enjoyed her health,' she said, 'they were welcome to bury her in effigy as often as they pleased; she was really glad to be able to afford amusement to so many people.'

"Night after night, during the whole of that winter, the same party beset her house with their diabolical music; but she only laughed at them.

"The leader of the mob was a young lawyer from these parts, a sad mischievous fellow; the widow became aware of this, and she invited him one evening

ROUGHING IT IN THE BUSH

to take tea with a small party at her house. He accepted the invitation, was charmed with her hearty and hospitable welcome, and soon found himself quite at home; but only think how ashamed he must have felt, when the same 'larum commenced, at the usual hour, in front of the lady's house!

"'Oh,' said Mrs. R——, smiling to her husband, 'here come our friends. Really, Mr. K——, they amuse us so much of an evening that I should feel quite dull without them.'

"From that hour the charivari ceased, and the old lady was left to enjoy the society of her young husband in quiet.

"I assure you, Mrs. M——, that the charivari often deters old people from making disgraceful marriages, so that it is not wholly without its use."

A few days after the charivari affair, Mrs. D—— stepped in to see me. She was an American; a very respectable old lady, who resided in a handsome framehouse on the main road. I was at dinner, the servantgirl, in the meanwhile, nursing my child at a distance. Mrs. D—— sat looking at me very seriously until I concluded my meal, her dinner having been taken several hours before. When I had finished, the girl gave me the child, and then removed the dinner-service into an outer room.

"You don't eat with your helps," said my visitor. "Is not that something like pride?"

"It is custom," said I; "we were not used to do so at home, and I think that keeping a separate table is more comfortable for both parties."

"Are you not both of the same flesh and blood? The

rich and the poor meet together, and the Lord is the maker of them all."

"True. Your quotation is just, and I assent to it with all my heart. There is no difference in the flesh and blood; but education makes a difference in the mind and manners, and till these can assimilate, it is better to keep apart."

"Ah! you are not a good Christian, Mrs. Moodie. The Lord thought more of the poor than He did of the rich, and He obtained more followers from among them. Now, *we* always take our meals with our people."

Presently after, while talking over the affairs of our households, I happened to say that the cow we had bought of Mollineux had turned out extremely well, and gave a great deal of milk.

"That man lived with us several years," she said; "he was an excellent servant, and D—— paid him his wages in land. The farm that he now occupies forms a part of our U. E. grant. But, for all his good conduct, I never could abide him, for being a *black*."

"Indeed! Is he not the same flesh and blood as the rest?"

The colour rose into Mrs. D——'s sallow face, and she answered with much warmth.

"What! do you want to compare *me* with a *nigger*?"

"Not exactly. But, after all, the colour makes the only difference between him and uneducated men of the same class."

"Mrs. Moodie!" she exclaimed, holding up her hands in pious horror; "they are the children of the devil! God never condescended to make a nigger."

ROUGHING IT IN THE BUSH

"Such an idea is an impeachment of the power and majesty of the Almighty. How can you believe in such an ignorant fable?"

"Well, then," said my monitress, in high dudgeon, "if the devil did not make them, they are descended from Cain."

"But all Cain's posterity perished in the flood."

My visitor was puzzled.

"The African race, it is generally believed, are the descendants of Ham, and to many of their tribes the curse pronounced against him seems to cling. To be the servant of servants is bad enough, without our making their condition worse by our cruel persecutions. Christ came to seek and to save that which was lost; and in proof of this inestimable promise, He did not reject the Ethiopian eunuch who was baptized by Philip, and who was, doubtless, as black as the rest of his people. Did you not admit Mollineux to your table with your other helps?"

"Mercy sake! do you think that I would sit down at the same table with a nigger? My helps would leave the house if I dared to put such an affront upon them. Sit down with a dirty black, indeed!"

"Do you think, Mrs. D ——, that there will be any negroes in heaven?"

"Certainly not, or I, for one, would never wish to go there;" and out of the house she sallied in high disdain.

Yet this was the woman who had given me such a plausible lecture on pride. Alas, for our fallen nature! Which is more subversive of peace and Christian fellowship—ignorance of our own characters, or of the characters of others?

THE CHARIVARI

Our departure for the woods became now a frequent theme of conversation. My husband had just returned from an exploring expedition to the backwoods, and was delighted with the prospect of removing thither.

CHAPTER TWELVE
ON A JOURNEY TO THE WOODS

CHAPTER   TWELVE
ON A JOURNEY TO THE WOODS

'Tis well for us poor denizens of earth
That God conceals the future from our gaze;
Or Hope, the blessed watcher on Life's tower,
Would fold her wings, and on the dreary waste
Close the bright eye that through the murky clouds
Of blank Despair still sees the glorious sun.

IT WAS A BRIGHT FROSTY MORNING when I bade adieu to the farm, the birthplace of my little Agnes, who, nestled beneath my cloak, was sweetly sleeping on my knee, unconscious of the long journey before us into the wilderness. The sun had not as yet risen. Anxious to get to our place of destination before dark, we started as early as we could. Our own fine team had been sold the day before for forty pounds; and one of our neighbours, a Mr. D——, was to convey us and our household goods to Douro for the sum of twenty dollars. During the week he had made several journeys, with furniture and stores; and all that now remained was to be conveyed to the woods in two large lumber sleighs, one driven by himself, the other by a younger brother.

It was not without regret that I left Melsetter, for so my husband had called the place, after his father's estate in Orkney. It was a beautiful, picturesque spot; and, in spite of the evil neighbourhood, I had learned to love it; indeed, it was much against my wish that it was sold. I had a great dislike to removing, which involves a necessary loss, and is apt to give to the emigrant roving and unsettled habits. But all regrets were now useless; and happily unconscious of the life of toil and anxiety that awaited us in those dreadful

269

woods, I tried my best to be cheerful, and to regard the future with a hopeful eye.

Our driver was a shrewd, clever man for his opportunities. He took charge of the living cargo, which consisted of my husband, our maid-servant, the two little children, and myself—besides a large hamper full of poultry, a dog, and a cat. The lordly sultan of the imprisoned seraglio thought fit to conduct himself in a very eccentric manner, for at every barn-yard we happened to pass, he clapped his wings, and crowed so long and loud that it afforded great amusement to the whole party, and doubtless was very edifying to the poor hens, who lay huddled together as mute as mice.

"That'ere rooster thinks he's on the top of the heap," said our driver, laughing. "I guess he's not used to travelling in a close conveyance. Listen! How all the crowers in the neighbourhood give him back a note of defiance! But he knows that he's safe enough at the bottom of the basket."

The day was so bright for the time of year (the first week in February), that we suffered no inconvenience from the cold. Little Katie was enchanted with the jingling of the sleigh-bells, and, nestled among the packages, kept singing or talking to the horses in her baby lingo. Trifling as these little incidents were, before we had proceeded ten miles on our long journey, they revived my drooping spirits, and I began to feel a lively interest in the scenes through which we were passing.

The first twenty miles of the way was over a hilly and well-cleared country; and as in winter the deep snow fills up the inequalities, and makes all roads a-like, we glided as swiftly and steadily along as if they had been the best highways in the world. Anon, the clearings began to diminish, and tall woods arose on either side of the path; their solemn aspect, and the deep silence that brooded over their vast solitudes, inspiring the mind with a strange awe. Not a breath of wind stirred the leafless branches, whose huge shadows —reflected upon the dazzling white covering of snow —lay so perfectly still, that it seemed as if Nature had suspended her operations, that life and motion had ceased, and that she was sleeping in her winding-sheet, upon the bier of death.

"I guess you will find the woods pretty lonesome," said our driver, whose thoughts had been evidently employed on the same subject as our own. "We were once in the woods, but emigration has stepped ahead of us, and made our'n a cleared part of the country. When I was a boy, all this country, for thirty miles on every side of us, was bush land. As to Peterborough, the place was unknown; not a settler had ever passed through the great swamp, and some of them believed that it was the end of the world."

"What swamp is that?" asked I.

"Oh, the great Cavan swamp. We are just two miles from it; and I tell you that the horses will need a good rest, and ourselves a good dinner, by the time we are through it. Ah! Mrs. Moodie, if ever you travel that way in summer, you will know something about corduroy roads. I was 'most jolted to death last fall; I thought it would have been no bad notion to have insured my teeth before I left C——. I really expected

271

that they would have been shook out of my head before we had done manœuvring over the big logs.

"How will my crockery stand it in the next sleigh?" quoth I. "If the road is such as you describe, I am afraid that I shall not bring a whole plate to Douro."

"Oh! the snow is a great leveller—it makes all rough places smooth. But with regard to this swamp I have something to tell you. About ten years ago, no one had ever seen the other side of it, and if pigs or cattle strayed away into it, they fell a prey to the wolves and bears, and were seldom recovered.

"An old Scotch emigrant, who had located himself on this side of it, so often lost his beasts that he determined during the summer season to try and explore the place, and see if there were any end to it. So he takes an axe on his shoulder, and a bag of provisions for a week, not forgetting a flask of whiskey, and off he starts all alone, and tells his wife that if he never returned, she and little Jock must try and carry on the farm without him; but he was determined to see the end of the swamp, even if it led to the other world. He fell upon a fresh cattle tract which he followed all that day; and towards night he found himself in the heart of a tangled wilderness of bushes, and himself half eaten up with mosquitoes and black flies. He was more than tempted to give in and return home by the first glimpse of light.

"The Scotch are a tough people; they are not easily daunted—a few difficulties only seem to make them more eager to get on; and he felt ashamed the next moment, as he told me, of giving up. So he finds out a large thick cedar-tree for his bed, climbs up, and coiling himself among the branches like a bear, he was soon fast asleep.

"The next morning, by daylight, he continued his journey, not forgetting to blaze with his axe the trees to the right and left as he went along. The ground was so spongy and wet that at every step he plunged up to his knees in water, but he seemed no nearer the end of the swamp than he had been the day before. He saw several deer, a racoon, and a ground-hog, during his walk, but was unmolested by bears or wolves. Having passed through several creeks, and killed a great many snakes, he felt so weary towards the close of the second day that he determined to go home the next morning. But just as he began to think his search was fruitless, he observed that the cedars and tamaracks which had obstructed his path became less numerous, and were succeeded by bass and soft maple. The ground, also, became less moist, and he was soon ascending a rising slope, covered with oak and beech, which shaded land of the very best quality. The old man was now fully convinced that he had cleared the great swamp, and that, instead of leading to the other world, it had conducted him to a country that would yield the very best returns for cultivation. His favourable report led to the formation of the road that we are about to cross, and to the settlement of Peterborough, which is one of the most promising new settlements in this district, and is surrounded by a splendid back country."

We were descending a very steep hill, and encountered an ox-sleigh, which was crawling slowly up it in a contrary direction. Three people were seated at the bottom of the vehicle upon straw, which made a cheap substitute for buffalo-robes. Perched, as we were, upon the crown of the height, we looked completely down into the sleigh, and during the whole course of my life I never saw three uglier mortals collected into such a narrow space. The man was blear-eyed, with a hare-lip, through which protruded two dreadful yellow teeth that resembled the tusks of a boar. The woman was long-faced, high cheek-boned, red-haired, and freckled all over like a toad. The boy resembled his hideous mother, but with the addition of a villainous obliquity of vision which rendered him the most disgusting object in this singular trio.

As we passed them, our driver gave a knowing nod to my husband, directing, at the same time, the most quizzical glance towards the strangers, as he exclaimed, "We are in luck, sir! I think that 'ere sleigh may be called Beauty's egg-basket!"

We made ourselves very merry at the poor people's expense, and Mr. D——, with his odd stories and Yankeefied expressions, amused the tedium of our progress through the great swamp, which in summer presents for several miles one uniform bridge of rough and unequal logs, all laid loosely across huge sleepers, so that they jump up and down, when pressed by the wheels, like the keys of a piano. The rough motion and jolting occasioned by this collision is so distressing, that it never fails to entail upon the traveller sore bones and an aching head for the rest of the day. The path is so narrow over these logs that two waggons cannot pass without great difficulty, which is rendered more dangerous by the deep natural ditches on either side of the bridge, formed by broad creeks that flow out of the swamp, and often terminate in mud-holes of very ominous dimensions. The snow, however, hid from us all the ugly features of the road, and Mr. D—— steered us through in perfect safety, and landed us at the door of a little log house which crowned the steep hill on the other side of the swamp, and which he dignified with the name of a tavern.

It was now two o'clock. We had been on the road since seven; and men, women, and children were all ready for the good dinner that Mr. D——had promised us at this splendid house of entertainment, where we were destined to stay for two hours, to refresh ourselves and rest the horses.

"Well, Mrs. J——, what have you got for our dinner?" said our driver, after he had seen to the accommodation of his teams.

"Pritters* and pork, sir. Nothing else to be had in the woods. Thank God, we have enough of that!"

D——shrugged up his shoulders, and looked at us.

"We've plenty of that same at home. But hunger's good sauce. Come, be spry, widow, and see about it, for I am very hungry."

I inquired for a private room for myself and the children, but there were no private rooms in the house. The apartment we occupied was like the cobbler's stall in the old song, and I was obliged to attend upon them in public.

"You have much to learn, ma'am, if you are going to the woods," said Mrs. J——.

"To unlearn, you mean," said Mr. D——. "To tell

* Vulgar Canadian for potatoes.

you the truth, Mrs. Moodie, ladies and gentlemen have no business in the woods. Eddication spoils man or woman for that location. So, widow (turning to our hostess), you are not tired of living alone yet?"

"No, sir; I have no wish for a second husband. I had enough of the first. I like to have my own way—to lie down mistress, and get up master."

"You don't like to be put out of your *old* way," returned he, with a mischievous glance.

She coloured very red; but it might be the heat of the fire over which she was frying the pork for our dinner.

I was very hungry, but I felt no appetite for the dish she was preparing for us. It proved salt, hard, and unsavoury.

D—— pronounced it very bad, and the whiskey still worse, with which he washed it down.

I asked for a cup of tea and a slice of bread. But they were out of tea, and the hop-rising had failed, and there was no bread in the house. For this disgusting meal we paid at the rate of a quarter of a dollar a-head.

I was glad when the horses being again put to, we escaped from the rank odour of the fried pork, and were once more in the fresh air.

"Well, mister; did not you grudge your money for that bad meat?" said D——, when we were once more seated in the sleigh. "But in these parts the worse the fare the higher the charge."

"I would not have cared," said I, "if I could have got a cup of tea."

"Tea! it's poor trash. I never could drink tea in

my life. But I like coffee, when 'tis boiled till it's quite black. But coffee is not good without plenty of trimmings."

"What do you mean by trimmings?"

He laughed. "Good sugar, and sweet cream. Coffee is not worth drinking without trimmings."

Often in after-years have I recalled the coffee trimmings, when endeavouring to drink the vile stuff which goes by the name of coffee in the houses of entertainment in the country.

We had now passed through the narrow strip of clearing which surrounded the tavern, and again entered upon the woods. It was near sunset, and we were rapidly descending a steep hill, when one of the traces that held our sleigh suddenly broke. D—— pulled up in order to repair the damage. His brother's team was close behind, and our unexpected standstill brought the horses upon us before J. D—— could stop them. I received so violent a blow from the head of one of them, just in the back of the neck, that for a few minutes I was stunned and insensible. When I recovered, I was supported in the arms of my husband, over whose knees I was leaning, and D—— was rubbing my hands and temples with snow.

"There, Mr. Moodie, she's coming to. I thought she was killed. I have seen a man before now killed by a blow from a horse's head in the like manner."

As soon as we could, we resumed our places in the sleigh; but all enjoyment of our journey, had it been otherwise possible, was gone.

When we reached Peterborough, Moodie wished us to remain at the inn all night, as we had still eleven

277

miles of our journey to perform, and that through a blazed forest-road, little travelled, and very much impeded by fallen trees and other obstacles; but D—— was anxious to get back as soon as possible to his own home, and he urged us very pathetically to proceed.

The moon arose during our stay at the inn, and gleamed upon the straggling frame-houses which then formed the now populous and thriving town of Peterborough. We crossed the wild, rushing beautiful Otonabee River by a rude bridge, and soon found ourselves journeying over the plains or level heights beyond the village, which were thinly wooded with picturesque groups of oak and pine, and very much resembled a gentleman's park at home.

Far below, to our right (for we were upon the Smith-town side) we heard the rushing of the river, whose rapid waters never receive curb from the iron chain of winter. Even while the rocky banks are coated with ice, and the frost-king suspends from every twig and branch the most beautiful and fantastic crystals, the black waters rush foaming along, a thick steam rising constantly above the rapids, as from a boiling pot. The shores vibrate and tremble beneath the force of the impetuous flood, as it whirls round cedar-crowned islands and opposing rocks, and hurries on to pour its tribute into the Rice Lake, to swell the calm, majestic grandeur of the Trent, till its waters are lost in the beautiful Bay of Quinté, and finally merged in the blue ocean of Ontario.

The most renowned of our English rivers dwindle into little muddy rills when compared with the sublimity of the Canadian waters. No language can adequately express the solemn grandeur of her lake and river scenery; the glorious islands that float, like visions from fairyland, upon the bosom of these azure mirrors of her cloudless skies. No dreary breadth of marshes, covered with flags, hides from our gaze the expanse of heavy-tinted waters; no foul mud-banks spread the unwholesome exhalations around. The rocky shores are crowned with the cedar, the birch, the alder, and soft maple, that dip their long tresses in the pure stream; from every crevice in the limestone the harebell and Canadian rose wave their graceful blossoms.

The fiercest droughts of summer may diminish the volume and power of these romantic streams, but it never leaves their rocky channels bare, nor checks the mournful music of their dancing waves.

Through the openings in the forest, we now and then caught the silver gleam of the river tumbling on in moonlight splendour, while the hoarse chiding of the wind in the lofty pines above us gave a fitting response to the melancholy cadence of the waters.

The children had fallen asleep. A deep silence pervaded the party. Night was above us with her mysterious stars. The ancient forest stretched around us on every side, and a foreboding sadness sunk upon my heart. Memory was busy with the events of many years. I retraced step by step the pilgrimage of my past life, until, arriving at this passage in the sombre history, I gazed through tears upon the singularly savage scene around me, and secretly marvelled, "What brought me here?"

"Providence," was the answer which the soul gave. "Not for your own welfare, perhaps, but for the welfare of your children, the unerring hand of the Great Father has led you here. You form a connecting link in the destinies of many. It is impossible for any human creature to live for himself alone. It may be your lot to suffer, but others will reap a benefit from your trials. Look up with confidence to Heaven, and the sun of hope will yet shed a cheering beam through the forbidding depths of this tangled wilderness."

The road now became so bad that Mr. D—— was obliged to dismount and lead his horses through the more intricate passages. The animals themselves, weary with their long journey and heavy load, proceeded at footfall. The moon, too, had deserted us, and the only light we had to guide us through the dim arches of the forest was from the snow and the stars, which now peered down upon us, through the leafless branches of the trees, with uncommon brilliancy.

"It will be past midnight before we reach your brother's clearing" (where we expected to spend the night), said D——. "I wish, Mr. Moodie, we had followed your advice and stayed at Peterborough. How fares it with you, Mrs Moodie, and the young ones? It is growing very cold."

We were now in the heart of a dark cedar swamp, and my mind was haunted with visions of wolves and bears; but beyond the long, wild howl of a solitary wolf, no other sound awoke the sepulchral silence of that dismal-looking wood.

"What a gloomy spot!" said I to my husband. "In

TORONTO

the old country, superstition would people it with ghosts."

"Ghosts! There are no ghosts in Canada!" said Mr. D——. "The country is too new for ghosts. No Canadian is afear'd of ghosts. It is only in old countries, like your'n, that are full of sin and wickedness, that people believe in such nonsense. No human habitation has ever been erected in this wood through which you are passing. Until a very few years ago, few white persons had ever passed through it; and the Red Man would not pitch his tent in such a place as this. Now, ghosts, as I understand the word, are the spirits of bad men that are not allowed by Providence to rest in their graves, but, for a punishment, are made to haunt the spots where their worst deeds were committed. I don't believe in all this; but, supposing it to be true, bad men must have died here before their spirits could haunt the place. Now, it is more than probable that no person ever ended his days in this forest, so that it would be folly to think of seeing his ghost."

This theory of Mr. D——'s had the merit of originality, and it is not improbable that the utter disbelief in supernatural appearances which is common to most native-born Canadians, is the result of the same very reasonable mode of arguing. The unpeopled wastes of Canada must present the same aspect to the new settler that the world did to our first parents after their expulsion from the Garden of Eden; all the sin which could defile the spot, or haunt it with the association of departed evil, is concentrated in their own persons. Bad spirits cannot be supposed to linger near a place where crime has never been committed. The belief in ghosts, so prevalent in old countries, must first have had its foundation in the consciousness of guilt.

After clearing the low, swampy portion of the woods, with much difficulty, and the frequent application of the axe to cut away the fallen timber that impeded our progress, our ears were assailed by a low, roaring, rushing sound, as of the falling of waters.

"That is Herriot's Falls," said our guide. "We are within two miles of our destination."

Oh, welcome sound! But those two miles appeared more lengthy than the whole journey. Thick clouds, that threatened a snow-storm, had blotted out the stars, and we continued to grope our way through a narrow, rocky path, upon the edge of the river, in almost total darkness. I now felt the chillness of the midnight hour and the fatigue of the long journey, with double force, and envied the servant and children, who had been sleeping ever since we left Peterborough. We now descended the steep bank, and prepared to cross the rapids.

Dark as it was, I looked with a feeling of dread upon the foaming waters as they tumbled over their bed of rocks, their white crests flashing, life-like, amid the darkness of the night.

"This is an ugly bridge over such a dangerous place," said D———, as he stood up in the sleigh and urged his tired team across the miserable, insecure log bridge, where darkness and death raged below, and one false step of his jaded horses would have plunged us into both. I must confess I drew a freer breath when the bridge was crossed, and D—— congratulated us on our safe arrival in Douro.

We now continued our journey along the left bank of the river, but when in sight of Mr. S——'s clearing, a large pine-tree, which had newly fallen across the narrow path, brought the teams to a standstill.

The mighty trunk which had lately formed one of the stately pillars in the sylvan temple of Nature, was of too large dimensions to chop in two with axes; and after about half an hour's labour, which to me, poor, cold, weary wight! seemed an age, the males of the party abandoned the task in despair. To go round it was impossible; its roots were concealed in an impenetrable wall of cedar-jungle on the right-hand side of the road, and its huge branches hung over the precipitous bank of the river.

"We must try and make the horses jump over it," said D——. "We may get an upset, but there is no help for it; we must either make the experiment, or stay here all night, and I am too cold and hungry for that—so here goes." He urged his horses to leap the log; restraining their ardour for a moment as the sleigh rested on the top of the formidable barrier, but so nicely balanced, that the difference of a straw would almost have overturned the heavily-laden vehicle and its helpless inmates. We, however, cleared it in safety. He now stopped, and gave directions to his brother to follow the same plan that he had adopted; but whether the young man had less coolness, or the horses in his team were more difficult to manage, I cannot tell: the sleigh, as it hung poised upon the top of the log, was overturned with a loud crash, and all my household goods and chattels were scattered over the road.

Alas, for my crockery and stone china! scarcely one article remained unbroken.

"Never fret about the china," said Moodie; "thank God, the man and the horses are uninjured."

I should have felt more thankful had the crocks been spared too; for, like most of my sex, I had a tender regard for china, and I knew that no fresh supply could be obtained in this part of the world. Leaving his brother to collect the scattered fragments, D—— proceeded on his journey. We left the road, and were winding our way over a steep hill, covered with heaps of brush and fallen timber, and as we reached the top, a light gleamed cheerily from the windows of a log house, and the next moment we were at my brother-in-law's door.

My brother-in-law and his family had retired to rest, but they instantly rose to receive the way-worn travellers; and I never enjoyed more heartily a warm welcome after a long day of intense fatigue, than I did that night of my first sojourn in the backwoods.

THE OTONABEE.

Dark, rushing, foaming river!
　I love the solemn sound
　That shakes thy shores around,
And hoarsely murmurs, ever,
　As thy waters onward bound,
　Like a rash, unbridled steed
Flying madly on its course;
That shakes with thundering force
　The vale and trembling mead.

A JOURNEY TO THE WOODS

So thy billows downward sweep,
　Nor rock nor tree can stay
　Their fierce, impetuous way;
Now in eddies whirling deep,
　Now in rapids white with spray.

I love thee, lonely river!
　Thy hollow restless roar,
　Thy cedar-girded * shore;
The rocky isles that sever
　The waves that round them pour.
　　Katchawanook † basks in light,
But thy currents woo the shade
By thy lofty pine-trees made,
　That cast a gloom like night,
Ere day's last glories fade.
　Thy solitary voice
The same bold anthem sung
When Nature's frame was young.
　No longer shall rejoice
The woods where erst it rung.

Lament, lament, wild river!
　A hand is on thy mane ‡
　That will bind thee in a chain
No force of thine can sever.
　Thy furious headlong tide,
In murmurs soft and low,
　Is destined yet to glide
To meet the lake below;
　And many a bark shall ride

---

　* The banks of the river have since been denuded of trees. The rocks that formed the falls and rapids have been blasted out. It is tame enough now.
　† This is the Indian name for one of the many expansions of this beautiful river.
　‡ Some idea of the rapidity of this river may be formed from the fact that heavy rafts of timber are floated down from Herriot's Falls, a distance of nine miles from Peterborough, in less than an hour. The shores are bold and rocky, and abound in beautiful and picturesque views.

285

ROUGHING IT IN THE BUSH

Securely on thy breast,
To waft across the main
Rich stores of golden grain
From the valleys of the West

CHAPTER THIRTEEN
THE WILDERNESS, AND OUR INDIAN FRIENDS

CHAPTER XIII. THE WILDERNESS, AND OUR INDIAN FRIENDS

Man of strange race! stern dweller of the wild!
Nature's free-born, untamed, and daring child!

THE CLOUDS OF THE PRECEDING NIGHT, instead of dissolving in snow, brought on a rapid thaw. A thaw in the middle of winter is the most disagreeable change that can be imagined. After several weeks of clear, bright, bracing, frosty weather, with a serene atmosphere and cloudless sky, you awake one morning surprised at the change in the temperature; and, upon looking out of the window, behold the woods obscured by a murky haze—not so dense as an English November fog, but more black and lowering—and the heavens shrouded in a uniform covering of leaden-coloured clouds, deepening into a livid indigo at the edge of the horizon. The snow, no longer hard and glittering, has become soft and spongy, and the foot slips into a wet and insidiously-yielding mass at every step. From the roof pours down a continuous stream of water, and the branches of the trees, collecting the moisture of the reeking atmosphere, shower it upon the earth from every dripping twig. The cheerless and uncomfortable aspect of things without never fails to produce a corresponding effect upon the minds of those within, and casts such a damp upon the spirits that it appears to destroy for a time all sense of enjoyment. Many persons (and myself among the number) are made aware of the approach of a thunderstorm by an intense pain and weight about the head; and I have heard numbers of Canadians complain that a thaw always made them feel bilious and heavy, and greatly depressed their animal spirits.

T

ROUGHING IT IN THE BUSH

I had a great desire to visit our new location, but when I looked out upon the cheerless waste, I gave up the idea, and contented myself with hoping for a better day on the morrow; but many morrows came and went before a frost again hardened the road sufficiently for me to make the attempt.

The prospect from the windows of my sister's log hut was not very prepossessing. The small lake in front, which formed such a pretty object in summer, now looked like an extensive field covered with snow, hemmed in from the rest of the world by a dark belt of sombre pine-woods. The clearing round the house was very small, and only just reclaimed from the wilderness, and the greater part of it was covered with piles of brushwood, to be burnt the first dry days of spring.

The charred and blackened stumps on the few acres that had been cleared during the preceding year were everything but picturesque; and I concluded, as I turned, disgusted, from the prospect before me, that there was very little beauty to be found in the backwoods. But I came to this decision during a Canadian thaw, be it remembered, when one is wont to view every object with jaundiced eyes.

Moodie had only been able to secure sixty-six acres of his government grant upon the Upper Katchawanook Lake, which, being interpreted, means in English, the "Lake of the Waterfalls," a very poetical meaning, which most Indian names have. He had, however, secured a clergy reserve of two hundred acres adjoining; and he afterwards purchased a fine lot, which likewise formed part of the same block, one

hundred acres, for £150.* This was an enormously
high price for wild land; but the prospect of opening
the Trent and Otonabee for the navigation of steam-
boats and other small craft, was at that period a favourite speculation, and its practicability, and the great
advantages to be derived from it, were so widely believed as to raise the value of the wild lands along
these remote waters to an enormous price; and settlers
in the vicinity were eager to secure lots, at any sacrifice, along their shores.

Our government grant was upon the lake shore,
and Moodie had chosen for the site of his log house a
bank that sloped gradually from the edge of the water.
until it attained to the dignity of a hill. Along the top
of this ridge, the forest road ran, and midway down
the hill, our humble home, already nearly completed,
stood, surrounded by the eternal forest. A few trees
had been cleared in its immediate vicinity, just sufficient to allow the workmen to proceed, and to prevent
the fall of any tree injuring the building, or the danger
of its taking fire during the process of burning the fallow

A neighbour had undertaken to build this rude
dwelling by contract, and was to have it ready for us
by the first week in the new year. The want of boards
to make the divisions in the apartments alone hindered him from fulfilling his contract. These had lately
been procured, and the house was to be ready for our
reception in the course of a week. Our trunks and bag-

---

* After a lapse of fifteen years, we have been glad to sell these lots of
land, after considerable clearings had been made upon them, for less than
they originally cost us.

gage had already been conveyed thither by Mr. D——; and, in spite of my sister's kindness and hospitality, I longed to find myself once more settled in a home of my own.

The day after our arrival, I was agreeably surprised by a visit from Monaghan, whom Moodie had once more taken into his service. The poor fellow was delighted that his nurse-child, as he always called little Katie, had not forgotten him, but evinced the most lively satisfaction at the sight of her dark friend.

Early every morning, Moodie went off to the house; and the first fine day, my sister undertook to escort me through the wood to inspect it. The proposal was joyfully accepted; and although I felt *rather* timid when I found myself with only my female companion in the vast forest, I kept my fears to myself, lest I should be laughed at.

The snow had been so greatly decreased by the late thaw, that it had been converted into a coating of ice, which afforded a dangerous and slippery footing. My sister, who had resided for nearly twelve months in the woods, was provided for her walk with Indian moccasins, which rendered her quite independent; but I stumbled at every step. The sun shone brightly, the air was clear and invigorating, and, in spite of the treacherous ground and my foolish fears, I greatly enjoyed my first walk in the woods. Naturally of a cheerful, hopeful disposition, my sister was enthusiastic in her admiration of the woods. She drew such a lively picture of the charms of a summer residence in the forest, that I began to feel greatly interested in her descriptions, and to rejoice that we, too, were to be her near neighbours and dwellers in the woods; and this circumstance not a little reconciled me to the change.

Hoping that my husband would derive an income equal to the one he had parted with from the investment of the price of his commission in the steam-boat stock, I felt no dread of want. Our legacy of £700 had afforded us means to purchase land, build our house, and give out a large portion of land to be cleared, and, with a considerable sum of money still in hand, our prospects for the future were in no way discouraging.

When we reached the top of the ridge that overlooked our cot, my sister stopped, and pointed out a log-house among the trees. "There, S——," she said, "is your house. When that black cedar swamp is cleared away, that now hides the lake from us, you will have a very pretty view." My conversation with her had quite altered the aspect of the country, and predisposed me to view things in the most favourable light. I found Moodie and Monaghan employed in piling up heaps of bush near the house, which they intended to burn off by hand, previous to firing the rest of the fallow, to prevent any risk to the building from fire. The house was made of cedar logs, and presented a superior air of comfort to most dwellings of the same kind. The dimensions were thirty-six feet in length, and thirty-two feet in breadth, which gave us a nice parlour, a kitchen, and two small bedrooms, which were divided by plank partitions. Pantry or storeroom there was none; some rough shelves in the kitchen, and a deal cupboard in a corner of the parlour, being the extent of our accommodations in that way.

293

ROUGHING IT IN THE BUSH

Our servant, Mary Tate, was busy scrubbing out the parlour and bedroom; but the kitchen, and the sleeping-room off it, were still knee-deep in chips, and filled with the carpenter's bench and tools, and all our luggage. Such as it was, it was a palace when compared to Old Satan's log hut, or the miserable cabin we had wintered in during the severe winter of 1833, and I regarded it with complacency as my future home.

While we were standing outside the building, conversing with my husband, a young gentleman, of the name of Morgan, who had lately purchased land in that vicinity, went into the kitchen to light his pipe at the stove, and, with true backwood carelessness, let the hot cinder fall among the dry chips that strewed the floor. A few minutes after, the whole mass was in a blaze, and it was not without great difficulty that Moodie and Mr. R—— succeeded in putting out the fire. Thus were we nearly deprived of our home before we had taken up our abode in it.

The indifference to the danger of fire in a country where most of the dwellings are composed of inflammable materials is truly astonishing. Accustomed to see enormous fires blazing on every hearth-stone, and to sleep in front of these fires, his bedding often riddled with holes made by hot particles of wood flying out during the night, and igniting beneath his very nose, the sturdy backwoodsman never dreads an enemy in the element that he is used to regard as his best friend. Yet what awful accidents, what ruinous calamities arise out of this criminal negligence, both to himself and others!

A few days after this adventure, we bade adieu to

my sister, and took possession of our new dwelling, and commenced "a life in the woods."

The first spring we spent in comparative ease and idleness. Our cows had been left upon our old place during the winter. The ground had to be cleared before it could receive a crop of any kind, and I had little to do but to wander by the lake shore, or among the woods, and amuse myself.

These were the halcyon days of the bush. My husband had purchased a very light cedar canoe, to which he attached a keel and a sail; and most of our leisure hours, directly the snows melted, were spent upon the water.

These fishing and shooting excursions were delightful. The pure beauty of the Canadian water, the sombre but august grandeur of the vast forest that hemmed us in on every side and shut us out from the rest of the world, soon cast a magic spell upon our spirits, and we began to feel charmed with the freedom and solitude around us. Every object was new to us. We felt as if we were the first discoverers of every beautiful flower and stately tree that attracted our attention, and we gave names to fantastic rocks and fairy isles, and raised imaginary houses and bridges on every picturesque spot which we floated past during our aquatic excursions. I learned the use of the paddle, and became quite a proficient in the gentle craft.

It was not long before we received visits from the Indians, a people whose beauty, talents, and good qualities have been somewhat overrated, and invested with a poetical interest which they scarcely deserve. Their honesty and love of truth are the finest traits in characters otherwise dark and unlovely. But these are two God-like attributes, and from them spring all that is generous and ennobling about them.

There never was a people more sensible of kindness, or more grateful for any little act of benevolence exercised towards them. We met them with confidence; our dealings with them were conducted with the strictest integrity; and they became attached to our persons, and in no single instance ever destroyed the good opinion we entertained of them.

The tribes that occupy the shores of all these inland waters, back of the great lakes, belong to the Chippewa or Missasagua Indians, perhaps the least attractive of all these wild people, both with regard to their physical and mental endowments.

The men of this tribe are generally small of stature, with very coarse and repulsive features. The forehead is low and retreating, the observing faculties large, the intellectual ones scarcely developed; the ears large, and standing off from the face; the eyes looking towards the temples, keen, snake-like, and far apart; the cheek bones prominent; the nose long and flat, the nostrils very round; the jaw-bone projecting, massy, and brutal; the mouth expressing ferocity and sullen determination; the teeth large, even, and dazzlingly white. The mouth of the female differs widely in expression from that of the male; the lips are fuller, the jaw less projecting, and the smile is simple and agreeable. The women are a merry, light-hearted set, and their constant laugh and incessant prattle form a strange contrast to the iron taciturnity of their grim lords.

THE WILDERNESS, AND OUR FRIENDS

Now I am upon the subject, I will recapitulate a few traits and sketches of these people, as they came under my own immediate observation.

A dry cedar swamp, not far from the house, by the lake shore, had been their usual place of encampment for many years. The whole block of land was almost entirely covered with maple trees, and had originally been an Indian sugar-bush. Although the favourite spot had now passed into the hands of strangers, they still frequented the place, to make canoes and baskets, to fish and shoot, and occasionally to follow their old occupation.

Scarcely a week passed away without my being visited by the dark strangers; and, as my husband never allowed them to eat with the servants (who viewed them with the same horror that Mrs. —— did black Mollineux), but brought them to his own table, they soon grew friendly and communicative, and would point to every object that attracted their attention, asking a thousand questions as to its use, the material of which it was made, and if we were inclined to exchange it for their commodities?

With a large map of Canada they were infinitely delighted. In a moment they recognized every bay and headland in Ontario, and almost screamed with delight when, following the course of the Trent with their fingers, they came to their own lake.

How eagerly each pointed out the spot to his fellows; how intently their black heads were bent down and their dark eyes fixed upon the map! What strange uncouth exclamations of surprise burst from their lips as they rapidly repeated the Indian names for every lake and river on this wonderful piece of paper!

The old chief Peter Nogan begged hard for the coveted treasure. He would give "Canoe, venison, duck, fish, for it; and more by and by."

I felt sorry that I was unable to gratify his wishes; but the map had cost upwards of six dollars, and was daily consulted by my husband, in reference to the names and situations of localities in the neighbourhood.

I had in my possession a curious Japanese sword, which had been given to me by an uncle of Tom Wilson's—a strange gift to a young lady; but it was on account of its curiosity, and had no reference to my warlike propensities. The sword was broad, and three-sided in the blade, and in shape resembled a moving snake. The hilt was formed of a hideous carved image of one of their war gods; and a more villainous-looking wretch was never conceived by the most distorted imagination. He was represented in a sitting attitude, the eagle's claws, that formed his hands, resting upon his knees; his legs terminated in lion's paws; and his face was a strange compound of beast and bird—the upper part of his person being covered with feathers, the lower with long, shaggy hair. The case of this awful weapon was made of wood, and, in spite of its serpentine form, fitted it exactly. No trace of a join could be found in the scabbard, which was of hard wood, and highly polished.

One of my Indian friends found this sword lying upon the bookshelf, and he hurried to communicate the important discovery to his companions. Moodie was absent, and they brought it to me to demand an explanation of the figure that formed the hilt.

I told them that it was a weapon that belonged to a very fierce people who lived in the East, far over the Great Salt Lake; that they were not Christians as we were, but said their prayers to images made of silver, and gold, and ivory, and wood, and that this was one of them; that before they went into battle they said their prayers to that hideous thing, which they had made with their own hands.

The Indians were highly amused by this relation and passed the sword from one to the other, exclaiming, "A god!—Owgh—A god!"

But, in spite of these outward demonstrations of contempt, I was sorry to perceive that this circumstance gave the weapon a great value in their eyes, and they regarded it with a sort of mysterious awe.

For several days they continued to visit the house, bringing along with them some fresh companion to look at Mrs. Moodie's *god*!—until, vexed and annoyed by the delight they manifested at the sight of the eagle-beaked monster, I refused to gratify their curiosity, by not producing him again.

The manufacture of the sheath, which had caused me much perplexity, was explained by old Peter in a minute. "'Tis burnt out," he said. "Instrument made like sword—heat red hot—burnt through—polished outside."

Had I demanded a whole fleet of canoes for my Japanese sword, I am certain they would have agreed to the bargain.

The Indian possesses great taste, which is displayed in the carving of his paddles, in the shape of his canoes, in the elegance and symmetry of his bows, in the cut of his leggings and moccasins, the sheath of his hunting knife, and in all the little ornaments in which he delights. It is almost impossible for a settler to imitate to perfection an Indian's cherry-wood paddle. My husband made very creditable attempts, but still there was something wanting—the elegance of the Indian finish was not there. If you show them a good print, they invariably point out the most natural, and the best executed figures in the group. They are particularly delighted with pictures, examine them long and carefully, and seem to feel an artist-like pleasure in observing the effect produced by light and shade.

I had been showing John Nogan, the eldest son of Old Peter, some beautiful coloured engravings of celebrated females; and, to my astonishment, he pounced upon the best, and grunted out his admiration in the most approved Indian fashion. After having looked for a long time at all the pictures very attentively, he took his dog Sancho upon his knee, and showed him the pictures, with as much gravity as if the animal really could have shared in his pleasure.

The vanity of these grave men is highly amusing. They seem perfectly unconscious of it themselves, and it is exhibited in the most child-like manner.

Peter and his son John were taking tea with us, when we were joined by my brother, Mr. S——. The latter was giving us an account of the marriage of Peter Jones, the celebrated Indian preacher.

"I cannot think," he said, "how any lady of property and education could marry such a man as Jones. Why, he's as ugly as Peter here."

This was said, not with any idea of insulting the red-skin on the score of his beauty, of which he possessed not the smallest particle, but in total forgetfulness that our guest understood English. Never shall I forget the red flash of that fierce dark eye, as it glared upon my unconscious brother. I would not have received such a fiery glance for all the wealth that Peter Jones obtained with his Saxon bride. John Nogan was high-ly amused by his father's indignation. He hid his face behind the chief; and, though he kept perfectly still, his whole frame was convulsed with suppressed laughter.

A plainer human being than poor Peter could scarcely be imagined; yet he certainly deemed himself handsome. I am inclined to think that their ideas of personal beauty differ very widely from ours.

Tom Nogan, the chief's brother, had a very large, fat, ugly squaw for his wife. She was a mountain of tawny flesh; and, but for the innocent, good-natured expression which, like a bright sunbeam penetrating a swarthy cloud, spread all around a kindly glow, she might have been termed hideous.

This woman they considered very handsome, call-ing her "a fine squaw—clever squaw—a much good woman"; though in what her superiority consisted, I never could discover, often as I visited the wigwam. She was very dirty, and appeared quite indifferent to the claims of common decency (in the disposal of the few filthy rags that covered her). She was, however, very expert in all Indian craft. No Jew could drive a

301

better bargain than Mrs. Tom; and her urchins, of whom she was the happy mother of five or six, were as cunning and avaricious as herself.

One day she visited me, bringing along with her a very pretty covered basket for sale. I asked her what she wanted for it, but could obtain from her no satisfactory answer. I showed her a small piece of silver. She shook her head. I tempted her with pork and flour, but she required neither. I had just given up the idea of dealing with her, in despair, when she suddenly seized upon me, and, lifting up my gown, pointed exultingly to my quilted petticoat, clapping her hands, and laughing immoderately.

Another time she led me all over the house, to show me what she wanted in exchange for *basket*. My patience was well-nigh exhausted in following her from place to place, in her attempt to discover the coveted article, when, hanging upon a peg in my chamber, she espied a pair of trousers belonging to my husband's logging-suit. The riddle was solved. With a joyful cry she pointed to them, exclaiming "Take basket. Give them!" It was with no small difficulty that I rescued the indispensables from her grasp.

From this woman I learned a story of Indian coolness and courage which made a deep impression on my mind. One of their squaws, a near relation of her own, had accompanied her husband on a hunting expedition into the forest. He had been very successful, and having killed more deer than they could well carry home, he went to the house of a white man to dispose of some of it, leaving the squaw to take care of the rest until his return. She sat carelessly upon the log with

302

his hunting-knife in her hand, when she heard the breaking of branches near her, and, turning round, beheld a great bear only a few paces from her.

It was too late to retreat; and seeing that the animal was very hungry, and determined to come to close quarters, she rose, and placed her back against a small tree, holding her knife close to her breast, and in a straight line with the bear. The shaggy monster came on. She remained motionless, her eyes steadily fixed upon her enemy, and, as his huge arms closed around her, she slowly drove the knife into his heart. The bear uttered a hideous cry, and sank dead at her feet. When the Indian returned, he found the courageous woman taking the skin from the carcass of the formidable brute. What iron nerves these people must possess, when even a woman could dare and do a deed like this!

The wolf they hold in great contempt, and scarcely deign to consider him as an enemy. Peter Nogan assured me that he never was near enough to one in his life to shoot it; that, except in large companies, and when greatly pressed by hunger, they rarely attack men. They hold the lynx, or wolverine, in much dread, as they often spring from trees upon their prey, fastening upon the throat with their sharp teeth and claws, from which a person in the dark could scarcely free himself without first receiving a dangerous wound. The cry of this animal is very terrifying, resembling the shrieks of a human creature in mortal agony.

My husband was anxious to collect some of the native Indian airs, as they all sing well, and have a fine ear for music, but all his efforts proved abortive. "John," he said to young Nogan (who played very

303

creditably on the flute, and had just concluded the popular air of "Sweet Home"), "cannot you play me one of your own songs?"

"Yes,—but no good."

"Leave me to be the judge of that. Cannot you give me a war song?"

"Yes,—but no good," with an ominous shake of the head.

"A hunting-song?"

"No fit for white man,"—with an air of contempt. "No good, no good!"

"Do, John, sing us a love-song," said I, laughing, "if you have such a thing in your language."

"Oh! much love-song—very much—bad—bad— no good for Christian man. Indian song no good for white ears." This was very tantalizing, as their songs sounded very sweetly from the lips of their squaws, and I had a great desire and curiosity to get some of them rendered into English.

To my husband they gave the name of "the musician," but I have forgotten the Indian word. It signified the maker of sweet sounds. They listened with intense delight to the notes of his flute, maintaining a breathless silence during the performance; their dark eyes flashing into fierce light at a martial strain, or softening with the plaintive and tender.

The cunning which they display in their contests with their enemies, in their hunting, and in making bargains with the whites (who are too apt to impose on their ignorance), seems to spring more from a law of necessity, forced upon them by their isolated position and precarious mode of life, than from any innate wish to betray. The Indian's face, after all, is a perfect index of his mind. The eye changes its expression with every impulse and passion, and shows what is passing within as clearly as the lightning in a dark night betrays the course of the stream. I cannot think that deceit forms any prominent trait in the Indian's character. They invariably act with the strictest honour towards those who never attempt to impose upon them. It is natural for a deceitful person to take advantage of the credulity of others. The genuine Indian never utters a falsehood, and never employs flattery (that powerful weapon in the hands of the insidious) in his communications with the whites.

His worst traits are those which he has in common with the wild animals of the forest, and which his intercourse with the lowest order of civilized men (who, in point of moral worth, are greatly his inferiors), and the pernicious effects of strong drink, have greatly tended to inflame and debase.

It is a melancholy truth, and deeply to be lamented, that the vicinity of European settlers has always produced a very demoralizing effect upon the Indians. As a proof of this, I will relate a simple anecdote.

John, of Rice Lake, a very sensible, middle-aged Indian, was conversing with me about their language, and the difficulty he found in understanding the books written in Indian for their use. Among other things, I asked him if his people ever swore, or used profane language towards the Deity.

The man regarded me with a sort of stern horror, as he replied, "Indian, till after he knew your people, never swore—no bad word in Indian. Indian must

305   U

learn your words to swear and take God's name in vain."

Oh, what a reproof to Christian men! I felt abashed and degraded in the eyes of this poor savage—who, ignorant as he was in many respects, yet possessed that first great attribute of the soul, a deep reverence for the Supreme Being. How inferior were thousands of my countrymen to him in this important point!

The affection of Indian parents to their children, and the deference which they pay to the aged, is another beautiful and touching trait in their character.

One extremely cold, wintry day, as I was huddled with my little ones over the stove, the door softly unclosed, and the moccasined foot of an Indian crossed the floor. I raised my head, for I was too much accustomed to their sudden appearance at any hour to feel alarmed, and perceived a tall woman standing silently and respectfully before me, wrapped in a large blanket. The moment she caught my eye she dropped the folds of her covering from around her, and laid at my feet the attenuated figure of a boy, about twelve years of age, who was in the last stage of consumption.

"Papoose die," she said, mournfully clasping her hands against her breast and looking down upon the suffering lad with the most heartfelt expression of maternal love, while large tears trickled down her dark face. "Moodie's squaw save papoose—poor Indian woman much glad."

Her child was beyond all human aid. I looked anxiously upon him, and knew, by the pinched-up features and purple hue of his wasted cheek, that he had not many hours to live. I could only answer with tears her agonizing appeal to my skill.

"Try and save him! All die but him." (She held up five of her fingers.) "Brought him all the way from Mutta Lake* upon my back, for white squaw to cure."

"I cannot cure him, my poor friend. He is in God's care; in a few hours he will be with Him."

The child was seized with a dreadful fit of coughing, which I expected every moment would terminate his frail existence. I gave him a teaspoonful of currant jelly, which he took with avidity, but could not retain a moment on his stomach.

"Papoose die," murmured the poor woman; "alone —alone! No papoose; the mother all alone."

She began re-adjusting the poor sufferer in her blanket. I got her some food, and begged her to stay and rest herself; but she was too much distressed to eat, and too restless to remain. She said little, but her face expressed the keenest anguish; she took up her mournful load, pressed for a moment his wasted, burning hand in hers, and left the room.

My heart followed her a long way on her melancholy journey. Think what this woman's love must have been for that dying son, when she had carried a lad of his age six miles through the deep snow upon her back, on such a day, in the hope of my being able to do him some good. Poor heart-broken mother! I learned from Joe Muskrat's squaw some days after that the boy died a few minutes after Elizabeth Iron, his mother, got home.

*Mud Lake, or Lake *Shemong*, in Indian.

ROUGHING IT IN THE BUSH

They never forget any little act of kindness. One cold night late in the fall, my hospitality was demanded by six squaws, and puzzled I was how to accommodate them all. I at last determined to give them the use of the parlour floor during the night. Among these women there was one very old, whose hair was as white as snow. She was the only grey-haired Indian I ever saw, and on that account I regarded her with peculiar interest. I knew that she was the wife of a chief, by the scarlet embroidered leggings, which only the wives and daughters of chiefs are allowed to wear. The old squaw had a very pleasing countenance, but I tried in vain to draw her into conversation. She evidently did not understand me; and the Muskrat squaw and Betty Cow were laughing at my attempts to draw her out. I administered supper to them with my own hands, and, after I had satisfied their wants (which is no very easy task, for they have great appetites), I told our servant to bring in several spare mattresses and blankets for their use. "Now mind, Jenny, and give the old squaw the best bed," I said; "the others are young, and can put up with a little inconvenience."

The old Indian glanced at me with her keen, bright eye; but I had no idea that she comprehended what I said.

Some weeks after this, as I was sweeping over my parlour floor, a slight tap drew me to the door. On opening it I perceived the old squaw, who immediately slipped into my hand a set of beautifully-embroidered bark trays, fitting one within the other, and exhibiting the very best sample of the porcupine-quill-work.

THE WILDERNESS, AND OUR FRIENDS

While I stood wondering what this might mean, the good old creature fell upon my neck, and kissing me, exclaimed, "You remember old squaw—make her comfortable! Old squaw no forget you. Keep them for her sake," and before I could detain her she ran down the hill with a swiftness which seemed to bid defiance to years. I never saw this interesting Indian again, and I concluded that she died during the winter, for she must have been of a great age.

My dear reader, I am afraid I shall tire you with my Indian stories; but you must bear with me patiently whilst I give you a few more. The real character of a people can be more truly gathered from such seemingly trifling incidents than from any ideas we may form of them from the great facts in their history, and this is my reason for detailing events which might otherwise appear insignificant and unimportant.

A friend was staying with us, who wished much to obtain a likeness of Old Peter. I promised to try and make a sketch of the old man the next time he paid us a visit. That very afternoon he brought us some ducks in exchange for pork, and Moodie asked him to stay and take a glass of whiskey with him and his friend Mr. K——. The old man had arrayed himself in a new blanket-coat, bound with red, and the seams all decorated with the same gay material. His leggings and moccasins were new, and elaborately fringed; and to cap the climax of the whole, he had a blue cloth conical cap upon his head ornamented with a deer's tail dyed blue, and several cock's feathers.

He was evidently very much taken up with the

magnificence of his own appearance, for he often glanced at himself in a small shaving glass that hung opposite, with a look of grave satisfaction. Sitting a-part, that I might not attract his observation, I got a tolerably faithful likeness of the old man, which, after slightly colouring, to show more plainly his Indian finery, I quietly handed over to Mr. K——. Sly as I thought myself, my occupation and the object of it had not escaped the keen eye of the old man. He rose, came behind Mr. K——'s chair and regarded the picture with a most affectionate eye. I was afraid that he would be angry at the liberty I had taken. No such thing! He was as pleased as Punch.

"That Peter?" he grunted. "Give me—put up in wigwam—make dog too! Owgh! owgh!" and he rubbed his hands together, and chuckled with delight. Mr. K—— had some difficulty in coaxing the picture from the old chief, so pleased was he with this rude representation of himself. He pointed to every particular article of his dress, and dwelt with peculiar glee on the cap and blue deer's tail.

A few days after this I was painting a beautiful little snow-bird that our man had shot out of a large flock that alighted near the door. I was so intent upon my task, to which I was putting the finishing strokes, that I did not observe the stealthy entrance (for they all walk like cats) of a stern-looking red man, till a slender, dark hand was extended over my paper to grasp the dead bird from which I was copying, and which as rapidly transferred it to the side of the painted one, accompanying the act with the deep guttural note of approbation, the unmusical, savage "Owgh."

THE WILDERNESS, AND OUR FRIENDS

My guest then seated himself with the utmost gravity in a rocking-chair, directly fronting me, and made the modest demand that I should paint a likeness of him, after the following quaint fashion:—

"Moodie's squaw know much—make Peter Nogan toder day on papare—make Jacob to-day—Jacob young—great hunter—give much duck—venison—to squaw."

Although I felt rather afraid of my fierce-looking visitor, I could scarcely keep my gravity; there was such an air of pompous self-approbation about the Indian, such a sublime look of conceit in his grave vanity.

"Moodie's squaw cannot do everything; she cannot paint young men," said I, rising, and putting away my drawing-materials, upon which he kept his eye intently fixed, with a hungry, avaricious expression. I thought it best to place the coveted objects beyond his reach. After sitting for some time, and watching all my movements, he withdrew, with a sullen, disappointed air.

This man was handsome, but his expression was vile. Though he often came to the house, I never could reconcile myself to his countenance.

Late one very dark, stormy night, three Indians begged to be allowed to sleep by the kitchen stove. The maid was frightened out of her wits at the sight of these strangers, who were Mohawks from the Indian woods upon the Bay of Quinté, and they brought along with them a horse and cutter. The night was so stormy, that, after consulting our man—Jacob Faithful, as we usually called him—I consented to grant their petition, although they were quite strangers, and taller and fiercer-looking than our friends the Missasaguas.

I was putting my children to bed, when the girl came rushing in, out of breath. "The Lord preserve us, madam, if one of these wild men has not pulled off his trousers, and is a-sitting mending them behind the stove! and what shall I do?"

"Do?—why, stay with me, and leave the poor fellow to finish his work."

The simple girl had never once thought of this plan of pacifying her outraged sense of propriety.

Their sense of hearing is so acute that they can distinguish sounds at an incredible distance, which cannot be detected by a European at all. I myself witnessed a singular exemplification of this fact. It was mid-winter; the Indians had pitched their tent, or wigwam, as usual, in our swamp. All the males were absent on a hunting expedition up the country, and had left two women behind to take care of the camp and its contents, Mrs. Tom Nogan and her children, and Susan Moore, a young girl of fifteen, and the only truly beautiful squaw I ever saw. There was something interesting about this girl's history, as well as her appearance. Her father had been drowned during a sudden hurricane, which swamped his canoe on Stony Lake; and the mother, who witnessed the accident from the shore, and was near her confinement with this child, boldly swam out to his assistance. She reached the spot where he sank, and even succeeded in recovering the body; but it was too late; the man was dead.

The soul of an Indian that has been drowned is

reckoned accursed, and he is never permitted to join his tribe on the happy hunting-grounds, but his spirit haunts the lake or river in which he lost his life. His body is buried on some lonely island, which the Indians never pass without leaving a small portion of food, tobacco, or ammunition, to supply his wants; but he is never interred with the rest of his people.

His children are considered unlucky, and few willingly unite themselves to the females of the family, lest a portion of the father's curse should be visited on them.

The orphan Indian girl generally kept aloof from the rest, and seemed so lonely and companionless, that she soon attracted my attention and sympathy, and a hearty feeling of good-will sprang up between us. Her features were small and regular, her face oval, and her large, dark, loving eyes were full of tenderness and sensibility, but as bright and shy as those of the deer. A rich vermilion glow burnt upon her olive cheek and lips, and set off the dazzling whiteness of her even and pearly teeth. She was small of stature, with delicate little hands and feet, and her figure was elastic and graceful. She was a beautiful child of nature, and her Indian name signified "The voice of angry waters." Poor girl, she had been a child of grief and tears from her birth! Her mother was a Mohawk, from whom she, in all probability, derived her superior personal attractions; for they are very far before the Missasaguas in this respect.

My friend and neighbour, Emilia S——, the wife of a naval officer, who lived about a mile distant from me, through the bush, had come to spend the day with me; and hearing that the Indians were in the swamp, and the men away, we determined to take a few trifles to the camp, in the way of presents, and spend an hour in chatting with the squaws.

What a beautiful moonlight night it was, as light as day!—the great forest sleeping tranquilly beneath the cloudless heavens—not a sound to disturb the deep repose of nature but the whispering of the breeze, which, during the most profound calm, creeps through the lofty pine tops. We bounded down the steep bank to the lake shore. Life is a blessing, a precious boon indeed, in such an hour, and we felt happy in the mere consciousness of existence—the glorious privilege of pouring out the silent adoration of the heart to the Great Father in His universal temple.

On entering the wigwam, which stood within a few yards of the clearing, in the middle of a thick group of cedars, we found Mrs. Tom, alone with her elfish children, seated before the great fire that burned in the centre of the camp; she was busy boiling some bark in an iron spider. The little boys, in red flannel shirts, which were their only covering, were tormenting a puppy, which seemed to take their pinching and pommelling in good part, for it neither attempted to bark nor to bite, but, like the eels in the story, submitted to the infliction because it was used to it. Mrs. Tom greeted us with a grin of pleasure, and motioned to us to sit down upon a buffalo-skin, which, with a courtesy so natural to the Indians, she had placed near her for our accommodation.

"You are all alone," said I, glancing round the camp.

THE WILDERNESS, AND OUR FRIENDS

"Ye'es; Indian away hunting — Upper Lakes. Come home with much deer."

"And Susan, where is she?"

"By and by," (meaning that she was coming). "Gone to fetch water—ice thick—chop with axe—take long time."

As she ceased speaking, the old blanket that formed the door of the tent was withdrawn, and the girl, bearing two pails of water, stood in the open space in the white moonlight. The glow of the fire streamed upon her dark, floating locks, danced in the black, glistening eye, and gave a deeper blush to the olive cheek! She would have made a beautiful picture; Sir Joshua Reynolds would have rejoiced in such a model —so simply graceful and unaffected, the very *beau idéal* of savage life and unadorned nature. A smile of recognition passed between us. She put down her burden beside Mrs. Tom, and noiselessly glided to her seat.

We had scarcely exchanged a few words with our favourite, when the old squaw, placing her hand against her ear, exclaimed, "Whist! whist!"

"What is it?" cried Emilia and I, starting to our feet. "Is there any danger?"

"A deer—a deer—in bush!" whispered the squaw, seizing a rifle that stood in a corner. "I hear sticks crack—a great way off. Stay here!"

A great way off the animal must have been, for though Emilia and I listened at the open door, an advantage which the squaw did not enjoy, we could not hear the least sound: all seemed still as death. The squaw whistled to an old hound, and went out.

315

ROUGHING IT IN THE BUSH

"Did you hear anything, Susan?"

She smiled, and nodded.

"Listen; the dog has found the track."

The next moment the discharge of a rifle, and the deep baying of the dog, woke up the sleeping echoes of the woods; and the girl started off to help the old squaw to bring in the game that she had shot.

The Indians are great imitators, and possess a nice tact in adopting the customs and manners of those with whom they associate. An Indian is Nature's gentleman—never familiar, coarse, or vulgar. If he takes a meal with you, he waits to see how you make use of the implements on the table, and the manner in which you eat, which he imitates with a grave decorum, as if he had been accustomed to the same usages from childhood. He never attempts to help himself, or demand more food, but waits patiently until you perceive what he requires. I was perfectly astonished at this innate politeness, for it seems natural to all the Indians with whom I have had any dealings.

There was one old Indian who belonged to a distant settlement, and only visited our lakes occasionally on hunting parties. He was a strange, eccentric, merry old fellow, with a skin like red mahogany, and a wiry, sinewy frame, that looked as if it could bid defiance to every change of temperature.

Old Snow-storm, for such was his significant name, was rather too fond of the whiskey-bottle, and when he had taken a drop too much, he became an unmanageable wild beast. He had a great fancy for my husband, and never visited the other Indians without extending the same favour to us. Once upon a time, he

THE WILDERNESS, AND OUR FRIENDS

broke the nipple of his gun; and Moodie repaired the injury for him by fixing a new one in its place, which little kindness quite won the heart of the old man, and he never came to see us without bringing an offering of fish, ducks, partridges, or venison, to show his gratitude.

One warm September day, he made his appearance bare-headed, as usual, and carrying in his hand a great checked bundle.

"Fond of grapes?" said he, putting the said bundle into my hands. "Fine grapes—brought them from island for my friend's squaw and papouse.

Glad of the donation, which I considered quite a prize, I hastened into the kitchen to untie the grapes and put them into a dish. But imagine my disappointment, when I found them wrapped up in a soiled shirt, only recently taken from the back of the owner. I called Moodie, and begged him to return Snow-storm his garment, and to thank him for the grapes.

The mischievous creature was highly diverted with the circumstance, and laughed immoderately.

"Snow-storm," said he, "Mrs. Moodie and the children are obliged to you for your kindness in bringing them the grapes; but how came you to tie them up in a dirty shirt?"

"Dirty!" cried the old man, astonished that we should object to the fruit on that score. "It ought to be clean; it has been washed often enough. Owgh! You see, Moodie," he continued, "I have no hat—never wear hat—want no shade to my eyes—love the sun—see all around me—up and down—much better widout hat. Could not put grapes in hat—blanket

317

coat too large, crush fruit, juice run out. I had noting but my shirt, so I takes off shirt, and brings grape safe over the water on my back. Papouse no care for dirty shirt; their *lee-tel bellies have no eyes.*"

In spite of this eloquent harangue, I could not bring myself to use the grapes, ripe and tempting as they looked, or give them to the children. Mr. W——— and his wife happening to step in at that moment fell into such an ecstasy at the sight of the grapes, that, as they were perfectly unacquainted with the circumstance of the shirt, I very *generously* gratified their wishes by presenting them with the contents of the large dish; and they never ate a bit less sweet for the novel mode in which they were conveyed to me!

The Indians, under their quiet exterior, possess a deal of humour. They have significant names for everything, and a nickname for every one, and some of the latter are laughably appropriate. A fat, pompous, ostentatious settler in our neighbourhood they called *Muckakee*, "the bull frog." Another, rather a fine young man, but with a very red face, they named *Segoskee*, "the rising sun." Mr. Wood, who had a farm above ours, was a remarkably slender young man, and to him they give the appellation of *Metig*, "thin stick." A woman, that occasionally worked for me, had a disagreeable squint; she was known in Indian by the name of *Sachàbò*, "cross-eye." A gentleman with a very large nose was *Choojas*, "big, or ugly nose." My little Addie, who was a fair, lovely creature, they viewed with great approbation, and called *Annoonk*, "a star"; while the rosy Katie was *Nogesigook*, "the northern lights." As to me, I was *Nono-*

cosiqui, a "humming-bird"; a ridiculous name for a tall woman, but it had reference to the delight I took in painting birds. My friend, Emilia, was "blue cloud"; my little Donald, "frozen face"; young C——, "the red-headed wood-pecker," from the colour of his hair; my brother, *Chippewa*, and "the bald-headed eagle." He was an especial favourite among them.

The Indians are often made a prey of and cheated by the unprincipled settlers, who think it no crime to overreach a red-skin. One anecdote will fully illustrate this fact. A young squaw, who was near becoming a mother, stopped at a Smith-town settler's house to rest herself. The woman of the house, who was Irish, was peeling for dinner some large white turnips, which her husband had grown in their garden. The Indian had never seen a turnip before, and the appearance of the firm, white, juicy root gave her such a keen craving to taste it that she very earnestly begged for a small piece to eat. She had purchased at Peterborough a large stone-china bowl, of a very handsome pattern (or, perhaps, got it at the store in exchange for *basket*), the worth of which might be half a dollar. If the poor squaw longed for the turnip, the value of which could scarcely reach a copper, the covetous European had fixed as longing a glance upon the china bowl, and she was determined to gratify her avaricious desire and obtain it on the most easy terms. She told the squaw, with some disdain, that her man did not grow turnips to give away to "Injuns," but she would sell her one. The squaw offered her four coppers, all the change she had about her. This the woman refused with contempt. She then proffered a basket; but that was not sufficient; nothing would satisfy her but the bowl. The Indian demurred; but opposition had only increased her craving for the turnip in a tenfold degree; and, after a short mental struggle, in which the animal propensity overcame the warnings of prudence, the squaw gave up the bowl, and received in return *one turnip*! The daughter of this woman told me this anecdote of her mother as a very clever thing. What ideas some people have of moral justice!

I have said before that the Indian never forgets a kindness. We had a thousand proofs of this, when overtaken by misfortune, and, withering beneath the iron grasp of poverty, we could scarcely obtain bread for ourselves and our little ones; then it was that the truth of the Eastern proverb was brought home to our hearts, and the goodness of God fully manifested towards us, "Cast thy bread upon the waters, and thou shalt find it after many days." During better times we had treated these poor savages with kindness and liberality, and they never forsook us. For many a good meal I have been indebted to them, when I had nothing to give in return, when the pantry was empty, and "the hearth-stone growing cold," as they term the want of provisions to cook at it. And their delicacy in conferring these favours was not the least admirable part of their conduct. John Nogan, who was much attached to us, would bring a fine bunch of ducks, and drop them at my feet "for the papouse," or leave a large maskinonge on the sill of the door, or place a quarter of venison just within it, and slip away without saying a word, thinking that receiving a present from a poor Indian might hurt our feelings, and he would spare us the mortification of returning thanks.

Often have I grieved that people with such generous impulses should be degraded and corrupted by civilized men; that a mysterious destiny involves and hangs over them, pressing them back into the wilderness, and slowly and surely sweeping them from the earth.

Their ideas of Christianity appeared to me vague and unsatisfactory. They will tell you that Christ died for men, and that He is the Saviour of the World, but they do not seem to comprehend the spiritual character of Christianity, nor the full extent of the requirements and application of the law of Christian love. These imperfect views may not be entertained by all Christian Indians, but they were very common amongst those with whom I conversed. Their ignorance upon theological, as well as upon other subjects, is, of course, extreme. One Indian asked me very innocently if I came from the land where Christ was born, and if I had ever seen Jesus. They always mention the name of the Persons in the Trinity with great reverence.

They are a highly imaginative people. The practical meaning of their names, and their intense admiration for the beauties of nature, are proof of this. Nothing escapes their observing eyes. There is not a flower that blooms in the wilderness, a bird that cuts the air with its wings, a beast that roams the

x

wood, a fish that stems the water, or the most minute insect that sports in the sunbeams, but it has an Indian name to illustrate its peculiar habits and qualities. Some of their words convey the direct meaning of the thing implied—thus, *ché-charm*, "to sneeze," is the very sound of that act; *toô-me-duh*, "to churn," gives the noise made by the dashing of the cream from side to side; and many others.

They believe in supernatural appearances—in spirits of the earth, the air, the waters. The latter they consider evil, and propitiate before undertaking a long voyage, by throwing small portions of bread, meat, tobacco, and gunpowder into the water.

When an Indian loses one of his children, he must keep a strict fast for three ays, abstaining from food of any kind. A hunter of the name of Young told me a curious story of their rigid observance of this strange rite.

"They had a chief," he said, "a few years ago, whom they called 'Handsome Jack,'—whether in derision, I cannot tell, for he was one of the ugliest Indians I ever saw. The scarlet fever got into the camp—a terrible disease in this country, and doubly terrible to those poor creatures who don't know how to treat it. His eldest daughter died. The chief had fasted two days when I met him in the bush. I did not know what had happened, but I opened my wallet, for I was on a hunting expedition, and offered him some bread and dried venison. He looked at me reproachfully.

"'Do white men eat bread the first night their papoose is laid in the earth?'

THE WILDERNESS, AND OUR FRIENDS

"I then knew the cause of his depression, and left him."

On the night of the second day of his fast another child died of the fever. He had now to accomplish three more days without tasting food. It was too much even for an Indian. On the evening of the fourth, he was so pressed by ravenous hunger, that he stole into the woods, caught a bull-frog, and devoured it alive. He imagined himself alone; but one of his people, suspecting his intention, had followed him, unperceived, to the bush. The act he had just committed was a hideous crime in their eyes, and in a few minutes the camp was in an uproar. The chief fled for protection to Young's house. When the hunter demanded the cause of his alarm, he gave for answer, "There are plenty of flies at my house. To avoid their stings I come to you."

It required all the eloquence of Mr. Young, who enjoyed much popularity among them, to reconcile the rebellious tribe to their chief.

They are very skilful in their treatment of wounds and many diseases. Their knowledge of the medicinal qualities of their plants and herbs is very great. They make excellent poultices from the bark of the bass and the slippery elm. They use several native plants in their dyeing of baskets and porcupine quills. The inner bark of the swamp-alder, simply boiled in water, makes a beautiful red. From the root of the black briony they obtain a fine salve for sores, and extract a rich yellow dye. The inner bark of the root of the sumach, roasted, and reduced to powder, is a good remedy for the ague, a tea-spoonful given be-

323

tween the hot and cold fit. They scrape the fine white powder from the large fungus that grows upon the bark of the pine, into whiskey, and take it for violent pains in the stomach. The taste of this powder strongly reminded me of quinine.

I have read much of the excellence of Indian cookery, but I never could bring myself to taste anything prepared in their dirty wigwams. I remember being highly amused in watching the preparation of a mess, which might have been called the Indian hotch-potch. It consisted of a strange mixture of fish, flesh, and fowl, all boiled together in the same vessel. Ducks, partridges, maskinonge, venison, and muskrats formed a part of this delectable compound. These were literally smothered in onions, potatoes, and turnips, which they had procured from me. They very hospitably offered me a dishful of the odious mixture, which the odour of the muskrat rendered everything but savoury; but I declined, simply stating that I was not hungry. My little boy tasted it, but quickly left the camp to conceal the effect it produced upon him.

Their method of broiling fish, however, is excellent. They take a fish, just fresh out of the water, cut out the entrails, and without removing the scales, wash it clean, dry it in a cloth, or in the grass, and cover it all over with clear hot ashes. When the flesh will part from the bone, they draw it out of the ashes, strip off the skin, and it is fit for the table of the most fastidious epicure.

The deplorable want of chastity that exists among the Indian women of this tribe seems to have been more the result of their intercourse with the settlers in the country, than from any previous disposition to this vice. The jealousy of their husbands has often been exercised in a terrible manner against the offending squaws; but this has not happened of late years. The men wink at these derelictions in their wives, and share with them the price of their shame.

The mixture of European blood adds greatly to the physical beauty of the half-race, but produces a sad falling-off from the original integrity of the Indian character. The half-caste is generally a lying, vicious rogue, possessing the worst qualities of both parents in an eminent degree. We have many of these half-Indians in the penitentiary, for crimes of the blackest dye.

The skill of the Indian in procuring his game, either by land or water, has been too well described by better writers than I could ever hope to be, to need any illustration from my pen, and I will close this long chapter with a droll anecdote which is told of a gentleman in this neighbourhood.

The early loss of his hair obliged Mr.—— to procure the substitute of a wig. This was such a good imitation of nature that none but his intimate friends and neighbours were aware of the fact.

It happened that he had had some quarrel with an Indian, which had to be settled in one of the petty courts. The case was decided in favour of Mr. ——, which so aggrieved the savage, who considered himself the injured party, that he sprang upon him with a furious yell, tomahawk in hand, with the intention of depriving him of his scalp. He twisted his hand in the locks which adorned the cranium of his adver-

325

sary, when—horror of horrors!—the treacherous wig came off in his hand. "Owgh! owgh!" exclaimed the affrighted savage, flinging it from him, and rushing from the court as if he had been bitten by a rattle-snake. His sudden exit was followed by peals of laughter from the crowd, while Mr. —— coolly pick-ed up his wig, and drily remarked that it had saved his head.

THE INDIAN FISHERMAN'S LIGHT.

The air is still, the night is dark,
  No ripple breaks the dusky tide;
From isle to isle the fisher's bark
  Like fairy meteor seems to glide;
Now lost in shade—now flashing bright
  On sleeping wave and forest tree;
We hail with joy the ruddy light,
Which far into the darksome night
  Shines red and cheerily!

With spear high poised, and steady hand,
  The centre of that fiery ray,
Behold the Indian fisher stand
  Prepared to strike the finny ray,
Hurrah! the shaft has sped below—
  Transfix'd the shining prize I see;
On swiftly darts the birch canoe;
Yon black rock shrouding from my view
  Its red light gleaming cheerily!

Around yon bluff, whose pine crest hides
  The noisy rapids from our sight,
Another bark—another glides—
  Red meteors of the murky night.
The bosom of the silent stream
  With mimic stars is dotted free;
The waves reflect the double gleam,
The tall woods lighten in the beam,
  Through darkness shining cheerily!

CHAPTER FOURTEEN
BURNING THE FALLOW

BURNING THE FALLOW

There is a hollow roaring in the air—
The hideous hissing of ten thousand flames,
That from the centre of yon sable cloud
Leap madly up, like serpents in the dark,
Shaking their arrowy tongues at Nature's heart.

IT IS NOT MY INTENTION TO GIVE A regular history of our residence in the bush, but merely to present to my readers such events as may serve to illustrate a life in the woods.

The winter and spring of 1834 had passed away. The latter was uncommonly cold and backward; so much so that we had a very heavy fall of snow upon the 14th and 15th of May, and several gentlemen drove down to Cobourg in a sleigh, the snow lying upon the ground to the depth of several inches.

A late, cold spring in Canada is generally succeeded by a burning hot summer; and the summer of '34 was the hottest I ever remember. No rain fell upon the earth for many weeks, till nature drooped and withered beneath one bright blaze of sunlight; and the ague and fever in the woods, and the cholera in the large towns and cities, spread death and sickness through the country.

Moodie had made during the winter a large clearing of twenty acres around the house. The progress of the workmen had been watched by me with the keenest interest. Every tree that reached the ground opened a wider gap in the dark wood, giving us a broader ray of light and a clearer glimpse of the blue sky. But when the dark cedar swamp fronting the house fell beneath the strokes of the axe, and we got a first view of the lake, my joy was complete; a new and beautiful object was now constantly before me,

329

which gave me the greatest pleasure. By night and day, in sunshine or in storm, water is always the most sublime feature in a landscape, and no view can be truly grand in which it is wanting. From a child, it always had the most powerful effect upon my mind, from the green ocean rolling in majesty, to the tinkling forest rill, hidden by the flowers and rushes along its banks. Half the solitude of my forest home vanished when the lake unveiled its bright face to the blue heavens, and I saw sun, and moon, and stars, and waving trees reflected there. I would sit for hours at the window as the shades of evening deepened round me, watching the massy foliage of the forests pictured in the waters, till fancy transported me back to England, and the songs of birds and the lowing of cattle were sounding in my ears. It was long, very long, before I could discipline my mind to learn and practise all the menial employments which are necessary in a good settler's wife.

The total absence of trees about the doors in all new settlements had always puzzled me, in a country where the intense heat of summer seems to demand all the shade that can be procured. My husband had left several beautiful rock-elms (the most picturesque tree in the country) near our dwelling, but, alas! the first high gale prostrated all my fine trees, and left our log cottage entirely exposed to the fierce rays of the sun.

The confusion of an uncleared fallow spread around us on every side. Huge trunks of trees and piles of brush gave a littered and uncomfortable appearance to the locality, and as the weather had been very dry for some weeks, I heard my husband daily talking with his choppers as to the expediency of firing the fallow. They still urged him to wait a little longer, until he could get a good breeze to carry the fire well through the brush.

Business called him suddenly to Toronto, but he left a strict charge with old Thomas and his sons, who were engaged in the job, by no means to attempt to burn it off until he returned, as he wished to be upon the premises himself, in case of any danger. He had previously burnt all the heaps immediately about the doors.

While he was absent, old Thomas and his second son fell sick with the ague, and went home to their own township, leaving John, a surly, obstinate young man, in charge of the shanty where they slept and kept their tools and provisions.

Monaghan I had sent to fetch up my three cows, as the children were languishing for milk, and Mary and I remained alone in the house with the little ones.

The day was sultry, and towards noon a strong wind sprang up that roared in the pine tops like the dashing of distant billows, but without in the least degree abating the heat. The children were lying listlessly upon the floor for coolness, and the girl and I were finishing sun-bonnets, when Mary suddenly exclaimed, "Bless us, mistress, what a smoke!" I ran immediately to the door, but was not able to distinguish ten yards before me. The swamp immediately below us was on fire, and the heavy wind was driving a dense black cloud of smoke directly towards us.

"What can this mean?" I cried. "Who can have set fire to the fallow?"

331

As I ceased speaking, John Thomas stood pale and trembling before me. "John, what is the meaning of this fire?"

"Oh, ma'am, I hope you will forgive me; it was I set fire to it, and I would give all I have in the world if I had not done it."

"What is the danger?"

"Oh, I'm terribly afear'd that we shall all be burnt up," said the fellow, beginning to whimper.

"Why did you run such a risk, and your master from home, and no one on the place to render the least assistance?"

"I did it for the best," blubbered the lad. "What shall we do?"

"Why, we must get out of it as fast as we can, and leave the house to its fate."

"We can't get out," said the man, in a low, hollow tone, which seemed the concentration of fear; "I would have got out of it if I could; but just step to the back door, ma'am, and see."

I had not felt the least alarm up to this minute; I had never seen a fallow burnt, but I had heard of it as a thing of such common occurrence that I had never connected with it any idea of danger. Judge, then, my surprise, my horror, when, on going to the back door, I saw that the fellow, to make sure of his work, had fired the field in fifty different places. Behind, before, on every side, we were surrounded by a wall of fire, burning furiously within a hundred yards of us, and cutting off all possibility of retreat; for could we have found an opening through the burning heaps, we could not have seen our way through the dense canopy of smoke; and, buried as we were in the heart of the forest, no one could discover our situation till we were beyond the reach of help.

I closed the door, and went back to the parlour. Fear was knocking loudly at my heart, for our utter helplessness annihilated all hope of being able to effect our escape—I felt stupefied. The girl sat upon the floor by the children, who, unconscious of the peril that hung over them, had both fallen asleep. She was silently weeping; while the fool who had caused the mischief was crying aloud.

A strange calm succeeded my first alarm; tears and lamentations were useless; a horrible death was impending over us, and yet I could not believe we were to die. I sat down upon the step of the door, and watched the awful scene in silence. The fire was raging in the cedar swamp immediately below the ridge on which the house stood, and it presented a spectacle truly appalling. From out the dense folds of a canopy of black smoke, the blackest I ever saw, leaped up continually red forks of lurid flame as high as the tree tops, igniting the branches of a group of tall pines that had been left standing for saw-logs.

A deep gloom blotted out the heavens from our sight. The air was filled with fiery particles which floated even to the door-step—while the crackling and roaring of the flames might have been heard at a great distance. Could we have reached the lake shore, where several canoes were moored at the landing, by launching out into the water we should have been in perfect safety; but, to attain this object, it was necessary to pass through this mimic hell; and not a bird could have flown over it with unscorched wings. There was no hope in that quarter, for, could we have escaped the flames, we should have been blinded and choked by the thick, black, resinous smoke.

The fierce wind drove the flames at the sides and back of the house up the clearing; and our passage to the road or to the forest, on the right and left, was entirely obstructed by a sea of flames. Our only ark of safety was the house, so long as it remained untouched by the consuming element. I turned to young Thomas and asked him how long he thought that would be.

"When the fire clears this little ridge in front, ma'am. The Lord have mercy upon us, then, or we must all go!"

"Cannot *you*, John, try and make your escape, and see what can be done for us and the poor children?"

My eye fell upon the sleeping angels, locked peacefully in each other's arms, and my tears flowed for the first time.

Mary, the servant-girl, looked piteously up in my face. The good, faithful creature had not uttered one word of complaint, but now she faltered forth—

"The dear, precious lambs!—Oh! such a death!"

I threw myself down upon the floor beside them, and pressed them alternately to my heart, while inwardly I thanked God that they were asleep, unconscious of danger, and unable by their childish cries to distract our attention from adopting any plan which might offer to effect their escape.

The heat soon became suffocating. We were parched with thirst, and there was not a drop of water in the house, and none to be procured nearer than the lake. I turned once more to the door, hoping that a passage might have been burnt through to the water. I saw nothing but a dense cloud of fire and smoke—could hear nothing but the crackling and roaring of the flames which were gaining so fast upon us that I felt their scorching breath in my face.

"Ah," thought I—and it was a most bitter thought —"what will my beloved husband say when he returns and finds that his poor Susy and his dear girls have perished in this miserable manner? But God can save us yet."

The thought had scarcely found a voice in my heart before the wind rose to a hurricane, scattering the flames on all sides into a tempest of burning billows. I buried my head in my apron, for I thought that our time was come, and that all was lost, when a most terrific crash of thunder burst over our heads, and, like the breaking of a water-spout, down came the rushing torrent of rain which had been pent up for so many weeks.

In a few minutes the chip-yard was all afloat, and the fire effectually checked. The storm which, un-noticed by us, had been gathering all day, and which was the only one of any note we had that summer, continued to rage all night, and before morning had quite subdued the cruel enemy whose approach we had viewed with such dread.

The imminent danger in which we had been placed struck me more forcibly after it was past than at the time, and both the girl and myself sank upon our knees and lifted up our hearts in humble thanksgiving to that God who had saved us by an act of His providence from an awful and sudden death. When all hope from human assistance was lost, His hand was mercifully stretched forth, making His strength more perfectly manifested in our weakness :—

> " He is their stay when earthly help is lost,
>   The light and anchor of the tempest-toss'd."

There was one person, unknown to us, who had watched the progress of that rash blaze, and had even brought his canoe to the landing, in the hope of getting us off. This was an Irish pensioner named Dunn, who had cleared a few acres on his government grant, and had built a shanty on the opposite shore of the lake.

"Faith, madam! an' I thought the captain was stark, staring mad to fire his fallow on such a windy day, and that blowing right from the lake to the house. When Old Wittals came in and towld us that the masther was not to the fore, but only one lad, an' the wife an' the childer at home,—thinks I, there's no time to be lost, or the crathurs will be burnt up intirely. We started instanther, but, by Jove! we were too late. The swamp was all in a blaze when we got to the landing, and you might as well have thried to get to heaven by passing through the other place."

This was the eloquent harangue with which the honest creature informed me the next morning of the efforts he had made to save us, and the interest he had felt in our critical situation. I felt comforted for my past anxiety, by knowing that one human being, however humble, had sympathized in our probable fate; while the providential manner in which we had been rescued will ever remain a theme of wonder and gratitude.

The next evening brought the return of my husband, who listened to the tale of our escape with a pale and disturbed countenance, not a little thankful to find his wife and children still in the land of the living.

For a long time after the burning of that fallow, it haunted me in my dreams. I would awake with a start, imagining myself fighting with the flames, and endeavouring to carry my little children through them to the top of the clearing, when invariably their garments and my own took fire just as I was within reach of a place of safety.

CHAPTER FIFTEEN
OUR LOGGING-BEE

CHAPTER XV.   OUR LOGGING-BEE

> There was a man in our town,
> In our town, in our town—
> There was a man in our town,
> He made a logging-bee;
> > And he bought lots of whiskey,
> > To make the loggers frisky—
> > To make the loggers frisky
> > At his logging-bee.
>
> The Devil sat on a log heap,
> A log heap, a log heap—
> A red hot burning log heap—
> A-grinning at the bee;
> > And there was lots of swearing,
> > Of boasting and of daring,
> > Of fighting and of tearing,
> > At that logging-bee.
>
> J. W. D. M.

A LOGGING-BEE FOLLOWED THE BURN-
ing of the fallow as a matter of course. In the bush,
where hands are few and labour commands an enormous rate of wages, these gatherings are considered
indispensable, and much has been written in their
praise; but to me, they present the most disgusting
picture of a bush life. They are noisy, riotous, drunk-
en meetings, often terminating in violent quarrels,
sometimes even in bloodshed. Accidents of the most
serious nature often occur, and very little work is
done when we consider the number of hands employed, and the great consumption of food and liquor.

I am certain, in our case, had we hired with the
money expended in providing for the bee, two or three
industrious, hard-working men, we should have got
through twice as much work, and have had it done
well, and have been the gainers in the end.

341

ROUGHING IT IN THE BUSH

People in the woods have a craze for giving and going to bees, and run to them with as much eagerness as a peasant runs to a racecourse or a fair; plenty of strong drink and excitement making the chief attraction of the bee.

In raising a house or barn, a bee may be looked upon as a necessary evil, but these gatherings are generally conducted in a more orderly manner than those for logging. Fewer hands are required, and they are generally under the control of the carpenter who puts up the frame, and if they get drunk during the raising they are liable to meet with very serious accidents.

Thirty-two men, gentle and simple, were invited to our bee, and the maid and I were engaged for two days preceding the important one, in baking and cooking for the entertainment of our guests. When I looked at the quantity of food we had prepared, I thought that it never could be all eaten, even by thirty-two men. It was a burning hot day towards the end of July when our loggers began to come in, and the "gee!" and "ha!" to encourage the oxen resounded on every side.

There was my brother S——, with his frank English face, a host in himself; Lieutenant —— in his blouse, wide white trousers, and red sash, his broad straw hat shading a dark manly face that would have been a splendid property for a bandit chief; the four gay, reckless, idle sons of ——, famous at any spree, but incapable of the least mental or physical exertion, who considered hunting and fishing as the sole aim and object of life. These young men rendered very little assistance themselves, and their example deterred others who were inclined to work.

There were the two R——s, who came to work and to make others work; my good brother-in-law, who had volunteered to be the Grog Boss, and a host of other settlers, among whom I recognized Moodie's old acquaintance, Dan Simpson, with his lank red hair and long freckled face; the Youngs, the hunters, with their round, black, curly heads and rich Irish brogue; poor C——, with his long, spare, consumptive figure, and thin, sickly face. Poor fellow, he has long since been gathered to his rest!

There was the ruffian squatter P——, from Clear Lake,—the dread of all honest men; the brutal M——, who treated oxen as if they had been logs, by beating them with handspikes; and there was Old Wittals, with his low forehead and long nose, a living witness of the truth of phrenology, if his large organ of acquisitiveness and his want of conscientiousness could be taken in evidence. Yet in spite of his derelictions from honesty, he was a hard-working, good-natured man, who, if he cheated you in a bargain, or took away some useful article in mistake from your homestead, never wronged his employer in his day's work.

He was a curious sample of cunning and simplicity —quite a character in his way—and the largest eater I ever chanced to know. From this ravenous propensity, for he ate his food like a famished wolf, he had obtained his singular name of "Wittals."

During the first year of his settlement in the bush, with a very large family to provide for, he had been often in want of food. One day he came to my brother with a very long face.

"Mr. S——, I'm no beggar, but I'd be obliged to you for a loaf of bread. I declare to you on my honour that I have not had a bit of wittals to dewour for two whole days."

He came to the right person with his petition. Mr. S—— with a liberal hand relieved his wants, but he entailed upon him the name of "Old Wittals," as part payment.

His daughter, who was a very pretty girl, had stolen a march upon him into the wood, with a lad whom he by no means regarded with a favourable eye. When she returned, the old man confronted her and her lover with this threat, which I suppose he considered "the most awful" punishment that he could devise—

"March into the house, Madam 'Ria (Maria); and if ever I catch you with that scamp again, I'll tie you up to a stump all day, and give you no wittals."

I was greatly amused by overhearing a dialogue between Old Wittals and one of his youngest sons, a sharp Yankeefied-looking boy, who had lost one of his eyes, but the remaining orb looked as if it could see all ways at once.

"I say, Sol, how came you to tell that tarnation tearing lie to Mr. S—— yesterday? Didn't you expect that you'd catch a good wallopping for the like of that? Lying may be excusable in a man, but 'tis a terrible bad habit in a boy."

"Lor', father, that worn't a lie. I told Mr. S——

NIGHT FISHING

our cow worn't in his peas. Nor more she wor; she was in his wheat.

"But she was in the peas all night, boy."

"That wor nothing to me; she worn't in just then. Sure I won't get a licking for that?"

"No, no, you are a good boy; but mind what I tell you, and don't bring me into a scrape with any of your real lies."

Prevarication, the worst of falsehoods, was a virtue in his eyes. So much for the old man's morality.

Monaghan was in his glory, prepared to work or fight, whichever should come uppermost; and there was old Thomas and his sons, the contractors for the clearing, to expedite whose movements the bee was called. Old Thomas was a very ambitious man in his way. Though he did not know A from B, he took it into his head that he had received a call from Heaven to convert the heathen in the wilderness; and every Sunday he held a meeting in our loggers' shanty, for the purpose of awakening sinners, and bringing over "Injun pagans" to the true faith. His method of accomplishing this object was very ingenious. He got his wife, Peggy— or "my Paggy," as he called her— to read aloud to him a text from the Bible, until he knew it by heart; and he had, as he said truly, "a good remembrancer," and never heard a striking sermon but he retained the most important passages, and retailed them second-hand to his bush audience.

I must say that I was not a little surprised at the old man's eloquence when I went one Sunday over to the shanty to hear him preach. Several wild young fellows had come on purpose to make fun of him; but his discourse, which was upon the text "We shall all meet before the judgment-seat of Christ," was rather too serious a subject to turn into a jest, with even old Thomas for the preacher. All went on very well until the old man gave out the hymn, and led off in such a loud, discordant voice, that my little Katie, who was standing between her father's knees, looked suddenly up and said, "Mamma, what a noise old Thomas makes!" This remark led to a much greater noise, and the young men, unable to restrain their long-suppressed laughter, ran tumultuously from the shanty.

I could have whipped the little elf; but small blame could be attached to a child of two years old, who had never heard a preacher, especially such a preacher as the old backwoodsman, in her life. Poor man! he was perfectly unconscious of the cause of the disturbance, and remarked to us after the service was over—

"Well, ma'am, did not we get on famously? Now, worn't that a *bootiful* discourse?"

"It was, indeed; much better than I expected."

"Yes, yes; I knew it would please you. It had quite an effect on those wild fellows. A few more such sermons will teach them good behaviour. Ah! the bush is a bad place for young men. The farther in the bush, say I, the farther from God, and the nearer to h—l. I told that wicked Captain L——, of Dummer, so the other Sunday; 'an',' says he, 'if you don't hold your confounded jaw, you old fool, I'll kick you there.' Now, ma'am—now, sir, was not that bad manners in a gentleman, to use such *appropriate epitaphs* to a humble servant of God, like I?"

OUR LOGGING-BEE

And thus the old man ran on for an hour, dilating upon his own merits and the sins of his neighbours.

There was John ——, from Smith-town, the most notorious swearer in the district; a man who esteemed himself clever, nor did he want for natural talent, but he had converted his mouth into such a sink of iniquity that it corrupted the whole man, and all the weak and thoughtless of his own sex who admitted him into their company. I had tried to convince John —— (for he often frequented the house under the pretence of borrowing books) of the great crime that he was constantly committing, and of the injurious effect it must produce upon his own family, but the mental disease had taken too deep a root to be so easily cured. Like a person labouring under some foul disease, he contaminated all he touched. Such men seem to make an ambitious display of their bad habits in such scenes, and if they afford a little help, they are sure to get intoxicated and make a row. There was my friend, old Ned Dunn, who had been so anxious to get us out of the burning fallow. There was a whole group of Dummer Pines: Levi, the little wiry, witty poacher; Cornish Bill, the honest-hearted old peasant, with his stalwart figure and uncouth dialect; and David, and Ned—all good men and true; and Malachi Chroak, a queer, withered-up, monkey-man, that seemed like some mischievous elf flitting from heap to heap to make work and fun for the rest; and many others were at that bee who have since found a rest in the wilderness: Adam T——, H——, J. M——, H. N——.

ROUGHING IT IN THE BUSH

These, at different times, lost their lives in those bright waters in which, on such occasions as these, they used to sport and frolic to refresh themselves during the noonday heat. Alas! how many, who were then young and in their prime, that river and its lakes have swept away!

Our men worked well until dinner-time, when, after washing in the lake, they all sat down to the rude board which I had prepared for them, loaded with the best fare that could be procured in the bush. Pea-soup, legs of pork, venison, eel, and raspberry pies, garnished with plenty of potatoes, and whiskey to wash them down, besides a large iron kettle of tea. To pour out the latter, and dispense it round, devolved upon me. My brother and his friends, who were all temperance men, and consequently the best workers in the field, kept me and the maid actively employed in replenishing their cups.

The dinner passed off tolerably well; some of the lower order of the Irish settlers were pretty far gone, but they committed no outrage upon our feelings by either swearing or bad language, a few harmless jokes alone circulating among them.

Some one was funning Old Wittalls for having eaten seven large cabbages at Mr. T——'s bee, a few days previous, and his son, Sol, thought himself, as in duty, bound to take up the cudgel for his father.

"Now, I guess that's a lie, anyhow. Fayther was sick that day, and I tell you he only ate five."

This announcement was followed by such an explosion of mirth that the boy looked fiercely round him, as if he could scarcely believe the fact that the whole party were laughing at him.

Malachi Chroak, who was good-naturedly drunk, had discovered an old pair of cracked bellows in a corner, which he placed under his arm, and applying his mouth to the pipe, and working his elbows to and fro, pretended that he was playing upon the bagpipes, every now and then letting the wind escape in a shrill squeak from this novel instrument.

"Arrah, ladies and jintlemen, do jist turn your swate little eyes upon me whilst I play for your iddifications the last illigant tune which my owld grandmother taught me. Och hone! 'tis a thousand pities that such musical owld crathers should be suffered to die, at all at all, to be poked away into a dirthy, dark hole, when their canthles shud be burnin' a-top of a bushel, givin' light to the house. An' then it is she that was the illigant dancer, stepping out so lively and frisky, just so."

And here he minced to and fro, affecting the airs of a fine lady. The supposititious bagpipe gave an uncertain, ominous howl, and he flung it down and started back with a ludicrous expression of alarm.

"Alive, is it ye are? Ye croaking owld divil, is that the tune you taught your son?"

"Och! my owld granny taught me, but now she is dead,
  That a dhrop of nate whiskey is good for the head;
  It would make a man spake when jist ready to dhie,
  If you doubt it—my boys!—I'd advise you to thry.
  Och! my owld granny sleeps with her head on a stone,—
  'Now, Malach, don't throuble the gals when I'm gone!'
  I thried to obey her; but, och, I am shure,
  There's no sorrow on earth that the angels can't cure.

Och! I took her advice—I'm a bachelor still;
And I dance, and I play, with such excellent skill,
      (*Taking up the bellows and beginning to dance.*)
That the dear little crathurs are striving in vain
Which first shall my hand or my fortin' obtain."

"Malach!" shouted a laughing group. "How was it that the old lady taught you to go a-courting?"

"Arrah, that's a sacret! I don't let out owld granny's sacrets," said Malachi, gracefully waving his head to and fro to the squeaking of the bellows; then suddenly tossing back the long, dangling black elf-locks that curled down the sides of his lank yellow cheeks, and winking knowingly with his comical little deep-seated black eyes, he burst out again—

"Wid the blarney I'd win the most dainty proud dame,
  No gal can resist the soft sound of that same;
  Wid the blarney, my boys—if you doubt it, go thry—
  But hand here the bottle, my whistle is dhry."

The men went back to the field, leaving Malachi to amuse those who remained in the house; and we certainly did laugh our fill at his odd capers and conceits.

Then he would insist upon marrying our maid. There could be no refusal—have her he would. The girl, to keep him quiet, laughingly promised that she would take him for her husband. This did not satisfy him. She must take her oath upon the Bible to that effect. Mary pretended that there was no Bible in the house, but he found an old spelling-book upon a shelf in the kitchen, and upon it he made her swear, and called upon me to bear witness to her oath, that she was now his betrothed, and he would go next day with her to the "praist." Poor Mary had reason to repent her frolic, for he stuck close to her the whole evening, tormenting her to fulfil her contract.

After the sun went down, the logging-band came in to supper, which was all ready for them. Those who remained sober ate the meal in peace, and quietly returned to their own homes, while the vicious and the drunken stayed to brawl and fight.

After having placed the supper on the table, I was so tired with the noise, and heat, and fatigue of the day, that I went to bed, leaving to Mary and my husband the care of the guests.

The little bed-chamber was only separated from the kitchen by a few thin boards; and, unfortunately for me and the girl, who was soon forced to retreat thither, we could hear all the wickedness and profanity going on in the next room. My husband, disgusted with the scene, soon left it, and retired into the parlour with the few of the loggers who, at that hour, remained sober. The house rang with the sound of unhallowed revelry, profane songs, and blasphemous swearing. It would have been no hard task to have imagined these miserable, degraded beings, fiends instead of men. How glad I was when they at last broke up and we were once more left in peace to collect the broken glasses and cups, and the scattered fragments of that hateful feast!

We were obliged to endure a second and a third repetition of this odious scene, before sixteen acres of land were rendered fit for the reception of our fall crop of wheat.

My hatred to these tumultuous, disorderly meetings was not in the least decreased by my husband being twice seriously hurt while attending them. After the second injury he received, he seldom went to them himself, but sent his oxen and servant in his place. In these odious gatherings, the sober, moral, and industrious man is more likely to suffer than the drunken and profane, as, during the delirium of drink, these men expose others to danger as well as themselves.

The conduct of many of the settlers, who considered themselves gentlemen, and would have been very much affronted to have been called otherwise, was often more reprehensible than that of the poor Irish emigrants, to whom they should have set an example of order and sobriety. The behaviour of these young men drew upon them the severe but just censures of the poorer class, whom they regarded in every way as their inferiors.

Just after the last of these logging-bees, we had to part with our good servant Mary, and just at a time when it was the heaviest loss to me. Her father, who had been a dairyman in the north of Ireland, an honest, industrious man, had brought out upwards of one hundred pounds to this country. With more wisdom than is generally exercised by Irish emigrants, instead of sinking all his means in buying a bush farm, he hired a very good farm in Cavan, stocked it with cattle, and returned to his old avocation. The services of his daughter, who was an excellent dairymaid, were required to take the management of the cows; and her brother brought a waggon and horses all the way from the front to take her home.

This event was perfectly unexpected, and left me

352

without a moment's notice to provide myself with another servant at a time when servants were not to be had, and I was perfectly unable to do the least thing. My little Addie was sick almost to death with the summer complaint, and the eldest still too young to take care of herself.

This was but the beginning of trouble.

Ague and lake fever had attacked our new settlement. The men in the shanty were all down with it, and my husband was confined to his bed on each alternate day, unable to raise hand or foot, and raving in the delirium of the fever.

In my sister and brother's families, scarcely a healthy person remained to attend upon the sick; and at Herriot's Falls, nine persons were stretched upon the floor of one log cabin, unable to help themselves or one another. After much difficulty, and only by offering enormous wages, I succeeded in procuring a nurse to attend upon me during my confinement. The woman had not been a day in the house before she was attacked by the same fever. In the midst of this confusion, and with my precious little Addie lying insensible on a pillow at the foot of my bed—expected every moment to breathe her last—on the night of the 26th of August the boy I had so ardently coveted was born. The next day, old Pine carried his wife (my nurse) away upon his back, and I was left to struggle through, in the best manner I could, with a sick husband, a sick child, and a new-born babe.

It was a melancholy season, one of severe mental and bodily suffering. Those who have drawn such agreeable pictures of a residence in the backwoods, never dwell upon the periods of sickness, when, far from medical advice, and often, as in my case, deprived of the assistance of friends by adverse circumstances, you are left to languish, unattended, upon the couch of pain.

The day that my husband was free of the fit, he did what he could for me and his poor sick babes, but, ill as he was, he was obliged to sow the wheat to enable the man to proceed with the drag, and was, therefore, necessarily absent in the field the greater part of the day.

I was very ill, yet, for hours at a time, I had no friendly voice to cheer me, to proffer me a drink of cold water, or to attend to the poor babe; and worse, still worse, there was no one to help that pale, marble child, who lay so cold and still, with "half-closed violet eyes," as if death had already chilled her young heart in his iron grasp.

There was not a breath of air in our close, burning bed-closet; and the weather was sultry beyond all that I have since experienced. How I wished that I could be transported to a hospital at home, to enjoy the common care that in such places is bestowed upon the sick! Bitter tears flowed continually over those young children. I had asked of Heaven a son, and there he lay helpless by the side of his almost equally helpless mother, who could not lift him up in her arms, or still his cries; while the pale, fair angel, with her golden curls, who had lately been the admiration of all who saw her, no longer recognized my voice, or was conscious of my presence. I felt that I could almost resign the long and eagerly-hoped-for son, to win one more smile from that sweet suffering creature. Often did I weep myself to sleep, and wake to weep again with renewed anguish.

And my poor little Katie, herself under three years of age, how patiently she bore the loss of my care and every comfort! How earnestly the dear thing strove to help me! She would sit on my sick-bed, and hold my hand, and ask me to look at her and speak to her; would inquire why Addie slept so long, and when she would wake again. Those innocent questions went like arrows to my heart.

Lieutenant ——, the husband of my dear Emilia, at length heard of my situation. His inestimable wife was from home, nursing her sick mother; but he sent his maid-servant up every day for a couple of hours, and the kind girl despatched a messenger nine miles through the woods to Dummer, to fetch her younger sister, a child of twelve years old.

Oh, how grateful I felt for these signal mercies! for my situation for nearly a week was one of the most pitiable that could be imagined. The sickness was so prevalent that help was not to be obtained for money; and without the assistance of that little girl, young as she was, it is more than probable that neither myself nor my children would ever have risen from that bed of sickness.

The conduct of our man Jacob, during this trying period, was marked with the greatest kindness and consideration. On the days that his master was confined to his bed with the fever, he used to place a vessel of cold water and a cup by his bedside, and then put his honest English face in at my door to know if he could make a cup of tea, or toast a bit of bread for the mistress, before he went into the field.

Katie was indebted to him for all her meals. He baked, and cooked, and churned, milked the cows, and made up the butter, as well and as carefully as the best female servant could have done. As to poor John Monaghan, he was down with the fever in the shanty, where four other men were all ill with the same terrible complaint.

I was obliged to leave my bed and endeavour to attend to the wants of my young family long before I was really able. When I made my first attempt to reach the parlour I was so weak, that, at every step, I felt as if I should pitch forward to the ground, which seemed to undulate beneath my feet, like the floor of a cabin in a storm at sea. My husband continued to suffer for many weeks with the ague; and when he was convalescent, all the children, even the poor babe, were seized with it; nor did it leave us till late in the spring of 1835.

CHAPTER SIXTEEN
A TRIP TO STONY LAKE

Oh, Nature! in thy ever-varying face,
   By rocky shore, or 'neath the forest tree,
What love divine, what matchless skill, I trace!
   My full warm heart responsive thrills to thee.
Yea, in my throbbing bosom's inmost core,
   Thou reign'st supreme; and, in thy sternest mood,
Thy votary bends in rapture to adore
   The Mighty Maker, who pronounced thee good.
Thy broad, majestic brow still bears His seal;
And when I cease to love, oh, may I cease to feel!

MY HUSBAND HAD LONG PROMISED ME a trip to Stony Lake, and in the summer of 1835, before the harvest commenced, he gave Mr. Y——, who kept the mill at the rapids below Clear Lake, notice of our intention, and the worthy old man and his family made due preparation for our reception. The little girls were to accompany us.

We were to start at sunrise, to avoid the heat of the day, to go up as far as Mr. Y——'s in our canoe, re-embark with his sons above the rapids in birch-bark canoes, go as far up the lake as we could accomplish by daylight, and return at night; the weather being very warm, and the moon at full. Before six o'clock we were all seated in the little craft, which spread her white sail to a smart breeze, and sped merrily over the blue waters. The lake on which our clearing stood was about a mile and a half in length, and about three-quarters of a mile in breadth; a mere pond when compared with the Bay of Quinté, Ontario, and the inland seas of Canada. But it was *our* lake, and, consequently, it had ten thousand beauties in our eyes which would scarcely have attracted the observation of a stranger.

At the head of the Katchawanook, the lake is di-

359

vided by a long neck of land that forms a small bay on the right-hand side, and a very brisk rapid on the left. The banks are formed of large masses of limestone; and the cardinal-flower and the tiger-lily seem to have taken an especial fancy to this spot, and to vie with each other in the display of their gorgeous colours.

It is an excellent place for fishing; the water is very deep close to the rocky pavement that forms the bank, and it has a pebbly bottom. Many a magic hour, at rosy dawn or evening grey, have I spent with my husband on this romantic spot, our canoe fastened to a bush, and ourselves intent upon ensnaring the black bass, a fish of excellent flavour that abounds in this place.

Our paddles soon carried us past the narrows and through the rapid water, the children sitting quietly at the bottom of the boat enchanted with all they heard and saw, begging papa to stop and gather water-lilies, or to catch one of the splendid butterflies that hovered over us; and often the little Addie darted her white hand into the water to grasp at the shadow of the gorgeous insects as they skimmed along the waves.

After passing the rapids, the river widened into another small lake, perfectly round in form, and having in its centre a tiny green island, in the midst of which stood, like a shattered monument of bygone storms, one blasted, black ash-tree.

The Indians call this lake *Bessikâkoon*, but I do not know the exact meaning of the word. Some say that it means "the Indian's grave," others "the lake of the one island." It is certain that an Indian girl is buried beneath that blighted tree; but I never could learn the particulars of her story, and perhaps there was no tale connected with it. She might have fallen a victim to disease during the wanderings of her tribe, and been buried on that spot; or she might have been drowned, which would account for her having been buried away from the rest of her people.

This little lake lies in the heart of the wilderness. There is but one clearing upon its shores, and that had been made by lumberers many years before; the place abounded with red cedar. A second growth of young timber had grown up in this spot, which was covered also with raspberry-bushes—several hundred acres being entirely overgrown with this delicious berry.

It was here annually that we used to come in large picnic parties, to collect this valuable fruit for our winter preserves, in defiance of black flies, mosquitoes, snakes, and even bears; all which have been encountered by berry-pickers upon this spot, as busy and as active as themselves, gathering an ample repast from Nature's bounteous lap.

And oh! what beautiful wild shrubs and flowers grew up in that neglected spot! Some of the happiest hours I spent in that bush are connected with reminiscences of " Irving's shanty," for so the raspberry-grounds were called. The clearing could not be seen from the shore. You had to scramble through a cedar swamp to reach the sloping ground which produced the berries.

The mill at the Clear Lake rapids was about three

miles distant from our own clearing; and after stemming another rapid, and passing between two beautiful wooded islands, the canoe rounded a point, and the rude structure was before us.

A wilder and more romantic spot than that which the old hunter had chosen for his homestead in the wilderness could scarcely be imagined. The waters of Clear Lake here empty themselves through a narrow, deep, rocky channel, not exceeding a quarter of a mile in length, and tumble over a limestone ridge of ten or twelve feet in height, which extends from one bank of the river to the other. The shores on either side are very steep, and the large oak-trees which have anchored their roots in every crevice of the rock, throw their fantastic arms far over the foaming waterfall, the deep green of their massy foliage forming a beautiful contrast with the white, flashing waters that foam over the chute at least fifty feet below the brow of the limestone rock. By a flight of steps cut in the banks we ascended to the platform above the river on which Mr. Y——'s house stood.

It was a large, rough-looking, log building, surrounded by barns and sheds of the same primitive material. The porch before the door was covered with hops, and the room of general resort, into which it immediately opened, was of large dimensions, the huge fireplace forming the most striking feature. On the hearth-stone, hot as was the weather, blazed a great fire, encumbered with all sorts of culinary apparatus, which, I am inclined to think, had been called into requisition for our sole benefit and accommodation.

The good folks had breakfasted long before we

started from home, but they would not hear of our proceeding to Stony Lake until after we had dined. It was only eight o'clock a.m., and we had still four hours to dinner, which gave us ample leisure to listen to the old man's stories, ramble round the premises, and observe all the striking features of the place.

Mr. Y—— was a Catholic, and the son of a respectable farmer from the south of Ireland. Some few years before, he had emigrated with a large family of seven sons and two daughters, and being fond of field sports, and greatly taken with the beauty of the locality in which he had pitched his tent in the wilderness, he determined to raise a mill upon the dam which Nature had provided to his hands, and wait patiently until the increasing immigration should settle the townships of Smith and Douro, render the property valuable, and bring plenty of grist to the mill.

He was not far wrong in his calculations, and though for the first few years he subsisted entirely by hunting, fishing, and raising what potatoes and wheat he required for his own family on the most fertile spots he could find on his barren lot, very little corn passed through the mill.

At the time we visited his place, he was driving a thriving trade, and all the wheat that was grown in the neighbourhood was brought by water to be ground at Y——'s mill.

He had lost his wife a few years after coming to the country; but his two daughters, Betty and Norah, were excellent housewives, and amply supplied her loss. From these amiable women we received a most kind and hearty welcome, and every comfort and luxury within their reach.

They appeared a most happy and contented family. The sons—a fine, hardy, independent set of fellows—were regarded by the old man with pride and affection. Many were his anecdotes of their prowess in hunting and fishing.

His method of giving them an aversion to strong drink while very young amused me greatly, but it is not every child that could have stood the test of his experiment.

"When they were little chaps, from five to six years of age, I made them very drunk," he said; "so drunk that it brought on severe headache and sickness, and this so disgusted them with liquor, that they never could abide the sight of it again. I have only one drunkard among the seven; and he was such a weak, puling crathur, that I dared not try the same game with him lest it should kill him. 'Tis his nature, I suppose, and he can't help it; but the truth is, that to make up for the sobriety of all the rest, he is killing himself with drink."

Norah gave us an account of her catching a deer that had got into the enclosure the day before.

"I went out," she said, "early in the morning, to milk the cows, and I saw a fine young buck struggling to get through the rail fence, in which having entangled his head and horns, I knew by the desperate efforts he was making to push aside the rails, that if I was not quick in getting hold of him, he would soon be gone."

"And did you dare to touch him?"

"If I had had Mat's gun I would have shot him, but

he would have made his escape long before I could run to the house for that, so I went boldly up to him and got him by the hind legs; and though he kicked and struggled dreadfully, I held on till Mat heard me call and ran to my help, and cut his throat with his hunting knife. So you see," she continued, with a good-natured laugh, "I can beat our hunters hollow —they hunt the deer, but I can catch a buck with my hands."

While we were chatting away, great were the preparations making by Miss Betty and a very handsome American woman who had recently come thither as a help. One little barefooted garsoon was shelling peas in an Indian basket, another was stringing currants into a yellow pie-dish, and a third was sent to the rapids with his rod and line to procure a dish of fresh fish to add to the long list of bush dainties that were preparing for our dinner.

It was in vain that I begged our kind entertainers not to put themselves to the least trouble on our account, telling them that we were now used to the woods, and contented with anything; they were determined to exhaust all their stores to furnish forth the entertainment. Nor can it be wondered at, that, with so many dishes to cook, and pies and custards to bake, instead of dining at twelve, it was past two o'clock before we were conducted to the dinner-table. I was vexed and disappointed at the delay, as I wanted to see all I could of the spot we were about to visit before night and darkness compelled us to return.

The feast was spread in a large outhouse, the table being formed of two broad deal boards laid together, and supported by rude carpenter's stools. A white linen cloth, a relic of better days, concealed these arrangements. The board was covered with an indescribable variety of roast and boiled, of fish, flesh, and fowl. My readers should see a table laid out in a wealthy Canadian farmer's house before they can have any idea of the profusion displayed in the entertainment of two visitors and their young children.

Besides venison, pork, chickens, ducks, and fish of several kinds, cooked in a variety of ways, there was a number of pumpkin, raspberry, cherry, and currant pies, with fresh butter and green cheese (as the new cream-cheese is called), maple molasses, preserves, and pickled cucumbers, besides tea and coffee—the latter, be it known, I had watched the American woman boiling in the *frying-pan*. It was a black-looking compound, and I did not attempt to discuss its merits. The vessel in which it had been prepared had prejudiced me, and rendered me very sceptical on that score.

We were all very hungry, having tasted nothing since five o'clock in the morning, and contrived, out of the variety of good things before us, to make an excellent dinner.

I was glad, however, when we rose to prosecute our intended trip up the lake. The old man, whose heart was now thoroughly warmed with whiskey, declared that he meant to make one of the party, and Betty, too, was to accompany us; her sister Norah kindly staying behind to take care of the children.

We followed a path along the top of the high ridge of limestone rock, until we had passed the falls and

the rapids above, when we found Pat and Mat Y——
waiting for us on the shore below, in two beautiful
new birch-bark canoes, which they had purchased
the day before from the Indians.

Miss Betty, Mat, and myself were safely stowed
into one, while the old miller, and his son Pat, and
my husband, embarked in the other, and our steers-
man pushed off into the middle of the deep and silent
stream, the shadow of the tall woods, towering so
many feet above us, casting an inky hue upon the
waters.

The scene was very imposing, and after paddling
for a few minutes in shade and silence, we suddenly
emerged into light and sunshine, and Clear Lake,
which gets its name from the unrivalled brightness of
its waters, spread out its azure mirror before us. The
Indians regard this sheet of water with peculiar reverence. It abounds in the finest sorts of fish, the
salmon-trout, the delicious white fish, maskinonge,
and black and white bass. There is no island in this
lake, no rice beds, nor stick nor stone to break its tranquil beauty, and, at the time we visited it, there was
but one clearing upon its shores.

The log hut of the squatter P——, commanding a
beautiful prospect up and down the lake, stood upon
a bold slope fronting the water; all the rest was
unbroken forest.

We had proceeded about a mile on our pleasant
voyage when our attention was attracted by a singular natural phenomenon, which Mat Y—— called
the battery.

On the right side of the shore rose a steep, perpendicular wall of limestone, that had the appearance of having been laid by the hand of man, so smooth and even was its surface. After attaining a height of about fifty feet, a natural platform of eight or ten yards broke the perpendicular line of the rock, when another wall, like the first, rose to a considerable height, terminating in a second and third platform of the same description.

Fire, at some distant period, had run over these singularly beautiful terraces, and a second growth of poplars and balm-of-gileads, relieved, by their tender green and light, airy foliage, the sombre indigo tint of the heavy pines that nodded like the plumes of a funeral-hearse over the fair young dwellers on the rock.

The water is forty feet deep at the base of this precipice, which is washed by the waves. After we had passed the battery, Mat Y—— turned to me and said, "That is a famous place for bears; many a bear have I shot among those rocks."

This led to a long discussion on the wild beasts of the country.

"I do not think that there is much danger to be apprehended from them," said he; "but I once had an ugly adventure with a wolf, two winters ago, on this lake."

I was all curiosity to hear the story, which sounded doubly interesting told on the very spot, and while gliding over those lovely waters.

"We were lumbering at the head of Stony Lake, about eight miles from here, my four brothers, myself, and several other hands. The winter was long and

368

severe; although it was the first week in March, there was not the least appearance of a thaw, and the ice on these lakes was firm as ever. I had been sent home to fetch a yoke of oxen to draw the saw-logs down to the water, our chopping being all completed and the logs ready for rafting.

"I did not think it necessary to encumber myself with my rifle, and was, therefore, provided with no weapon of defence but the long gad I used to urge on the cattle. It was about four o'clock in the afternoon when I rounded Sandy Point, that long point which is about a mile ahead of us on the left shore, when I first discovered that I was followed, but at a great distance, by a large wolf. At first I thought little of the circumstance, beyond a passing wish that I had brought my gun. I knew that he would not attack me before dark, and it was still two long hours to sundown; so I whistled, and urged on my oxen, and soon forgot the wolf—when, on stopping to repair a little damage to the peg of the yoke, I was surprised to find him close at my heels. I turned, and ran towards him, shouting as loud as I could, when he slunk back, but showed no inclination to make off. Knowing that he must have companions near, by his boldness, I shouted as loud as I could, hoping that my cries might be heard by my brothers, who would imagine that the oxen had got into the ice and would come to my assistance. I was now winding my way through the islands in Stony Lake; the sun was setting red before me, and I had still three miles of my journey to accomplish. The wolf had become so impudent that I kept him off by pelting him

2 A

with snowballs; and once he came so near that I struck him with the gad. I now began to be seriously alarmed, and, from time to time, shouted with all my strength; and you may imagine my joy when these cries were answered by the report of a gun. My brothers had heard me, and the discharge of a gun, for a moment, seemed to daunt the wolf. He uttered a long howl, which was answered by the cries of a large pack of the dirty brutes from the wood. It was only just light enough to distinguish objects, and I had to stop and face my enemy, to keep him at bay.

"I saw the skeleton forms of half a dozen more of them slinking among the bushes that skirted a low island; and tired and cold, I gave myself and the oxen up for lost, when I felt the ice tremble on which I stood, and heard men running at a little distance. 'Fire your guns!' I cried out, as loud as I could. My order was obeyed, and such a yelling and howling immediately filled the whole forest as would have chilled your very heart. The thievish varmints instantly fled away into the bush.

"I never felt the least fear of wolves until that night; but when they meet in large bands, like cowardly dogs, they trust to their numbers and grow fierce. If you meet with one wolf, you may be certain that the whole pack is at no great distance."

We were fast approaching Sandy Point, a long white ridge of sand running half across the lake, and though only covered with scattered groups of scrubby trees and brush, it effectually screened Stony Lake from our view. There were so many beautiful flowers peeping through the dwarf, green bushes, that wishing to inspect them nearer, Mat kindly ran the canoe ashore, and told me that he would show me a pretty spot where an Indian, who had been drowned during a storm off that point, was buried. I immediately recalled the story of Susan Moore's father, but Mat thought that he was interred upon one of the islands farther up.

"It is strange," he said, "that they are such bad swimmers. The Indian, though unrivalled by us whites in the use of the paddle, is an animal that does not take readily to the water, and those among them who can swim seldom use it as a recreation."

Pushing our way through the bushes, we came to a small opening in the underwood, so thickly grown over with wild Canadian roses in full blossom, that the air was impregnated with a delightful odour. In the centre of this bed of sweets rose the humble mound that protected the bones of the red man from the ravenous jaws of the wolf and the wild cat. It was completely covered with stones, and from among the crevices had sprung a tuft of blue harebells, waving as wild and free as if they grew among the bonny red heather on the glorious hills of the North or shook their tiny bells to the breeze on the broom-encircled commons of England.

The harebell had always from a child been with me a favourite flower; and the first sight of it in Canada, growing upon that lonely grave, so flooded my soul with remembrances of the past, that in spite of myself the tears poured freely from my eyes. There are moments when it is impossible to repress those outgushings of the heart—

ROUGHING IT IN THE BUSH

"Those flood-gates of the soul that sever,
In passion's tide to part for ever."

If Mat and his sister wondered at my tears, they must have suspected the cause, for they walked to a little distance and left me to the indulgence of my feelings. I gathered those flowers and placed them in my bosom, and kept them for many a day; they had become holy, when connected with sacred home recollections, and the never-dying affections of the heart which the sight of them recalled.

A shout from our companions in the other canoe made us retrace our steps to the shore. They had already rounded the point, and were wondering at our absence.

Oh, what a magnificent scene of wild and lonely grandeur burst upon us as we swept round the little peninsula, and the whole majesty of Stony Lake broke upon us at once, another Lake of the Thousand Isles in miniature, and in the heart of the wilderness! Imagine a large sheet of water, some fifteen miles in breadth and twenty-five in length, taken up by islands of every size and shape, from the lofty naked rock of red granite to the rounded hill covered with oak-trees to its summit, while others were level with the waters, and of a rich emerald green, only fringed with a growth of aquatic shrubs and flowers. Never did my eyes rest on a more lovely or beautiful scene. Not a vestige of man or of his works was there. The setting sun, that cast such a gorgeous flood of light upon this exquisite panorama, bringing out some of these lofty islands in strong relief, and casting others into intense shade, shed no cheery beam upon church spire or cottage pane. We beheld the landscape, savage and grand in its primeval beauty.

As we floated among the channels between those rocky picturesque isles, I asked Mat how many of them there were.

"I never could succeed," he said, "in counting them all. One Sunday, Pat and I spent a whole day in going from one to the other, to try and make out how many there were, but we could only count up to one hundred and forty before we gave up the task in despair. There are a great many of them, more than any one would think—and, what is very singular, the channel between them is very deep, sometimes above forty feet, which accounts for the few rapids to be found in this lake. It is a glorious place for hunting, and the waters, undisturbed by steam-boats, abound in all sorts of fish.

"Most of these islands are covered with huckleberries, while grapes, high and low-bush cranberries, blackberries, wild cherries, gooseberries, and several sorts of wild currants grow here in profusion. There is one island among these groups (but I never could light upon the identical one) where the Indians yearly gather their wampum-grass. They come here to collect the best birch-bark for their canoes, and to gather wild onions. In short, from the game, fish, and fruit which they collect among the islands of this lake, they chiefly depend for their subsistence. They are very jealous of the settlers in the country coming to hunt and fish here, and tell many stories of wild beasts and rattlesnakes that abound along its shores; but I, who have frequented the lake for years, was never disturbed by anything beyond the adventure with the wolf, which I have already told you. The banks of this lake are all steep and rocky, and the land along the shore is barren and totally unfit for cultivation.

"Had we time to run up a few miles farther, I could have showed you some places well worth a journey to look at; but the sun is already down, and it will be dark before we get back to the mill."

The other canoe now floated alongside, and Pat agreed with his brother that it was high time to return. With reluctance I turned from this strangely fascinating scene. As we passed under one bold rocky island, Mat said laughingly, "That is Mount Rascal."

"How did it obtain that name?"

"Oh, we were out here berrying with our good priest, Mr. B——. This island promised so fair, that we landed upon it, and, after searching for an hour, we returned to the boat without a single berry, upon which Mr. B—— named it 'Mount Rascal.'"

The island was so beautiful, it did not deserve the name, and I christened it "Oak Hill," from the abundance of oak-trees which clothed its steep sides. The wood of this oak is so heavy and hard that it will not float in the water, and it is in great request for the runners of lumber-sleighs, which have to pass over very bad roads.

The breeze, which had rendered our sail up the lakes so expeditious and refreshing, had stiffened into a pretty high wind, which was dead against us all the way down. Betty now knelt in the bow and assisted her brother, squaw fashion, in paddling the canoe; but, in spite of all their united exertions, it was past ten o'clock before we reached the mill. The good Norah was waiting tea for us. She had given the children their supper four hours ago, and the little creatures, tired with using their feet all day, were sound asleep upon her bed.

After supper, several Irish songs were sung, while Pat played upon the fiddle, and Betty and Mat enlivened the company with an Irish jig.

It was midnight when the children were placed on my cloak at the bottom of the canoe, and we bade adieu to this hospitable family. The wind being dead against us, we were obliged to dispense with the sail, and take to our paddles. The moonlight was as bright as day, the air warm and balmy; and the aromatic, resinous smell exuded by the heat from the balm-of-gilead and the pine-trees of the forest, added greatly to our sense of enjoyment as we floated past scenes so wild and lonely—isles that assumed a mysterious look and character in that witching hour. In moments like these I ceased to regret my separation from my native land, and, filled with the love of Nature, my heart forgot for the time the love of home. The very spirit of peace seemed to brood over the waters, which were broken into a thousand ripples of light by every breeze that stirred the rice blossoms, or whispered through the shivering aspen-trees. The far-off roar of the rapids, softened by distance, and the long, mournful cry of the night owl, alone broke the silence of the night. Amid these lonely wilds the soul draws nearer to God, and is filled to overflowing by the overwhelming sense of His presence.

It was two o'clock in the morning when we fastened the canoe to the landing, and Moodie carried up the children to the house. I found the girl still up with my boy, who had been very restless during our absence. My heart reproached me, as I caught him to my breast, for leaving him so long; in a few minutes he was consoled for past sorrows, and sleeping sweetly in my arms.

A CANADIAN SONG.

Come, launch the light canoe;
　The breeze is fresh and strong:
The summer skies are blue,
　And 'tis joy to float along;
　　Away o'er the waters,
　　The bright-glancing waters,
　　The many-voiced waters,
　As they dance in light and song.

When the great Creator spoke,
　On the long unmeasured night,
The living day-spring broke,
　And the waters own'd His might;
　　The voice of many waters,
　　Of glad, rejoicing waters,
　　Of living, leaping waters,
　First hailed the dawn of light.

Where foaming billows glide
　To earth's remotest bound;
The rushing ocean tide
　Rolls on the solemn sound;
　　God's voice is in the waters;
　　The deep, mysterious waters,
　　The sleepless, dashing waters,
　Still breathe its tones around.

CHAPTER SIXTEEN
THE "OULD DHRAGOON"

IT IS DELIGHTFUL TO OBSERVE A FEEL-
ing of contentment under adverse circumstances.
We may smile at the rude and clumsy attempts of
the remote and isolated backwoodsman to attain
something like comfort, but happy he who, with the
buoyant spirits of the light-hearted Irishman, con-
trives to make himself happy even when all others
would be miserable.

A certain degree of dissatisfaction with our present circumstances is necessary to stimulate us to
exertion, and thus to enable us to secure future
comfort; but where the delusive prospect of future
happiness is too remote for any reasonable hope of
ultimate attainment, then, surely it is true wisdom
to make the most of the present and to cultivate a
spirit of happy contentment with the lot assigned to
us by Providence.

"Ould Simpson," or the "Ould Dhragoon," as he
was generally called, was a good sample of this
happy character; and I shall proceed to give the
reader a sketch of his history, and a description of
his establishment. He was one of that unfortunate
class of discharged soldiers who are tempted to sell
their pensions often far below their true value, for
the sake of getting a lot of land in some remote
settlement, where it is only rendered valuable by the
labour of the settler, and where they will have the
unenviable privilege of expending the last remains
of their strength in clearing a patch of land for the
benefit of some grasping storekeeper who has given
them credit while engaged in the work.

The old dragoon had fixed his abode on the verge

379

of an extensive beaver-meadow, which was considered a sort of natural curiosity in the neighbourhood;
and where he managed by cutting the rank grass in
the summer time, to support several cows, which afforded the chief subsistence of his family. He had
also managed, with the assistance of his devoted partner, Judy, to clear a few acres of poor rocky land on
the sloping margin of the level meadow, which he
planted year after year with potatoes. Scattered over
this small clearing, here and there, might be seen the
but-end of some half-burnt hemlock tree, which had
escaped the general combustion of the log heaps, and
now formed a striking contrast to the white limestone rocks which showed their rounded surfaces a-
bove the meagre soil.

The "ould dhragoon" seemed, moreover, to have
some taste for the picturesque, and by way of ornament, had left standing sundry tall pines and hem-
locks neatly girdled to destroy their foliage, the shade
of which would have been detrimental to the "blessed
praties" which he designed to grow in his clearing,
but which, in the meantime, like martyrs at the stake,
stretched their naked branches imploringly towards
the smiling heavens. As he was a kind of hermit,
from choice, and far removed from other settlers,
whose assistance is so necessary in new settlements,
old Simpson was compelled to resort to the most
extraordinary contrivances while clearing his land.
Thus, after felling the trees, instead of chopping them
into lengths, for the purpose of facilitating the operation of piling them preparatory to burning, which
would have cost him too much labour, he resorted

to the practice of "niggering," as it is called; which is simply laying light pieces of round timber across the trunks of the trees, and setting fire to them at the point of contact, by which means the trees are slowly burned through.

It was while busily engaged in this interesting operation that I first became acquainted with the subject of this sketch.

Some twenty or thirty little fires were burning briskly in different parts of the blackened field, and the old fellow was watching the slow progress of his silent "niggers," and replacing them from time to time as they smouldered away. After threading my way among the uncouth logs, blazing and smoking in all directions, I encountered the old man, attired in an old hood, or bonnet, of his wife Judy, with his patched canvas trousers rolled up to his knees, one foot bare, and the other furnished with an old boot, which from its appearance had once belonged to some more aristocratic foot. His person was long, straight, and sinewy, and there was a light springiness and elasticity in his step which would have suited a younger man, as he skipped along with a long handspike over his shoulder. He was singing a stave from the "Enniskillen Dragoon" when I came up with him.

"With his silver-mounted pistols, and his long carbine,
Long life to the brave Inniskillen dragoon."

His face would have been one of the most lugubrious imaginable, with his long, tangled hair hanging confusedly over it, in a manner which has been happily compared to a "bewitched haystack," had it not been for a certain humorous twitch or convulsive movement which affected one side of his countenance whenever any droll idea passed through his mind. It was with a twitch of this kind, and a certain indescribable twinkle of his somewhat melancholy eye, as he seemed intuitively to form a hasty conception of the oddity of his appearance to a stranger unused to the bush, that he welcomed me to his clearing. He instantly threw down his handspike, and leaving his "niggers" to finish their work at their leisure, insisted on our going to his house to get something to drink.

On the way, I explained to him the object of my visit, which was to mark out, or "blaze," the sidelines of a lot of land I had received as part of a military grant, immediately adjoining the beaver-meadow, and I asked him to accompany me, as he was well acquainted with the different lots.

"Och! by all manner of manes, and welcome; the dhevil a foot of the way but I know as well as my own clearing; but come into the house, and get a dhrink of milk, an' a bite of bread an' butther, for sorrow a dhrop of the whiskey has crossed my teeth for the last month; an' it's but poor intertainment for man or baste I can offer you, but shure you're heartily welcome."

The precincts of the homestead were divided and subdivided into an infinity of enclosures of all shapes and sizes. The outer enclosure was a bush fence, formed of trees felled on each other in a row, and the gaps filled up with brushwood. There was a large gate, swung with wooden hinges, and a wooden latch to fasten it; the smaller enclosures were made with round poles tied together with bark. The house was of the rudest description of "shanty," with hollowed basswood logs, fitting into each other somewhat in the manner of tiles for a roof, instead of shingles. No iron was to be seen, in the absence of which there were plenty of leathern hinges, wooden latches for locks and bark-strings instead of nails. There was a large fireplace at one end of the shanty, with a chimney, constructed of split laths, plastered with a mixture of clay and cowdung. As for windows, these were luxuries which could well be dispensed with; the open door was an excellent substitute for them in the daytime, and at night none were required. When I ventured to object to this arrangement, that he would have to keep the door shut in the winter time, the old man replied, in the style so characteristic of his country, "Shure it will be time enough to think of that when the could weather sets in." Everything about the house wore a Robinson Crusoe aspect, and though there was not any appearance of original plan or foresight, there was no lack of ingenious contrivance to meet every want as it arose.

Judy dropped us a low curtsey as we entered, which was followed by a similar compliment from a stout girl of twelve, and two or three more of the children, who all seemed to share the pleasure of their parents in receiving strangers in their unpretending tenement. Many were the apologies that poor Judy offered for the homely cheer she furnished us, and great was her delight at the notice we took of the "childher." She set little Biddy, who was the pride of her heart, to reading the Bible; and she took down a curious machine from a shelf, which she had "conthrived out

383

of her own head," as she said, for teaching the children to read. This was a flat box, or frame, filled with sand, which saved paper, pens, and ink. Poor Judy had evidently seen better days, but, with a humble and contented spirit, she blessed God for the food and scanty raiment their labour afforded them. Her only sorrow was the want of "idication" for the children.

She would have told us a long story about her trials and sufferings, before they had attained their present comparative comfort and independence, but, as we had a tedious scramble before us, through cedar swamps, beaver-meadows, and piny ridges, the "ould dhragoon" cut her short, and we straightway started on our toilsome journey.

Simpson, in spite of a certain dash of melancholy in his composition, was one of those happy fellows of the "light heart and thin pair of breeches" school, who, when they meet with difficulty or misfortune, never stop to measure its dimensions, but hold in their breath and run lightly over, as in crossing a bog, where to stand still is to sink.

Off, then, we went, with the "ould dhragoon" skipping and bounding on before us, over fallen trees and mossy rocks; now ducking under the low, tangled branches of the white cedar, then carefully piloting us along rotten logs covered with green moss, to save us from the discomfort of wet feet. All this time he still kept one of his feet safely ensconced in the boot, while the other seemed to luxuriate in the water, as if there was something amphibious in his nature.

We soon reached the beaver-meadow, which extended two or three miles; sometimes contracting into a narrow gorge between the wooded heights, then spreading out again into an ample field of verdure, and presenting everywhere the same unvarying level surface, surrounded with rising grounds, covered with the dense unbroken forest, as if its surface had formerly been covered by the waters of a lake, which in all probability has been the case at some not very remote period. In many places the meadow was so wet that it required a very large share of faith to support us in passing over its surface; but our friend, the dragoon, soon brought us safe through all dangers to a deep ditch, which he had dug to carry off the superfluous water from the part of the meadow which he owned. When we had obtained firm footing on the opposite side, we sat down to rest ourselves before commencing the operation of "blazing," or marking the trees with our axes, along the side-line of my lot. Here the mystery of the boot was explained. Simpson very coolly took it off from the hitherto favoured foot and drew it on the other.

He was not a bit ashamed of his poverty, and candidly owned that this was the only boot he possessed, and he was desirous of giving each of his feet fair play.

Nearly the whole day was occupied in completing our job, in which the "dhragoon" assisted us, with the most hearty good-will, enlivening us with his inexhaustible fund of good-humour and drollery. It was nearly dark when we got back to his "shanty," where the kind-hearted Judy was preparing a huge pot of potatoes and other "combustibles," as Simpson called the other eatables, for our entertainment.

2B

ROUGHING IT IN THE BUSH

Previous to starting on our surveying expedition, we had observed Judy very earnestly giving some important instructions to one of her little boys, on whom she seemed to be most seriously impressing the necessity of using the utmost diligence. The happy contentment which now beamed in poor Judy's still comely countenance bespoke the success of the messenger. She could not "call up spirits from the vasty deep" of the cellar, but she had procured some whiskey from her next-door neighbour—some five or six miles off; and there it stood somewhat ostentatiously on the table in a "greybeard," with a "corn cob," or ear of Indian corn stripped of its grain, for a cork, smiling most benevolently on the family circle, and looking a hundred welcomes to the strangers.

An indescribably enlivening influence seemed to exude from every pore of that homely earthen vessel, diffusing mirth and good-humour in all directions. The old man jumped and danced about on the rough floor of the "shanty"; and the children sat giggling and nudging each other in a corner, casting a timid look, from time to time, at their mother, for fear she might check them for being "over bould."

"Is it crazy ye are intirely, ye ould omadhawn!" said Judy, whose notions of propriety were somewhat shocked with the undignified levity of her partner; "the likes of you I never see'd; ye are too foolidge intirely. Have done now wid your diviltries, and set the stools for the gintlemens, while I get the supper for yees."

Our plentiful though homely meal was soon discussed, for hunger, like a good conscience, can laugh

THE "OULD DHRAGOON"

at luxury; and the "greybeard" made its appearance, with the usual accompaniments of hot water and maple sugar, which Judy had scraped from the cake, and placed in a saucer on the table before us.

The "ould dhragoon," despising his wife's admonitions, gave way freely to his feelings, and knew no bounds to his hilarity. He laughed and joked, and sang snatches of old songs picked up in the course of his service at home and abroad. At length Judy, who looked on him as a "raal janius," begged him to "sing the gintlemens the song he made when he first came to the counthry." Of course we ardently seconded the motion, and nothing loth, the old man, throwing himself back on his stool, and stretching out his long neck, poured forth the following ditty, with which I shall conclude my hasty sketch of the "ould dhragoon":—

Och! it's here I'm intirely continted,
   In the wild woods of swate 'Mericay;
God's blessing on him that invinted
   Big ships for our crossing the say!

Here praties grow bigger nor turnips;
   And though cruel hard is our work,
In ould Ireland we'd nothing but praties,
   But here we have praties and pork.

I live on the banks of a meadow,
   Now see that my maning you take;
It bates all the bogs of ould Ireland—
   Six months in the year it's a lake.

Bad luck to the beavers that dammed it,
   I wish them all kilt for their pains;
For shure though the craters are clever,
   'Tis sartin they've drown'd my domains.

ROUGHING IT IN THE BUSH

I've built a log hut of the timber
   That grows on my charmin' estate;
And an illigant root-house erected,
   Just facing the front of my gate.

And I've made me an illigant pig-sty,
   Well litter'd with straw and wid hay;
And it's there, free from noise of the chilther,
   I sleep in the heat of the day.

It's there I'm intirely at aise, Sir,
   And enjoy all the comforts of home;
I stretch out my legs as I plase, sir,
   And dhrame of the pleasures to come.

Shure, it's pleasant to hear the frogs croakin',
   When the sun's going down in the sky,
And my Judy sits quietly smokin'
   While the praties are boil'd till they're dhry.

Och! thin, if you love indepindence,
   And have money your passage to pay,
You must quit the ould counthry intirely,
   And start in the middle of May.

J. W. D. M.

CHAPTER EIGHTEEN
DISAPPOINTED HOPES

Stern Disappointment, in thy iron grasp
The soul lies stricken.   So the timid deer,
Who feels the foul fangs of the felon wolf
Clench'd in his throat, grown desperate for life,
Turns on his foes, and battles with the fate
That hems him in—and only yields in death.

THE SUMMER OF '35 WAS VERY WET; A circumstance so unusual in Canada that I have seen no season like it during my sojourn in the country. Our wheat crop promised to be both excellent and abundant; and the clearing and seeding sixteen acres, one way or another, had cost us more than fifty pounds; still we hoped to realize something handsome by the sale of the produce; and, as far as appearances went, all looked fair. The rain commenced about a week before the crop was fit for the sickle, and from that time until nearly the end of September was a mere succession of thunder showers; days of intense heat, succeeded by floods of rain. Our fine crop shared the fate of all other fine crops in the country; it was totally spoiled; the wheat grew in the sheaf, and we could scarcely save enough to supply us with bad sickly bread; the rest was exchanged at the distillery for whisky, which was the only produce which could be obtained for it. The storekeepers would not look at it, or give either money or goods for such a damaged article.

My husband and I had worked hard in the field; it was the first time I had ever tried my hand at field-labour, but our ready money was exhausted, and the steam-boat stock had not paid us one farthing; we could not hire, and there was no help for it. I had a hard struggle with my pride before I would consent to render the least assistance on the farm, but reflection convinced me that I was wrong—that Providence had placed me in a situation where I was called upon to work—that it was not only my duty to obey that call, but to exert myself to the utmost to assist my husband and help to maintain my family.

Ah, poverty! thou art a hard taskmaster, but in thy soul-ennobling school I have received more god-like lessons, have learned more sublime truths, than ever I acquired in the smooth highways of the world!

The independent in soul can rise above the seeming disgrace of poverty, and hold fast their integrity, in defiance of the world and its selfish and unwise maxims. To them, no labour is too great, no trial too severe; they will unflinchingly exert every faculty of mind and body before they will submit to become a burden to others.

The misfortunes that now crowded upon us were the result of no misconduct or extravagance on our part, but arose out of circumstances which we could not avert nor control. Finding too late the error into which we had fallen, in suffering ourselves to be cajoled and plundered out of our property by interested speculators, we braced our minds to bear the worst, and determined to meet our difficulties calmly and firmly, nor suffer our spirits to sink under calamities which energy and industry might eventually repair. Having once come to this resolution, we cheerfully shared together the labours of the field. One in heart and purpose, we dared remain true to

A JOURNEY TO THE WOODS

ourselves, true to our high destiny as immortal creatures, in our conflict with temporal and physical wants.

We found that manual toil, however distasteful to
those unaccustomed to it, was not after all such a
dreadful hardship; that the wilderness was not without its rose, the hard face of poverty without its smile.
If we occasionally suffered severe pain, we as often
experienced great pleasure, and I have contemplated
a well-hoed ridge of potatoes on that bush farm with
as much delight as in years long past I had experienced in examining a fine painting in some well-
appointed drawing-room.

I can now look back with calm thankfulness on
that long period of trial and exertion—with thankfulness that the dark clouds that hung over us, threat-
ening to blot us from existence, when they did burst
upon us, were full of blessings. When our situation
appeared perfectly desperate, then were we on the
threshold of a new state of things, which was born
out of that very distress.

In order more fully to illustrate the necessity of
a perfect and childlike reliance upon the mercies of
God—who, I most firmly believe, never deserts those
who have placed their trust in Him—I will give a
brief sketch of our lives during the years 1836 and
1837.

Still confidently expecting to realize an income,
however small, from the steam-boat stock, we had involved ourselves considerably in debt, in order to pay
our servants and obtain the common necessaries of
life; and we owed a large sum to two Englishmen
in Dummer, for clearing ten more acres upon the

farm. Our utter inability to meet these demands weighed very heavily upon my husband's mind. All superfluities in the way of groceries were now given up, and we were compelled to rest satisfied upon the produce of the farm. Milk, bread, and potatoes during the summer became our chief, and often, for months, our only fare. As to tea and sugar, they were luxuries we would not think of, although I missed the tea very much; we rang the changes upon peppermint and sage, taking the one herb at our breakfast, the other at our tea, until I found an excellent substitute for both in the root of the dandelion.

The first year we came to this country, I met with an account of dandelion coffee, published in the *New York Albion*, given by a Dr. Harrison, of Edinburgh, who earnestly recommended it as an article of general use.

"It possesses," he says, "all the fine flavour and exhilarating properties of coffee, without any of its deleterious effects. The plant being of a soporific nature, the coffee made from it when drunk at night produces a tendency to sleep, instead of exciting wakefulness, and may be safely used as a cheap and wholesome substitute for the Arabian berry, being equal in substance and flavour to the best Mocha coffee."

I was much struck with this paragraph at the time, and for several years felt a great inclination to try the Doctor's coffee; but something or other always came in the way, and it was put off till another opportunity. During the fall of '35, I was assisting my husband in taking up a crop of potatoes in the field, and observing a vast number of fine dandelion roots among the potatoes, it brought the dandelion coffee back to my memory, and I determined to try some for our supper. Without saying anything to my husband, I threw aside some of the roots, and when we left work, collecting a sufficient quantity for the experiment, I carefully washed the roots quite clean, without depriving them of the fine brown skin which covers them, and which contains the aromatic flavour which so nearly resembles coffee that it is difficult to distinguish it from it while roasting.

I cut my roots into small pieces, the size of a kidney-bean, and roasted them on an iron baking-pan in the stove-oven, until they were as brown and crisp as coffee. I then ground and transferred a small cupful of the powder to the coffee-pot, pouring upon it scalding water, and boiling it for a few minutes briskly over the fire. The result was beyond my expectations. The coffee proved excellent—far superior to the common coffee we procured at the stores.

To persons residing in the bush, and to whom tea and coffee are very expensive articles of luxury, the knowledge of this valuable property in a plant scattered so abundantly through their fields, would prove highly beneficial. For years we used no other article; and my Indian friends who frequented the house gladly adopted the root, and made me show them the whole process of manufacturing it into coffee.

Experience taught me that the root of the dandelion is not so good when applied to this purpose in the spring as it is in the fall. I tried it in the spring, but the juice of the plant, having contributed to the production of leaves and flowers, was weak, and destitute of the fine bitter flavour so peculiar to coffee. The time of gathering in the potato crop is the best suited for collecting and drying the roots of the dandelion; and as they always abound in the same hills, both may be accomplished at the same time. Those who want to keep a quantity for winter use may wash and cut up the roots, and dry them on boards in the sun. They will keep for years, and can be roasted when required.

Few of our colonists are acquainted with the many uses to which this neglected but most valuable plant may be applied. I will point out a few which have come under my own observation, convinced as I am that the time will come when this hardy weed, with its golden flowers and curious seed-vessels, which form a constant plaything to the little children rolling about and luxuriating among the grass in the sunny month of May, will be transplanted into our gardens and tended with due care.

The dandelion planted in trenches, and blanched to a beautiful cream-colour with straw, makes an excellent salad, quite equal to endive, and is more hardy and requires less care.

In many parts of the United States, particularly in new districts where vegetables are scarce, it is used early in the spring, and boiled with pork as a substitute for cabbage. During our residence in the bush we found it, in the early part of May, a great addition to the dinner-table. In the township of Dummer, the settlers boil the tops, and add hops to the liquor, which they ferment, and from which they obtain excellent beer. I have never tasted this simple beverage, but I have been told by those who use it that it is equal to the table-beer used at home.

Necessity has truly been termed the mother of invention, for I contrived to manufacture a variety of dishes almost out of nothing, while living in her school. When entirely destitute of animal food, the different varieties of squirrels supplied us with pies, stews, and roasts. Our barn stood at the top of the hill near the bush, and in a trap set for such "small deer," we often caught from ten to twelve a day.

The flesh of the black squirrel is equal to that of the rabbit, and the red, and even the little chipmunk, is palatable when nicely cooked. But from the lake, during the summer, we derived the larger portion of our food. The children called this piece of water "Mamma's pantry"; and many a good meal has the munificent Father given to his poor dependent children from its well-stored depths. Moodie and I used to rise by daybreak, and fish for an hour after sunrise, when we returned, he to the field, and I to dress the little ones, clean up the house, assist with the milk, and prepare the breakfast.

Oh, how I enjoyed these excursions on the lake; the very idea of our dinner depending upon our success added double zest to our sport!

One morning we started as usual before sunrise; a thick mist still hung like a fine veil upon the water when we pushed off, and anchored at our accustomed place. Just as the sun rose, and the haze parted and drew up like a golden sheet of transparent gauze, through which the dark woods loomed out like giants, a noble buck dashed into the water, followed by four Indian hounds.

We then discovered a canoe full of Indians, just below the rapids, and another not many yards from us, that had been concealed by the fog. It was a noble sight, that gallant deer exerting all his energy, and stemming the water with such matchless grace, his branching horns held proudly aloft, his broad nostrils distended, and his fine eye fixed intently upon the opposite shore. Several rifle-balls whizzed past him, the dogs followed hard upon his track, but my very heart leaped for joy when, in spite of all his foes, his glassy hoofs spurned the opposite bank and he plunged headlong into the forest.

My beloved partner was most skilful in trolling for bass and maskinonge. His line he generally fastened to the paddle, and the motion of the oar gave a life-like vibration to the queer-looking mice and dragon-flies I used to manufacture from squirrel fur, or scarlet and white cloth, to tempt the finny wanderers of the wave.

When too busy himself to fish for our meals, little Katie and I ventured out alone in the canoe, which we anchored in any promising fishing spot by fastening a harrow tooth to a piece of rope, and letting it drop from the side of the little vessel. By the time she was five years old, my little mermaid could both steer and paddle the light vessel, and catch small fish, which were useful for soup.

During the winter of '36, we experienced many privations. The ruffian squatter P——, from Clear Lake, drove from the barn a fine young bull we were rearing, and for several weeks all trace of the animal was lost. We had almost forgotten the existence of poor Whiskey, when a neighbour called and told Moodie that his yearling was at P——'s and that he would advise him to get it back as soon as possible.

Moodie had to take some wheat to Y——'s mill, and as the squatter lived only a mile farther, he called at his house; and there, sure enough, he found the lost animal. With the greatest difficulty he succeeded in regaining his property, but not without many threats of vengeance from the parties who had stolen it. To these he paid no regard; but a few days after, six fat hogs, on which we depended for all our winter store of animal food, were driven into the lake and destroyed.

The death of these animals deprived us of three barrels of pork, and half-starved us through the winter. That winter of '36, how heavily it wore away! The grown flour, frosted potatoes, and scant quantity of animal food rendered us all weak, and the children suffered much from the ague.

One day, just before the snow fell, Moodie had gone to Peterborough for letters; our servant was sick in bed with the ague, and I was nursing my little boy, Dunbar, who was shaking with the cold fit of his miserable fever, when Jacob put his honest, round, rosy face in at the door.

"Give me the master's gun, ma'am; there's a big buck feeding on the rice-bed near the island."

I took down the gun, saying, "Jacob, you have no chance; there is but one charge of buck-shot in the house."

"One chance is better nor none," said Jacob, as he

commenced loading the gun. "Who knows what may happen to oie? Mayhap oie may chance to kill 'un; and you and the measter and the wee bairns may have zummat zavory for zupper yet."

Away walked Jacob with Moodie's "Manton" over his shoulder. A few minutes after, I heard the report of the gun, but never expected to see anything of the game, when Jacob suddenly bounced into the room, half-wild with delight.

"Thae beast iz dead az a door-nail. Zure how the measter will laugh when he sees the fine buck that oie a'zhot."

"And have you really shot him?"

"Come and zee! 'Tis worth your while to walk down to the landing to look at 'un."

Jacob got a rope, and I followed him to the landing, where, sure enough, lay a fine buck fastened in tow of the canoe. Jacob soon secured him by the hind legs to the rope he had brought; and, with our united efforts, we at last succeeded in dragging our prize home. All the time he was engaged in taking off the skin, Jacob was anticipating the feast that we were to have; and the good fellow chuckled with delight when he hung the carcass quite close to the kitchen door, that his "measter" might run against it when he came home at night. This event actually took place. When Moodie opened the door, he struck his head against the dead deer.

"What have you got here?"

"A fine buck, zur," said Jacob, bringing forward the light, and holding it up in such a manner that all the merits of the prize could be seen at a glance.

400

"A fine one, indeed! How did we come by it?"

"It was zhot by oie," said Jacob, rubbing his hands in a sort of ecstasy. "Thae beast iz the first oie ever zhot in my life. He! he! he!"

"You shot that fine deer, Jacob?—and there was only one charge in the gun! Well done; you must have taken a good aim."

"Why, zur, oie took no aim at all. Oie just pointed the gun at the deer, and zhut my oeys and let fly at 'un. 'Twas Providence kill'd 'un, not oie."

"I believe you," said Moodie; "Providence has hitherto watched over us and kept us from actual starvation."

The flesh of the deer, and the good broth that I was able to obtain from it, greatly assisted in restoring our sick to health; but long before that severe winter terminated we were again out of food. Mrs.—— had given to Katie, in the fall, a very pretty little pig, which she had named Spot. The animal was a great favourite with Jacob and the children, and he always received his food from their hands at the door, and followed them all over the place like a dog. We had a noble hound called Hector, between whom and the pet pig there existed the most tender friendship. Spot always shared with Hector the hollow log which served him for a kennel, and we often laughed to see Hector lead Spot round the clearing by his ear. After bearing the want of animal food until our souls sickened at the bad potatoes and grown flour bread, we began—that is, the elders of the family—to cast very hungry eyes upon Spot; but no one liked to propose having him killed. At last Jacob spoke his mind upon the subject.

"Oi've heard, zur, that the Jews never eat pork; but we Christians dooz, and are right glad ov the chance. Now, zur, oi've been thinking that 'tis no manner ov use our keeping that beast Spot. If he wor a zow, now there might be zome zenze in the thing; and we all feel weak for a morzel of meat. S'poze I kill him? He won't make a bad piece of pork."

Moodie seconded the move; and, in spite of the tears and prayers of Katie, her uncouth pet was sacrificed to the general wants of the family; but there were two members of the house who disdained to eat a morsel of the victim; poor Katie and the dog Hector. At the self-denial of the first I did not at all wonder, for she was a child full of sensibility and warm affections, but the attachment of the brute creature to his old playmate filled us all with surprise. Jacob first drew our attention to the strange fact.

"That dog," he said, as we were passing through the kitchen while he was at dinner, "do teach uz Christians a lesson how to treat our friends. Why, zur, he'll not eat a morzel of Spot. Oie have tried and tempted him in all manner ov ways, and he only do zneer and turn up his nose when oie hould him a bit to taste." He offered the animal a rib of the fresh pork as he finished speaking, and the dog turned away with an expression of aversion, and, on a repetition of the act, walked from the table.

Human affection could scarcely have surpassed the love felt by this poor animal for his playfellow. His attachment to Spot, that could overcome the pangs of hunger—for, like the rest of us, he was half-starved —must have been strong indeed.

Jacob's attachment to us, in its simplicity and fidelity, greatly resembled that of the dog; and sometimes, like the dog, he would push himself in where he was not wanted, and gratuitously give his advice, and make remarks which were not required.

Mr. K——, from Cork, was asking Moodie many questions about the partridges of the country; and, among other things, he wanted to know by what token you were able to discover their favourite haunts. Before Moodie could answer this last query a voice responded, through a large crack in the boarded wall which separated us from the kitchen, "They always bides where they's drum." This announcement was received with a burst of laughter that greatly disconcerted the natural philosopher in the kitchen.

On the 21st of May of this year, my second son, Donald, was born. The poor fellow came in hard times. The cows had not calved, and our bill of fare, now minus the deer and Spot, only consisted of bad potatoes and still worse bread. I was rendered so weak by want of proper nourishment that my dear husband, for my sake, overcame his aversion to borrowing, and procured a quarter of mutton from a friend. This, with kindly presents from neighbours—often as badly off as ourselves—a loin of a young bear, and a basket containing a loaf of bread, some tea, some fresh butter, and oatmeal, went far to save my life.

Shortly after my recovery, Jacob—the faithful, good Jacob—was obliged to leave us, for we could no longer afford to pay wages. What was owing to him had to be settled by sacrificing our best cow, and a great many valuable articles of clothing from my husband's wardrobe. Nothing is more distressing than being obliged to part with articles of dress which you know that you cannot replace. Almost all my clothes had been appropriated to the payment of wages, or to obtain garments for the children, excepting my wedding dress, and the beautiful baby-linen which had been made by the hands of dear and affectionate friends for my first-born. These were now exchanged for coarse, warm flannels, to shield her from the cold.

Moodie and Jacob had chopped eight acres during the winter, but these had to be burnt off and logged up before we could put in a crop of wheat for the ensuing fall. Had we been able to retain this industrious, kindly English lad, this would have been soon accomplished; but his wages, at the rate of thirty pounds per annum, were now utterly beyond our means.

Jacob had formed an attachment to my pretty maid, Mary Pine, and before going to the Southern States, to join an uncle who resided in Louisville, an opulent tradesman, who had promised to teach him his business, Jacob thought it as well to declare himself. The declaration took place on a log of wood near the back door, and from my chamber window I could both hear and see the parties, without being myself observed. Mary was seated very demurely at one end of the log, twisting the strings of her checked apron, and the loving Jacob was busily whittling the other extremity of their rustic seat. There was a long silence. Mary stole a look at Jacob, and he heaved a tremendous sigh, something between a yawn and a groan. "Meary," he said, "I must go."

"I know that afore," returned the girl.

"I had zummat to zay to you, Meary. Do you think you will miss oie?" (looking very affectionately, and twitching nearer).

"What put that into your head, Jacob?" This was said very demurely.

"Oie thowt, may be, Meary, that your feelings might be zummat loike my own. I feel zore about the heart, Meary, and it's all com' of parting with you. Don't you feel queerish too?"

"Can't say that I do, Jacob. I shall soon see you again" (pulling violently at her apron-string).

"Meary, oie'm afeard you don't feel loike oie."

"P'r'aps not—women can't feel like men. I'm sorry that you are going, Jacob, for you have been very kind and obliging, and I wish you well."

"Meary," cried Jacob, growing desperate at her coyness, and getting quite close up to her, "will you marry oie? Say yeez or noa?"

This was coming close to the point. Mary drew farther from him, and turned her head away.

"Meary," said Jacob, seizing upon the hand that held the apron-string, "do you think you can better yoursel'? If not—why, oie'm your man. Now, do just turn about your head and answer oie."

The girl turned round, and gave him a quick, shy glance, then burst out into a simpering laugh.

"Meary, will you take oie?" (jogging her elbow).

"I will," cried the girl, jumping up from the log and running into the house.

"Well, that bargain's made," said the lover, rubbing his hands; "and now oie'll go and bid measter and missus good-buy."

The poor fellow's eyes were full of tears, for the children, who loved him very much, clung, crying, about his knees. "God bless yees all," sobbed the kind-hearted creature. "Doan't forget Jacob, for he'll neaver forget you. Good-buy!"

Then turning to Mary, he threw his arms round her neck, and bestowed upon her fair cheek the most audible kiss I ever heard.

"And doan't you forget me, Meary. In two years oie will be back to marry you; and may be oie may come back a rich man."

Mary, who was an exceedingly pretty girl, shed some tears at the parting; but in a few days she was as gay as ever, and listening with great attention to the praises bestowed upon her beauty by an old bachelor, who was her senior by five-and-twenty years. But then he had a good farm, a saddle mare, and plenty of stock, and was reputed to have saved money. The saddle mare seemed to have great weight in old Ralph T——h's wooing; and I used laughingly to remind Mary of her absent lover, and beg her not to marry Ralph T——h's mare.

THE CANADIAN HUNTER'S SONG.

The northern lights are flashing,
　On the rapids' restless flow;
And o'er the wild waves dashing,
　Swift darts the light canoe.

DISAPPOINTED HOPES

The merry hunters come.
    "What cheer?—what cheer?"—
    "We've slain the deer!"
"Hurrah!—You're welcome home!"

The blithesome horn is sounding,
    And the woodman's loud halloo;
And joyous steps are bounding
    To meet the birch canoe.
        "Hurrah!—The hunters come."
        And the woods ring out
        To their merry shout
    As they drag the dun deer home!

The hearth is brightly burning,
    The rustic board is spread;
To greet the sire returning.
    The children leave their bed.
        With laugh and shout they come—
        That merry band—
        To grasp his hand,
    And bid him welcome home!

CHAPTER NINETEEN
THE LITTLE STUMPY MAN

There was a little man—
I'll sketch him if I can,
For he clung to mine and me
Like the old man of the sea;
And in spite of taunt and scoff
We could not pitch him off,
For the cross-grained, waspish elf
Cared for no one but himself.

BEFORE I DISMISS FOR EVER THE TROU-
bles and sorrows of 1836, I would fain introduce to
the notice of my readers some of the odd characters
with whom we became acquainted during that period.
The first that starts vividly to my recollection is the
picture of a short, stumpy, thickset man—a British
sailor, too—who came to stay one night under our
roof, and took quiet possession of his quarters for nine
months, and whom we were obliged to tolerate, from
the simple fact that we could not get rid of him.

During the fall, Moodie had met this individual
(whom I will call Mr. Malcolm) in the mail-coach,
going up to Toronto. Amused with his eccentric and
blunt manners and finding him a shrewd, clever fellow
in conversation, Moodie told him that if ever he came
into his part of the world he should be glad to renew
their acquaintance. And so they parted, with mutual
goodwill, as men often part who have travelled a
long journey in good-fellowship together, without
thinking it probable they should ever meet again.

The sugar season had just commenced with the
spring thaw; Jacob had tapped a few trees in order
to obtain sap to make molasses for the children, when
his plans were frustrated by the illness of my husband, who was again attacked with the ague. Towards

the close of a wet, sloppy day, while Jacob was in the wood, chopping, and our servant gone to my sister, who was ill, to help to wash, as I was busy baking bread for tea, my attention was aroused by a violent knocking at the door, and the furious barking of our dog, Hector. I ran to open it, when I found Hector's teeth clenched in the trousers of a little, dark, thick-set man, who said, in a gruff voice—

"Call off your dog. What the devil do you keep such an infernal brute about the house for? Is it to bite people who come to see you?"

Hector was the best-behaved, best-tempered animal in the world; he might have been called a gentlemanly dog. So little was there of the unmannerly puppy in his behaviour, that I was perfectly astonished at his ungracious conduct. I caught him by the collar, and, not without some difficulty, succeeded in dragging him off.

"Is Captain Moodie within?" said the stranger.

"He is, sir. But he is ill in bed—too ill to be seen."

"Tell him a friend" (he laid a strong stress upon the last word), "a particular friend must speak to him."

I now turned my eyes to the face of the speaker with some curiosity. I had taken him for a mechanic, from his dirty, slovenly appearance; and his physiognomy was so unpleasant that I did not credit his assertion that he was a friend of my husband, for I was certain that no man who possessed such a forbidding aspect could be regarded by Moodie as a friend. I was about to deliver his message, but the moment I let go Hector's collar, the dog was at him again.

THE LITTLE STUMPY MAN

"Don't strike him with your stick," I cried, throwing my arms over the faithful creature. "He is a powerful animal, and, if you provoke him, he will kill you."

I at last succeeded in coaxing Hector into the girl's room, where I shut him up, while the stranger came into the kitchen, and walked to the fire to dry his wet clothes.

I immediately went into the parlour, where Moodie was lying upon a bed near the stove, to deliver the stranger's message; but before I could say a word, he dashed in after me, and, going up to the bed, held out his broad, coarse hand, with, "How are you, Mr. Moodie? You see I have accepted your kind invitation sooner than either you or I expected. If you will give me house-room for the night, I shall be obliged to you."

This was said in a low, mysterious voice; and Moodie, who was struggling with the hot fit of his disorder, and whose senses were not a little confused, stared at him with a look of vague bewilderment. The countenance of the stranger grew dark.

"You cannot have forgotten me—my name is Malcolm."

"Yes, yes; I remember you now," said the invalid, holding out his burning, feverish hand. "To my home, *such as it is*, you are welcome."

I stood by in wondering astonishment, looking from one to the other, as I had no recollection of ever hearing my husband mention the name of the stranger; but as he had invited him to share our hospitality, I did my best to make him welcome, though in

413

what manner he was to be accommodated puzzled me not a little. I placed the arm-chair by the fire, and told him that I would prepare tea for him as soon as I could.

"It may be as well to tell you, Mrs. Moodie," said he sulkily, for he was evidently displeased by my husband's want of recognition on his first entrance, "that I have had no dinner."

I sighed to myself, for I well knew that our larder boasted of no dainties; and, from the animal expression of our guest's face, I rightly judged that he was fond of good living.

By the time I had fried a rasher of salt pork, and made a pot of dandelion coffee, the bread I had been preparing was baked; but grown flour will not make light bread, and it was unusually heavy. For the first time I felt heartily ashamed of our humble fare. I was sure that he for whom it was provided was not one to pass it over in benevolent silence. "He might be a gentleman," I thought, "but he does not look like one;" and a confused idea of who he was, and where Moodie had met with him, began to float through my mind. I did not like the appearance of the man, but I consoled myself that he was only to stay for one night, and I could give up my bed for that one night, and sleep on a bed on the floor by my sick husband. When I re-entered the parlour to cover the table, I found Moodie fallen asleep, and Mr. Malcolm reading. As I placed the tea-things on the table, he raised his head, and regarded me with a gloomy stare. He was a strange-looking creature; his features were tolerably regular, his complexion dark, with a good colour; his very broad and round head was covered with a perfect mass of close, black, curling hair, which, in growth, texture, and hue, resembled the wiry, curly hide of a water-dog. His eyes and mouth were both well shaped, but gave, by their sinister expression, an odious and doubtful meaning to the whole of his physiognomy. The eyes were cold, insolent and cruel, and as green as the eyes of a cat. The mouth bespoke a sullen, determined, and sneering disposition, as if it belonged to one brutally obstinate, one who could not by any gentle means be persuaded from his purpose. Such a man, in a passion, would have been a terrible wild beast; but the current of his feelings seemed to flow in a deep, sluggish channel, rather than in a violent or impetuous one; and, like William Penn, when he reconnoitred his unwelcome visitors through the keyhole of the door, I looked at my strange guest, and liked him not. Perhaps my distant and constrained manner made him painfully aware of the fact, for I am certain that, from that first hour of our acquaintance, a deep-rooted antipathy existed between us, which time seemed rather to strengthen than diminish.

He ate of his meal sparingly, and with evident disgust; the only remarks which dropped from him were—

"You make bad bread in the bush. Strange that you can't keep your potatoes from the frost! I should have thought that you could have had things more comfortable in the woods."

"We have been very unfortunate," I said, "since we came to the woods. I am sorry that you should be obliged to share the poverty of the land. It would have given me much pleasure could I have set before you a more comfortable meal."

"Oh, don't mention it. So that I get good pork and potatoes I shall be contented."

What did these words imply?—an extension of his visit? I hoped that I was mistaken; but before I could lose any time in conjecture my husband awoke. The fit had left him, and he rose and dressed himself, and was soon chatting cheerfully with his guest.

Mr. Malcolm now informed him that he was hiding from the sheriff of the N—— district's officers, and that it would be conferring upon him a great favour if he would allow him to remain at his house for a few weeks.

"To tell you the truth, Malcolm," said Moodie, "we are so badly off that we can scarcely find food for ourselves and the children. It is out of our power to make you comfortable, or to keep an additional hand, without he is willing to render some little help on the farm. If you can do this, I will endeavour to get a few necessaries on credit, to make your stay more agreeable."

To this proposition Malcolm readily assented, not only because it released him from all sense of obligation, but because it gave him a privilege to grumble.

Finding that his stay might extend to an indefinite period, I got Jacob to construct a rude bedstead out of two large chests that had transported some of our goods across the Atlantic, and which he put up in a corner of the parlour. This I provided with a small hair-mattress, and furnished with what bedding I could spare.

THE LITTLE STUMPY MAN

For the first fortnight of his sojourn, our guest did nothing but lie upon that bed, and read, and smoke, and drink whiskey-and-water from morning until night. By degrees he let out part of his history; but there was a mystery about him which he took good care never to clear up. He was the son of an officer in the navy, who had not only attained a very high rank in the service, but, for his gallant conduct, had been made a Knight-Companion of the Bath.

He had himself served his time as a midshipman on board his father's flag-ship, but had left the navy and accepted a commission in the Buenos-Ayrean service during the political struggles in that province; he had commanded a sort of privateer under the Government, to whom, by his own account, he had rendered many very signal services. Why he left South America and came to Canada he kept profound secret. He had indulged in very vicious and dissipated courses since he came to the province, and by his own account had spent upwards of four thousand pounds, in a manner not over creditable to himself. Finding that his friends would answer his bills no longer, he took possession of a grant of land obtained through his father's interest, up in Harvey, a barren township on the shores of Stony Lake ; and, after putting up his shanty, and expending all his remaining means, he found that he did not possess one acre out of the whole four hundred that would yield a crop of potatoes. He was now considerably in debt, and the lands, such as they were, had been seized, with all his effects, by the sheriff, and a warrant was out for his own apprehension, which he contrived to elude during his

417   2D

sojourn with us. Money he had none; and, beyond the dirty fearnought blue seaman's jacket which he wore, a pair of trousers of the coarse cloth of the country, an old black vest that had seen better days, and two blue-checked shirts, clothes he had none. He shaved but once a week, never combed his hair, and never washed himself. A dirtier or more sloven-ly creature never before was dignified by the title of a gentleman. He was, however, a man of good edu-cation, of excellent abilities, and possessed a bitter, sarcastic knowledge of the world; but he was selfish and unprincipled in the highest degree.

His shrewd observations and great conversational powers had first attracted my husband's attention, and, as men seldom show their bad qualities on a journey, he thought him a blunt, good fellow, who had travelled a great deal, and could render himself a very agreeable companion by a graphic relation of his ad-ventures. He could be all this, when he chose to re-lax from his sullen, morose mood; and, much as I disliked him, I have listened with interest for hours to his droll descriptions of South American life and manners.

Naturally indolent, and a constitutional grumbler, it was with the greatest difficulty that Moodie could get him to do anything beyond bringing a few pails of water from the swamp for the use of the house, and he has often passed me carrying water up from the lake without offering to relieve me of the burden. Mary, the betrothed of Jacob, called him a perfect "beast"; but he, returning good for evil, considered *her* a very pretty girl, and paid her so many uncouth attentions that he roused the jealousy of honest Jake, who vowed that he would give him a good "loomping" if he only dared to lay a finger upon his sweetheart. With Jacob to back her, Mary treated the "zea-bear," as Jacob termed him, with vast disdain, and was so saucy to him that, forgetting his admiration, he declared he would like to serve her as the Indians had done a scolding woman in South America. They attacked her house during the absence of her husband, cut out her tongue, and nailed it to the door, by way of knocker; and he thought that all women who could not keep a civil tongue in their head should be served in the same manner.

"And what should be done to men who swear and use ondacent language?" quoth Mary indignantly. "Their tongues should be slit, and given to the dogs. Faugh! You are such a nasty fellow that I don't think Hector would eat your tongue."

"I'll kill that beast," muttered Malcolm, as he walked away.

I remonstrated with him on the impropriety of bandying words with our servants. "You see," I said, "the disrespect with which they treat you; and if they presume upon your familiarity, to speak to our guest in this contemptuous manner, they will soon extend the same conduct to us."

"But, Mrs. Moodie, you should reprove them."

"I cannot, sir, while you continue, by taking liberties with the girl, and swearing at the man, to provoke them to retaliation."

"Swearing! What harm is there in swearing? A sailor cannot live without oaths."

419

"But a gentleman might, Mr. Malcolm. I should be sorry to consider you in any other light."

"Ah, you are such a prude—so methodistical—you make no allowance for circumstances! Surely, in the woods we may dispense with the hypocritical, conventional forms of society, and speak and act as we please."

"So you seem to think; but you see the result."

"I have never been used to the society of ladies, and I cannot fashion my words to please them; and I won't, that's more!" he muttered to himself as he strode off to Moodie in the field. I wished from my very heart that he was once more on the deck of his piratical South American craft.

One night he insisted on going out in the canoe to spear maskinonge with Moodie. The evening turned out very chill and foggy, and, before twelve, they returned, with only one fish, and half frozen with cold. Malcolm had got twinges of rheumatism, and he fussed, and sulked, and swore, and quarrelled with everybody and everything, until Moodie, who was highly amused by his petulance, advised him to go to his bed, and pray for the happy restoration of his temper.

"Temper!' he cried; "I don't believe there's a good-tempered person in the world. It's all hypocrisy! I never had a good temper! My mother was an ill-tempered woman, and ruled my father, who was a confoundedly severe, domineering man. I was born in an ill-temper. I was an ill-tempered child; I grew up an ill-tempered man. I feel worse than ill-tempered now, and when I die it will be in an ill-temper."

THE LITTLE STUMPY MAN

"Well," quoth I, "Moodie has made you a tumbler of hot punch, which may help to drive out the cold and the ill-temper, and cure the rheumatism."

"Ay; your husband's a good fellow, and worth two of you, Mrs. Moodie. He makes some allowance for the weakness of human nature, and can excuse even my ill-temper."

I did not choose to bandy words with him, and the next day the unfortunate creature was shaking with the ague. A more untractable, outrageous, *im*-patient I never had the ill-fortune to nurse. During the cold fit, he did nothing but swear at the cold, and wished himself roasting; and during the fever, he swore at the heat, and wished that he was sitting, in no other garment than his shirt, on the north side of an iceberg. And when the fit at last left him, he got up, and ate such quantities of fat pork, and drank so much whiskey-punch, that you would have imagined he had just arrived from a long journey, and had not tasted food for a couple of days.

He would not believe that fishing in the cold night-air upon the water had made him ill, but raved that it was all my fault for having laid my baby down on his bed while it was shaking with the ague.

Yet, if there were the least tenderness mixed up in his iron nature, it was the affection he displayed for that young child. Dunbar was just twenty months old, with bright dark eyes, dimpled cheeks, and soft, flowing golden hair, which fell round his infant face in rich curls. The merry, confiding little creature formed such a contrast to his own surly, unyielding temper, that, perhaps, that very circumstance made the bond

421

of union between them. When in the house, the little boy was seldom out of his arms, and whatever were Malcolm's faults, he had none in the eyes of the child, who used to cling around his neck and kiss his rough, unshaven cheeks with the greatest fondness.

"If I could afford it, Moodie," he said one day to my husband, "I should like to marry. I want some one upon whom I could wreak my affections." And wanting that some one in the form of a woman, he contented himself with venting them upon the child.

As the spring advanced, and after Jacob left us, he seemed ashamed of sitting in the house doing nothing, and therefore undertook to make us a garden, or "to make garden," as the Canadians term preparing a few vegetables for the season. I procured the necessary seeds, and watched with no small surprise the industry with which our strange visitor commenced operations. He repaired the broken fence, dug the ground with the greatest care, and laid it out with a skill and neatness of which I had believed him perfectly incapable. In less than three weeks, the whole plot presented a very pleasing prospect, and he was really elated by his success.

"At any rate," said he, "we shall no longer be starved on bad flour and potatoes. We shall have peas, and beans, and beets, and carrots, and cabbage in abundance, besides the plot I have reserved for cucumbers and melons."

"Ah," thought I, "does he, indeed, mean to stay with us until the melons are ripe?" and my heart died within me, for he not only was a great additional ex-

THE LITTLE STUMPY MAN

pense, but he gave a great deal of additional trouble,
and entirely robbed us of all privacy, as our very parlour was converted into a bedroom for his accommodation; besides that, a man of his singularly dirty
habits made a very disagreeable inmate.

The only redeeming point in his character, in my
eyes, was his love for Dunbar. I could not entirely
hate a man who was so fondly attached to my child.
To the two little girls he was very cross, and often
chased them from him with blows.

He had, too, an odious way of finding fault with
everything. I never could cook to please him; and he
tried in the most malicious way to induce Moodie to
join in his complaints. All his schemes to make strife
between us, however, failed, and were generally visited
upon himself. In no way did he ever seek to render
me the least assistance. Shortly after Jacob left us,
Mary Pine was offered higher wages by a family at
Peterborough, and for some time I was left with four
little children, and without a servant. Moodie always
milked the cows, because I never could overcome my
fear of cattle; and though I had occasionally milked
when there was no one else in the way, it was in fear
and trembling.

Moodie had to go down to Peterborough; but before he went, he begged Malcolm to bring me what
water and wood I required, and to stand by the cattle
while I milked the cows, and he would himself be home
before night.

He started at six in the morning, and I got the pail
to go and milk. Malcolm was lying upon his bed,
reading.

423

"Mr. Malcolm, will you be so kind as to go with me to the fields for a few minutes while I milk?"

"Yes!" (then, with a sulky frown), "but I want to finish what I am reading."

"I will not detain you long."

"Oh no! I suppose about an hour. You are a shocking bad milker."

"True; I never went near a cow until I came to this country; and I have never been able to overcome my fear of them."

"More shame for you! A farmer's wife and afraid of a cow! Why, these little children would laugh at you."

I did not reply, nor would I ask him again. I walked slowly to the field, and my indignation made me forget my fear. I had just finished milking, and with a brimming pail was preparing to climb the fence and return to the house, when a very wild ox we had came running with headlong speed from the wood. All my fears were alive again in a moment. I snatched up the pail, and, instead of climbing the fence and getting to the house, I ran with all the speed I could command down the steep hill towards the lake shore; my feet caught in a root of the many stumps in the path, and I fell to the ground, my pail rolling many yards ahead of me. Every drop of my milk was spilt upon the grass. The ox passed on. I gathered myself up and returned home. Malcolm was very fond of new milk, and he came to meet me at the door.

"Hi! Hi!—Where's the milk?"

"No milk for the poor children to-day," said I, showing him the inside of the pail, with a sorrowful shake of the head, for it was no small loss to them and me.

THE LITTLE STUMPY MAN

"How the devil's that? So you were afraid to milk the cows. Come away, and I will keep off the bugga-boos."

"I did milk them—no thanks to your kindness, Mr. Malcolm—but——"

"But what?"

"The ox frightened me, and I fell and spilt all the milk."

"Whew! Now don't go and tell your husband that it was all my fault; if you had had a little patience, I would have come when you asked me, but I don't choose to be dictated to, and I won't be made a slave by you or any one else."

"Then why do you stay, sir, where you consider yourself so treated?" said I. "We are all obliged to work to obtain bread; we give you the best share— surely the return we ask for it is but small."

"You make me feel my obligations to you when you ask me to do anything; if you left it to my better feelings we should get on better."

"Perhaps you are right. I will never ask you to do anything for me in future."

"Oh, now, that's all mock-humility. In spite of the tears in your eyes, you are as angry with me as ever; but don't go to make mischief between me and Moodie. If you'll say nothing about my refusing to go with you, I'll milk the cows for you myself to-night."

"And can you milk?" said I, with some curiosity.

"Milk! Yes; and if I were not so confoundedly low-spirited and——lazy, I could do a thousand other

425

things too. But now, don't say a word about it to Moodie."

I made no promise; but my respect for him was not increased by his cowardly fear of reproof from Moodie, who treated him with a kindness and consideration which he did not deserve.

The afternoon turned out very wet, and I was sorry that I should be troubled with his company all day in the house. I was making a shirt for Moodie from some cotton that had been sent me from home, and he placed himself by the side of the stove, just opposite, and continued to regard me for a long time with his usual sullen stare. I really felt half afraid of him.

"Don't you think me mad?" said he. "I have a brother deranged; he got a stroke of the sun in India, and lost his senses in consequence; but sometimes I think it runs in the family."

What answer could I give to this speech but mere evasive commonplace!

"You won't say what you really think," he continued; "I know you hate me, and that makes me dislike you. Now what would you say if I told you I had committed a murder, and that it was the recollection of that circumstance that made me at times so restless and unhappy?

I looked up in his face, not knowing what to believe.

"'Tis fact," said he, nodding his head; and I hoped that he would not go mad, like his brother, and kill me.

"Come, I'll tell you all about it; I know the world would laugh at me for calling such an act *murder*;

426

and yet I have been such a miserable man ever since that I *feel* it was.

"There was a noted leader among the rebel Buenos-Ayreans, whom the government wanted much to get hold of. He was a fine, dashing, handsome fellow; I had often seen him, but we never came to close quarters. One night I was lying wrapped up in my poncho at the bottom of my boat, which was rocking in the surf, waiting for two of my men, who were gone on shore. There came to the shore this man and one of his people, and they stood so near the boat, which I suppose they thought empty, that I could distinctly hear their conversation. I suppose it was the devil who tempted me to put a bullet through that man's heart. He was an enemy to the flag under which I fought, but he was no enemy to me—I had no right to become his executioner; but still the desire to kill him, for the mere devilry of the thing, came so strongly upon me that I no longer tried to resist it. I rose slowly upon my knees; the moon was shining very bright at the time, both he and his companion were too earnestly engaged to see me, and I deliberately shot him through the body. He fell with a heavy groan back into the water; but I caught the last look he threw up to the moonlight skies before his eyes glazed in death. Oh, that look! —so full of despair and unutterable anguish; it haunts me yet—it will haunt me for ever. I would not have cared if I had killed him in strife—but in cold blood, and he so unsuspicious of his doom! Yes, it was murder; I know by this constant tugging at my heart that it was murder. What do you say to it?"

ROUGHING IT IN THE BUSH

"I should think as you do, Mr. Malcolm. It is a terrible thing to take away the life of a fellow-creature without the least provocation."

"Ah! I knew you would blame me; but he was an enemy after all; I had a right to kill him; I was hired by the government under whom I served to kill him; and who shall condemn me?"

"No one more than your own heart."

"It is not the heart, but the brain, that must decide in questions of right and wrong," said he. "I acted from impulse, and shot that man; had I reasoned upon it for five minutes, the man would be living now. But what's done cannot be undone. Did I ever show you the work I wrote upon South America?"

"Are you an author," said I incredulously.

"To be sure I am. Murray offered me £100 for my manuscript, but I would not take it. Shall I read to you some passages from it?"

I am sorry to say that his behaviour in the morning was uppermost in my thoughts, and I had no repugnance in refusing.

"No, don't trouble yourself. I have the dinner to cook, and the children to attend to, which will cause a constant interruption; you had better defer it to some other time."

"I shan't ask you to listen to me again," said he, with a look of offended vanity; but he went to his trunk and brought out a large MS., written on foolscap, which he commenced reading to himself with an air of great self-importance, glancing from time to time at me, and smiling disdainfully. Oh, how glad I was when the door opened, and the return of Moodie broke up this painful *tête-à-tête*.

From the sublime to the ridiculous is but a step. The very next day, Mr. Malcolm made his appearance before me, wrapped in a great-coat belonging to my husband, which literally came down to his heels. At this strange apparition, I fell a-laughing.

"For God's sake, Mrs. Moodie, lend me a pair of inexpressibles. I have met with an accident in crossing the fence, and mine are torn to shreds—gone to the devil entirely."

"Well, don't swear. I'll see what can be done for you."

I brought him a new pair of fine, drab-coloured kersey-mere trousers that had never been worn. Although he was eloquent in his thanks, I had no idea that he meant to keep them for his sole individual use from that day thenceforth. But after all, what was the man to do? He had no trousers, and no money, and he could not take to the woods. Certainly his loss was not our gain. It was the old proverb reversed.

The season for putting in the potatoes had now arrived. Malcolm volunteered to cut the sets, which was easy work that could be done in the house, and over which he could lounge and smoke; but Moodie told him that he must take his share in the field, that I had already sets enough saved to plant half an acre, and would have more prepared by the time they were required. With many growls and shrugs, he felt obliged to comply; and he performed his part pretty well, the execrations bestowed upon the mosquitoes and black flies forming a sort of safety-valve to let off the concentrated venom of his temper. When he came in to dinner, he held out his hands to me.

"Look at these hands."

"They are blistered with the hoe."

"Look at my face."

"You are terribly disfigured by the black flies. But Moodie suffers just as much, and says nothing."

"Bah!—The only consolation one feels for such annoyances is to complain. Oh, the woods!—the cursed woods!—how I wish I were out of them." The day was very warm, but in the afternoon I was surprised by a visit from an old maiden lady, a friend of mine from C——. She had walked up with a Mr. Crowe, from Peterborough, a young, brisk-looking farmer, in breeches and top-boots, just out from the old country, who, naturally enough, thought he would like to roost among the woods.

He was a little, lively, good-natured manny, with a real Anglo-Saxon face,—rosy, high cheek-boned, with full lips, and a turned-up nose; and, like most little men, was a great talker, and very full of himself. He had belonged to the secondary class of farmers, and was very vulgar, both in person and manners. I had just prepared tea for my visitors, when Malcolm and Moodie returned from the field. There was no affectation about the former. He was manly in his person, and blunt even to rudeness, and I saw by the quizzical look which he cast upon the spruce little Crowe that he was quietly quizzing him from head to heel. A neighbour had sent me a present of maple molasses, and Mr. Crowe was so fearful of spilling some of the rich syrup upon his drab shorts that he spread a large pocket-handkerchief over his knees, and tucked another under his chin. I felt very much inclined to laugh, but restrained the inclination as well as I could—and if the little creature would have sat still, I could have quelled my rebellious propensity altogether; but up he would jump at every word I said to him, and make me a low, jerking bow, often with his mouth quite full, and the treacherous molasses running over his chin.

Malcolm sat directly opposite to me and my volatile next-door neighbour. He saw the intense difficulty I had to keep my gravity, and was determined to make me laugh out. So, coming slyly behind my chair, he whispered in my ear, with the gravity of a judge, "Mrs. Moodie, that must have been the very chap who first jumped Jim Crowe."

This appeal obliged me to run from the table. Moodie was astonished at my rudeness; and Malcolm, as he resumed his seat, made the matter worse by saying, "I wonder what is the matter with Mrs. Moodie; she is certainly very hysterical this afternoon."

The potatoes were planted, and the season of strawberries, green-peas, and young potatoes had come, but still Malcolm remained our constant guest. He had grown so indolent, and gave himself so many airs, that Moodie was heartily sick of his company, and gave him many gentle hints to change his quarters; but our guest was determined to take no hint. For some reason best known to himself, perhaps out of sheer contradiction, which formed one great element in his character, he seemed obstinately bent upon remaining where he was.

Moodie was busy under-brushing for a fall fallow. Malcolm spent much of his time in the garden, or lounging about the house. I had baked an eel-pie for dinner, which if prepared well is by no means an unsavoury dish. Malcolm had cleaned some green-peas and washed the first young potatoes we had drawn that season, with his own hands, and he was reckoning upon the feast he should have on the potatoes with childish glee. The dinner at length was put upon the table. The vegetables were remarkably fine, and the pie looked very nice.

Moodie helped Malcolm, as he always did, very largely, and the other covered his plate with a portion of peas and potatoes, when, lo and behold! my gentleman began making a very wry face at the pie.

"What an infernal dish!" he cried, pushing away his plate with an air of great disgust. "These eels taste as if they had been stewed in oil. Moodie, you should teach your wife to be a better cook."

The hot blood burnt upon Moodie's cheek. I saw indignation blazing in his eye.

"If you don't like what is prepared for you, sir, you may leave the table and my house, if you please. I will put up with your ungentlemanly and ungrateful conduct to Mrs. Moodie no longer."

Out stalked the offending party. I thought, to be sure, we had got rid of him; and though he deserved what was said to him, I was sorry for him. Moodie took his dinner, quietly remarking, "I wonder he could find it in his heart to leave those fine peas and potatoes."

He then went back to his work in the bush, and I

cleared away the dishes, and churned, for I wanted butter for tea.

About four o'clock, Mr. Malcolm entered the room. "Mrs. Moodie," said he, in a more cheerful voice than usual, "where's the boss?"

"In the wood, under-brushing." I felt dreadfully afraid that there would be blows between them.

"I hope, Mr. Malcolm, that you are not going to him with any intention of a fresh quarrel?"

"Don't you think I have been punished enough by losing my dinner?" said he, with a grin. "I don't think we shall murder one another." He shouldered his axe, and went whistling away.

After striving for a long while to stifle my foolish fears, I took the baby in my arms, and little Dunbar by the hand, and ran up to the bush where Moodie was at work.

At first I only saw my husband, but the strokes of an axe at a little distance soon guided my eyes to the spot where Malcolm was working away as if for dear life. Moodie smiled, and looked at me significantly.

"How could the fellow stomach what I said to him? Either great necessity or great meanness must be the cause of his knocking under. I don't know whether most to pity or despise him."

"Put up with it, dearest, for this once. He is not happy, and must be greatly distressed."

Malcolm kept aloof, ever and anon casting a furtive glance towards us; at last little Dunbar ran to him, and held up his arms to be kissed. The strange man snatched him to his bosom, and covered him with caresses. It might be love to the child that had quelled his sullen spirit, or he might really have cherished an affection for us deeper than his ugly temper would allow him to show. At all events, he joined us at tea as if nothing had happened, and we might truly say that he had obtained a new lease of his long visit.

But what could not be effected by words or hints of ours was brought about a few days after by the silly observation of a child. He asked Katie to give him a kiss, and he would give her some raspberries he had gathered in the bush.

"I don't want them. Go away; I don't like you, *you little stumpy man*!"

His rage knew no bounds. He pushed the child from him, and vowed that he would leave the house that moment—that she could not have thought of such an expression herself; she must have been taught it by us. This was an entire misconception on his part; but he would not be convinced that he was wrong. Off he went, and Moodie called after him, "Malcolm, as I am sending to Peterborough to-morrow, the man shall take in your trunk." He was too angry even to turn and bid us good-bye; but we had not seen the last of him yet.

Two months after, we were taking tea with a neighbour, who lived a mile below us on the small lake. Who should walk in but Mr. Malcolm? He greeted us with great warmth for him, and, when we rose to take leave, he rose and walked home by our side. "Surely the little stumpy man is not returning to his old quarters?" I am still a babe in the affairs of men. Human nature has more strange varieties than any one menagerie can contain, and Malcolm was one of the oddest of her odd species.

That night he slept in his old bed below the parlour window, and for three months afterwards he stuck to us like a beaver.

He seemed to have grown more kindly, or we had got more used to his eccentricities, and let him have his own way; certainly he behaved himself much better.

He neither scolded the children nor interfered with the maid, nor quarrelled with me. He had greatly discontinued his bad habit of swearing, and he talked of himself and his future prospects with more hope and self-respect. His father had promised to send him a fresh supply of money, and he proposed to buy of Moodie the clergy reserve, and that they should farm the two places on shares. This offer was received with great joy, as an unlooked-for means of paying our debts and extricating ourselves from present and overwhelming difficulties, and we looked upon the little stumpy man in the light of a benefactor.

So matters continued until Christmas Eve, when our visitor proposed walking into Peterborough in order to give the children a treat of raisins to make a Christmas pudding.

"We will be quite merry to-morrow," he said. "I hope we shall eat many Christmas dinners together, and continue good friends."

He started after breakfast, with the promise of coming back at night; but night came, the Christmas passed away, months and years fled away, but we never saw the little stumpy man again!

ROUGHING IT IN THE BUSH

He went away that day with a stranger in a waggon from Peterborough, and never afterwards was seen in that part of Canada. We afterwards learned that he went to Texas, and it is thought that he was killed at St. Antonio; but this is a mere conjecture. Whether dead or living, I feel convinced that—

"We ne'er shall look upon his like again."

CHAPTER TWENTY
THE FIRE

CHAPTER TWENTY   THE FIRE

Now, Fortune, do thy worst! For many years,
Thou, with relentless and unsparing hand,
Hast sternly pour'd on our devoted heads
The poison'd phials of thy fiercest wrath.

THE EARLY PART OF THE WINTER OF 1837, a year never to be forgotten in the annals of Canadian history, was very severe. During the month of February, the thermometer often ranged from eighteen to twenty-seven degrees below zero. Speaking of the coldness of one particular day, a genuine brother Jonathan remarked, with charming simplicity, that it was thirty degrees below zero that morning, and it would have been much colder if the thermometer had been longer.

The morning of the seventh was so intensely cold that everything liquid froze in the house. The wood that had been drawn for the fire was green, and it ignited too slowly to satisfy the shivering impatience of women and children; I vented mine in audibly grumbling over the wretched fire, at which I in vain endeavoured to thaw frozen bread, and to dress crying children.

It so happened that an old friend, the maiden lady before alluded to, had been staying with us for a few days. She had left us for a visit to my sister, and as some relatives of hers were about to return to Britain, by the way of New York, and had offered to convey letters to friends at home, I had been busy all the day before preparing a packet for England.

It was my intention to walk to my sister's with this packet, directly the important affair of breakfast had been discussed; but the extreme cold of the morning had occasioned such delay, that it was late before the breakfast-things were cleared away.

After dressing, I found the air so keen that I could not venture out without some risk to my nose, and my husband kindly volunteered to go in my stead.

I had hired a young Irish girl the day before. Her friends were only just located in our vicinity, and she had never seen a stove until she came to our house. After Moodie left, I suffered the fire to die away in the Franklin stove in the parlour, and went into the kitchen to prepare bread for the oven.

The girl, who was a good-natured creature, had heard me complain bitterly of the cold and the impossibility of getting the green wood to burn, and she thought that she would see if she could not make a good fire for me and the children, against my work was done. Without saying one word about her intention, she slipped out through a door that opened from the parlour into the garden, ran round to the woodyard, filled her lap with cedar chips, and, not knowing the nature of the stove, filled it entirely with the light wood.

Before I had the least idea of my danger, I was aroused from the completion of my task by the crackling and roaring of a large fire, and a suffocating smell of burning soot. I looked up at the kitchen cooking-stove. All was right there. I knew I had left no fire in the parlour stove; but not being able to account for the smoke and smell of burning, I opened the door, and, to my dismay, found the stove red-hot, from the front plate to the topmost pipe that let out the smoke through the roof.

THE LOG CABIN OF THE EARLY SETTLER

THE FIRE

My first impulse was to plunge a blanket, snatched from the servant's bed, which stood in the kitchen, into cold water. This I thrust into the stove, and upon it I threw water, until all was cool below. I then ran up to the loft, and, by exhausting all the water in the house, even to that contained in the boilers upon the fire, contrived to cool down the pipes which passed through the loft. I then sent the girl out of doors to look at the roof, which, as a very deep fall of snow had taken place the day before, I hoped would be completely covered, and safe from all danger of fire.

She quickly returned, stamping, and tearing her hair, and making a variety of uncouth outcries, from which I gathered that the roof was in flames.

This was terrible news, with my husband absent, no man in the house, and a mile and a quarter from any other habitation. I ran out to ascertain the extent of the misfortune, and found a large fire burning in the roof between the two stove pipes. The heat of the fires had melted off all the snow, and a spark from the burning pipe had already ignited the shingles. A ladder, which for several months had stood against the house, had been moved two days before to the barn, which was at the top of the hill near the road; there was no reaching the fire through that source. I got out the dining-table, and tried to throw water upon the roof by standing on a chair placed upon it, but I only expended the little water that remained in the boiler, without reaching the fire. The girl still continued weeping and lamenting.

"You must go for help," I said. "Run as fast as you can to my sister's, and fetch your master."

"And lave you, ma'arm, and the childher alone wid the burnin' house?"

"Yes, yes! Don't stay one moment."

"I have no shoes, ma'arm, and the snow is so deep."

"Put on your master's boots; make haste, or we shall be lost before help comes."

The girl put on the boots and started, shrieking "Fire!" the whole way. This was utterly useless, and only impeded her progress by exhausting her strength. After she had vanished from the head of the clearing into the wood, and I was left quite alone, with the house burning over my head, I paused one moment to reflect what had best be done.

The house was built of cedar logs; in all probability it would be consumed before any help could arrive. There was a brisk breeze blowing up from the frozen lake, and the thermometer stood at eighteen degrees below zero. We were placed between the two extremes of heat and cold, and there was as much danger to be apprehended from the one as the other. In the bewilderment of the moment, the direful extent of the calamity never struck me; we wanted but this to put the finishing stroke to our misfortunes, to be thrown naked, houseless, and penniless, upon the world. " *What shall I save first?* " was the thought just then uppermost in my mind. Bedding and clothing appeared the most essentially necessary, and, without another moment's pause, I set to work with a right good will to drag all that I could from my burning home.

While little Agnes, Dunbar, and baby Donald filled the air with their cries, Katie, as if fully conscious of the importance of exertion, assisted me in carrying

442

out sheets and blankets, and dragging trunks and boxes some way up the hill, to be out of the way of the burning brands when the roof should fall in.

How many anxious looks I gave to the head of the clearing as the fire increased, and large pieces of burning pine began to fall through the boarded ceiling about the lower rooms where we were at work. The children I had kept under a large dresser in the kitchen, but it now appeared absolutely necessary to remove them to a place of safety. To expose the young, tender things to the direful cold, was almost as bad as leaving them to the mercy of the fire. At last I hit upon a plan to keep them from freezing. I emptied all the clothes out of a large, deep chest of drawers, and dragged the empty drawers up the hill; these I lined with blankets, and placed a child in each drawer, covering it well over with the bedding, giving to little Agnes the charge of the baby to hold between her knees, and keep well covered until help should arrive. Ah, how long it seemed coming!

The roof was now burning like a brush-heap, and, unconsciously, the child and I were working under a shelf upon which were deposited several pounds of gunpowder, which had been procured for blasting a well, as all our water had to be brought uphill from the lake. This gunpowder was in a stone jar, secured by a paper stopper; the shelf upon which it stood was on fire, but it was utterly forgotten by me at the time, and even afterwards, when my husband was working on the burning loft over it.

I found that I should not be able to take many more trips for goods. As I passed out of the parlour for the last time, Katie looked up at her father's flute, which was suspended upon two brackets, and said—

"Oh, dear mamma! do save papa's flute; he will be so sorry to lose it."

God bless the dear child for the thought! the flute was saved; and, as I succeeded in dragging out a heavy chest of clothes, and looked up once more despairingly to the road, I saw a man running at full speed. It was my husband. Help was at hand, and my heart uttered a deep thanksgiving as another and another figure came upon the scene.

I had not felt the intense cold, although without cap, or bonnet, or shawl, with my hands bare and exposed to the bitter biting air. The intense excitement, the anxiety to save all I could, had so totally diverted my thoughts from myself, that I had felt nothing of the danger to which I had been exposed; but now that help was near, my knees trembled under me, I felt giddy and faint, and dark shadows seemed dancing before my eyes.

The moment my husband and brother-in-law entered the house, the latter exclaimed—

"Moodie, the house is gone; save what you can of your winter stores and furniture."

Moodie thought differently. Prompt and energetic in danger, and possessing admirable presence of mind and coolness when others yield to agitation and despair, he sprang upon the burning loft and called for water. Alas, there was none!

"Snow, snow; hand me up pailfuls of snow!"

Oh! it was bitter work filling those pails with frozen

snow; but Mr. T—— and I worked at it as fast as we were able.

The violence of the fire was greatly checked by covering the boards of the loft with this snow. More help had now arrived. Young B—— and S—— had brought the ladder down with them from the barn, and were already cutting away the burning roof, and flinging the flaming brands into the deep snow.

"Mrs. Moodie, have you any pickled meat?"

"We have just killed one of our cows and salted it for winter stores."

"Well, then, fling the beef into the snow, and let us have the brine."

This was an admirable plan. Wherever the brine wetted the shingles, the fire turned from it, and concentrated into one spot.

But I had not time to watch the brave workers on the roof. I was fast yielding to the effects of over excitement and fatigue, when my brother's team dashed down the clearing, bringing my excellent old friend, Miss B——, and the servant-girl.

My brother sprang out, carried me back into the house, and wrapped me up in one of the large blankets scattered about. In a few minutes I was seated with the dear children in the sleigh, and on the way to a place of warmth and safety.

Katie alone suffered from the intense cold. The dear little creature's feet were severely frozen, but were fortunately restored by her uncle discovering the fact before she approached the fire, and rubbing them well with snow.

In the meanwhile, the friends we had left so actively employed at the house, succeeded in getting the fire under before it had destroyed the walls. The only accident that occurred was to a poor dog that Moodie had called Snarleyowe. He was struck by a burning brand thrown from the house, and crept under the barn and died.

Beyond the damage done to the building, the loss of our potatoes and two sacks of flour, we had escaped in a manner almost miraculous. This fact shows how much can be done by persons working in union, without bustle and confusion, or running in each other's way. Here were six men, who, without the aid of water, succeeded in saving a building, which, at first sight, almost all of them had deemed past hope. In after years, when entirely burnt out in a disastrous fire that consumed almost all we were worth in the world, some four hundred persons were present, with a fire-engine to second their endeavours, yet all was lost. Every person seemed in the way; and though the fire was discovered immediately after it took place, nothing was done beyond saving some of the furniture.

Our party was too large to be billeted upon one family. Mrs. T—— took compassion upon Moodie, myself, and the baby, while their uncle received the three children to his hospitable home.

It was some weeks before Moodie succeeded in repairing the roof, the intense cold preventing any one from working in such an exposed situation.

The news of our fire travelled far and wide. I was reported to have done prodigies and to have saved the greater part of our household goods before help arrived. Reduced to plain prose, these prodigies shrink into the simple and by no mean marvellous fact, that during the excitement I dragged out chests which, under ordinary circumstances, I could not have moved; and that I was unconscious both of the cold and the danger to which I was exposed while working under a burning roof, which, had it fallen, would have buried both the children and myself under its ruins.

These circumstances appeared far more alarming, as all real danger does, after they were past. The fright and over-exertion gave my health a shock from which I did not recover for several months, and made me so fearful of fire, that from that hour it haunts me like a nightmare. Let the night be ever so serene, all stoves must be shut up, and the hot embers covered with ashes, before I dare retire to rest; and the sight of a burning edifice, so common a spectacle in large towns in this country, makes me really ill. This feeling was greatly increased after a second fire, when, for some torturing minutes, a lovely boy, since drowned, was supposed to have perished in the burning house.

Our present fire led to a new train of circumstances, for it was the means of introducing to Moodie a young Irish gentleman who was staying at my brother's house. John E—— was one of the best and gentlest of human beings. His father, a captain in the army, had died while his family were quite young, and had left his widow with scarcely any means, beyond the pension she received at her husband's death, to bring up and educate a family of five children. A handsome, showy woman, Mrs. E—— soon married again; and

447

the poor lads were thrown upon the world. The eldest, who had been educated for the Church, first came to Canada in the hope of getting some professorship in the college, or of opening a classical school. He was a handsome, gentlemanly, well-educated young man, but constitutionally indolent—a natural defect which seemed common to all the males of the family, and which was sufficiently indicated by their soft, silky, fair hair and milky complexions. R—— had the good sense to perceive that Canada was not the country for him. He spent a week under our roof, and we were much pleased with his elegant tastes and pursuits; but my husband strongly advised him to try and get a situation as a tutor in some family at home. This he afterwards obtained. He became tutor and travelling companion to the young Lord M——, and has since got an excellent living.

John, who had followed his brother to Canada without the means of transporting himself back again, was forced to remain, and was working with Mr. S—— for his board. He proposed to Moodie working his farm upon shares; and, as we were unable to hire a man, Moodie gladly closed with his offer; and, during the time he remained with us, we had every reason to be pleased with the arrangement.

It was always a humiliating feeling to our proud minds, that hirelings should witness our dreadful struggles with poverty, and the strange shifts we were forced to make in order to obtain even food. But John E—— had known and experienced all that we had suffered, in his own person, and was willing to share our home with all its privations. Warm-hearted, sincere, and truly affectionate—a gentleman in word, thought, and deed— we found his society and cheerful help a great comfort. Our odd meals became a subject of merriment, and the peppermint and sage tea drank with a better flavour when we had one who sympathized in all our trials, and shared all our toils, to partake of it with us.

The whole family soon became attached to our young friend; and after the work of the day was over, greatly we enjoyed an hour's fishing on the lake. John E—— said that we had no right to murmur, as long as we had health, a happy home, and plenty of fresh fish, milk, and potatoes. Early in May we received an old Irishwoman into our service, who for four years proved a most faithful and industrious creature. And what with John E—— to assist my husband on the farm, and old Jenny to help me to nurse the children and manage the house, our affairs, if they were no better in a pecuniary point of view, at least presented a more pleasing aspect at home. We were always cheerful, and sometimes contented and even happy.

How great was the contrast between the character of our new inmate and that of Mr. Malcolm! The sufferings of the past year had been greatly increased by the intolerable nuisance of his company, while many additional debts had been contracted in order to obtain luxuries for him which we never dreamed of purchasing for ourselves. Instead of increasing my domestic toils, John did all in his power to lessen them; and it always grieved him to see me iron a shirt, or wash the least article of clothing for him.

"You have too much to do already; I cannot bear to give you the least additional work," he would say. And he generally expressed the greatest satisfaction at my method of managing the house, and preparing our simple fare. The little ones he treated with the most affectionate kindness, and gathered the whole flock about his knees the moment he came in to his meals.

On a wet day, when no work could be done abroad, Moodie took up his flute, or read aloud to us, while John and I sat down to work. The young emigrant, early cast upon the world and his own resources, was an excellent hand at the needle. He would make or mend a shirt with the greatest precision and neatness, and cut out and manufacture his canvas trousers and loose summer-coats with as much adroitness as the most experienced tailor, darn his socks, and mend his boots and shoes, and often volunteered to assist me in knitting the coarse yarn of the country into socks for the children, while he made them moccasins from the dressed deer-skins that we obtained from the Indians.

Scrupulously neat and clean in his person, the only thing which seemed to ruffle his calm temper was the dirty work of logging; he hated to come in from the field with his person and clothes begrimed with charcoal and smoke. Old Jenny used to laugh at him for not being able to eat his meals without first washing his hands and face.

"Och! my dear heart, yer too particular intirely; we've no time in the woods to be clane." She would say to him in answer to his request for soap and a

THE FIRE

towel, "An' is it soap yer a-wantin'? I tell yer that that same is not to the fore; bating the throuble of makin', it's little soap that the misthress can get to wash the clothes for us and the childher, without yer wastin' it in makin' yer purty skin as white as a leddy's. Do, darlint, go down to the lake and wash there; that basin is big enough, anyhow." And John would laugh and go down to the lake to wash, in order to appease the wrath of the old woman. John had a great dislike to cats, and even regarded with an evil eye, our old pet cat, Peppermint, who had taken a great fancy to share his bed and board.

"If I tolerate our own cat," he would say, "I will not put up with such a nuisance as your friend Emilia sends us in the shape of her ugly Tom. Why, where in the world do you think I found that beast sleeping last night?"

I expressed my ignorance.

"In our potato-pot. Now, you will agree with me that potatoes dressed with cat's hair is not a very nice dish. The next time I catch Master Tom in the potato-pot, I will kill him."

"John, you are not in earnest. Mrs. —— would never forgive any injury done to Tom, who is a great favourite."

"Let her keep him at home, then. Think of the brute coming a mile through the woods to steal from us all he can find, and then sleeping off the effects of his depredations in the potato-pot."

I could not help laughing, but I begged John by no means to annoy Emilia by hurting her cat.

The next day, while sitting in the parlour at work,

451

I heard a dreadful squall, and rushed to the rescue. John was standing, with a flushed cheek, grasping a large stick in his hand, and Tom was lying dead at his feet.

"Oh, the poor cat!"

"Yes, I have killed him; but I am sorry for it now. What will Mrs. —— say?"

"She must not know it. I have told you the story of the pig that Jacob killed. You had better bury it with the pig."

John was really sorry for having yielded, in a fit of passion, to do so cruel a thing; yet a few days after he got into a fresh scrape with Mrs. ——'s animals.

The hens were laying up at the barn. John was very fond of fresh eggs, but some strange dog came daily and sucked the eggs. John had vowed to kill the first dog he found in the act. Mr. —— had a very fine bull-dog which he valued very highly; but with Emilia, Chowder was an especial favourite. Bitterly had she bemoaned the fate of Tom, and many were the inquiries she made of us as to his sudden disappearance.

One afternoon John ran into the room. "My dear Mrs. Moodie, what is Mrs. ——'s dog like?"

" A large bull-dog, brindled black and white."

"Then, by Jove, I've shot him!"

"John, John! you mean me to quarrel in earnest with my friend. How could you do it?"

"Why, how the deuce should I know her dog from another? I caught the big thief in the very act of devouring the eggs from under your sitting hen, and I shot him dead without another thought. But I will bury him, and she will never find it out a bit more than she did who killed the cat."

Some time after this, Emilia returned from a visit at P——. The first thing she told me was the loss of the dog. She was so vexed at it, she had had him advertised, offering a reward for his recovery.

I, of course, was called upon to sympathize with her, which I did with a very bad grace. "I did not like the beast," I said; "he was cross and fierce, and I was afraid to go up to her house while he was there."

"Yes; but to lose it so. It is so provoking; and him such a valuable animal. I could not tell how deeply she felt the loss. She would give four dollars to find out who had stolen him."

How near she came to making the grand discovery the sequel will show.

Instead of burying him with the murdered pig and cat, John had scratched a shallow grave in the garden, and concealed the dead brute.

After tea, Emilia requested to look at the garden; and I, perfectly unconscious that it contained the remains of the murdered Chowder, led the way. Mrs. ——, whilst gathering a handful of fine green-peas, suddenly stooped, and looking earnestly at the ground, called to me—

"Come here, Susanna, and tell me what has been buried here. It looks like the tail of a dog."

She might have added, "Of my dog." Murder, it seems, will out. By some strange chance, the grave that covered the mortal remains of Chowder had been disturbed, and the black tail of the dog was sticking out.

453

ROUGHING IT IN THE BUSH

"What can it be?" said I, with an air of perfect innocence. "Shall I call Jenny, and dig it up?"

"Oh no, my dear; it has a shocking smell, but it does look very much like Chowder's tail."

"Impossible! How could it come among my peas?"

"True. Besides, I saw Chowder, with my own eyes, yesterday, following a team; and George C——hopes to recover him for me."

"Indeed! I am glad to hear it. How these mosquitoes sting. Shall we go back to the house?"

While we returned to the house, John, who had overheard the whole conversation, hastily disinterred the body of Chowder, and placed him in the same mysterious grave with Tom and the pig.

Moodie and his friend finished logging-up the eight acres which the former had cleared the previous winter, besides putting in a crop of peas and potatoes, and an acre of Indian corn, reserving the fallow for fall wheat, while we had the promise of a splendid crop of hay off the sixteen acres that had been cleared in 1834. We were all in high spirits, and everything promised fair, until a very trifling circumstance again occasioned us much anxiety and trouble, and was the cause of our losing most of our crop.

Moodie was asked to attend a bee, which was called to construct a corduroy-bridge over a very bad piece of road. He and J. E—— were obliged to go that morning with wheat to the mill, but Moodie lent his yoke of oxen for the work.

The driver selected for them at the bee was the

THE FIRE

brutal M——y, a man noted for his ill-treatment of cattle, especially if the animals did not belong to him. He gave one of the oxen such a severe blow over the loins with a handspike that the creature came home perfectly disabled, just as we wanted his services in the hay-field and harvest.

Moodie had no money to purchase, or even to hire, a mate for the other ox; but he and John hoped that by careful attendance upon the injured animal he might be restored to health in a few days. They conveyed him to a deserted clearing, a short distance from the farm, where he would be safe from injury from the rest of the cattle; and early every morning we went in the canoe to carry poor Duke a warm mash, and to watch the progress of his recovery.

Ah! ye who revel in this world's wealth, how little can you realize the importance which we, in our poverty, attached to the life of this valuable animal! Yes, it even became the subject of prayer, for the bread for ourselves and our little ones depended greatly upon his recovery. We were doomed to disappointment. After nursing him with the greatest attention and care for some weeks, the animal grew daily worse, and suffered such intense agony, as he lay groaning upon the ground, unable to rise, that John shot him to put him out of pain.

Here, then, were we left without oxen to draw in our hay, or secure our other crops. A neighbour, who had an odd ox, kindly lent us the use of him when he was not employed on his own farm; and John and Moodie gave their own work for the occasional loan of a yoke of oxen for a day. But with all these

455

drawbacks, and in spite of the assistance of old Jenny and myself in the field, a great deal of the produce was damaged before it could be secured. The whole summer we had to labour under this disadvantage. Our neighbours were all too busy to give us any help, and their own teams were employed in saving their crops. Fortunately, the few acres of wheat we had to reap were close to the barn, and we carried the sheaves thither by hand, old Jenny proving an invaluable help, both in the harvest and hay-field.

Still, with all these misfortunes, Providence watched over us in a signal manner. We were never left entirely without food. Like the widow's cruse of oil, our means, though small, were never suffered to cease entirely. We had been for some days without meat, when Moodie came running in for his gun. A great she-bear was in the wheat-field at the edge of the wood, very busily employed in helping to harvest the crop. There was but one bullet, and a charge or two of buckshot, in the house; but Moodie started to the wood with the single bullet in his gun, followed by a little terrier dog that belonged to John E——. Old Jenny was busy at the wash-tub, but the moment she saw her master running up the clearing and knew the cause, she left her work and, snatching up the carving-knife, ran after him, that in case the bear should have the best of the fight, she would be there to help "the masther." Finding her shoes incommode her, she flung them off, in order to run faster. A few minutes after came the report of the gun, and I heard Moodie halloo to E——, who was cutting stakes for a fence in the wood. I hardly

THE FIRE

thought it possible that he could have killed the bear, but I ran to the door to listen. The children were all excitement, which the sight of the black monster, borne down the clearing upon two poles, increased to the wildest demonstrations of joy. Moodie and John were carrying the prize, and old Jenny, brandishing her carving-knife, followed in the rear.

The rest of the evening was spent in skinning, and cutting up, and salting the ugly creature, whose flesh filled a barrel with excellent meat, in flavour resembling beef, while the short grain and juicy nature of the flesh gave to it the tenderness of mutton. This was quite a Godsend, and lasted us until we were able to kill two large fat hogs in the fall.

A few nights after, Moodie and I encountered the mate of Mrs. Bruin, while returning from a visit to Emilia, in the very depth of the wood.

We had been invited to meet our friend's father and mother, who had come up on a short visit to the woods; and the evening passed away so pleasantly that it was near midnight before the little party of friends separated. The moon was down. The wood, through which we had to return, was very dark, the ground being low and swampy, and the trees thick and tall. There was, in particular, one very ugly spot where a small creek crossed the road. This creek could only be passed by foot-passengers scrambling over a fallen tree, which, in a dark night, was not very easy to find.

I begged a torch of Mr.——; but no torch could be found. Emilia laughed at my fears; still, knowing what a coward I was in the bush of a night, she

457

found about an inch of candle, which was all that remained from the evening's entertainment. This she put into an old lanthorn.

"It will not last you long, but it will carry you over the creek."

This was something gained, and off we set.

It was so dark in the bush, that our dim candle looked like a solitary red spark in the intense surrounding darkness, and scarcely served to show us the path.

We went chatting along, talking over the news of the evening, Hector running on before us, when I saw a pair of eyes glare upon us from the edge of the swamp, with the green, bright light emitted by the eyes of a cat.

"Did you see those terrible eyes, Moodie?" and I clung, trembling, to his arm.

"What eyes?" said he, feigning ignorance. "It's too dark to see anything. The light is nearly gone, and, if you don't quicken your pace and cross the tree before it goes out, you will, perhaps, get your feet wet by falling into the creek."

"Good Heavens! I saw them again; and do just look at the dog."

Hector stopped suddenly, and, stretching himself along the ground, his nose resting between his fore-paws, began to whine and tremble. Presently he ran back to us, and crept under our feet. The cracking of branches and the heavy tread of some large animal sounded close beside us.

Moodie turned the open lanthorn in the direction from whence the sounds came, and shouted as loud

458

THE FIRE

as he could, at the same time endeavouring to urge forward the fear-stricken dog, whose cowardice was only equalled by my own.

Just at that critical moment the wick of the candle flickered a moment in the socket, and expired. We were left, in perfect darkness, alone with the bear— for such we supposed the animal to be.

My heart beat audibly; a cold perspiration was streaming down my face, but I neither shrieked nor attempted to run. I don't know how Moodie got me over the creek. One of my feet slipped into the water, but expecting, as I did every moment, to be devoured by Master Bruin, that was a thing of no consequence. My husband was laughing at my fears, and every now and then he turned towards our companion, who continued following us at no great distance, and gave him an encouraging shout. Glad enough was I when I saw the gleam of the light from our little cabin window shine out among the trees; and, the moment I got within the clearing I ran, without stopping, until I was safely within the house. John was sitting up for us, nursing Donald. He listened with great interest to our adventure with the bear, and thought that Bruin was very good to let us escape without one affectionate hug.

"Perhaps it would have been otherwise had he known, Moodie, that you had not only killed his good lady, but were dining sumptuously off her carcass every day."

The bear was determined to have something in return for the loss of his wife. Several nights after this, our slumbers were disturbed about midnight by

459

an awful yell, and old Jenny shook violently at our chamber door.

"Masther, masther, dear! Get up wid you this moment, or the bear will desthroy the cattle intirely."

Half asleep, Moodie sprang from his bed, seized his gun, and ran out. I threw my large cloak round me, struck a light, and followed him to the door. The moment the latter was unclosed, some calves that we were rearing rushed into the kitchen, closely followed by the larger beasts, who came bellowing headlong down the hill, pursued by the bear.

It was a laughable scene, as shown by that paltry tallow-candle. Moodie, in his night-shirt, taking aim at something in the darkness, surrounded by the terrified animals; old Jenny, with a large knife in her hand, holding on to the white skirts of her master's garment, making outcry loud enough to frighten away all the wild beasts in the bush—herself almost in a state of nudity.

"Och, masther, dear! don't timpt the ill-conditioned crathur wid charging too near; think of the wife and the childher. Let me come at the rampaging baste an' I'll stick the knife into the heart of him."

Moodie fired. The bear retreated up the clearing with a low growl. Moodie and Jenny pursued him some way, but it was too dark to discern any object at a distance. I, for my part, stood at the open door, laughing until the tears ran down my cheeks, at the glaring eyes of the oxen, their ears erect, and their tails carried gracefully on a level with their backs, as they stared at me and the light in blank astonishment. The noise of the gun had just roused John

THE FIRE

E—— from his slumbers. He was no less amused than myself, until he saw that a fine yearling heifer was bleeding, and found, upon examination, that the poor animal, having been in the claws of the bear, was dangerously, if not mortally hurt.

"I hope," he cried, "that the brute has not touched my foal!" I pointed to the black face of the filly peeping over the back of an elderly cow.

"You see, John, that Bruin preferred veal; there's your 'horsey,' as Dunbar calls her, safe, and laughing at you."

Moodie and Jenny now returned from the pursuit of the bear. E—— fastened all the cattle into the back yard, close to the house. By daylight he and Moodie started in chase of Bruin, whom they tracked by his blood some way into the bush, but here he entirely escaped their search.

THE BEARS OF CANADA.

Oh! *bear* me from this savage land of *bears*,
　For 'tis indeed *unbearable* to me;
I'd rather cope with vilest worldly cares,
　Or writhe with cruel sickness of the sea.
Oh! *bear* me to my own *bare* land of hills,*
　Where I'd be sure brave *bare*-legg'd lads to see—
Bear cakes, *bare* rocks, and whiskey stills,
　And *bare*-legg'd nymphs, to smile once more on me.

I'd *bear* the heat, I'd *bear* the freezing air
　Of equatorial realm or Arctic Sea,
I'd sit all *bare* at night, and watch the Northern *Bear*,
　And bless my soul that he was far from me.
　　　　　　* The Orkney Isles.

461

ROUGHING IT IN THE BUSH

I'd *bear* the poor-rates, tithes, and all the ills
   John Bull must *bear* (who takes them all, poor sinner!
As patients do when forced to gulp down pills,
   And water-gruel drink in lieu of dinner).

I'd *bear* the *bareness* of all barren lands
   Before I'd *bear* the *bearishness* of this;
Bare head, *bare* feet, *bare* legs, *bare* hands,
   Bear everything, but want of social bliss.
But should I die in this drear land of *bears*,
   Oh! ship me off, my friends, discharge the sable wearers,
For if you don't, in spite of priests and prayers,
The *bears* will come, and eat up corpse and *bearers*.

                         J. W. D. M.

CHAPTER TWENTY-ONE
THE OUTBREAK

CHAPTER XXI. THE OUTBREAK

Can a corrupted stream pour through the land
Health-giving waters? Can the slave, who lures
His wretched followers with the hope of gain,
Feel in his bosom the immortal fire
That bound a Wallace to his country's cause,
And bade the Thracian shepherd cast away
Rome's galling yoke; while the astonished world—
Rapt into admiration at the deed—
Paused, ere she crush'd, with overwhelming force,
The man who fought to win a glorious grave?

THE LONG-PROTRACTED HARVEST WAS at length brought to a close. Moodie had procured another ox from Dummer, by giving a note at six months' date for the payment; and he and John E—— were in the middle of sowing their fall crop of wheat, when the latter received a letter from the old country, which conveyed to him intelligence of the death of his mother, and of a legacy of two hundred pounds. It was necessary for him to return to claim the property, and though we felt his loss severely, we could not, without great selfishness, urge him to stay. John had formed an attachment to a young lady in the country, who, like himself, possessed no property. Their engagement, which had existed several years, had been dropped, from its utter hopelessness, by mutual consent. Still the young people continued to love each other, and to look forward to better days, when their prospects might improve so far that E—— would be able to purchase a bush-farm, and raise a house, however lowly, to shelter his Mary.

He, like our friend Malcolm, had taken a fancy to buy a part of our block of land which he could cultivate in partnership with Moodie, without being ob-

2G

liged to hire, when the same barn, cattle, and implements would serve for both. Anxious to free himself from the thraldom of debts which pressed him sore, Moodie offered to part with two hundred acres at less than they cost us, and the bargain was to be considered as concluded directly the money was forthcoming.

It was a sorrowful day when our young friend left us; he had been a constant inmate in the house for nine months, and not one unpleasant word had ever passed between us. He had rendered our sojourn in the woods more tolerable by his society, and sweetened our bitter lot by his friendship and sympathy. We both regarded him as a brother, and parted with him with sincere regret. As to old Jenny, she lifted up her voice and wept, consigning him to the care and protection of all the saints in the Irish calendar.

For several days after John left us, a deep gloom pervaded the house. Our daily toil was performed with less cheerfulness and alacrity; we missed him at the evening board, and at the evening fire; and the children asked each day, with increasing earnestness, when dear E—— would return.

Moodie continued sowing his fall wheat. The task was nearly completed, and the chill October days were fast verging upon winter, when towards the evening of one of them he contrived—I know not how— to crawl down from the field at the head of the hill, faint and pale, and in great pain. He had broken the small bone of his leg. In dragging among the stumps, the heavy machine (which is made in the form of the letter V, and is supplied with large iron teeth) had hitched upon a stump, and being swung off again by the motion of the oxen, had come with great force against his leg. At first he was struck down, and for some time was unable to rise; but at length he contrived to unyoke the team, and crawled partly on his hands and knees down the clearing.

What a sad, melancholy evening that was! Fortune seemed never tired of playing us some ugly trick. The hope which had so long sustained me seemed about to desert me altogether; when I saw him on whom we all depended for subsistence, and whose kindly voice ever cheered us under the pressure of calamity, smitten down helpless, all my courage and faith in the goodness of the Divine Father seemed to forsake me, and I wept long and bitterly.

The next morning I went in search of a messenger, to send to Peterborough for the doctor; but though I found and sent the messenger, the doctor never came. Perhaps he did not like to incur the expense of a fatiguing journey, with small chance of obtaining a sufficient remuneration.

Our dear sufferer contrived, with assistance, to bandage his leg; and after the first week of rest had expired, he amused himself with making a pair of crutches, and in manufacturing Indian paddles for the canoe, axe-handles, and yokes for the oxen. It was wonderful with what serenity he bore this unexpected affliction.

Buried in the obscurity of those woods, we knew nothing, heard nothing of the political state of the country, and were little aware of the revolution which was about to work a great change for us and for Canada.

467

ROUGHING IT IN THE BUSH

The weather continued remarkably mild. The first great snow, which for years had ordinarily fallen between the 10th and 15th of November, still kept off. November passed on; and as all our firewood had to be chopped by old Jenny during the lameness of my husband, I was truly grateful to God for the continued mildness of the weather.

On the 4th of December—that great day of the outbreak—Moodie was determined to take advantage of the open state of the lake to carry a large grist up to Y——'s mill. I urged upon him the danger of a man attempting to manage a canoe in rapid water who was unable to stand without crutches; but Moodie saw that the children would need bread, and he was anxious to make the experiment.

Finding that I could not induce him to give up the journey, I determined to go with him. Old Wittals, who happened to come down that morning, assisted in placing the bags of wheat in the little vessel, and helped to place Moodie at the stern. With a sad, foreboding spirit, I assisted to push off from the shore.

The air was raw and cold, but our sail was not without its pleasure.

The lake was very full from the heavy rains, and the canoe bounded over the waves with a free, springy motion. A slight frost had hung every little bush and spray along the shores with sparkling crystals. The red pigeon-berries, shining through their coating of ice, looked like cornelian beads set in silver, and strung from bush to bush. We found the rapids at the entrance of Bessikakoon Lake very hard to stem, and were so often carried back by the force of the water, that, cold as the air was, the great exertion which Moodie had to make use of to attain the desired object brought the perspiration out in big drops upon his forehead. His long confinement to the house and low diet had rendered him very weak.

The old miller received us in the most hearty and hospitable manner, and complimented me upon my courage in venturing upon the water in such cold, rough weather. Norah was married, but the kind Betty provided us an excellent dinner, while we waited for the grist to be ground.

It was near four o'clock when we started on our return. If there had been danger in going up the stream, there was more in coming down. The wind had changed, the air was frosty, keen, and biting, and Moodie's paddle came up from every dip into the water loaded with ice. For my part, I had only to sit still at the bottom of the canoe, as we floated rapidly down with wind and tide. At the landing we were met by old Jenny, who had a long story to tell us, of which we could make neither head nor tail—how some gentleman had called during our absence, and left a large paper, all about the Queen and the Yankees; that there was war between Canada and the States; that Toronto had been burnt, and the governor killed, and I know not what other strange and monstrous statements. After much fatigue, Moodie climbed the hill, and we were once more safe by our own fireside. Here we found the elucidation of Jenny's marvellous tales: a copy of the Queen's proclamation, calling upon all loyal gentlemen to join in putting down the unnatural rebellion.

ROUGHING IT IN THE BUSH

A letter from my sister explained the nature of the outbreak, and the astonishment with which the news had been received by all the settlers in the bush. My brother and my sister's husband had already gone off to join some of the numerous bands of gentlemen who were collecting from all quarters to march to the aid of Toronto, which it was said was besieged by the rebel force. She advised me not to suffer Moodie to leave home in his present weak state; but the spirit of my husband was aroused, he instantly obeyed what he considered the imperative call of duty, and told me to prepare him a few necessaries, that he might be ready to start early in the morning.

Little sleep visited our eyes that night. We talked over the strange news for hours; our coming separation, and the probability that, if things were as bad as they appeared to be, we might never meet again. Our affairs were in such a desperate condition that Moodie anticipated that any change must be for the better; it was impossible for them to be worse. But the poor, anxious wife thought only of a parting which to her put a finishing stroke to all her misfortunes.

Before the cold, snowy morning broke, we were all stirring. The children, who had learned that their father was preparing to leave them, were crying and clinging round his knees. His heart was too deeply affected to eat; the meal passed over in silence, and he rose to go. I put on my hat and shawl to accompany him through the wood as far as my sister Mrs. T——'s. The day was like our destiny, cold, dark, and lowering. I gave the dear invalid his crutches, and we commenced our sorrowful walk. Then old Jenny's lamentations burst forth, as flinging her arms round my husband's neck, she kissed and blessed him after the fashion of her country.

"Och hone! och hone!" she cried, wringing her hands, "masther dear, why will you lave the wife and the childher? The poor crathur is breakin' her heart intirely at partin' wid you. Shure an' the war is nothin' to you, that you must be goin' into danger, an' you wid a broken leg. Och hone! och hone! come back to your home—you will be kilt, and thin what will become of the wife and the wee bairns?"

Her cries and lamentations followed us into the wood. At my sister's, Moodie and I parted; and with a heavy heart I retraced my steps through the wood. For once I forgot all my fears. I never felt the cold. Sad tears were flowing over my cheeks; when I entered the house, hope seemed to have deserted me, and for upwards of an hour I lay upon the bed and wept.

Poor Jenny did her best to comfort me, but all joy had vanished with him who was my light of life.

Left in the most absolute uncertainty as to the real state of public affairs, I could only conjecture what might be the result of this sudden outbreak. Several poor settlers called at the house during the day, on their way down to Peterborough; but they brought with them the most exaggerated accounts. There had been a battle, they said, with the rebels, and the loyalists had been defeated; Toronto was besieged by sixty thousand men, and all the men in the backwoods were ordered to march instantly to the relief of the city.

In the evening I received a note from Emilia, who

was at Peterborough, in which she informed me that my husband had borrowed a horse of Mr. S——, and had joined a large party of two hundred volunteers, who had left that morning for Toronto; that there had been a battle with the insurgents; that Colonel Moodie had been killed, and the rebels had retreated; and that she hoped my husband would return in a few days.

The honest backwoodsmen, perfectly ignorant of the abuses that had led to the present position of things, regarded the rebels as a set of monsters, for whom no punishment was too severe, and obeyed the call to arms with enthusiasm. The leader of the insurgents must have been astonished at the rapidity with which a large force was collected, as if by magic, to repel his designs. A great number of those volunteers were half-pay officers, many of whom had fought in the continental wars with the armies of Napoleon, and would have been found a host in themselves. I must own that my British spirit was fairly aroused, and, as I could not aid in subduing the enemies of my beloved country with my arm, I did what little I could to serve the good cause with my pen. It may probably amuse my readers to give them a specimen of these loyal staves, which were widely circulated through the Colony at the time:—

THE OATH OF THE CANADIAN VOLUNTEERS.

> Huzza for England!—May she claim
>   Our fond devotion ever;
> And, by the glory of her name,
> Our brave forefathers' honest fame,
>   We swear—no foe shall sever

THE OUTBREAK

Her children from their parent's side;
　　Though parted by the wave,
In weal or woe, whate'er betide,
　　We swear to die, or save
Her honour from the rebel band
Whose crimes pollute our injured land!

Let the foe come—we will not shrink
　　To meet them if they dare;
Well must they fight, ere rashly think
To rend apart one sacred link
　　That binds our country fair
To that dear isle, from whence we sprung,
　　Which gave our fathers birth;
Whose glorious deeds her bards have sung;
　　The unrivall'd of the earth.
The highest privilege we claim,
To own her sway—to bear her name.

Then, courage, loyal volunteers!
　　God will defend the right;
That thought will banish slavish fears,
That blessed consciousness still cheers
　　The soldier in the fight.
The stars for us shall never burn,
　　The stripes may frighten slaves,
The Briton's eye will proudly turn
　　Where Britain's standard waves.
Beneath its folds, if Heaven requires,
We'll die, as died of old our sires!

In a week, Moodie returned. So many volunteers
had poured into Toronto that the number of friends
was likely to prove as disastrous as that of enemies,
on account of the want of supplies to maintain them
all. The companies from the back townships had been
remanded, and I received with delight my own again.
But this re-union did not last long. Several regiments

473

of militia were formed to defend the colony, and to my husband was given the rank of captain in one of those then stationed in Toronto.

On the 20th of January 1838, he bade us a long a-dieu. I was left with old Jenny and the children to take care of the farm. It was a sad, dull time. I could bear up against all trials with him to comfort and cheer me, but his long-continued absence cast a gloom upon my spirit not easily to be shaken off. Still his very appointment to this situation was a signal act of mercy. From his full pay, he was enabled to liquidate many pressing debts and to send home from time to time sums of money to procure necessaries for me and the little ones. These remittances were greatly wanted; but I demurred before laying them out for comforts which we had been so long used to dispense with. It seemed almost criminal to purchase any article of luxury, such as tea and sugar, while a debt remained unpaid.

The Y——y's were very pressing for the thirty pounds that we owed them for the clearing; but they had such a firm reliance upon the honour of my husband, that, poor and pressed for money as we were, they never sued us. I thought it would be a pleasing surprise to Moodie, if, with the sums of money which I occasionally received from him, I could diminish this debt, which had always given him the greatest uneasiness; and, my resolution once formed, I would not allow any temptation to shake it.

The money was always transmitted to Dummer. I only reserved the sum of two dollars a month, to pay a little lad to chop wood for us. After a time, I began to think the Y——y's were gifted with second-sight, for I never received a money-letter but the very next day I was sure to see some of the family.

Just at this period I received a letter from a gentleman, requesting me to write for a magazine (the *Literary Garland*), just started in Montreal, with promise to remunerate me for my labours. Such an application was like a gleam of light springing up in the darkness; it seemed to promise the dawning of a brighter day. I had never been able to turn my thoughts towards literature during my sojourn in the bush. When the body is fatigued with labour, unwonted and beyond its strength, the mind is in no condition for mental occupation.

The year before, I had been requested by an American author, of great merit, to contribute to the *North American Review*, published for several years in Philadelphia; and he promised to remunerate me in proportion to the success of the work. I had contrived to write several articles after the children were asleep, though the expense even of the stationery and the postage of the manuscripts was severely felt by one so destitute of means; but the hope of being the least service to those dear to me cheered me to the task. I never realized anything from that source; but I believe it was not the fault of the editor. Several other American editors had written to me to furnish them with articles, but I was unable to pay the postage of heavy packets to the States, and they could not reach their destination without being paid to the frontier. Thus, all chance of making anything in that way had been abandoned. I wrote to Mr. L——, and frankly

ROUGHING IT IN THE BUSH

informed him how I was situated. In the most liberal manner, he offered to pay the postage on all manuscripts to his office, and left me to name my own terms of remuneration. This opened up a new era in my existence, and for many years I have found in this generous man, to whom I am still personally unknown, a steady friend. I actually shed tears of joy over the first twenty-dollar bill I received from Montreal. It was my own; I had earned it with my own hand; and it seemed to my delighted fancy to form the nucleus out of which a future independence for my family might arise. I no longer retired to bed when the labours of the day were over. I sat up and wrote by the light of a strange sort of candle that Jenny called "sluts," and which the old woman manufactured out of pieces of old rags twisted together and dipped in pork lard, and stuck in a bottle. They did not give a bad light, but it took a great many of them to last me for a few hours.

The faithful old creature regarded my writings with a jealous eye.

"An', shure, it's killin' yerself that you are intirely. You were thin enough before you took to the pen; scriblin' an' scrablin' when you should be in bed an' asleep. What good will it be to your childher, dear heart! if you die afore your time, by wastin' your strength afther that fashion?"

Jenny never could conceive the use of books. "Shure we can live and die widout them. It's only a waste of time botherin' your brains wid the like of them; but, thank goodness! the lard will soon be all done, an' thin we shall hear you spakin' again, instead of sittin' there doubled up all night, destroying your eyes wid porin' over the dirthy writin'."

As the sugar-making season drew near, Jenny conceived the bold thought of making a good *lump* of sugar, that the "childher" might have something to "ate" with their bread during the summer. We had no sugar-kettle, but a neighbour promised to lend us his, and to give us twenty-eight troughs, on condition that we gave him half the sugar we made.

The very first day a terrible accident happened to us; a large log fell upon the sugar-kettle—the borrowed sugar-kettle—and cracked it, spilling all the sap, and rendering the vessel, which had cost four dollars, useless. We were all in dismay. Just at that time Old Wittals happened to pass on his way to Peterborough. He very good-naturedly offered to get the kettle repaired for us, which, he said, could be easily done by a rivet and an iron hoop. But where was the money to come from? I thought awhile. Katie had a magnificent coral and bells, the gift of her godfather; I asked the dear child if she would give it to buy another kettle for Mr. T——. She said, "I would give ten times as much to help mamma."

I wrote a little note to Emilia, who was still at her father's; and Mr. W——, the storekeeper, sent us a fine sugar-kettle back by Wittals, and also the other mended, in exchange for the useless piece of finery. We had now two kettles at work, to the joy of Jenny, who declared that it was a lucky fairy who had broken the old kettle.

While Jenny was engaged in boiling and gathering the sap in the bush, I sugared off the syrup in the house, an operation watched by the children with intense interest. After standing all day over the hot stove-fire, it was quite a refreshment to breathe the pure air at night. Every evening I ran up to see Jenny in the bush, singing and boiling down the sap in the front of her little shanty. The old woman was in her element, and afraid of nothing under the stars; she slept beside her kettles at night, and snapped her fingers at the idea of the least danger. She was sometimes rather despotic in her treatment of her attendant, Sol. One morning, in particular, she bestowed upon the lad a severe cuffing.

I ran up the clearing to the rescue, when my ears were assailed by the "boo-hooing" of the boy.

"What has happened? Why do you beat the child, Jenny?"

"It's jist, thin, I that will bate him—the unlucky omadhawn! Has not he spilt and spiled two buckets of syrup, that I have been the live-long night bilin'? Sorra wid him; I'd like to strip the skin off him, I would! Musha! but 'tis enough to vex a saint."

"Ah, Jenny!" blubbered the poor boy, "but you have no mercy. You forget that I have but one eye, and that I could not see the root which caught my foot and threw me down."

"Faix! an' 'tis a pity that you have the one eye, when you don't know how to make a betther use of it," muttered the angry dame, as she picked up the pails, and pushing him on before her, beat a retreat into the bush.

I was heartily sick of the sugar-making long before the season was over; however, we were well paid for

478

our trouble. Besides one hundred and twelve pounds of fine soft sugar, as good as Muscovado, we had six gallons of molasses, and a keg containing six gallons of excellent vinegar. There was no lack, this year, of nice preserves and pickled cucumbers, dainties found in every native Canadian establishment.

Besides gaining a little money with my pen, I practised a method of painting birds and butterflies upon the white, velvety surface of the large fungi, that grow plentifully upon the bark of the sugar-maple. These had an attractive appearance, and my brother, who was a captain in one of the provisional regiments, sold a great many of them among the officers, without saying by whom they were painted. One rich lady in Peterborough, long since dead, ordered two dozen to send as curiosities to England. These, at one shilling each, enabled me to buy shoes for the children, who, during our bad times, had been forced to dispense with these necessary coverings. How often, during the winter season, have I wept over their little chapped feet, literally washing them with my tears! But these days were to end; Providence was doing great things for us; and Hope raised at last her drooping head, to regard with a brighter glance the far-off future.

Slowly the winter rolled away; but he to whom every thought turned was still distant from his humble home. The receipt of an occasional letter from him was my only solace during his long absence, and we were still too poor to indulge often in this luxury. My poor Katie was as anxious as her mother to hear from her father; and when I did get the long-looked-for prize, she would kneel down before me, her little elbows resting on my knees, her head thrown back, and the tears trickling down her innocent cheeks, eagerly drinking in every word.

The spring brought us plenty of work; we had potatoes and corn to plant, and the garden to cultivate. By lending my oxen for two days' work, I got Wittals, who had no oxen, to drag me in a few acres of oats, and to prepare the land for potatoes and corn. The former I dropped into the earth, while Jenny covered them up with the hoe.

Our garden was well dug and plentifully manured, the woman bringing the manure, which had lain for several years at the barn door, down to the plot in a large Indian basket placed upon a hand-sleigh. We had soon every sort of vegetable sown, with plenty of melons and cucumbers, and all our beds promised a good return. There were large flights of ducks upon the lake every night and morning, but though we had guns, we did not know how to use them. However, I thought of a plan which, I flattered myself, might prove successful; I got Sol to plant two stakes in the shallow water near the rice beds, and to these I attached a slender rope, made by braiding long strips of the inner bark of the basswood together; to these again I fastened, at regular intervals, about a quarter of a yard of whipcord, headed by a strong perch-hook. These hooks I baited with fish offal, leaving them to float just under the water. Early next morning, I saw a fine black duck fluttering upon the line. The boy ran down with the paddles, but before he could reach the spot, the captive got away, by carrying the hook and line with him. At the next stake he found upon the hooks a large eel and a catfish.

I had never before seen one of those whiskered, toad-like natives of the Canadian waters (so common to the Bay of Quinté, where they grow to a great size), that I was really terrified at the sight of the hideous beast, and told Sol to throw it away. In this I was very foolish, for they are esteemed good eating in many parts of Canada, but to me the sight of the reptile-like thing is enough—it is uglier and far more disgusting-looking than a toad.

When the trees came into leaf, and the meadows were green and flushed with flowers, the poor children used to talk constantly to me of their father's return; their innocent prattle made me very sad. Every evening we walked into the wood, along the path that he must come whenever he did return home, to meet him; and, though it was a vain hope, and the walk was taken just to amuse the little ones, I used to be silly enough to feel deeply disappointed when we returned alone. Donald, who was a mere baby when his father left us, could just begin to put words together. "Who is papa?" "When will he come?" "Will he come by the road?" "Will he come in a canoe?" The little creature's curiosity to see this unknown father was really amusing; and oh! how I longed to present the little fellow, with his rosy cheeks and curling hair, to his father; he was so fair, so altogether charming in my eyes. Emilia had called him Cedric the Saxon; and he well suited the name, with his frank, honest disposition, and large, loving, blue eyes.

ROUGHING IT IN THE BUSH

June had commenced; the weather was very warm, and Mr. T—— had sent for the loan of old Jenny to help him for a day with his potatoes. I had just prepared dinner when the old woman came shrieking like a mad thing down the clearing, and waving her hands towards me. I could not imagine what had happened.

"Ninny's mad!" whispered Dunbar; "she's the old girl for making a noise."

"Joy! joy!" bawled out the old woman, now running breathlessly towards us. "The masther's come —the masther's come!"

"Where?—where?"

"Jist above in the wood. Goodness gracious! I have run to let you know—so fast—that my heart— is like to—break."

Without stopping to comfort poor Jenny, off started the children and myself, at the very top of our speed; but I soon found that I could not run—I was too much agitated. I got to the head of the bush, and sat down upon a fallen tree. The children sprang forward like wild kids, all but Donald, who remained with his old nurse. I covered my face with my hands, my heart, too, was beating audibly, and now that he was come, and was so near me, I scarcely could command strength to meet him. The sound of happy young voices roused me up; the children were leading him along in triumph, and he was bending down to them, all smiles, but hot and tired with his long journey. It was almost worth our separation, that blissful meeting. In a few minutes he was at home, and the children upon his knees. Katie stood silently

482

holding his hand, but Addie and Dunbar had a thousand things to tell him. Donald was frightened at his military dress, but he peeped at him from behind my gown, until I caught and placed him in his father's arms.

His leave of absence only extended to a fortnight. It had taken him three days to come all the way from Lake Erie, where his regiment was stationed at Point Abino; and the same time would be consumed in his return. He could only remain with us eight days. How soon they fled away! How bitter was the thought of parting with him again! He had brought money to pay the Y——y's. How surprised he was to find their large debt more than half liquidated. How gently did he chide me for depriving myself and the children of the little comforts he had designed for us, in order to make this sacrifice. But never was self-denial more fully rewarded; I felt happy in having contributed in the least to pay a just debt to kind and worthy people. You must become poor yourself before you can fully appreciate the good qualities of the poor—before you can sympathize with them, and fully recognize them as your brethren in the flesh. Their benevolence to each other, exercised amidst want and privation, as far surpasses the munificence of the rich towards them, as the exalted philanthropy of Christ and His disciples does the Christianity of the present day. The rich man gives from his abundance; the poor man shares with a distressed comrade his all.

One short, happy week too soon fled away, and we were once more alone. In the fall, my husband

483

expected the regiment in which he held his commission would be reduced, which would again plunge us into the same distressing poverty. Often of a night I revolved these things in my mind, and perplexed myself with conjectures as to what in future was to become of us. Although he had saved all he could from his pay, it was impossible to pay several hundreds of pounds of debt; and the steam-boat stock still continued a dead letter. To remain much longer in the woods was impossible, for the returns from the farm scarcely fed us, and but for the clothing sent us by our friends from home, who were not aware of our real difficulties, we should have been badly off indeed.

I pondered over every plan that thought could devise; at last, I prayed to the Almighty to direct me as to what would be the best course for us to pursue. A sweet assurance stole over me, and soothed my spirit, that God would provide for us, as He had hitherto done—that a great deal of our distress arose from want of faith. I was just sinking into a calm sleep when the thought seemed whispered into my soul, "Write to the Governor; tell him candidly all you have suffered during your sojourn in this country, and trust to God for the rest."

At first I paid little heed to this suggestion; but it became so importunate that at last I determined to act upon it as if it were a message sent from heaven. I rose from my bed, struck a light, sat down, and wrote a letter to the Lieutenant-Governor, Sir George Arthur, a simple statement of facts, leaving it to his benevolence to pardon the liberty I had taken in addressing him.

THE OUTBREAK

I asked of him to continue my husband in the militia service, in the same regiment in which he now held the rank of captain, which, by enabling him to pay our debts, would rescue us from our present misery. Of the political character of Sir George Arthur I knew nothing. I addressed him as a man and a Christian; and I acknowledge, with the deepest and most heartfelt gratitude, the generous kindness of his conduct towards us.

Before the day dawned, my letter was ready for the post. The first secret I ever had from my husband was the writing of that letter; and, proud and sensitive as he was, and averse to asking the least favour of the great, I was dreadfully afraid that the act I had just done would be displeasing to him; still, I felt resolutely determined to send it. After giving the children their breakfast, I walked down and read it to my brother-in-law, who was not only much pleased with its contents, but took it down himself to the post-office.

Shortly after, I received a letter from my husband, informing me that the regiment had been reduced, and that he should be home in time to get in the harvest. Most anxiously I awaited a reply to my application from the Governor, but no reply came.

The first week in August our dear Moodie came home, and brought with him, to our no small joy, J. E——, who had just returned from Ireland. E—— had been disappointed about the money, which was subject to litigation; and, tired of waiting at home until the tedious process of the law should terminate,

485

he had come back to the woods, and, before night, was reinstated in his old quarters.

His presence made Jenny all alive; she dared him at once to a trial of skill with her in the wheat-field, which E—— prudently declined. He did not expect to stay longer in Canada than the fall, but, whilst he did stay, he was to consider our house his home.

That harvest was the happiest we ever spent in the bush. We had enough of the common necessaries of life. A spirit of peace and harmony pervaded our little dwelling, for the most affectionate attachment existed among its members. We were not troubled with servants, for the good old Jenny we regarded as an humble friend, and were freed, by that circumstance, from many of the cares and vexations of a bush life. Our evening excursions on the lake were doubly enjoyed after the labours of the day, and night brought us calm and healthful repose.

The political struggles that convulsed the country were scarcely echoed in the depths of those primeval forests, though the expulsion of Mackenzie from Navy Island, and the burning of the Caroline by Captain Drew, had been discussed on the farthest borders of civilization.

CHAPTER TWENTY-TWO
THE WHIRLWIND

RICE LAKE

CHAPTER XXII. THE WHIRLWIND*

"Dark heavy clouds were gathering in the west,
  Wrapping the forest in funereal gloom;
Onward they roll'd, and rear'd each livid crest,
  Like Death's murk shadows frowning o'er earth's tomb.
From out the inky womb of that deep night
  Burst livid flashes of electric flame.
Whirling and circling with terrific might,
  In wild confusion on the tempest came.
Nature, awakening from her still repose,
  Shudders responsive to the whirlwind's shock,
Feels at her mighty heart convulsive throes;
  Her groaning forests to earth's centre rock."

S. S.

THE 19th OF AUGUST CAME, AND OUR harvest was all safely housed. Business called Moodie away for a few days to Cobourg. Jenny had gone to Dummer to visit her friends, and J. E—— had taken a grist of the new wheat, which he and Moodie had threshed the day before, to the mill. I was consequently left alone with the children, and had a double portion of work to do. During their absence it was my lot to witness the most awful storm I ever beheld, and a vivid recollection of its terrors was permanently fixed upon my memory.

The weather had been intensely hot during the three preceding days, although the sun was entirely obscured by a bluish haze, which seemed to render the unusual heat of the atmosphere more oppressive. Not a breath of air stirred the vast forest, and the waters of the lake assumed a leaden hue. After passing a sleepless night, I arose, a little after daybreak, to superintend my domestic affairs. E—— took his

* For the poem that heads this chapter, I am indebted to my brother, Mr. Sutherland, of Douro, C. W.

489

breakfast and went off to the mill, hoping that the rain would keep off until after his return.

"It is no joke," he said, "being upon these lakes in a small canoe, heavily laden, in a storm."

Before the sun rose, the heavens were covered with hard-looking clouds of a deep blue and black cast, fading away to white at their edges, and in form resembling the long, rolling waves of a heavy sea—but with this difference, that the clouds were perfectly motionless, piled in long curved lines, one above the other, and so remained until four o'clock in the afternoon. The appearance of these clouds, as the sun rose above the horizon, was the most splendid that can be imagined, tinged up to the zenith with every shade of saffron, gold, rose-colour, scarlet, and crimson, fading away into the deepest violet. Never did the storm-fiend shake in the face of day a more gorgeous banner; and, pressed as I was for time, I stood gazing like one entranced upon the magnificent pageant.

As the day advanced, the same blue haze obscured the sun, which frowned redly through his misty veil. At ten o'clock the heat was suffocating, and I extinguished the fire in the cooking-stove, determined to make our meals upon bread and milk rather than add to the oppressive heat. The thermometer in the shade ranged from ninety-six to ninety-eight degrees, and I gave over my work and retired with the little ones to the coolest part of the house. The young creatures stretched themselves upon the floor, unable to jump about or play; the dog lay panting in the shade; the fowls half-buried themselves in the dust, with open beaks and outstretched wings. All nature seemed to droop beneath the scorching heat.

Unfortunately for me, a gentleman arrived about one o'clock from Kingston, to transact some business with my husband. He had not tasted food since six o'clock, and I was obliged to kindle the fire to prepare his dinner. It was one of the hardest tasks I ever performed; I almost fainted with the heat, and most inhospitably rejoiced when his dinner was over and I saw him depart. Shortly after, my friend Mrs. C—— and her brother called in, on their way from Peterborough.

"How do you bear the heat?" asked Mrs. C——. "This is one of the hottest days I ever remember to have experienced in this part of the province. I am afraid that it will end in a hurricane, or what the Lower Canadians term 'l'orage.'"

About four o'clock they rose to go. I urged them to stay longer. "No," said Mrs. C——, "the sooner we get home the better. I think we can reach it before the storm breaks."

I took Donald in my arms, and my eldest boy by the hand, and walked with them to the brow of the hill, thinking that the air would be cooler in the shade. In this I was mistaken. The clouds over our heads hung so low, and the heat was so great, that I was soon glad to retrace my steps.

The moment I turned round to face the lake, I was surprised at the change that had taken place in the appearance of the heavens. The clouds, that had before lain so motionless, were now in rapid motion, hurrying and chasing each other round the horizon.

491

ROUGHING IT IN THE BUSH

It was a strangely awful sight. Before I felt a breath of the mighty blast that had already burst on the other side of the lake, branches of trees, leaves, and clouds of dust were whirled across the lake, whose waters rose in long sharp furrows, fringed with foam, as if moved in their depths by some unseen but powerful agent.

Panting with terror, I just reached the door of the house as the hurricane swept up the hill, crushing and overturning everything in its course. Spell-bound, I stood at the open door with clasped hands, unable to speak, rendered dumb and motionless by the terrible grandeur of the scene, while little Donald, who could not utter many intelligible words, crept to my feet, appealing to me for protection, and his rosy cheeks paled even to marble whiteness. The hurrying clouds gave to the heavens the appearance of a pointed dome, round which the lightning played in broad ribbons of fire. The roaring of the thunder, the rushing of the blast, the impetuous downpouring of the rain, and the crash of falling trees were perfectly deafening; and in the midst of this uproar of the elements, old Jenny burst in, drenched with wet, and half-dead with fear.

"The Lord preserve us!" she cried, "this surely is the day of judgment. Fifty trees fell across my very path, between this an' the creek. Mrs. C—— just reached her brother's clearing a few minutes before a great oak fell on her very path. What thunder!— what lightning! Misthress, dear!—it's turn'd so dark, I can only jist see yer face."

Glad enough was I of her presence; for to be alone

in the heart of the great forest, in a log hut, on such a night, was not a pleasing prospect. People gain courage by companionship, and in order to reassure each other, struggle to conceal their fears.

"And where is Mr. E——?"

"I hope not on the lake. He went early this morning to get the wheat ground at the mill."

"Och, the crathur! He's surely drowned. What boat could stan' such a scrimmage as this?"

I had my fears for poor John; but as the chance that he had to wait at the mill till others were served was more than probable, I tried to still my apprehensions for his safety.

The storm soon passed over, after having levelled several acres of wood near the house, and smitten down in its progress two gigantic pines in the clearing, which must have withstood the force of a thousand winters.

A few minutes after our household had retired to rest, my first sleep was broken by the voice of J. E——, speaking to old Jenny in the kitchen. He had been overtaken by the storm, but had run his canoe ashore upon an island before its full fury burst, and turned it over the flour; while he had to brave the terrors of the pitiless tempest—buffeted by the wind, and drenched with torrents of rain. I got up and made him a cup of tea, while Jenny prepared a rasher of bacon and eggs for his supper.

Shortly after this, J. E—— bade a final adieu to Canada, with his cousin C. W——. He volunteered into the Scots Greys, and we never saw him more; but I have been told that he was so highly respected by the officers of the regiment, that they subscribed for his commission; that he rose to the rank of lieutenant; accompanied the regiment to India, and was at the taking of Cabul; but from himself we never heard again.

The 16th of October, my third son was born; and a few days after, my husband was appointed paymaster to the militia regiments in the V. District, with the rank and full pay of captain.

This was Sir George Arthur's doings. He returned no answer to my application, but he did not forget us.

As the time that Moodie might retain his situation was very doubtful, he thought it advisable not to remove me and the family until he could secure some permanent situation; by so doing, he would have a better opportunity of saving the greater part of his income to pay off his old debts.

This winter of 1839 was one of severe trial to me. Hitherto I had enjoyed the blessing of health; but both the children and myself were now doomed to suffer from dangerous attacks of illness. All the little things had malignant scarlet fever, and, for several days, I thought it would please the Almighty to take from me my two girls. This fever is so fatal to children in Canada, that none of my neighbours dared approach the house. For three weeks Jenny and I were never undressed; our whole time was taken up in nursing the five little helpless creatures through the successive stages of their alarming disease. I sent for Dr. Taylor; but he did not come, and I was obliged to trust to the mercy of God, and my own judgment and good nursing. Though I escaped the fever, mental anxiety and fatigue brought on other illness, which, for nearly ten weeks, rendered me perfectly helpless. When I was again able to creep from my sick-bed, the baby was seized with an illness which Dr. B—— pronounced mortal. Against all hope, he recovered, but these severe mental trials rendered me weak and nervous, and more anxious than ever to be re-united to my husband. To add to these troubles, my sister and her husband sold their farm, and removed from our neighbourhood. Mr. —— had returned to England, and had obtained a situation in the Customs; and his wife, my friend Emilia, was keeping a school in the village; so that I felt more solitary than ever, thus deprived of so many kind, sympathizing friends.

CHAPTER TWENTY-THREE
THE WALK TO DUMMER

We trod a weary path, through silent woods,
Tangled and dark, unbroken by a sound
Of cheerful life. The melancholy shriek
Of hollow winds careering o'er the snow,
Or tossing into waves the green pine tops,
Making the ancient forest groan and sigh
Beneath their mocking voice, awoke alone
The solitary echoes of the place.

READER! HAVE YOU EVER HEARD OF A
place situated in the forest-depths of this far western
wilderness, called Dummer? Ten years ago, it might
not inaptly have been termed "The *last* clearing in
the world." Nor to this day do I know of any in that
direction which extends beyond it. Our bush-farm
was situated on the border-line of a neighbouring
township, only one degree less wild, less out of the
world, or nearer to the habitations of civilization than
the far-famed "English Line," the boast and glory of
this *terra incognita*.

This place, so named by the emigrants who had
pitched their tents in that solitary wilderness, was a
long line of cleared land, extending upon either side
for some miles through the darkest and most interminable forest. The English Line was inhabited
chiefly by Cornish miners, who, tired of burrowing
like moles underground, had determined to emigrate
to Canada, where they could breathe the fresh air of
Heaven, and obtain the necessaries of life upon the
bosom of their mother earth. Strange as it may appear, these men made good farmers, and steady, industrious colonists, working as well above ground as
they had toiled in their early days beneath it. All
our best servants came from Dummer; and although

499

they spoke a language difficult to be understood, and were uncouth in their manners and appearance, they were faithful and obedient, performing the tasks assigned to them with patient perseverance; good food and kind treatment rendering them always cheerful and contented.

My dear old Jenny, that most faithful and attached of all humble domestic friends, came from Dummer, and I was wont to regard it with complacency for her sake. But Jenny was not English; she was a generous, warm-hearted daughter of the Green Isle—the Emerald gem set in the silver of ocean. Yes, Jenny was one of the poorest children of that impoverished but glorious country where wit and talent seem indigenous, springing up spontaneously in the rudest and most uncultivated minds; showing what the land could bring forth in its own strength, unaided by education, and unfettered by the conventional rules of society. Jenny was a striking instance of the worth, noble self-denial, and devotion which are often met with—and, alas! but too often disregarded—in the poor and ignorant natives of that deeply-injured and much-abused land. A few words about my old favourite may not prove uninteresting to my readers.

Jenny Buchanan, or as she called it, Bohánon, was the daughter of a petty exciseman of Scotch extraction who, at the time of her birth, resided near the old town of Inniskillen. Her mother died a few months after she was born, and her father, within the twelve months, married again. In the meanwhile the poor orphan babe had been adopted by a kind neighbour, the wife of a small farmer in the vicinity.

THE WALK TO DUMMER

In return for coarse food and scanty clothing, the little Jenny became a servant-of-all-work. She fed the pigs, herded the cattle, assisted in planting potatoes, and digging peat from the bog, and was undisputed mistress of the poultry-yard. As she grew up to womanhood, the importance of her labours increased. A better reaper in the harvest-field, or footer of turf in the bog, could not be found in the district, or a woman more thoroughly acquainted with the management of cows and the rearing of young cattle; but here poor Jenny's accomplishments terminated.

Her usefulness was all abroad. Within the house she made more dirt than she had the inclination or the ability to clear away. She could neither read, nor knit, nor sew; and although she called herself a Protestant, and a Church of England woman, she knew no more of religion, as revealed to man through the Word of God, than the savage who sinks to the grave in ignorance of a Redeemer. Hence she stoutly resisted all idea of being a sinner, or of standing the least chance of receiving hereafter the condemnation of one.

"Och, shure thin," she would say, with simple earnestness of look and manner, almost irresistible. "God will never throuble Himsel' about a poor, hard-working crathur like me, who never did any harm to the manest of His makin'."

One thing was certain, that a benevolent Providence had "throubled Himsel'" about poor Jenny in times past, for the warm heart of this neglected child of nature contained a stream of the richest benevolence, which, situated as she had been, could not have been derived from any other source. Honest, faithful, and industrious, Jenny became a law unto herself, and practically illustrated the golden rule of her blessed Lord, "to do unto others as we would they should do unto us." She thought it was impossible that her poor services could ever repay the debt of gratitude that she owed to the family who had brought her up, although the obligation must have been entirely on their side. To them she was greatly attached— for them she toiled unceasingly; and when evil days came, and they were not able to meet the rent-day, or to occupy the farm, she determined to accompany them in their emigration to Canada, and formed one of the stout-hearted band that fixed its location in the lonely and unexplored wilds now known as the township of Dummer.

During the first year of their settlement, the means of obtaining the common necessaries of life became so precarious, that, in order to assist her friends with a little ready money, Jenny determined to hire out into some wealthy house as a servant. When I use the term wealth as applied to any bush-settler, it is of course only comparatively; but Jenny was anxious to obtain a place with settlers who enjoyed a small income independent of their forest means.

Her first speculation was a complete failure. For five long, hopeless years she served a master from whom she never received a farthing of her stipulated wages. Still her attachment to the family was so strong and had become so much the necessity of her life, that the poor creature could not make up her mind to leave them. The children whom she had received into her arms at their birth, and whom she had nursed with maternal tenderness, were as dear to her as if they had been her own; she continued to work for them although her clothes were worn to tatters, and her own friends were too poor to replace them.

Her master, Captain N———, a handsome, dashing officer, who had served many years in India, still maintained the carriage and appearance of a gentleman, in spite of his mental and moral degradation arising from a constant state of intoxication; he still promised to remunerate at some future day her faithful services; and although all his neighbours well knew that his means were exhausted, and that that day would never come, yet Jenny, in the simplicity of her faith, still toiled on, in the hope that the better day he spoke of would soon arrive.

And now a few words respecting this master, which I trust may serve as warning to others. Allured by the bait that has been the ruin of so many of his class, the offer of a large grant of land, Captain N——— had been induced to form a settlement in this remote and untried township, laying out much, if not all, of his available means in building a log house, and clearing a large extent of barren and stony land. To this uninviting home he conveyed a beautiful young wife, and a small and increasing family. The result may be easily anticipated. The want of society—a dreadful want to a man of his previous habits—the total absence of all the comforts and decencies of life, produced inaction, apathy, and, at last, despondency, which was only alleviated by a constant and immoderate use of ardent spirits. As long as Captain N———

retained his half-pay, he contrived to exist. In an evil hour he parted with this, and quickly trod the downhill path to ruin.

And here I would remark that it is always a rash and hazardous step for any officer to part with his half-pay, although it is almost every day done, and generally followed by the same disastrous results. A certain income, however small, in a country where money is so hard to be procured, and where labour cannot be attained but at a very high pecuniary remuneration, is invaluable to a gentleman unaccustomed to agricultural employment; who, without this reserve to pay his people, during the brief but expensive seasons of seed-time and harvest, must either work himself or starve. I have known no instance in which such sale has been attended with ultimate advantage; but, alas! too many in which it has terminated in the most distressing destitution. These government grants of land, to half-pay officers, have induced numbers of this class to emigrate to the backwoods of Canada, who are totally unfit for pioneers; but tempted by the offer of finding themselves landholders of what, on paper, appear to them fine estates, they resign a certainty, to waste their energies and die half-starved and broken-hearted in the depths of the pitiless wild.

If a gentleman so situated would give up all idea of settling on his grant, but hire a good farm in a favourable situation—that is, not too far from a market—and with his half-pay hire efficient labourers, of which plenty are now to be had, to cultivate the land, with common prudence and economy, he would soon obtain a comfortable subsistence for his family. And if

504

SUGAR MAKING

the males were brought up to share the burthen and heat of the day, the expense of hired labour, as it yearly diminished, would add to the general means and well-being of the whole, until the hired farm became the real property of the industrious tenants. But the love of show, the vain boast of appearing richer and better dressed than our neighbours, too often involves the emigrant's family in debt, from which they are seldom able to extricate themselves without sacrificing the means which would have secured their independence.

This, although a long digression, will not, I hope, be without its use; and if this book is regarded not as a work of amusement but one of practical experience, written for the benefit of others, it will not fail to convey some useful hints to those who have contemplated emigration to Canada, the best country in the world for the industrious and well-principled man, who really comes out to work, and to better his condition by the labour of his hands; but a gulf of ruin to the vain and idle, who only set foot upon these shores to accelerate their ruin.

But to return to Captain N——. It was at this disastrous period that Jenny entered his service. Had her master adapted his habits and expenditure to his altered circumstances, much misery might have been spared, both to himself and his family. But he was a proud man—too proud to work, or to receive with kindness the offers of service tendered to him by his half-civilized but well-meaning neighbours.

"Hang him!" cried an indignant English settler (Captain N—— was an Irishman), whose offer of drawing wood had been rejected with unmerited contempt. "Wait a few years, and we shall see what his pride will do for him. I *am* sorry for his poor wife and children; but for himself, I have no pity for him."

This man had been uselessly insulted, at the very moment when he was anxious to perform a kind and benevolent action; when, like a true Englishman, his heart was softened by witnessing the sufferings of a young, delicate female and her infant family. Deeply affronted by the captain's foolish conduct, he now took a malignant pleasure in watching his arrogant neighbour's progress to ruin.

The year after the sale of his commission, Captain N—— found himself considerably in debt. "Never mind, Ella," he said to his anxious wife; "the crops will pay all."

The crops were a failure that year. Creditors pressed hard; the captain had no money to pay his workmen, and he would not work himself. Disgusted with his location, but unable to change it for a better; without friends in his own class (for he was the only gentleman then resident in the new township), to relieve the monotony of his existence with their society, or to afford him advice or assistance in his difficulties, the fatal whiskey-bottle became his refuge from gloomy thoughts.

His wife, an amiable and devoted creature, wellborn, well-educated, and deserving of a better lot, did all in her power to wean him from the growing vice. But, alas! the pleadings of an angel, in such circumstances, would have had little effect upon the mind of such a man. He loved her as well as he could love

506

anything, and he fancied that he loved his children, while he was daily reducing them, by his favourite vice, to beggary.

For awhile he confined his excesses to his own fire-side, but this was only for as long a period as the sale of his stock and land would supply him with the means of criminal indulgence. After a time, all these resources failed, and his large grant of eight hundred acres of land had been converted into whiskey, except the one hundred acres on which his house and barn stood, embracing the small clearing from which the family derived their scanty supply of wheat and pot-atoes. For the sake of peace, his wife gave up all her ornaments and household plate, and the best articles of a once handsome and ample wardrobe, in the hope of hiding her sorrows from the world, and keeping her husband at home.

The pride that had rendered him so obnoxious to his humbler neighbours, yielded at length to the in-ordinate craving for drink; the man who had held himself so high above his honest and industrious fellow-settlers, could now unblushingly enter their cabins and beg for a drop of whiskey. The feeling of shame once subdued, there was no end to his audaci-ous mendicity. His whole time was spent in wander-ing about the country, calling upon every new set-tler, in the hope of being asked to partake of the cov-eted poison. He was even known to enter by the window of an emigrant's cabin, during the absence of the owner, and remain drinking in the house while a drop of spirits could be found in the cupboard. When driven forth by the angry owner of the hut, he

ROUGHING IT IN THE BUSH

wandered on to the distant town of P——, and lived there in a low tavern, while his wife and children were starving at home.

"He is the filthiest beast in the township," said the afore-mentioned neighbour to me; "it would be a good thing for his wife and children if his worthless neck were broken in one of his drunken sprees."

This might be the melancholy fact, but it was not the less dreadful on that account. The husband of an affectionate wife—the father of a lovely family—and his death to be a matter of rejoicing!—a blessing, instead of being an affliction!—an agony not to be thought upon without the deepest sorrow.

It was at this melancholy period of her sad history, that Mrs. N—— found, in Jenny Buchanan, a help in her hour of need. The heart of the faithful creature bled for the misery which involved the wife of her degraded master, and the children she so dearly loved. Their want and destitution called all the sympathies of her ardent nature into active operation; they were long indebted to her labour for every morsel of food which they consumed. For them she sowed, she planted, she reaped. Every block of wood which shed a cheering warmth around their desolate home was cut from the forest by her own hands, and brought up a steep hill to the house upon her back. For them she coaxed the neighbours, with whom she was a general favourite, out of many a mess of eggs for their especial benefit; while with her cheerful songs, and hearty, hopeful disposition, she dispelled much of the cramping despair which chilled the heart of the unhappy mother in her deserted home.

508

THE WALK TO DUMMER

For several years did this great, poor woman keep the wolf from the door of her beloved mistress, toiling for her with the strength and energy of a man. When was man ever so devoted, so devoid of all selfishness, so attached to employers yet poorer than herself, as this uneducated Irishwoman?

A period was at length put to her unrequited services. In a fit of intoxication her master beat her severely with the iron ramrod of his gun, and turned her, with abusive language, from his doors. Oh, hard return, for all her unpaid labours of love! She forgave this outrage for the sake of the helpless beings who depended upon her care. He repeated the injury, and the poor creature returned almost heartbroken to her former home.

Thinking that his spite would subside in a few days, Jenny made a third effort to enter his house in her usual capacity; but Mrs N—— told her, with many tears, that her presence would only enrage her husband, who had threatened herself with the most cruel treatment if she allowed the faithful servant again to enter the house. Thus ended her five years' service to the ungrateful master. Such was her reward!

I heard of Jenny's worth and kindness from the Englishman who had been so grievously affronted by Captain N——, and sent for her to come to me. She instantly accepted my offer, and returned with my messenger. She had scarcely a garment to cover her. I was obliged to find her a suit of clothes before I could set her to work. The smiles and dimples of my curly-headed, rosy little Donald, then a baby-boy of fifteen months, consoled the old woman for her separation from Ellie N——; and the good-will with which all the children (now four in number) regarded the kind old body, soon endeared to her the new home which Providence had assigned to her.

Her accounts of Mrs. N——, and her family, soon deeply interested me in her fate; and Jenny never went to visit her friends in Dummer without an interchange of good wishes passing between us.

The year of the Canadian rebellion came, and brought with it sorrow into many a bush dwelling. Old Jenny and I were left alone with the little children, in the depths of the dark forest, to help ourselves in the best way we could. Men could not be procured in that thinly-settled spot for love nor money, and I now fully realized the extent of Jenny's usefulness. Daily she yoked the oxen, and brought down from the bush fuel to maintain our fires, which she felled and chopped up with her own hands. She fed the cattle, and kept all things snug about the doors, not forgetting to load her master's two guns, "in case," as she said, "the ribels should attack us in our retreat."

The months of November and December of 1838 had been unnaturally mild for this iron climate; but the opening of the ensuing January brought a short but severe spell of frost and snow. We felt very lonely in our solitary dwelling, crouching round the blazing fire, that scarcely chased the cold from our miserable log-tenement, until this dreary period was suddenly cheered by the unexpected presence of my beloved friend, Emilia, who came to spend a week with me in my forest home.

THE WALK TO DUMMER

She brought her own baby-boy with her, and an ample supply of buffalo robes, not forgetting a treat of baker's bread, and "sweeties" for the children. Oh, dear Emilia! best and kindest of women, though absent in your native land, long, long shall my heart cherish with affectionate gratitude all your visits of love, and turn to you as a sister, tried, and found most faithful, in the dark hour of adversity, and amidst the almost total neglect of those from whom nature claimed a tenderer and holier sympathy.

Great was the joy of Jenny at this accession to our family party; and after Mrs. S—— was well warmed and had partaken of tea—the only refreshment we could offer her—we began to talk over the news of the place.

"By the bye, Jenny," said she, turning to the old servant, who was undressing the little boy by the fire, "have you heard lately from poor Mrs. N——? We have been told that she and the family are in a dreadful state of destitution. That worthless man has left them for the States, and it is supposed that he has joined Mackenzie's band of ruffians on Navy Island; but whether this be true or false, he has deserted his wife and children, taking his eldest son along with him (who might have been of some service at home), and leaving them without money or food."

"The good Lord! What will become of the cra-thurs?" responded Jenny, wiping her wrinkled cheek with the back of her hard, brown hand. "An' thin they have not a sowl to chop and draw them fire-wood; an' the weather so oncommon savare. Och, hone! what has not that *baste* of a man to answer for?"

ROUGHING IT IN THE BUSH

"I heard," continued Mrs. S——, "that they have tasted no food but potatoes for the last nine months, and scarcely enough of them to keep soul and body together; that they have sold their last cow, and the poor young lady and her second brother, a lad of only twelve years old, bring all the wood for the fire from the bush on a hand-sleigh."

"Oh dear!—oh dear!" sobbed Jenny; an' I not there to hilp them! An' poor Miss Mary, the tinder thing! Oh, 'tis hard, terribly hard upon the crathurs, an' they not used to the like."

"Can nothing be done for them?" said I.

"That is what we want to know," returned Emilia, "and that was one of my reasons for coming up to D——. I wanted to consult you and Jenny upon the subject. You, who are an officer's wife, and I, who am both an officer's wife and daughter, ought to devise some plan of rescuing this unfortunate lady and her family from her present forlorn situation.

The tears sprang to my eyes, and I thought, in the bitterness of my heart, upon my own galling poverty, that my pockets did not contain even a single copper, and that I had scarcely garments enough to shield me from the inclemency of the weather. By unflinching industry, and taking my part in the toil of the field, I had bread for myself and family, and this was more than poor Mrs. N—— possessed; but it appeared impossible for me to be of any assistance to the unhappy sufferer, and the thought of my incapacity gave me severe pain. It was only in moments like the present that I felt the curse of poverty.

THE WALK TO DUMMER

"Well," continued my friend, "you see, Mrs. Moodie, that the ladies of P—— are all anxious to do what they can for her; but they first want to learn if the miserable circumstances in which she is said to be placed are true. In short, my dear friend, they want you and me to make a pilgrimage to Dummer, to see the poor lady herself; and then they will be guided by our report."

"Then let us lose no time in going upon our own mission of mercy."

"Och, my dear heart, you will be lost in the woods!" said old Jenny. "It is nine long miles to the first clearing, and that through a lonely, blazed path. After you are through the beaver-meadow, there is not a single hut for you to rest or warm yourselves. It is too much for the both of yees; you will be frozen to death on the road."

"No fear," said my benevolent friend; "God will take care of us, Jenny. It is on His errand we go; to carry a message of hope to one about to perish."

"The Lord bless you for a darlint," cried the old woman, devoutly kissing the velvet cheek of the little fellow sleeping upon her lap. "May your own purty child never know the want and sorrow that is around her."

Emilia and I talked over the Dummer scheme until we fell asleep. Many were the plans we proposed for the immediate relief of the unfortunate family. Early the next morning, my brother-in-law, Mr. T——, called upon my friend. The subject next our heart was immediately introduced, and he was called into the general council. His feelings, like

513   2K

our own, were deeply interested; and he proposed that we should each provide something from our own small stores to satisfy the pressing wants of the distressed family, while he promised to bring his cutter the next morning, and take us through the beaver-meadow, and to the edge of the great swamp, which would shorten four miles, at least, of our long and hazardous journey.

We joyfully acceded to his proposal, and set cheerfully to work to provide for the morrow. Jenny baked a batch of her very best bread, and boiled a large piece of beef, and Mr. T—— brought with him, the next day, a fine cooked ham, in a sack, into the bottom of which he stowed the beef and loaves, besides some sugar and tea, which his own kind wife, the author of *The Backwoods of Canada*, had sent. I had some misgivings as to the manner in which these good things could be introduced to the poor lady, who, I had heard, was reserved and proud.

"Oh, Jenny," I said, "how shall I be able to ask her to accept provisions from strangers? I am afraid of wounding her feelings."

"Oh, darlint, never fear that! She is proud, I know; but 'tis not a stiff pride, but jist enough to consale her disthress from her ignorant English neighbours, who think so manely of poor folk like her who were once rich. She will be very thankful to you for your kindness, for she has not experienced much of it from the Dummer people in her throuble, though she may have no words to tell you so. Say that old Jenny sent the bread to dear wee Ellie, 'cause she knew she would like a loaf of Jenny's bakin'."

514

THE WALK TO DUMMER

"But the meat?"

"Och, the mate, is it? May be, you'll think of some excuse for the mate when you get there."

"I hope so; but I'm a sad coward with strangers, and I have lived so long out of the world that I am at a great loss what to do. I will try and put a good face on the matter. Your name, Jenny, will be no small help to me."

All was now ready. Kissing our little bairns who crowded around us with eager and inquiring looks, and charging Jenny for the hundredth time to take especial care of them during our absence, we mounted the cutter, and set off, under the care and protection of Mr. T——, who determined to accompany us on the journey.

It was a black, cold day; no sun visible in the grey dark sky; a keen, cutting wind, and hard frost. We crouched close to each other.

"Good heavens, how cold it is!" whispered Emilia. "What a day for such a journey!"

She had scarcely ceased speaking, when the cutter went upon a stump which lay concealed under the drifted snow; and we, together with the ruins of our conveyance, were scattered around.

"A bad beginning," said my brother-in-law, with a rueful aspect, as he surveyed the wreck of the cutter from which we had promised ourselves so much benefit. "There is no help for it but to return home."

"Oh no," said Mrs. S——; "bad beginnings make good endings, you know. Let us go on; it will be far better walking than riding such a dreadful day. My feet are half-frozen already with sitting still."

"But, my dear madam," expostulated Mr. T——, "consider the distance, the road, the dark, dull day, and our imperfect knowledge of the path. I will get the cutter mended to-morrow; and the day after we may be able to proceed."

"Delays are dangerous," said the pertinacious Emilia, who, woman-like, was determined to have her own way. "Now, or never. While we wait for the broken cutter, the broken-hearted Mrs. N—— may starve. We can stop at Colonel C——'s and warm ourselves, and you can leave the cutter at his house until our return."

"It was upon your account that I proposed the delay," said the good Mr. T——, taking the sack, which was no inconsiderable weight, upon his shoulder, and driving his horse before him into neighbour W——'s stable. "Where you go, I am ready to follow."

When we arrived, Colonel C——'s family were at breakfast, of which they made us partake; and after vainly endeavouring to dissuade us from what appeared to them our Quixotic expedition, Mrs. C—— added a dozen fine white fish to the contents of the sack, and sent her youngest son to help Mr. T—— along with his burthen, and to bear us company on our desolate road.

Leaving the Colonel's hospitable house on our left we again plunged into the woods, and after a few minutes' brisk walking, found ourselves upon the brow of a steep bank that overlooked the beaver-meadow, containing within its area several hundred acres.

There is no scenery in the bush that presents such a novel appearance as those meadows or openings, surrounded, as they invariably are, by dark, intricate forests, their high, rugged banks covered with the light, airy tamarack and silver birch. In summer they look like a lake of soft, rich verdure, hidden in the bosom of the barren and howling waste. Lakes they certainly have been, from which the waters have receded, "ages, ages long ago"; and still the whole length of these curious level valleys is traversed by a stream of no inconsiderable dimensions.

The waters of the narrow, rapid creek, which flowed through the meadow we were about to cross, were of sparkling brightness, and icy cold. The frost-king had no power to check their swift, dancing movements, or stop their perpetual song. On they leaped, sparkling and flashing beneath their ice-crowned banks, rejoicing as they revelled on in their lonely course. In the prime of the year, this is a wild and lovely spot, the grass is of the richest green, and the flowers of the most gorgeous dyes. The gayest butterflies float above them upon painted wings, and the whip-poor-will pours forth from the neighbouring woods, at the close of dewy eve, his strange but sadly plaintive cry. Winter was now upon the earth, and the once green meadow looked like a small forest lake covered with snow.

The first step we made into it plunged us up to the knees in the snow, which was drifted to a great height in the open space. Mr. T—— and our young friend C—— walked on ahead of us, in order to break a track through the untrodden snow. We soon reached the cold creek, but here a new difficulty presented itself. It was too wide to jump across, and we could see no other way of passing to the other side.

517

ROUGHING IT IN THE BUSH

"There must be some sort of a bridge here about," said young C——, "or how can the people from Dummer pass constantly during the winter to and fro. I will go along the bank, and halloo to you if I find one."

In a few minutes he gave the desired signal, and on reaching the spot, we found a round, slippery log flung across the stream by way of bridge. With some trouble, and after various slips, we got safely on the other side. To wet our feet would have been to ensure their being frozen, and as it was, we were not without serious apprehension on that score. After crossing the bleak, snowy plain, we scrambled over another brook, and entered the great swamp which occupied two miles of our dreary road.

It would be vain to attempt giving any description of this tangled maze of closely-interwoven cedars, fallen trees, and loose-scattered masses of rock. It seemed the fitting abode of wolves and bears and every other unclean beast. The fire had run through it during the summer, making the confusion doubly confused. Now we stooped, half-doubled, to crawl under fallen branches that hung over our path, then again we had to clamber over prostrate trees of great bulk, descending from which we plumped down into holes in the snow, sinking mid-leg into the rotten trunk of some treacherous, decayed pine-tree. Before we were half through the great swamp, we began to think ourselves sad fools, and to wish that we were safe again by our own firesides. But, then, a great object was in view,—the relief of a distressed fellow-creature, and like the "full of hope, misnamed forlorn," we determined to overcome every difficulty and toil on.

THE WALK TO DUMMER

It took us an hour at least to clear the great swamp, from which we emerged into a fine wood, composed chiefly of maple-trees. The sun had, during our immersion in the dark shades of the swamp, burst through his leaden shroud, and cast a cheery gleam along the rugged boles of the lofty trees. The squirrel and chipmunk occasionally bounded across our path; the dazzling snow which covered it reflected the branches above us in an endless variety of dancing shadows. Our spirits rose in proportion. Young C—— burst out singing, and Emilia and I laughed and chatted as we bounded along our narrow road. On, on for hours, the same interminable forest stretched away to the right and left, before and behind us.

"It is past twelve," said my brother T—— thoughtfully; "if we do not soon come to a clearing, we may chance to spend the night in the forest."

"Oh, I am dying with hunger," cried Emilia. "Do, C——, give us one or two of the cakes your mother put into the bag for us to eat upon the road."

The ginger-cakes were instantly produced. But where were the teeth to be found that could masticate them? The cakes were frozen as hard as stones; this was a great disappointment to us tired and hungry wights; but it only produced a hearty laugh. Over the logs we went again; for it was a perpetual stepping up and down, crossing the fallen trees that obstructed our path. At last we came to a spot where two distinct blazed roads diverged.

"What are we to do now?" said Mr. T——.

We stopped, and a general consultation was held, and without one dissenting voice we took the branch to the right, which, after pursuing for about half a mile, led us to a log hut of the rudest description.

"Is this the road to Dummer?" we asked a man, who was chopping wood outside the fence.

"I guess you are in Dummer," was the answer.

My heart leaped for joy, for I was dreadfully fatigued.

"Does this road lead through the English Line?"

"That's another thing," returned the woodman. "No, you turned off from the right path when you came up here." We all looked very blank at each other. "You will have to go back, and keep the other road, and that will lead you straight to the English Line."

"How many miles is it to Mrs. N——'s?"

"Some four, or thereabouts," was the cheering rejoinder. "'Tis one of the last clearings on the line. If you are going back to Douro to-night, you must look sharp."

Sadly and dejectedly we retraced our steps. There are few trifling failures more bitter in our journey through life than that of a tired traveller mistaking his road. What effect must that tremendous failure produce upon the human mind, when, at the end of life's unretraceable journey, the traveller finds that he has fallen upon the wrong track through every stage, and instead of arriving at a land of blissful promise, sinks for ever into the gulf of despair!

The distance we had trodden in the wrong path, while led on by hope and anticipation, now seemed to double in length, as with painful steps we toiled on to reach the right road. This object once attained, soon led us to the dwellings of men.

THE WALK TO DUMMER

Neat, comfortable log houses, surrounded by well-fenced patches of clearing, arose on either side of the forest road; dogs flew out and barked at us, and children ran shouting indoors to tell their respective owners that strangers were passing their gates, a most unusual circumstance, I should think, in that location.

A servant who had lived two years with my brother-in-law, we knew must live somewhere in this neighbourhood, at whose fireside we hoped not only to rest and warm ourselves, but to obtain something to eat. On going up to one of the cabins to inquire for Hannah J——, we fortunately happened to light upon the very person we sought. With many exclamations of surprise, she ushered us into her neat and comfortable log dwelling.

A blazing fire, composed of two huge logs, was roaring up the wide chimney, and the savoury smell that issued from a large pot of pea-soup was very agreeable to our cold and hungry stomachs. But, alas, the refreshment went no further! Hannah most politely begged us to take seats by the fire, and warm and rest ourselves; she even knelt down and assisted in rubbing our half-frozen hands, but she never once made mention of the hot soup, or of the tea which was drawing in a tin teapot upon the hearth-stone, or of a glass of whiskey, which would have been thankfully accepted by our male pilgrims.

Hannah was not an Irishwoman, no, nor a Scotch lassie, or her very first request would have been for us to take "a pickle of soup," or "a sup of thae warm broths." The soup was no doubt cooking for Hannah's husband and two neighbours, who were chop-

521

ping for him in the bush, and whose want of punctuality she feelingly lamented.

As we left her cottage and jogged on, Emilia whispered, laughing, "I hope you are satisfied with your good dinner? Was not the pea-soup excellent?—and that cup of nice hot tea!—I never relished anything more in my life. I think we should never pass that house without giving Hannah a call, and testifying our gratitude for her good cheer."

Many times did we stop to inquire the way to Mrs. N——'s, before we ascended the steep, bleak hill upon which her house stood. At the door, Mr. T—— deposited the sack of provisions, and he and young C—— went across the road to the house of an English settler (who, fortunately for them, proved more hospitable than Hannah J——), to wait until our errand was executed.

The house before which Emilia and I were standing had once been a tolerably comfortable log dwelling. It was larger than such buildings generally are, and was surrounded by dilapidated barns and stables, which were not cheered by a solitary head of cattle. A black pine-forest stretched away to the north of the house, and terminated in a dismal, tangled cedar swamp, the entrance to the house not having been constructed to face the road.

The spirit that had borne me up during the journey died within me. I was fearful that my visit would be deemed an impertinent intrusion. I knew not in what manner to introduce myself, and my embarrassment had been greatly increased by Mrs. S—— declaring that I must break the ice, for she had not courage to go in. I remonstrated, but she was firm. To hold any longer parley was impossible. We were standing on the top of a bleak hill, with the thermometer many degrees below zero, and exposed to the fiercest biting of the bitter, cutting blast. With a heavy sigh, I knocked slowly but decidedly at the crazy door. I saw the curly head of a boy glance for a moment against the broken window. There was a stir within, but no one answered our summons. Emilia was rubbing her hands together, and beating a rapid tattoo with her feet upon the hard and glittering snow, to keep them from freezing.

Again I appealed to the inhospitable door, with a vehemence which seemed to say, "We are freezing, good people; in mercy let us in!"

Again there was a stir, and a whispered sound of voices, as if in consultation, from within; and after waiting a few minutes longer—which, cold as we were, seemed an age—the door was cautiously opened by a handsome, dark-eyed lad of twelve years of age, who was evidently the owner of the curly head that had been sent to reconnoitre us through the window. Carefully closing the door after him, he stepped out upon the snow, and asked us coldly but respectfully what we wanted. I told him that we were two ladies, who had walked all the way from Douro to see his mamma, and that we wished very much to speak to her. The lad answered us, with the ease and courtesy of a gentleman, that he did not know whether his mamma could be seen by strangers, but he would go in and see. So saying he abruptly left us, leaving behind him an ugly skeleton of a dog, who, after expressing his disapprobation at our presence in the most disagreeable and unequivocal manner, pounced like a famished wolf upon the sack of good things which lay at Emilia's feet, and our united efforts could scarcely keep him off.

"A cold, doubtful reception this!" said my friend, turning her back to the wind, and hiding her face in her muff. "This is worse than Hannah's liberality, and the long weary walk."

I thought so too, and began to apprehend that our walk had been in vain, when the lad again appeared, and said that we might walk in, for his mother was dressed.

Emilia, true to her determination, went no farther than the passage. In vain were all my entreating looks and mute appeals to her benevolence and friendship; I was forced to enter alone the apartment that contained the distressed family.

I felt that I was treading upon sacred ground, for a pitying angel hovers over the abode of suffering virtue, and hallows all its woes. On a rude bench before the fire sat a lady, between thirty and forty years of age, dressed in a thin, coloured muslin gown, the most inappropriate garment for the rigour of the season, but, in all probability, the only decent one that she retained. A subdued melancholy looked forth from her large, dark, pensive eyes. She appeared like one who, having discovered the full extent of her misery, had proudly steeled her heart to bear it. Her countenance was very pleasing and, in early life (but she was still young), she must have been eminently handsome. Near her, with her head bent down, and shaded by her thin, slender hand, her slight figure scarcely covered by her scanty clothing, sat her eldest daughter, a gentle sweet-looking girl, who held in her arms a baby brother, whose destitution she endeavoured to conceal. It was a touching sight; that suffering girl, just stepping into womanhood, hiding against her young bosom the nakedness of the little creature she loved. Another fine boy, whose neatly-patched clothes had not one piece of the original stuff apparently left in them, stood behind his mother, with dark, glistening eyes fastened upon me, as if amused, and wondering who I was, and what business I could have there. A pale and attenuated, but very pretty, delicately-featured little girl was seated on a low stool before the fire. This was old Jenny's darling, Ellie, or Eloise. A rude bedstead of home manufacture, in a corner of the room, covered with a coarse woollen quilt, contained two little boys, who had crept into it to conceal their wants from the eyes of the stranger. On the table lay a dozen peeled potatoes, and a small pot was boiling on the fire, to receive this their scanty and only daily meal. There was such an air of patient and enduring suffering in the whole group, that, as I gazed heart-stricken upon it, my fortitude quite gave way, and I burst into tears.

Mrs. N—— first broke the painful silence, and, rather proudly, asked me to whom she had the pleasure of speaking. I made a desperate effort to regain my composure, and told her, but with much embarrassment, my name; adding that I was so well acquainted with her and her children, through Jenny, that I could not consider her as a stranger; that I hoped that, as I was the wife of an officer, and, like her, a resident in the bush, and well acquainted with all its trials and privations, she would look upon me as a friend.

She seemed surprised and annoyed, and I found no small difficulty in introducing the object of my visit'; but the day was rapidly declining, and I knew that not a moment was to be lost. At first she coldly rejected all offers of service, and said that she was contented, and wanted for nothing.

I appealed to the situation in which I beheld herself and her children, and implored her, for their sakes, not to refuse help from friends who felt for her distress. Her maternal feelings triumphed over her assumed indifference, and when she saw me weeping, for I could no longer restrain my tears, her pride yielded, and for some minutes not a word was spoken. I heard the large tears, as they slowly fell from her daughter's eyes, drop one by one upon her garments.

At last the poor girl sobbed out, "Dear mamma, why conceal the truth? You know that we are nearly naked and starving."

Then came the sad tale of domestic woes: the absence of the husband and eldest son; the uncertainty as to where they were, or in what engaged; the utter want of means to procure the common necessaries of life; the sale of the only remaining cow that used to provide the children with food. It had been sold for twelve dollars, part to be paid in cash, part in potatoes; the potatoes were nearly exhausted, and they were allowanced to so many a day. But the six dollars she had retained as their last resource. Alas! she had sent the eldest boy the day before to P —— to get a letter out of the post-office, which she hoped contained some tidings of her husband and son. She was all anxiety and expectation—but the child returned late at night without the letter which they had longed for with such feverish impatience. The six dollars upon which they had depended for a supply of food were in notes of the Farmer's Bank, which at that time would not pass for money, and which the roguish purchaser of the cow had passed off upon this distressed family.

Oh! imagine, ye who revel in riches—who can daily throw away a large sum upon the merest toy—the cruel disappointment, the bitter agony of this poor mother's heart, when she received this calamitous news, in the midst of her starving children. For the last nine weeks they had lived upon a scanty supply of potatoes; they had not tasted raised bread or animal food for eighteen months.

"Ellie," said I, anxious to introduce the sack, which had lain like a nightmare upon my mind, "I have something for you; Jenny baked some loaves last night, and sent them to you with her best love."

The eyes of all the children grew bright. "You will find the sack with the bread in the passage," said I to one of the boys. He rushed joyfully out, and returned with Mrs. —— and the sack. Her bland and affectionate greeting restored us all to tranquillity.

The delighted boy opened the sack. The first thing he produced was the ham.

"Oh," said I, "that is a ham that my sister sent to Mrs. N——; 'tis of her own curing, and she thought that it might be acceptable."

527

Then came the white fish, nicely packed in a clean cloth. "Mrs. C—— thought fish might be a treat to Mrs. N——, as she lived so far from the great lakes." Then came Jenny's bread, which had already been introduced. The beef, and tea, and sugar fell upon the floor without any comment. The first scruples had been overcome, and the day was ours.

"And now, ladies," said Mrs. N——, with true hospitality, "since you have brought refreshments with you, permit me to cook something for your dinner."

The scene I had just witnessed had produced such a choking sensation that all my hunger had vanished. Before we could accept or refuse Mrs. N——'s kind offer, Mr. T—— arrived, to hurry us off.

It was two o'clock when we descended the hill in front of the house, that led by a side-path round to the road, and commenced our homeward route. I thought the four miles of clearings would never be passed; and the English Line appeared to have no end. At length we entered once more the dark forest.

The setting sun gleamed along the ground; the necessity of exerting our utmost speed, and getting through the great swamp before darkness surrounded us, was apparent to all. The men strove vigorously forward, for they had been refreshed with a substantial dinner of potatoes and pork, washed down with a glass of whiskey, at the cottage in which they had waited for us; but poor Emilia and I, faint, hungry, and foot-sore, it was with the greatest difficulty we could keep up. I thought of Rosalind, as our march up and down the fallen logs recommenced, and often exclaimed with her, "'Oh, Jupiter! how weary are my legs!'"

THE WALK TO DUMMER

Night closed in just as we reached the beaver-meadow. Here our ears were greeted with the sound of well-known voices. James and Henry C—— had brought the ox-sleigh to meet us at the edge of the bush. Never was splendid equipage greeted with such delight. Emilia and I, now fairly exhausted with fatigue, scrambled into it, and lying down on the straw which covered the bottom of the rude vehicle, we drew the buffalo robes over our faces, and actually slept soundly until we reached Colonel C——'s hospitable door.

An excellent supper of hot fish and fried venison was smoking on the table, with other good cheer, to which we did ample justice. I, for one, never was so hungry in my life. We had fasted for twelve hours, and that on an intensely cold day, and had walked during that period upwards of twenty miles. Never, never shall I forget that weary walk to Dummer; but a blessing followed it.

It was midnight when Emilia and I reached my humble home; our good friends the oxen being again put in requisition to carry us there. Emilia went immediately to bed, from which she was unable to rise for several days. In the meanwhile I wrote to Moodie an account of the scene I had witnessed, and he raised a subscription among the officers of the regiment for the poor lady and her children, which amounted to forty dollars. Emilia lost no time in making a full report to her friends at P——; and before a week passed away, Mrs. N—— and her family were removed thither by several benevolent individuals in the place. A neat cottage was hired for her: and, to the honour

2L

of Canada be it spoken, all who could afford a donation gave cheerfully. Farmers left at her door, pork, beef, flour, and potatoes; the storekeepers sent groceries, and goods to make clothes for the children; the shoemakers contributed boots for the boys; while the ladies did all in their power to assist and comfort the gentle creature thus thrown by Providence upon their bounty.

While Mrs. N—— remained at P—— she did not want for any comfort. Her children were clothed and her rent paid by her benevolent friends, and her house supplied with food and many comforts from the same source. Respected and beloved by all who knew her, it would have been well had she never left the quiet asylum where for several years she enjoyed tranquillity and a respectable competence from her school; but in an evil hour she followed her worthless husband to the Southern States, and again suffered all the woes which drunkenness inflicts upon the wives and children of its degraded victims.

CHAPTER TWENTY-FOUR
OF A CHANGE IN OUR PROSPECTS

CHAPTER TWENTY-FOUR
OF A CHANGE IN OUR PROSPECTS

The future flower lies folded in the bud,—
Its beauty, colour, fragrance, graceful form,
Carefully shrouded in that tiny cell;
Till time and circumstance, and sun and shower,
Expand the embryo blossom—and it bursts
Its narrow cerements, lifts its blushing head,
Rejoicing in the light and dew of heaven.
But if the canker-worm lies coil'd around
The heart o' the bud, the summer sun and dew
Visit in vain the sear'd and blighted flower.

DURING MY ILLNESS, A KIND NEIGH-
bour, who had not only frequently come to see me,
but had brought me many nourishing things made
by her own fair hands, took a great fancy to my
second daughter, who, lively and volatile, could not
be induced to remain quiet in the sick chamber. The
noise she made greatly retarded my recovery, and
Mrs. H——took her home with her, as the only means
of obtaining for me necessary rest. During that winter, and through the ensuing summer, I only received occasional visits from my little girl, who, fairly
established with her new friends, looked upon their
house as her home.

The removal of my sister rendered my separation
from my husband doubly lonely and irksome. Sometimes the desire to see and converse with him would
press so painfully on my heart that I would get up in
the night, strike a light, and sit down and write him
a long letter, and tell him all that was in my mind;
and when I had thus unburthened my spirit, the letter was committed to the flames, and, after fervently
commending him to the care of the Great Father

of mankind, I would lay down my throbbing head on my pillow beside our first-born son, and sleep tranquilly.

It is a strange fact that many of my husband's letters to me were written at the very time when I felt those irresistible impulses to hold communion with him. Why should we be ashamed to admit openly our belief in this mysterious intercourse between the spirits of those who are bound to each other by the tender ties of friendship and affection, when the experience of every day proves its truth? Proverbs, which are the wisdom of ages collected into a few brief words, tell us in one pithy sentence that "if we talk of the devil he is sure to appear." While the name of a long-absent friend is in our mouth, the next moment brings him into our presence. How can this be, if mind did not meet mind, and the spirit had not a prophetic consciousness of the vicinity of another spirit, kindred with its own? This is an occurrence so common that I never met with any person to whom it had not happened; few will admit it to be a spiritual agency, but in no other way can they satisfactorily explain its cause. If it were a mere coincidence, or combination of ordinary circumstances, it would not happen so often, and people would not be led to speak of the long-absent always at the moment when they are just about to present themselves before them. My husband was no believer in what he termed my fanciful, speculative theories; yet at the time when his youngest boy and myself lay dangerously ill, and hardly expected to live, I received from him a letter, written in great haste, which commenced with this sentence: "Do write to me, dear S——, when you receive this. I have felt very uneasy about you for some days past, and am afraid that all is not right at home."

Whence came this sudden fear? Why at that particular time did his thoughts turn so despondingly towards those so dear to him? Why did the dark cloud in his mind hang so heavily above his home? The burden of my weary and distressed spirit had reached him, and, without knowing of our sufferings and danger, his own responded to the call.

The holy and mysterious nature of man is yet hidden from himself; he is still a stranger to the movements of that inner life, and knows little of its capabilities and powers. A purer religion, a higher standard of moral and intellectual training, may in time reveal all this. Man still remains a half-reclaimed savage; the leaven of Christianity is slowly and surely working its way, but it has not yet changed the whole lump, or transformed the deformed into the beauteous child of God. Oh, for that glorious day! It is coming. The dark clouds of humanity are already tinged with the golden radiance of the dawn, but the sun of righteousness has not yet arisen upon the world with healing on his wings; the light of truth still struggles in the womb of darkness, and man stumbles on to the fulfilment of his sublime and mysterious destiny.

This spring I was not a little puzzled how to get in the crops. I still continued so weak that I was quite unable to assist in the field, and my good old Jenny was sorely troubled with inflamed feet, which

535

required constant care. At this juncture, a neighbouring settler, who had recently come among us, offered to put in my small crop of peas, potatoes, and oats, in all not comprising more than eight acres, if I would lend him my oxen to log-up a large fallow of ten acres and put in his own crops. Trusting to his fair dealing, I consented to this arrangement; but he took advantage of my isolated position, and not only logged-up his fallow, but put in all his spring crops before he sowed an acre of mine. The oxen were worked down so low that they were almost unfit for use, and my crops were put in so late, and with such little care, that they all proved a failure. I should have felt this loss more severely had it happened in any previous year; but I had ceased to feel that deep interest in the affairs of the farm from a sort of conviction in my own mind that it would not long remain my home.

Jenny and I did our best in the way of hoeing and weeding; but no industry on our part could repair the injury done to the seed by being sown out of season.

We therefore confined our attention to the garden, which, as usual, was very productive, and with milk, fresh butter, and eggs, supplied the simple wants of our family. Emilia enlivened our solitude by her company for several weeks during the summer, and we had many pleasant excursions on the water together.

My knowledge of the use of the paddle, however, was not entirely without its danger.

One very windy Sunday afternoon, a servant-girl, who lived with my friend Mrs. C——, came crying

RESIDENCE OF THE LATE COL. STRICKLANDS, FOUNDER OF LAKEFIELD, ONTARIO

to the house, and implored the use of my canoe and paddles to cross the lake to see her dying father. The request was instantly granted; but there was no man upon the place to ferry her across, and she could not manage the boat herself—in short, had never been in a canoe in her life.

The girl was deeply distressed. She said that she had got word that her father could scarcely live till she could reach Smith-town; that if she went round by the bridge, she must walk five miles, while if she crossed the lake she could be home in half an hour.

I did not much like the angry swell upon the water, but the poor creature was in such grief that I told her, if she was not afraid of venturing with me, I would try and put her over.

She expressed her thanks in the warmest terms, accompanied by a shower of blessings; and I took the paddles and went down to the landing. Jenny was very averse to my *tempting Providence*, as she termed it, and wished that I might get back as safe as I went. However, the old woman launched the canoe for me, pushed us from the shore, and away we went. The wind was in my favour, and I found so little trouble in getting across that I began to laugh at my own timidity. I put the girl on shore, and endeavoured to shape my passage home. But this I found was no easy task. The water was rough, and the wind high, and the strong current, which runs through that part of the lake to the Smith rapids, was dead against me. In vain I laboured to cross this current; it resisted all my efforts, and at each repulse I was carried farther down towards the rapids, which were full of sunken rocks, and hard for the strong arm of a man to stem—to the weak hand of a woman their safe passage was impossible. I began to feel rather uneasy at the awkward situation in which I found myself placed, and for some time I made desperate efforts to extricate myself by paddling with all my might. I soon gave this up, and contented myself by steering the canoe in the path that it thought fit to pursue. After drifting down with the current for some little space, until I came opposite a small island, I put out all my strength to gain the land. In this I fortunately succeeded, and getting on shore, I contrived to drag the canoe so far round the headland that I got her out of the current. All now was smooth sailing, and I joyfully answered old Jenny's yells from the landing, that I was safe, and would join her in a few minutes.

This fortunate manœuvre stood me in good stead upon another occasion when crossing the lake, some weeks after this, in company with a young female friend, during a sudden storm.

Two Indian women, heavily laden with their packs of dried venison, called at the house to borrow the canoe, to join their encampment upon the other side. It so happened that I wanted to send to the mill that afternoon, and the boat could not be returned in time without I went over with the Indian women and brought it back. My young friend was delighted at the idea of the frolic, and as she could both steer and paddle, and the day was calm and bright, though excessively warm, we both agreed to accompany the squaws to the other side, and bring back the canoe.

A CHANGE IN OUR PROSPECTS

Mrs. Muskrat had fallen in love with a fine fat kitten, whom the children had called "Buttermilk," and she begged so hard for the little puss, that I presented it to her, rather marvelling how she would contrive to carry it so many miles through the woods, and she loaded with such an enormous pack; when, lo! the squaw took down the bundle, and in the heart of the piles of dried venison she deposited the cat in a small basket, giving it a thin slice of the meat to console it for its close confinement. Puss received the donation with piteous mews; it was evident that mice and freedom were preferred by her to venison and the honour of riding on a squaw's back.

The squaws paddled us quickly across, and we laughed and chatted as we bounded over the blue waves, until we were landed in a dark cedar swamp, in the heart of which we found the Indian encampment.

A large party were lounging around the fire, superintending the drying of a quantity of venison which was suspended on forked sticks. Besides the flesh of the deer, a number of musk-rats were skinned, and extended as if standing bolt upright before the fire, warming their paws. The appearance they cut was most ludicrous. My young friend pointed to the musk-rats, as she sank down, laughing, upon one of the skins.

Old Snow-storm, who was present, imagined that she wanted one of them to eat, and very gravely handed her the unsavoury beast, stick and all.

"Does the old man take me for a cannibal?" she said. "I would as soon eat a child."

539

Among the many odd things cooking at that fire there was something that had the appearance of a bull-frog.

"What can that be?" she said, directing my eyes to the strange monster. "Surely they don't eat bull-frogs!"

This sally was received by a grunt of approbation from Snow-storm; and, though Indians seldom forget their dignity so far as to laugh, he for once laid aside his stoical gravity, and, twirling the thing round with a stick, burst into a hearty peal.

"*Muckakee?* Indian eat *muckakee?*—Ha! ha! Indian no eat *muckakee!* Frenchmans eat his hind legs; they say the speckled beast much good. This no *muckakee!*—the liver of deer, dried—very nice—Indian eat him."

"I wish him much joy of the delicate morsel," said the saucy girl, who was intent upon quizzing and examining everything in the camp.

We had remained the best part of an hour, when Mrs. Muskrat laid hold of my hand, and leading me through the bush to the shore, pointed up significantly to a cloud, as dark as night, that hung loweringly over the bush.

"Thunder in that cloud—get over the lake—quick, before it breaks." Then motioning for us to jump into the canoe, she threw in the paddles, and pushed us from the shore.

We saw the necessity of haste, and both plied the paddle with diligence to gain the opposite bank, or at least the shelter of the island, before the cloud poured down its fury upon us. We were just in the middle of the current when the first peal of thunder broke with startling nearness over our heads. The storm frowned darkly upon the woods; the rain came down in torrents; and there were we exposed to its utmost fury in the middle of a current too strong for us to stem.

"What shall we do? We shall be drowned!" said my young friend, turning her pale, tearful face towards me.

"Let the canoe float down the current till we get close to the island, then run her into the land. I saved myself once before by this plan."

We did so, and were safe; but there we had to remain, wet to our skins, until the wind and the rain abated sufficiently for us to manage our little craft. "How do you like being upon the lake in a storm like this?" I whispered to my shivering, dripping companion.

"Very well in romance, but terribly dull in reality. We cannot, however, call it a dry joke," continued she, wringing the rain from her dress. "I wish we were suspended over Old Snow-storm's fire with the bull-frog, for I hate a shower-bath with my clothes on."

I took warning by this adventure never to cross the lake again without a stronger arm than mine in the canoe to steer me safely through the current.

I received much kind attention from my new neighbour, the Rev. W. W——, a truly excellent and pious clergyman of the English Church. The good, white-haired old man expressed the kindest sympathy in all my trials, and strengthened me greatly with his benevolent counsels and gentle charity. Mr. W——

was a true follower of Christ. His Christianity was not confined to his own denomination; and every Sabbath his log cottage was filled with attentive auditors, of all persuasions, who met together to listen to the word of life delivered to them by a Christian minister in the wilderness.

He had been a very fine preacher, and, though considerably turned of seventy, his voice was still excellent, and his manner solemn and impressive.

His only son, a young man of twenty-eight years of age, had received a serious injury in the brain by falling upon a turf-spade from a loft window when a child, and his intellect had remained stationary from that time. Poor Harry was an innocent child; he loved his parents with the simplicity of a child, and all who spoke kindly to him he regarded as friends. Like most persons of his cast of mind, his predilection for pet animals was a prominent instinct. He was always followed by two dogs, whom he regarded with especial favour. The moment he caught your eye, he looked down admiringly upon his four-footed attendants, patting their sleek necks, and murmuring, "Nice dogs—nice dogs." Harry had singled out myself and my little ones as great favourites. He would gather flowers for the girls, and catch butterflies for the boys; while to me he always gave the title of "dear aunt."

It so happened that one fine morning I wanted to walk a couple of miles through the bush, to spend the day with Mrs. C——; but the woods were full of the cattle belonging to the neighbouring settlers, and of these I was terribly afraid. Whilst I was dressing the

542

little girls to accompany me, Harry W—— came in with a message from his mother. "Oh," thought I, "here is Harry W——. He will walk with us through the bush, and defend us from the cattle."

The proposition was made, and Harry was not a little proud of being invited to join our party. We had accomplished half the distance without seeing a single hoof, and I was beginning to congratulate myself upon our unusual luck, when a large red ox, maddened by the stings of the gad-flies, came headlong through the bush, tossing up the withered leaves and dried moss with his horns, and making directly toward us. I screamed to my champion for help; but where was he?—running like a frightened chipmunk along the fallen timber, shouting to my eldest girl at the top of his voice—

"Run, Katty, run!—The bull, the bull! Run, Katty! —The bull, the bull!"—leaving us poor creatures far behind in the chase.

The bull, who cared not one fig for us, did not even stop to give us a passing stare, and was soon lost among the trees; while our valiant knight never stopped to see what had become of us, but made the best of his way home. So much for taking an innocent for a guard.

The next month most of the militia regiments were disbanded. My husband's services were no longer required at B——, and he once more returned to help to gather in our scanty harvest. Many of the old debts were paid off by his hard-saved pay; and though all hope of continuing in the militia service was at an end, our condition was so much improved that we

543

looked less to the dark than to the sunny side of the landscape.

The potato crop was gathered in, and I had collected my store of dandelion-roots for our winter supply of coffee, when one day brought a letter to my husband from the Governor's secretary, offering him the situation of sheriff of the V——district. Though perfectly unacquainted with the difficulties and responsibilities of such an important office, my husband looked upon it as a gift sent from heaven to remove us from the sorrows and poverty with which we were surrounded in the woods.

Once more he bade us farewell; but it was to go and make ready a home for us, that we should no more be separated from each other.

Heartily did I return thanks to God that night for all His mercies to us; and Sir George Arthur was not forgotten in those prayers.

From B——, my husband wrote to me to make what haste I could in disposing of our crops, household furniture, stock, and farming implements; and to prepare myself and the children to join him on the first fall of snow that would make the roads practicable for sleighing. To facilitate this object, he sent me a box of clothing to make up for myself and the children.

For seven years I had lived out of the world entirely; my person had been rendered coarse by hard work and exposure to the weather. I looked double the age I really was, and my hair was already thickly sprinkled with grey. I clung to my solitude. I did not like to be dragged from it to mingle in gay scenes, in a busy town, and with gaily dressed people. I was no longer fit for the world; I had lost all relish for the pursuits and pleasures which are so essential to its votaries; I was contented to live and die in obscurity.

My dear Emilia rejoiced, like a true friend, in my changed prospects, and came up to help me to cut clothes for the children, and to assist me in preparing them for the journey.

I succeeded in selling off our goods and chattels much better than I expected. My old friend, Mr. W——, who was a newcomer, became the principal purchaser, and when Christmas arrived I had not one article left upon my hands save the bedding, which it was necessary to take with us.

CHAPTER TWENTY-FIVE
ADIEU TO THE WOODS

Adieu!—Adieu!—when quivering lips refuse
  The bitter pangs of parting to declare;
And the full bosom feels that it must lose
  Friends who were wont its inmost thoughts to share;
When hands are tightly clasp'd, 'mid struggling sighs
And streaming tears, those whisper'd accents rise,
  Leaving to God the objects of our care
In that short, simple, comprehensive prayer—
                                        ADIEU!

NEVER DID EAGER BRITISH CHILDREN look for the first violets and primroses of spring with more impatience than my baby boys and girls watched, day after day, for the first snowflakes that were to form the road to convey them to their absent father.

"Winter never means to come this year. It will never snow again!" exclaimed my eldest boy, turning from the window on Christmas Day, with the most rueful aspect that ever greeted the broad, gay beams of the glorious sun. It was like a spring day. The little lake in front of the window glittered like a mirror of silver, set in its dark frame of pine woods.

I, too, was wearying for the snow, and was tempted to think that it did not come as early as usual, in order to disappoint us. But I kept this to myself, and comforted the expecting child with the oft-repeated assertion that it would certainly snow upon the morrow.

But the morrow came and passed away, and many other morrows, and the same mild, open weather prevailed. The last night of the old year was ushered in with furious storms of wind and snow; the rafters of our log cabin shook beneath the violence of the gale, which swept up from the lake like a lion roaring for his prey, driving the snowflakes through every open crevice, of which there were not a few, and powdering the floor until it rivalled in whiteness the ground without.

"Oh, what a dreadful night!" we cried, as we huddled, shivering, around the old broken stove. "A person abroad in the woods to-night would be frozen. Flesh and blood could not long stand this cutting wind."

"It reminds me of a laughable extempore ditty," said I to my young friend, A. C——, who was staying with me, "composed by my husband during the first very cold night we spent in Canada"—

> Oh, the cold of Canada nobody knows,
> The fire burns our shoes without warming our toes;
> Oh, dear, what shall we do?
> Our blankets are thin, and our noses are blue—
> Our noses are blue, and our blankets are thin,
> It's at zero without, and we're freezing within!
>
> (*Chorus*)—Oh, dear, what shall we do?

"But, joking apart, my dear A——, we ought to be very thankful that we are not travelling this night to B——."

"But to-morrow," said my eldest boy, lifting up his curly head from my lap. "It will be fine to-morrow, and we shall see dear papa again."

In this hope he lay down on his little bed upon the floor, and was soon fast asleep; perhaps dreaming of that eagerly-anticipated journey, and of meeting his beloved father.

Sleep was a stranger to my eyes. The tempest raged so furiously without that I was fearful the roof would be carried off the house, or that the chimney would take fire. The night was far advanced when old Jenny and myself retired to bed.

My boy's words were prophetic; that was the last night I ever spent in the bush—in the dear forest home which I had loved in spite of all the hardships which we had endured since we pitched our tent in the backwoods. It was the birthplace of my three boys, the school of high resolve and energetic action in which we had learned to meet calmly, and successfully to battle with the ills of life. Nor did I leave it without many regretful tears, to mingle once more with a world to whose usages, during my long solitude, I had become almost a stranger, and to whose praise or blame I felt alike indifferent.

When the day dawned, the whole forest scenery lay glittering in a mantle of dazzling white; the sun shone brightly, the heavens were intensely blue, but the cold was so severe that every article of food had to be thawed before we could get our breakfast. The very blankets that covered us during the night were stiff with our frozen breath. "I hope the sleighs won't come to-day," I cried; "we should be frozen on the long journey."

About noon two sleighs turned into our clearing. Old Jenny ran screaming into the room, "The masther has sent for us at last! The sleighs are come! Fine large sleighs, and illigant teams of horses! Och, and it's a cowld day for the wee things to lave the bush."

The snow had been a week in advance of us at B——, and my husband had sent up the teams to remove us. The children jumped about, and laughed aloud for joy. Old Jenny did not know whether to

551

laugh or cry, but she set about helping me to pack up trunks and bedding as fast as our cold hands would permit.

In the midst of the confusion, my brother arrived, like a good genius, to our assistance, declaring his determination to take us down to B—— himself in his large lumber-sleigh. This was indeed joyful news. In less than three hours he despatched the hired sleighs with their loads, and we all stood together in the empty house, striving to warm our hands over the embers of the expiring fire.

How cold and desolate every object appeared! The small windows, half blocked up with snow, scarcely allowed a glimpse of the declining sun to cheer us with his serene aspect. In spite of the cold, several kind friends had waded through the deep snow to say, "God bless you!—Good-bye"; while a group of silent Indians stood together, gazing upon our proceedings with an earnestness which showed that they were not uninterested in the scene. As we passed out to the sleigh, they pressed forward, and silently held out their hands, while the squaws kissed me and the little ones with tearful eyes. They had been true friends to us in our dire necessity, and I returned their mute farewell from my very heart.

Mr. S—— sprang into the sleigh. One of our party was missing. "Jenny!" shouted my brother, at the top of his voice, "it is too cold to keep your mistress and the little children waiting."

"Och, shure, thin, it is I that am coming!" returned the old body, as she issued from the house.

Shouts of laughter greeted her appearance. The

ADIEU TO THE WOODS

figure she cut upon that memorable day I shall never forget. My brother dropped the reins upon the horses' necks, and fairly roared. Jenny was about to commence her journey to the front in three hats. Was it to protect her from the cold? Oh no; Jenny was not afraid of the cold! She could have eaten her breakfast on the north side of an iceberg, and always dispensed with shoes, during the most severe of our Canadian winters. It was to protect these precious articles from injury.

Our good neighbour, Mrs. W——, had presented her with an old sky-blue drawn-silk bonnet, as a parting benediction. This, by way of distinction, for she never had possessed such an article of luxury as a silk bonnet in her life, Jenny had placed over the coarse calico cap, with its full furbelow of the same yellow, ill-washed, homely material, next to her head; over this, as second in degree, a sun-burnt straw hat, with faded pink ribbons, just showed its broken rim and tawdry trimmings; and, to crown all, and serve as a guard to the rest, a really serviceable grey-beaver bonnet, once mine, towered up as high as the celebrated crown in which brother Peter figures in Swift's *Tale of a Tub*.

"Mercy, Jenny! Why, old woman, you don't mean to go with us that figure!"

"Och, my dear heart! I've no band-box to kape the cowld from desthroying my illigant bonnets," returned Jenny, laying her hand upon the side of the sleigh.

"Go back, Jenny; go back," cried my brother. "For God's sake take all that tomfoolery from off

553

your head. We shall be the laughing-stock of every village we pass through."

"Och, shure, now, Mr. S——, who'd think of looking at an owld crathur like me! It's only yersel' that would notice the like."

"All the world, everybody would look at you, Jenny. I believe that you put on those hats to draw the attention of all the young fellows that we shall happen to meet on the road. Ha, Jenny!"

With an air of offended dignity, the old woman returned to the house to re-arrange her toilet, and provide for the safety of her "illigant bonnets," one of which she suspended to the strings of her cloak, while she carried the third dangling in her hand; and no persuasion of mine would induce her to put them out of sight.

Many painful and conflicting emotions agitated my mind, but found no utterance in words, as we entered the forest path, and I looked my last upon that humble home consecrated by the memory of a thousand sorrows. Every object had become endeared to me during my long exile from civilized life. I loved the lonely lake, with its magnificent belt of dark pines sighing in the breeze; the cedar swamp, the summer home of my dark Indian friends; my own dear little garden, with its rugged snake-fence which I had helped Jenny to place with my own hands, and which I had assisted the faithful woman in cultivating for the last three years, where I had so often braved the tormenting mosquitoes, black flies, and intense heat, to provide vegetables for the use of the family. Even the cows, that had given a breakfast for the last time to my children, were now regarded with mournful affection. A poor labourer stood in the doorway of the deserted house, holding my noble water-dog, Rover, in a string. The poor fellow gave a joyous bark as my eyes fell upon him.

"James J——, take care of my dog."

"Never fear, ma'am, he shall bide with me as long as he lives."

"He and the Indians at least feel grieved for our departure," I thought. Love is so scarce in this world that we ought to prize it, however lowly the source from whence it flows.

We accomplished only twelve miles of our journey that night. The road lay through the bush, and along the banks of the grand, rushing, foaming Otonabee river, the wildest and most beautiful of forest streams. We slept at the house of kind friends, and early in the morning resumed our long journey, but minus one of our party. Our old favourite cat, Peppermint, had made her escape from the basket in which she had been confined, and had scampered off, to the great grief of the children.

As we passed Mrs. H——'s house, we called for dear Addie. Mr. H—— brought her in his arms to the gate, well wrapped up in a large fur cape and a warm woollen shawl.

"You are robbing me of my dear little girl," he said. "Mrs. H—— is absent; she told me not to part with her if you should call; but I could not detain her without your consent. Now that you have seen her, allow me to keep her for a few months longer?"

Addie was in the sleigh. I put my arm about her.

I felt I had my child again, and I secretly rejoiced in the possession of my own. I sincerely thanked him for his kindness, and Mr. S—— drove on.

At Mr. R——'s, we found a parcel from dear Emilia, containing a plum-cake and other good things for the children. Her kindness never flagged.

We crossed the bridge over the Otonabee, in the rising town of Peterborough, at eight o'clock in the morning. Winter had now set in fairly. The children were glad to huddle together in the bottom of the sleigh, under the buffalo skins and blankets; all but my eldest boy, who, just turned of five years old, was enchanted with all he heard and saw, and continued to stand up and gaze around him. Born in the forest, which he had never quitted before, the sight of a town was such a novelty that he could find no words wherewith to express his astonishment.

"Are the houses come to see one another?" he asked. "How did they all meet here?"

The question greatly amused his uncle, who took some pains to explain the difference between town and country. During the day, we got rid of old Jenny and her bonnets, whom we found a very refractory travelling companion, as wilful, and far more difficult to manage than a young child. Fortunately, we overtook the sleighs with the furniture, and Mr. S—— transferred Jenny to the care of one of the drivers; an arrangement that proved satisfactory to all parties.

We had been most fortunate in obtaining comfortable lodgings for the night. The evening had closed in so intensely cold that although we were only two miles from C——, Addie was so much affected by it that the child lay sick and pale in my arms, and, when spoken to, seemed scarcely conscious of our presence.

My brother jumped from the front seat, and came round to look at her. "That child is ill with the cold; we must stop somewhere to warm her, or she will hardly hold out till we get to the inn at C——."

We were just entering the little village of A——, in the vicinity of the court-house, and we stopped at a pretty green cottage, and asked permission to warm the children. A stout, middle-aged woman came to the sleigh, and in the kindest manner requested us to alight.

"I think I know that voice," I said. "Surely it cannot be Mrs. S——, who once kept the —— hotel at C——?"

"Mrs. Moodie, you are welcome," said the excellent woman, bestowing upon me a most friendly embrace; "you and your children. I am heartily glad to see you again after so many years. God bless you all!"

Nothing could exceed the kindness and hospitality of this generous woman; she would not hear of our leaving her that night, and, directing my brother to put up his horses in her stable, she made up an excellent fire in a large bedroom, and helped me to undress the little ones who were already asleep, and to warm and feed the rest before putting them to bed.

This meeting gave me real pleasure. In their station of life, I seldom have found a more worthy couple than this American and his wife; and, having witnessed so many of their acts of kindness, both to ourselves and others, I entertained for them a sincere

557

respect and affection, and truly rejoiced that Providence had once more led me to the shelter of their roof.

Mr. S—— was absent, but I found little Mary—the sweet child who used to listen with such delight to Moodie's flute—grown up into a beautiful girl; and the baby that was, a fine child of eight years old. The next morning was so intensely cold that my brother would not resume the journey until past ten o'clock, and even then it was a hazardous experiment.

We had not proceeded four miles before the horses were covered with icicles. Our hair was frozen as white as old Time's solitary forelock, our eyelids stiff, and every limb aching with cold.

"This will never do," said my brother, turning to me, "the children will freeze. I never felt the cold more severe than this."

"Where can we stop?" said I; "we are miles from C——, and I see no prospect of the weather becoming milder."

"Yes, yes; I know, by the very intensity of the cold, that a change is at hand. We seldom have more than three very severe days running, and this is the third. At all events, it is much warmer at night in this country than during the day; the wind drops, and the frost is more bearable. I know a worthy farmer who lives about a mile ahead; he will give us house-room for a few hours; and we will resume our journey in the evening. The moon is at full; and it will be easier to wrap the children up, and keep them warm when they are asleep. Shall we stop at Old Woodruff's?"

"With all my heart." My teeth were chattering with

the cold, and the children were crying over their aching fingers at the bottom of the sleigh.

A few minutes' ride brought us to a large farmhouse, surrounded by commodious sheds and barns. A fine orchard opposite, and a yard well stocked with fat cattle and sheep, sleek geese, and plethoric-looking swine, gave promise of a land of abundance and comfort. My brother ran into the house to see if the owner was at home, and presently returned, accompanied by the staunch Canadian yeoman and his daughter, who gave us a truly hearty welcome, and assisted in removing the children from the sleigh to the cheerful fire that made all bright and cosy within.

Our host was a shrewd, humorous-looking Yorkshireman. His red, weather-beaten face, and tall, athletic figure, bent as it was with hard labour, gave indications of great personal strength; and a certain knowing twinkle in his small, clear grey eyes, which had been acquired by long dealing with the world, with a quiet, sarcastic smile that lurked round the corners of his large mouth, gave you the idea of a man who could not easily be deceived by his fellows; one who, though no rogue himself, was quick in detecting the roguery of others. His manners were frank and easy, and he was such a hospitable entertainer that you felt at home with him in a minute.

"Well, how are you, Mr. S——?" cried the farmer, shaking my brother heartily by the hand. "Toiling in the bush still, eh?"

"Just in the same place."

"And the wife and children?"

"Hearty. Some half-dozen have been added to the flock since you were our way."

"So much the better—so much the better. The more the merrier, Mr. S——; children are riches in this country."

"I know not how that may be; I find it hard to clothe and feed mine."

"Wait till they grow up; they will be brave helps to you then. The price of labour—the price of labour, Mr. S——, is the destruction of the farmer."

"It does not seem to trouble you much, Woodruff," said my brother, glancing round the well-furnished apartment.

"My son and S—— do it all," cried the old man. "Of course the girls help in busy times, and take care of the dairy, and we hire occasionally; but small as the sum is which is expended in wages during seed-time and harvest, I feel it, I can tell you."

"You are married again, Woodruff?"

"No, sir," said the farmer, with a peculiar smile, "not yet;" which seemed to imply the probability of such an event. "That tall gal is my eldest daughter; she manages the house, and an excellent housekeeper she is. But I cannot keep her for ever." With a knowing wink, "Gals will think of getting married, and seldom consult the wishes of their parents upon the subject when once they have taken the notion into their heads. But 'tis natural, Mr. S——, it is natural; we did just the same when we were young."

My brother looked laughingly towards the fine, handsome young woman, as she placed upon the table hot water, whiskey, and a huge plate of plum-cake, which did not lack a companion, stored with the finest apples which the orchard could produce.

The young girl looked down, and blushed.

"Oh, I see how it is, Woodruff! You will soon lose your daughter. I wonder that you have kept her so long. But who are these young ladies?" he continued, as three girls very demurely entered the room.

"The two youngest are my darters, by my last wife, who, I fear, mean soon to follow the bad example of their sister. The other *lady*," said the old man, with a reverential air, "is a *particular* friend of my eldest darter's."

My brother laughed slily, and the old man's cheek took a deeper glow as he stooped forward to mix the punch.

"You said that these two young ladies, Woodruff, were by your last wife. Pray how many wives have you had?"

"Only three. It is impossible, they say in my country, to have too much of a good thing."

"So I suppose you think," said my brother, glancing first at the old man and then towards Miss Smith. "Three wives! You have been a fortunate man, Woodruff, to survive them all."

"Ay, have I not, Mr. S——? but to tell you the truth, I have been both lucky and unlucky in the wife way," and then he told us the history of his several ventures in matrimony, with which I shall not trouble my readers.

When he had concluded, the weather was somewhat milder, the sleigh was ordered to the door, and we proceeded on our journey, resting for the night at a small

2N

village about twenty miles from B——, rejoicing that the long distance, which separated us from the husband and father, was diminished to a few miles, and that, with the blessing of Providence, we should meet on the morrow.

About noon we reached the distant town, and were met at the inn by him whom one and all so ardently longed to see. He conducted us to a pretty, neat cottage, which he had prepared for our reception, and where we found old Jenny already arrived. With great pride the old woman conducted me over the premises, and showed me the furniture "the masther" had bought; especially recommending to my notice a china tea-service, which she considered the most wonderful acquisition of the whole.

"Och! who would have thought, a year ago, misthress dear, that we should be living in a mansion like this, and ating off raal chaney? It is but yesterday that we were hoeing praties in the field."

"Yes, Jenny, God has been very good to us, and I hope that we shall never learn to regard with indifference the many benefits which we have received at His hands."

Reader! it is not my intention to trouble you with the sequel of our history. I have given you a faithful picture of a life in the backwoods of Canada, and I leave you to draw from it your own conclusions. To the poor, industrious working man it presents many advantages; to the poor gentleman, *none!* The former works hard, puts up with coarse, scanty fare, and submits, with a good grace, to hardships that would kill a domesticated animal at home. Thus he becomes independent, inasmuch as the land that he has cleared finds him in the common necessaries of life; but it seldom, if ever, in remote situations, accomplishes more than this. The gentleman can neither work so hard, live so coarsely, nor endure so many privations as his poorer but more fortunate neighbour. Unaccustomed to manual labour, his services in the field are not of a nature to secure for him a profitable return. The task is new to him, he knows not how to perform it well; and, conscious of his deficiency, he expends his little means in hiring labour, which his bush-farm can never repay. Difficulties increase, debts grow upon him, he struggles in vain to extricate himself, and finally sees his family sink into hopeless ruin.

If these sketches should prove the means of deterring one family from sinking their property, and shipwrecking all their hopes, by going to reside in the backwoods of Canada, I shall consider myself amply repaid for revealing the secrets of the prison-house, and feel that I have not toiled and suffered in the wilderness in vain.

BOOKPLATE OF J. W. DUNBAR MOODIE

CHAPTER TWENTY-SIX
THE MAPLE-TREE

CHAPTER XXVI. THE MAPLE-TREE
A CANADIAN SONG

HAIL TO THE PRIDE OF THE FOREST
—hail
To the maple, tall and green;
It yields a treasure which ne'er shall fail
While leaves on its boughs are seen.
When the moon shines bright,
On the wintry night,
And silvers the frozen snow;
And echo dwells
On the jingling bells
As the sleighs dart to and fro;
Then it brightens the mirth
Of the social hearth
With its red and cheery glow.

Afar, 'mid the bosky forest shades,
It lifts its tall head on high;
When the crimson-tinted evening fades
From the glowing saffron sky;
When the sun's last beams
Light up woods and streams,
And brighten the gloom below;
And the deer springs by
With his flashing eye,
And the shy, swift-footed doe;
And the sad winds chide
In the branches wide,
With a tender plaint of woe.

The Indian leans on its ragged trunk,
With the bow in his red right-hand,
And mourns that his race, like a stream, has sunk
From the glorious forest land.
But, blythe and free,
The maple-tree,
Still tosses to sun and air
Its thousand arms,
While in countless swarms

ROUGHING IT IN THE BUSH

The wild bee revels there;
But soon not a trace
Of the red man's race
Shall be found in the landscape fair.

When the snows of winter are melting fast,
And the sap begins to rise,
And the biting breath of the frozen blast
Yields to the spring's soft sighs,
Then away to the wood,
For the maple, good,
Shall unlock its honied store;
And boys and girls,
With their sunny curls,
Bring their vessels brimming o'er
With the luscious flood
Of the brave tree's blood,
Into cauldrons deep to pour.

The blaze from the sugar-bush gleams red;
Far down in the forest dark,
A ruddy glow on the tree is shed,
That lights up the rugged bark;
And with merry shout,
The busy rout
Watch the sap as it bubbles high;
And they talk of the cheer
Of the coming year,
And the jest and the song pass by;
And brave tales of old
Round the fire are told,
That kindle youth's beaming eye.

Hurrah! for the sturdy maple-tree!
Long may its green branches wave;
In native strength sublime and free,
Meet emblem for the brave.
May the nation's peace
With its growth increase,

THE MAPLE-TREE

And its worth be widely spread;
    For it lifts not in vain
    To the sun and rain
Its tall, majestic head.
    May it grace our soil,
    And reward our toil,
Till the nation's heart is dead.